COMPLETE GUIDE TO THE
ROBINSON-PATMAN ACT

Every man who knows how to read has it in his power to magnify himself, to multiply the ways in which he exists, to make his life full, significant, and interesting.

ALDOUS HUXLEY

COMPLETE GUIDE TO THE
ROBINSON-PATMAN ACT

WRIGHT PATMAN, 1883-1976

Englewood Cliffs, N.J.
PRENTICE-HALL, INC.

PREFACE

The purpose of this volume is to bring up-to-date an analysis of the Robinson-Patman Act which I authored in 1938. Even at that early date when the Act, of which the late Senator Joseph P. Robinson and I were co-authors, was only two years old, we had thousands of requests for information. We received these requests from manufacturers, sales managers, advertising men, retailers, wholesalers and others who represented businessmen or were engaged in business. These inquiries evidenced a widespread desire characteristic of American businessmen to operate honestly within the spirit as well as the letter of the law. Businessmen needed information on how to do that, and my first volume was designed to fill that need.

Now the Act has attained maturity. Its Silver Anniversary has been celebrated. In these 25 years, the Act has been subjected to interpretations through findings and opinions handed down in more than one thousand law cases which arose under the Act. The Federal Trade Commission alone has issued decisions in more than 700 cases. The Act has stood the test of time and the challenges made to it in these cases, and it has become more and more important that representatives of manufacturers, wholesalers, retailers, and others affected by the Act be provided with up-to-date information about the law and the interpretations given to it by the Federal Trade Commission and the courts. This book provides such information, and I am hopeful that it will prove of benefit to users in understanding the Robinson-Patman Act.

While this volume was prepared with a view to making it useful to members of the legal and accounting professions, thought and effort was devoted also to making it a helpful tool for businessmen who need at hand a ready explanation of the Robinson-Patman Act and how to comply with its provisions.

This volume is not intended to render or serve as a substitute for legal,

v

accounting, or other professional service. Many problems arise where the advice of expert professionals is not only desirable but necessary, and, of course, lawyers are indispensable in the handling of cases arising under the Robinson-Patman Act and in litigating the issues therein.

The material has been so organized that the presentation demonstrating the history and the purpose of the law in Chapter I is clearly separated from the discussion of the various provisions appearing in the subsequent chapters. Likewise, in each of the subsequent chapters full and separate discussions appear, not only regarding the provisions of the law but also on the Federal Trade Commission and court interpretations of the provisions. The discussion of each provision of the Act is made separately from the discussions of other provisions. For example, Chapter II contains the discussion of subsection 2(a) and its enforcement.

Chapter VIII is devoted entirely to the discussion of how the Act is enforced. There many questions are answered about how the Federal Trade Commission proceeds with its enforcement of the Robinson-Patman Act.

A special feature of this volume is the discussion of many problems in question and answer form. The volume contains 133 well defined questions along with full answers. These questions and answers are indexed according to the subject matter to which they relate. The Index appears immediately following the Table of Contents.

Another special feature of the volume is the information appearing in the Appendix. Appendix A contains tables of all Robinson-Patman Act cases decided by the Federal Trade Commission from June 19, 1936 through June 30, 1961. Appendix B provides information about the Federal Trade Commission's statement of policy and rules of practice. In this way the reader is informed about the nature of procedures and his rights in cases brought by the Federal Trade Commission for Robinson-Patman Act violations. Appendix C contains references to the record regarding the Robinson-Patman Act. This includes references to debates and the reports by committees and the conference reports on the Robinson-Patman Act and related bills. This vital and valuable information about the Robinson-Patman Act is not available elsewhere at this time. My earlier volume on the Robinson-Patman Act contained information of this kind, but that volume is now out of print and unavailable.

In the concluding chapters of this volume reference is made to the strong support given to the Robinson-Patman Act by representatives of business at all levels. It has been made clear by representatives of business that the discriminatory practices against which the Robinson-Patman Act is directed are unsound practices. They are harmful to business enterprises endeavoring to maintain high ethical standards and are destructive of competition generally. For these reasons countless businessmen have abandoned these practices and are urging full enforcement of the Act.

In Chapter IX, reference is made to opponents of the Act and their critical and deprecatory comments about it. The volume concludes with a discussion of current price discrimination problems and proposals for amending and strengthening the price discrimination law.

A personal word or two must be added. The Robinson-Patman Act has withstood test after test. This has been made possible because of the skill and the devotion to public interest of many able Members of Congress and Mr. Everette MacIntyre, former General Counsel of the House Small Business Committee and now Commissioner of the Federal Trade Commission. In May, 1935, Mr. MacIntyre was loaned to me by the Federal Trade Commission to serve as Chief Counsel to a Special Investigating Committee of the House of Representatives, a committee which was under my chairmanship. The work of Mr. MacIntyre as Chief Counsel, and of the investigating committee produced much of the evidence which was considered by the Judiciary Committees of the House of Representatives and the Senate in 1935–36 when the Robinson and Patman bills were under consideration. Mr. MacIntyre has worked for the enforcement of the Act ever since. Through the years, I have relied upon him in a substantial way for advice, counsel, and assistance in considering the legislative problems which have arisen regarding the Robinson-Patman Act.

Thus, many Members of Congress and Mr. MacIntyre share with me the credit for the Robinson-Patman Act, which has long served a constructive purpose in our free enterprise system. My deepest appreciation is extended to them for their prodigious and skilled labors in aiding me at every step of the development and enforcement of the Act.

CONTENTS

INDEX OF QUESTIONS AND ANSWERS

This is an index of the questions and answers appearing in the various chapters. The index is by the subject matter to which the questions relate and shows for each question the number which has been assigned it and the page on which it appears.

Chapter I

BACKGROUND AND HISTORY OF THE ACT

PRICE DISCRIMINATION AS A PROBLEM

Today we read and hear much about discrimination. Although not all discrimination involves discrimination in price, this volume is concerned only with price discrimination.

Problems arising from the practice of price discrimination motivated Congress to enact the Clayton Act (1914),[1] as amended by the Robinson-Patman Act (1936).[2] It is clear that Congress was troubled by the problem of price discrimination and that it thought it was solving that problem through the enactment of these acts; the legislative history of this legislation leaves no room for dispute or argument about that fact.

SIGNIFICANCE OF PRICE DISCRIMINATION

In the course of its consideration of proposed legislation against price discrimination, Congress became quite well informed on the economic significance of price discrimination. It was found that price discrimination had been a weapon of sellers who held some degree of monopoly power. This power had been effectively employed by powerful sellers, with the effect of destroying competition and the tendency to create stronger monopolies.

These legislative findings regarding the economic significance of price discrimination were made only after due consideration of arguments presented by proponents and opponents of the proposals for legislation against discriminatory pricing practices, which involved even the meaning of the

[1] 15 U.S.C. §§ 12–27.
[2] 15 U.S.C. § 13.

1

term "price discrimination." In view of this, it would seem worthwhile to discuss some aspects of the arguments that were considered by the Congress.

Webster defines "discrimination" as "a distinction, as in treatment; especially, an unfair or injurious distinction." The injury attaches to the person who receives disfavor in treatment. In considering price discrimination, therefore, we should direct our attention to the action of a seller of commodities who discriminates in price between and among the purchasers to whom he sells, distinguishing some purchasers with disfavor by charging them higher prices than he charges other purchasers for goods of like grade and quality. This definition of "price discrimination" will serve as the basis for discussion here.

This discussion is concerned not only with the meaning of the term, but also with the significance of the practice. Recently, we have heard much argument about the economic significance of price discrimination. According to one school of thought, the practice is a manifestation of competition. Another school of thought holds that it is the antithesis of competition—a destroyer of competition and a creator of monopolies. How did Congress perceive the practice of price discrimination when it viewed it as a problem to be dealt with in 1914 and again in 1936—and how does it perceive it today?

The Commissioner of Corporations, in a report on the transportation of petroleum (May 2, 1906), informed Congress about the Standard Oil Company's practice of inducing and receiving the advantages of rebates from several railroads on a very large volume of business in the transportation of petroleum. In that report, it was stated:[3]

> The Standard has therefore been able by reason of its discriminating freight rates to sell oil, when necessary to meet competition, at prices which were profitable to itself, but which left no profit to a competitor. Having thus destroyed competition in large sections of the country, the Standard there charges prices several cents above the cost of manufacture. Railway discriminations, in connection with price cutting, have thus enabled the Standard to obtain monopoly profits of enormous amount.

This price discrimination in favor of a large multiple-market operator, and the company's use of those advantages in discriminating between and among its customers in widely separated markets to destroy its competitors, was the outstanding aspect of price discrimination brought to the attention of the Congress before enactment of the Clayton Act in 1914. The history of that discrimination paralleled the history of the operations of the Standard Oil Trust and the Standard Oil Co. of New Jersey.

---

[3] GARFIELD, TRANSPORTATION OF PETROLEUM 3 (1906).

In a report dated August 5, 1907, the Commissioner of Corporations informed Congress that the business of each of Standard's competitors was largely confined to a limited area and to a limited number of towns within that area—first, because their volume of business was small, and second, because their resources did not permit the direct delivery methods utilized by Standard. These direct delivery methods enabled Standard to make sales and deliveries of kerosene to all sections of the country. In the markets where it faced no competition, Standard could, and did, charge monopoly prices, and these high prices, in turn, enabled the company to reduce its prices in competitive areas and towns to a point that left no profit for the independent concerns.[4]

In the course of its investigations of trusts, Congress found that Standard first acquired its position as a multiple-market operator through merger with a number of previously independent competitors. In order to effectuate the control of these companies, the Standard Oil Trust was organized in 1879. It encompassed about 40 companies that controlled a large percentage of the total oil refining capacity in the United States. Thus, what started out in the period of 1860–1865 as only one of about 30 small refining companies had by 1879 grown to a position where it exercised monopoly control over prices in many local markets that previously enjoyed the benefits of price competition.

Powerful monopoly control such as this in a number of separate markets is what enables a large seller to discriminate in price regularly, or at will, between and among its customers and the communities in which the customers are located. Of course, a small seller without market power can, and on rare occasions does, engage in spasmodic price discriminations, but these discriminations ordinarily do not have any economic significance. Price discriminations that are practiced frequently or regularly, and at will, with devastating effects, can only be employed by a seller who has market power approaching monopoly control over prices in the markets in which he operates. It is clear from the record that the Standard Oil Co. had such market power and control of prices in many local markets.

As a result of its investigations of trusts, Congress was informed that the trail blazed by Standard in the petroleum industry—which included the acquisition of market power and multiple-market control through merger with competitors, then the use of that market power to discriminate in price to destroy the remaining competition—had shown the way to monopolists and would-be monopolists in other industries, who quickly proceeded to

---

[4] COMMISSIONER OF CORPORATIONS, REPORT ON THE PETROLEUM INDUSTRY, Part II at 28 (August 5, 1907).

imitate Standard's practice of price discrimination in such industries as tobacco, sugar, biscuits, and steel.

The monopoly power acquired and abused by companies in the petroleum and tobacco industries was challenged as a violation of the Sherman Antitrust Act. In 1911, the Supreme Court of the United States disposed of those challenges. It held that the Standard Oil Co. of New Jersey was a monopoly in violation of Section 2 of the Sherman Act, and it decreed a dissolution of that combination.[5] The Standard Oil Companies of today resulted from the dissolution. A similar ruling was handed down against the American Tobacco Co.[6] Later, the combination in restraint of trade having monopoly control over prices in the sugar industry was challenged successfully under the Sherman Act.[7]

In some of these cases, effort was made to defend the challenged monopoly control over prices on the ground that this power and position had been acquired as a result of the use of a lawful practice—namely, the practice of price discrimination. For example, attorneys for the Standard Oil Co. of New Jersey argued before the Supreme Court of the United States that Standard should not be broken up as a monopoly because it had acquired its position as a result of lawful competitive methods.[8] In the later Sugar Institute case, representatives of the defendants expressed a strange idea of just what constituted discriminatory treatment. They confused discrimination with competition and condemned price reductions because the sellers were either not willing or able to provide all buyers with the same reductions. Therefore, they undertook to maintain all prices at a high "competitive" level, contending that any seller who reduced prices below that "competitive" level, even though he treated all his buyers equally, was engaging in unethical, noncompetitive, and discriminatory conduct.[9]

Many of these ideas about the economic significance of price discrimination have persisted and have served as the wellspring for other ideas from which has arisen the argument that the Clayton Act, the Robinson-Patman Act, and other legislation against price discrimination constitute legislation against competition and are, therefore, basically in conflict with the Sher-

---

5 Standard Oil v. United States, 221 U.S. 1 (1911).
6 United States v. American Tobacco Co., 221 U.S. 106 (1911).
7 Sugar Institute, Inc. v. U.S., 297 U.S. 553.
8 Standard Oil Co. v. U.S., 221 U.S. 1, 84. The attorneys argued that: "(Defendant's) control was but the result of lawful competitive methods, guided by economic genius of the higher order, sustained by courage, by a keen insight into commercial situations, resulting in the acquisition of great wealth, but at the same time serving to stimulate and increase production, to widely extend the distribution of the products of petroleum at a cost largely below that which would have otherwise prevailed, thus proving to be at one and the same time a benefaction to the general public as well as of enormous advantage to individuals."
9 15 F. Supp. 817, 865–879.

man Antitrust Act and the national antimonopoly policy underlying it. It is for this reason the definition of the term "price discrimination" and the recorded expressions of Congress regarding the economic significance of price discrimination are being discussed at length.

In the course of its study of price discrimination, Congress found that the practice was springing up in various industries. It was in that setting in 1911 that the Supreme Court of the United States approved the action brought by the government under the Sherman Act to subdivide the Standard Oil Company.[10]

The order of the Court breaking up the Standard Oil Trust did not provide for ending Standard Oil's practice of price discrimination. In fact, the Sherman Act contains no provision prohibiting that practice. Therefore, it is not strange that Standard's attorneys argued that the Court should not order a breakup of Standard's monopoly, which had been acquired in "good faith" and through the lawful means of price discrimination.[11]

At the opening of the 63d Congress in 1913, President Wilson, in one of his first messages, called for legislation to prohibit price discrimination and other unfair trade practices. In that connection, he said:

> We are sufficiently familiar with the actual processes and methods of monopoly and of the many hurtful restraints of trade to make definition possible, at any rate up to the limit of which experience has disclosed. These practices, being now abundantly disclosed, can be explicitly and item by item forbidden by statute in such terms as will practically eliminate uncertainty, the law itself and the penalty being made equally plain.

Congress was responsive to that call for legislation. First, it enacted the Federal Trade Commission Act, which became law September 26, 1914.[12] In that law, unfair methods of competition were made unlawful. Congress also enacted the Clayton Antitrust Act,[13] Section 2 of which made price discrimination unlawful when the effect might be substantially to lessen competition or to tend to create a monopoly in any line of commerce. That law was approved October 15, 1914. President Wilson was highly elated over the prospects provided by this legislation for action against monopolistic practices and conditions.[14]

---

[10] Standard Oil Co. v. U.S., 221 U.S. 1 (1911).

[11] See fn. 8.

[12] 15 U.S.C. §§ 41–50 (1958).

[13] 15 U.S.C. §§ 12–33 (1958).

[14] Shortly after President Wilson signed the Clayton Antitrust Act and the Federal Trade Commission Act, he wrote in a private letter: "With similar purpose and in a like temper the Congress has sought, in the Trade Commission bill and in the Clayton bill, to make men in a small way of business as free to succeed as men in a big way, and to kill monopoly in

The conclusions of Congress regarding the economic significance of the practice of price discrimination were vividly recorded in the committee reports on the bill that became the Clayton Act.[15] In those reports, references were made to the price-discrimination practices of the Standard Oil Co. of New Jersey and the American Tobacco Co., and to the great market power that these multiple-market operators had acquired and abused through the use of price discrimination, with the result of destroying competition and creating monopolies. The practice of price discrimination was viewed as evil and as contributing to prices far above the market value in some sections of the country. It was noted that those who had sufficient market power to discriminate in price had charged high prices in some markets to subsidize the lower prices involved in the discriminations, with the effect of eliminating competition in the areas where the lower prices were charged.

---

the seed . . . It is our purpose to destroy monopoly and maintain competition as an only effectual instrument of business liberty . . ." Letter of Woodrow Wilson, October 17, 1914, in THE PUBLIC PAPERS OF WOODROW WILSON, 1926, vol. 2, 189–90.

[15] The Clayton Act of 1914 originated with the bill H.R. 15657, introduced by Mr. Clayton on April 14, 1914, 51 CONG. REC. 6714 (1914). Section 2 of this bill prohibited discrimination in price between different purchasers, with the purpose or intent to destroy or wrongfully injure the business of a competitor of either the purchaser or the seller. Section 2 did not contain any proviso excepting discriminations made in good faith to meet competition.

H.R. 15657 was reported out on May 6, 1914, and the report, H.R. REP. No. 627, 63d Cong., 2d Sess., 1914, 8–9, showed that the Sec. 2 prohibition of price discrimination was confined to a well-known, common particular form of discrimination. Thus, the report stated in part: "Section 2 of the bill is intended to prevent unfair discrimination. The necessity for legislation needs little argument to sustain the wisdom of it. In the past it has been a most common practice of great and powerful combinations engaged in commerce—notably the Standard Oil Co. and the American Tobacco Co., and others of less notoriety, but of great influence—to lower prices of their commodities, oftentimes below the cost of prices of production in certain communities and sections where they had competition, with the intent to destroy and make unprofitable the business of their competitors, and with the ultimate purpose in view of thereby acquiring a monopoly in the particular locality or section in which the discrimination price is made. Every concern that engaged in this evil practice must of necessity recoup its losses in the particular communities or sections where their commodities are sold below cost or without a fair profit by raising the price of the same class of commodities above their fair market value in other sections or communities. Such a system or practice is so manifestly unfair and unjust, not only to competitors who are directly injured thereby, but to the general public, that your committee is strongly of the opinion that the present antitrust laws ought to be supplemented by making this particular form of discrimination a specific offense under the law when practiced by those engaged in commerce."

S. Doc. No. 583, 63d Cong., 2d Sess. (1914) made the same statement for the Senate Judiciary Committee in its report on H.R. 15657.

In its report on the bill to enact the Clayton Act, S. REP. No. 695, 83d Cong., 2d Sess., 1 (1914), to accompany H.R. 15657, the Senate Committee on the Judiciary said: "Broadly stated, the bill, in its treatment of unlawful restraints and monopolies, seeks to prohibit and make unlawful certain trade practices which, as a rule, singly and in themselves are not covered by the Act of July 2, 1890 (the Sherman Act) or other existing antitrust acts and thus, by making these practices illegal, to arrest the creation of trusts, conspiracies, and monopolies in their incipiency and before consummation."

CONGRESS INTENDED THROUGH THE ENACTMENT OF THE ROBINSON-PATMAN ACT TO MAKE INJURIOUS PRICE DISCRIMINATIONS UNLAWFUL

The legislation Congress enacted in 1914, making it unlawful to practice price discrimination in certain situations, was hailed not only by President Wilson, but by small business enterprises and the public generally as a step in the right direction. However, the champions of the free and competitive enterprise system were in for some unpleasant surprises. It was found that somehow someone had slipped into the antidiscrimination provision of Section 2 of the Clayton Antitrust Act a proviso that made that section of the law unoperative against price discriminations made "in good faith to meet competition." When that proviso was being debated in Congress, concern was expressed about the possibility of it pulling the teeth from the law. The fears that were expressed about the possible effect of the "good faith" proviso of the Clayton Antitrust Act of 1914 have proved to be well founded. In the first 20-year period after the enactment of the legislation, it was found the "good faith" proviso had made the law somewhat ineffective for use against destructive price discriminations.

Congress wanted more information about the ineffectiveness of the Clayton Act and about the practice of price discrimination, and it requested the Federal Trade Commission to investigate the matter. This was done pursuant to Senate Resolution 224, 70th Congress. On December 14, 1934, the Commission submitted its final report on the investigation.[16] In the report, the Commission stated that the then-existing law, as it had been interpreted, permitted destructive price discriminations "when made in good faith to meet competition," and that this "good faith" provision of the law virtually nullified the provisions in the Clayton Act that were directed against price discriminations.[17] The Commission recommended that the law be amended and the nullifying provisions eliminated.[18]

In its report, the Federal Trade Commission unequivocally stated:

> Should the trend of the past 20 years and particularly of the last decade continue for a like period, we shall have a condition in some lines of chain-store merchandising that few will dispute is monopolistic.

It has been shown that the original Section 2 of the Clayton Act, as approved in 1914, was considered and enacted in large part because of terri-

---

[16] Senate Document S. Doc. No. 4, 74th Cong., 1st Sess., 1934, *The Federal Trade Commission Final Report on the Chain Store Investigation.*
[17] *Id.* at 90.
[18] *Id.* at 96–97.

torial price discrimination of sellers who were making the primary sales of the merchandise in question. Therefore, the discrimination is commonly referred to as having occurred in the primary line of commerce. The competition affected by that type of discrimination, of course, was the competition provided by competing primary sellers at the manufacturing or producing level. Only incidentally was competition at the secondary level, or that between the sellers and customers, said to be involved. As a result, many thought that Section 2 of the Clayton Act, as approved in 1914, did not apply to price discriminations that only affected competition between and among the customers, or the secondary line of commerce, and in 1923 the U.S. Circuit Court of Appeals for the Second Circuit so held.[19] The Supreme Court of the United States held that the law was not so restricted in its application, but could be applied to price discriminations that affect "any line of commerce."[20]

These differences in view left in doubt whether Section 2 of the Clayton Act of 1914 could effectively be applied in cases where the price discriminations affected only competition in the secondary line of commerce.

These circumstances contributed to the growth and spread of the practice of price discrimination in all lines of commerce. In many instances, big buyers were demanding special price concessions and coercing small suppliers into granting special concessions with threats of putting up their own manufacturing plants. In other instances, they were playing the suppliers off against one another, forcing suppliers of nationally advertised products to meet the prices of small, exclusive suppliers who could not, in practice, market to the independent trade.

Resolutions were introduced in the House of Representatives providing for a Congressional investigation of the trade practices of big-scale buying and selling organizations. These resolutions provided for investigations to be made by a special investigating committee, consisting of seven members of the House—four Democrats and three Republicans—under the chairmanship of the author.

In the light of the facts uncovered during the course of this investigation of big-scale buying and selling in 1935–1936, it was not difficult to see why the law against price discrimination had broken down. One of the main reasons was the defect in the law pointed out by the Federal Trade Commission in its report on the chain-store investigation: the provision that allowed the sellers who were discriminating in price to defend on the ground that they were meeting competition in good faith.

Bills were introduced in both the House and the Senate to overcome the

---

[19] Mennen Co. v. FTC, 288 Fed. 774.
[20] Van Camp & Son v. American Can Co., 278 U.S. 245, 254.

defects in the laws against price discrimination, including the loophole that permitted discriminations "made in good faith to meet competition."[21]

Extensive hearings were held by the Committee on the Judiciary of the House of Representatives and by the Committee on the Judiciary of the Senate on these proposals to strengthen the laws against destructive price discriminations. Representatives of many of the large corporations that had been practicing price discrimination voiced strong opposition to these legislative proposals. However, the Committees reported favorably on the Robinson and Patman bills and recommended their enactment into law. The report of the Committee on the Judiciary to the House on the Patman bill contained the following statement:

> Your committee is of the opinion that the evidence is overwhelming that price discrimination practices exist to such an extent that the survival of independent merchants, manufacturers, and other business-men is seriously imperiled and that remedial legislation is necessary.

The House Committee on the Judiciary, in reporting H.R. 8442 (the Patman bill), stated:[22]

> Section 2 (a) attaches to competitive relations between a given seller and his several customers. It concerns discrimination between customers of the same seller. It has nothing to do with fixing prices nor does it require the maintenance of any relationship in prices charged by a competing seller.
>
> Discriminations in excess of sound economic differences between the customers concerned, in the treatment accorded them, involve generally an element of loss, whether only of the necessary minimum of profits or of actual costs, that must be recouped from the business of customers not granted them. When granted by a given seller to his customers in other States, and denied to those within the State, they involve the use of that interstate commerce to the burden and injury of the latter. When granted to customers within the State and denied to those beyond, they involve conversely a direct resulting burden upon his interstate commerce with the latter. Both are within the proper and well-recognized power of Congress to suppress . . .

The same House report on the proposed legislation made it equally clear that the bill was intended to reach price discriminations that affected the primary line of commerce. It was stated:[23]

> . . . The existing law has in practice been too restrictive in requir-ing a showing of general injury to competitive conditions in the line of

---

[21] H.R. 8442, introduced by Rep. Wright Patman (D., Tex.), and S. 3154, introduced by Senator Joseph Robinson (D., Ark.), 74th Cong. 2d Sess. (1935).

[22] H.R. REP. No. 2287, 74th Cong., 2d Sess. 8 (1935). See also S. REP. No. 1502, 74th Cong., 2d Sess. 2 (1935), accompanying S. 3154 in the Robinson bill).

[23] *Id.* at 8.

commerce concerned, whereas the more immediately important concern is in injury to the competitor victimized by the discrimination. Only through such injury in fact can the larger, general injury result. Through this broadening of the jurisdiction of the act, a more effective suppression of such injuries is possible and the more effective protection of the public interest at the same time is achieved.

Congress passed the Robinson and Patman bills overwhelmingly. Only 16 votes were recorded in opposition in the House of Representatives, and none in the Senate. The enactment was completed on June 16, 1936, and President Roosevelt signed the Robinson-Patman Act on June 19, 1936.

Chapter II

PRICE DISCRIMINATION, A DISCUSSION
OF SUBSECTION 2(a) AND ITS ENFORCEMENT

THE PROHIBITIONS CONTAINED IN SUBSECTION 2(A)

Sec. 2(a) That it shall be unlawful for any person engaged in commerce, in the course of such commerce, either directly or indirectly, to discriminate in price between different purchasers of commodities of like grade and quality, where either or any of the purchases involved in such discrimination are in commerce, where such commodities are sold for use, consumption, or resale within the United States or any Territory thereof or the District of Columbia or in any insular possession or other place under the jurisdiction of the United States, and where the effect of such discrimination may be substantially to lessen competition or tend to create a monopoly in any line of commerce, or to injure, destroy, or prevent competition with any person who either grants or knowingly receives the benefit of such discrimination, or with customers of either of them.

REQUIREMENTS FOR A PRIMA FACIE CASE UNDER SUBSECTION 2(A)

The word "person" as used in subsection 2(a) of the Robinson-Patman Act is defined in Section 1 of the Clayton Act.[24] It includes persons and partnerships. Also, it includes corporations and associations existing under or authorized by the laws either of the United States, the laws of any of the territories, the laws of any State, or the laws of any foreign country.

A case of a violation of the Robinson-Patman Act can be made out by showing that some "person" has discriminated in price between different

---

[24] 15 U.S.C. Sec. 12.

11

purchasers of commodities of like grade and quality. Additionally, it must be shown that a number of other necessary propositions have been answered in the affirmative or statements of ultimate facts (i.e. conclusions of facts) have been established. Only in this way may a prima facie case arising under Subsection 2(a) of the Robinson-Patman Act be proved.

The first proposition that must be considered is the one that charges that a person has *discriminated in price*. The subsection makes it unlawful for any person, either directly or indirectly, to discriminate in price between different purchasers. At first glance, it does not appear the definition of the term "discrimination" in this context should present any difficulty; the term "discrimination" ordinarily is considered to be a simple word of the English language. Webster defines it as "a distinction, as in treatment," and as "an unfair or injurious distinction."

A number of writers who have defined the term "discrimination" as used in the Robinson-Patman Act have fallen back on the definition given by Congressman Utterback, Chairman of the House managers. In reporting the bill to the House, he stated:[25]

> In its meaning as simple English, a discrimination is more than a mere difference. Underlying the meaning of the word is the idea that some relationship exists between the parties to the discrimination which entitles them to equal treatment, whereby the difference granted to one casts some burden or disadvantage upon the other. If the two are competing in the resale of the goods concerned, that relationship exists. Where, also, the price to one is so low as to involve a sacrifice of some part of the seller's necessary costs and profit as applied to that business, it leaves that deficit inevitably to be made up in higher prices to his other customers; and there, too, a relationship may exist upon which to base the charge of discrimination. But where no such relationship exists, where the goods are sold in different markets and the conditions affecting those markets set different price levels for them, the sale to different customers at those different prices would not constitute a discrimination within the meaning of this bill.

From this definition by Congressman Utterback, it is clear that he has elaborated on the definition provided by Webster. In doing so, he expresses the thought that discrimination is more than a mere difference in price—that some relationship should exist whereby the differences in price involved would cast a burden or disadvantage upon some person. Through that line of reasoning, Congressman Utterback supplies an explanation for the "unfair or injurious distinction" part of Webster's definition. However, he does not explain the nature of the relationship that should exist between the parties affected by the discrimination in order to give rise to the unfair

---

[25] 80 CONG. REC. 9416 (1936).

and injurious aspect of the distinction. On this point, courts and text writers have differed. Some have indicated a belief that a relationship should exist between and among all purchasers of goods of like grade and quality from the same seller.[26] The United States Court of Appeals for the Seventh Circuit, in the case of *Anheuser-Busch v. Federal Trade Commission*,[27] held that there must be a relationship between different purchasers that entitles them to comparable treatment, and it reasoned that such a relationship would exist only in situations where different prices are charged to *competing* purchasers. In that case, Anheuser-Busch was not shown to have discriminated between and among different competing customers, and the Court consequently concluded that, even assuming the price differences involved were directed at Anheuser-Busch's local competitors, they were not discriminatory. The Supreme Court of the United States, in reviewing that case, disagreed with the Seventh Circuit Court of Appeals and held neither the language of subsection 2(a), its legislative history, nor its judicial application countenanced a construction that could draw strength from even a lingering doubt as to the purpose of the Congress of protecting primary-line competition through the passage of the Robinson-Patman Act. In doing so, it ruled that it is not necessary to show that the different customers of a seller, who are charged different prices, are *competing* customers.[28]

From the interpretations provided by the Supreme Court of the United States in the *Anheuser-Busch* case and previous cases, we have learned what relationship is required in order for price differences to become "discrimination." These decisions by the Court have supplied explanations omitted by Congressman Utterback when he referred to the fact that some relationship should exist. Through the decisions of the Court, we are informed that the relationship requirement is met if a seller making differences in prices is in competition with other sellers in the sale of competitive merchandise, or if his customers pay him different prices for goods of like grade and quality and they are in competition with each other.

Did the Person Charged with Violating Subsection 2(a), in the Course of Commerce, Charge Some of His Customers Higher Prices Than He Charged Other Customers?

Of course, the first factor to be considered in determining whether a seller has discriminated in price between different purchasers is the differential, if any, between the prices charged and paid by the different cus-

[26] Austin, Price Discrimination 19 (1959). Compare Edwards, The Price Discrimination Law 30–31, 215–36 (1959).
[27] 265 F.2d 677.
[28] FTC v. Anheuser-Busch, 363 U.S. 536 (1960).

tomers. The term "price," as used in the Robinson-Patman Act, means the amount paid by the buyer to the seller for the merchandise involved in an actual transaction; that is, the amount paid by the buyer to the seller for the merchandise located at the place, in the condition, and under the circumstances that exist at the passing of the title to the goods, as provided for in the sale. Thus, as ordinarily applies in the law of sales, the price paid for the merchandise could apply at the location of the place of business of the vendor or at the place of business of the vendee.

This definition of the term "price" as used in subsection 2(a) would provide for application of the statute to discriminations in price, irrespective of whether the discriminations occurred on a f.o.b. factory basis or on a delivered basis.

"Price" could therefore mean the amount paid for the merchandise f.o.b. the place of business of the seller or f.o.b. the place of business of the buyer, depending on the terms and conditions applying to the transaction. In order properly to compare two or more transactions of a seller with two or more of his customers, for the purpose of determining whether discrimination is involved, the prices must be reduced to a common denominator. In other words, an effort should be made to determine whether the difference in the prices reflects an allowance for the cost of the transportation involved. Then we have a common denominator: the net price received by the seller from the two buyers in question.

Terms and conditions other than those involving transportation must also be considered. For example, if a seller charged a price of $1.00 per unit for an item and then allowed a 10 per cent trade or quantity discount, it is obvious the net price would not be $1.00, but 90 cents per unit. The net price is what would be used in making comparisons with prices charged other customers for the purpose of determining whether a price difference or discrimination had occurred under the Robinson-Patman Act. The statute provides a latitude for this interpretation in that it prohibits a seller from "either directly or indirectly" discriminating in price between different purchasers.

The statement of the managers on the part of the House on the conference report made to the House of Representatives by Mr. Utterback,[29] accompanying H.R. 8442, contained the following statement:

> The Senate amendment made it unlawful to discriminate between purchasers "in price or terms of sale." The House bill did not contain the words "or terms of sale." The Senate receded, and the words "or terms of sale" were stricken. The managers were of the opinion that the bill should be inapplicable to terms of sale except as they amount

---

[29] H.R. Rep. No. 2951, 74th Cong., 2d Sess. (1935).

in effect to indirect discriminations in price within the meaning of the remainder of subsection (a).

Terms or conditions of sale providing for the seller to pass on to the buyer discounts, rebates, or allowances that depend not only on volumes of goods in particular shipments, but also on volumes of goods in future purchases, the furnishing of advertising or promotional allowances, and other such related conditions and terms should be regarded as directly or indirectly affecting and becoming a part of the price charged.

Many forms and types of terms and conditions of sale may involve indirect price discriminations. The following questions and answers bear on various types of possible indirect price discriminations.

TERMS OF SALE—CASH DISCOUNTS

No. 1. Question. Is discrimination in terms of sale forbidden by the Act?

Opinion. Under a strict definition of "terms of sale," where the discrimination actually represents a discrimination in price, it may come within the provisions of the Act.

No. 2. Question. For illustration, consider the case of a man who buys $500 worth of merchandise over a period of six months. He receives the 2 per cent cash discount made to all our customers, regardless of how much they purchase. For this volume of business, would it be legal for us to give him an extra 1 per cent, the purchaser of $5,000 in the same period an additional 2 per cent, and the purchaser of $10,000 in a like period an additional 3 per cent? These discounts would be volume discounts, in addition to the regular 2 per cent cash discount.

Opinion. If the purchasers are not in competition with each other, the Act is not concerned. If some of them should happen to be in competition and should receive different rates of volume discounts to the extent that injury would result to the less favored, then—should you be challenged— you must be prepared to show that the larger discount did not exceed the savings in selling or handling cost that the larger volume made possible.

No. 3. Question. Do variations in the length of time of delivery on contracts for merchandise involve a discrimination in price?

Opinion. It is possible that an indirect discrimination within the meaning of the Act may result in this manner.

No. 4. Question. May a manufacturer classify his customers by the promptness with which they pay their bills, and sell to slow-pay customers at a higher price than he sells to prompt-pay customers?

Opinion. If injury develops, an unlawful discrimination may result. His only defense would be the difference in cost of carrying and collecting the accounts and absorbing bad-debt losses.

No. 5. Question. Assuming that terms are a part of the price, is there anything in the Act to compel the customer to adhere to terms?

Opinion. Ordinarily, no, especially with respect to payment days. If a customer "steals" an extra discount and by reason of it injures a competing customer's business, the injured party may recover damages from any or all parties who may be guilty of the unlawful act in question.

No. 6. Question. When a manufacturer publishes credit terms and cash discount terms and enforces them with 90 per cent of his customers, does he violate the Act when: (1) he continues to sell on open account to those 10 per cent of his customers who have not settled their accounts in compliance with his published terms; (2) he allows a cash discount to that 10 per cent of his customers after the expiration of the cash discount period?

Opinion. In neither of the above cases does there appear to have been a discrimination in price. Therefore, the Act would not apply.

No. 7. Question. Is discrimination in credit or cash discount terms permissible under the Act?

Opinion. Yes. Granting of unlawful price discriminations or other allowances in the guise of cash discounts, however, is prohibited by the Act. They are treated not as cash discounts, but as allowances through subterfuge.

No. 8. Question. Is a cash discount for prompt payment permissible?

Opinion. The Act does not prohibit the granting of cash discounts, unless they are granted as a subterfuge to circumvent the provisions of the Act.

No. 9. Question. Our terms of sale are 2 per cent, 30 days. We have some customers who deduct the 2 per cent for longer periods, and others who settle by note and likewise deduct the 2 per cent. Would the granting of these special arrangements constitute a discrimination under the Robinson-Patman Act?

Opinion. The Act would not apply to negligible exceptions in the absence of intent to discriminate.

No. 10. Question. A manufacturer prints on his billheads that he will allow a cash discount of 1 per cent for payment in ten days. Most customers willingly conform to these terms, but occasionally a large customer insists on taking a cash discount of 2 per cent. If the manufacturer, rather than risk the loss of the customer's business, allows the 2 per cent discount, has he committed an infraction of the Robinson-Patman Act?

Opinion. This represents a price discrimination in which both buyer and seller are guilty. If liability is to be escaped, all other customers in competition with the big buyer must be extended the same consideration.

No. 11. Question. There are situations where a one-price policy to all our customers prevails. Yet many customers persist in sending in checks in payment of invoices and taking off 5 or 10 per cent discount, claiming over-charging and things of that sort. Is this a violation of the Act, and who may be held responsible?

Opinion. Yes. Both buyer and seller are responsible.

No. 12. Question. Is the extension of varying cash discount terms to buyers a violation of the Act?

Opinion. Where customers in competition with each other are injured, you would be liable. It depends on whether the discrimination results in a measurable injury.

No. 13. Question. When a customer ignores the cash discount terms of the manufacturer, is such action a violation of the Robinson-Patman Act? Is the manufacturer equally guilty with the buyer?

Opinion. If it results in a net price discrimination between customers who are in competition with each other under conditions stated by the Act, both buyer and seller are liable under the Act.

No. 14. Question. Does the Robinson-Patman Law prohibit the allowance of unearned cash discount? If so, what section?

Opinion. Where the cash discount actually represents an unlawful price discrimination, Section 2(a) would apply.

No. 15. Question. A customer has three definite payment dates each month when he pays his bills and deducts the cash discount allowed by the seller. This arrangement has been satisfactory with everyone with whom the customer does business. Does the Robinson-Patman Act forbid such an arrangement?

Opinion. This does not appear to be a violation.

CONSIGNMENT SALES

No. 16. Question. Does the Robinson-Patman law prohibit discrimination resulting from giving longer terms or consigning goods to certain buyers if the consignor does not offer the same proposition to other buyers?

Opinion. It is not believed the Act applies in such cases, unless the consignment policy results in giving one group of ultimate buyers an unfair advantage over others in competition with them.

No. 17. Question. Does the Act forbid consignment sales?

Opinion. It does not.

No. 18. Question. Is special dating on consigned goods considered a price discrimination?

Opinion. It is presumed that what is meant here is that a shipment of goods may be consigned to a party for a specified length of time, within which it must be sold or returned. The Act does not apply.

No. 19. Question. Suppose a manufacturer consigns to a wholesaler on a *del credere* basis. The manufacturer allows a discount of 40 per cent on gross lots; the wholesaler consignee allows a discount of 10 per cent on dozen lots. Is the variable discount—10 per cent as against 40 per cent— a violation of the Robinson-Patman Act, when applied to competing purchasers?

Opinion. What seems to be involved here is a case where the manufacturer has a 40 per cent discount on gross lots to all direct purchasers and does not make direct delivery in smaller quantities. He also consigns in gross lots to a wholesaler-agent, who receives the 40 per cent discount as a commission. The wholesaler-agent, in turn, handles dozen-lot orders and gives a 10 per cent discount on them, retaining the balance of the 40 per cent as his compensation. Because of the agency relationship, all the customers of the wholesale-agent are, in fact, customers of the manufacturer. Customers purchasing through the agent in dozen lots are discriminated against in favor of competing customers who buy direct in gross lots. Injury results, but whether or not the discrimination—10 per cent as against 40 per cent— exceeds the difference in cost of manufacture, sale, and delivery due to the differing methods of purchase and sale depends on the facts in the case. If the manufacturer cannot substantiate the differences in accordance with the limitations defining legal price differentials, he is liable to the injured customers.

PACKAGING

No. 20. Question. Is the following discrimination a violation of the Robinson-Patman Act? A manufacturer regularly sells an item packed 30 units in a box for 60 cents throughout the northern states. In order to promote volume in the South, he packs the same item 34 units to the box for 60 cents.

Opinion. Under the primary test of an unlawful price discrimination, this is not a violation of the Act if all purchasers who may be in competition with each other are treated alike and receive the same number of units per box. However, if the effect or result is to destroy competition in primary lines of commerce, the seller is definitely liable under the Act.

VOLUME OR QUANTITY DISCOUNTS

No. 21. Question. Are quantity discounts forbidden under the law?

Opinion. They are not. The Act, however, limits them to economic differences in cost.

No. 22. Question. May any manufacturer have a graduated scale of discounts?

Opinion. He may, but the scale must keep within the limitations of the Act.

No. 23. Question. I make a full line of products and give a special quantity discount when total purchases equal 6,000 units on the entire line and certain minimums are reached in each line. This discount is not given to a purchaser who purchases 6,000 units in a single line. Every buyer must reach the minimum set in each line and the total set for all lines, otherwise he does not receive the discount. May I continue this plan under the Robinson-Patman Act?

Opinion. It would appear that the plan is not illegal if injury does not result to any competitor of the purchaser or competitor of the discriminating seller. The discounts should not exceed the difference in cost of handling the different quantities.

No. 24. Question. Would it be a violation of the Robinson-Patman Act to have a schedule of graduated discounts according to the monthly volume of business, discount being determined by total business handled in each month?

Opinion. This plan does not appear essentially illegal unless it is arbitrary. If, however, the discount goals are set so high that only a few favored purchasers may take advantage of them, it would be discriminatory in effect.

No. 25. Question. Are quantity discounts based on annual, seasonal, or quarterly purchases allowed under the Act? For example, if all customers are sent a quantity credit memorandum based on $5,000 worth of shipments in a certain length of time, and all customers who attained this volume received that credit memo, would this violate the law?

Opinion. The setting of a flat amount such as that is arbitrary, dangerous, and often illegal, since there would be some customers whose purchases would fall just below the arbitrary limit. Any form of quantity discounts is permissible under the Act where they do not exceed the difference or savings in handling costs. All customers should know, however, they are entitled to the discount under specified conditions equally applicable to all. A series of graduated breaks is safer and fairer than one or two arbitrary limits.

No. 26. Question. A dealer is given, at the end of the year, a graduated cash rebate according to his accumulated purchases during the year. Is this now prohibited?

Opinion. No, if the graduated scale does not result in injury or does not exceed the difference-in-cost limitation.

No. 27. Question. May a manufacturer classify his customers by their volume of purchases for a definite period?

Opinion. Yes, but the mere classification would not excuse price discriminations prohibited by the Act.

No. 28. Question. If one dealer buys 3,000 gallons of ice cream annually, and another only 300 gallons in the same time, the larger dealer can receive a better price to the extent of the differential in cost of selling, manufacturing, or delivery. Is this correct?

Opinion. Yes.

No. 29. Question. In the event that a manufacturer offers a volume discount, does the law provide that such a discount must be published as a part of the price list?

Opinion. The Act does not require either a published price list or the publication of volume discounts. With regard to price discriminations, the Act is concerned only with your treatment of purchasers who may be in competition with each other. But if an injured customer shows that you gave a discount to a competitor without letting him know that such a discount was equally obtainable by him, you may be in trouble.

This is not like the provisions governing allowances for advertising and use of facilities. Within the meaning of those clauses, such allowances must be made available to all other purchasers on proportionally equal terms. This implies that they must be made known, which implies some form of publication.

No. 30. Question. May a special quantity discount be made at different times of the year?

Opinion. Quantity discounts may be offered for short periods and at any time. The Act is only concerned with the effect of the resulting price discriminations themselves.

No. 31. Question. A manufacturer sells products of the same quality, style, and finish in interstate commerce to several customers competing with each other. Some purchase in small quantities, some in large quantities. Does the Robinson-Patman Act make it mandatory that all customers be sold at the same price and under the same terms, regardless of the quantity they buy?

Opinion. The Act does not require that all competing customers be sold at the same price. It only prescribes the limitations beyond which differences in price shall not be lawful.

No. 32. Question. Suppose a manufacturer sells on a discount basis of 3 per cent for carload shipments as against no discount on orders even as small as a dozen quantity. May the carload buyer, alleging that his larger purchase represents a greater economy than 3 per cent savings to the manufacturer as compared with the purchaser of only a dozen, claim to have been discriminated against under the Robinson-Patman Act?

Opinion. The carload buyer has no case whatsoever. The Act does not *require* a seller to make any difference in price to any sellers under any condition. He may name one and the same price to every purchaser. He may give a purchaser part of the savings effected by the purchaser's method of buying, but that does not imply, under the law, he must give him all the savings. The Act is not concerned with forcing sellers to grant discounts or price discriminations. It is only concerned with seeing that no unfair discrimination is made between competing purchasers, if the seller does elect, or is forced, to grant price differences.

No. 33. Question. In our kind of retail business, nearly everything we buy comes packed in standard quantities—so many to a carton or case. The quantities in which the products are packed frequently vary, but they are generally convenient quantities so the customer is not required to overstock. Therefore, purchases are made in the standard case or carton lot. It costs the seller just about the same per carton to handle one carton or a dozen cartons. Yet on some products he offers such large discounts on large quantities that only one big retailer with several stores in a trading area can meet those quantity requirements. As a result, to meet that competition the small buyer has to cut the price on these goods in order to sell them at all. Seller delivers direct to both the large buyer and the small one in about the same quantity at a time. Isn't this a point where the quantity price idea is all cockeyed?

Opinion. The law of diminishing returns applies to quantity discounts, as it does to taxes or any other comparable factor. Up to a certain point, volume business from a single buyer is inviting and generally deemed profitable. There are pronounced savings in cost involved. As an illustration, the business of a retailer is usually considered unprofitable if he only purchases occasionally and in broken lots. On the other hand, a retailer who buys with reasonable regularity and in standard quantities is accepted as a profitable dealer. Usually, the volume that a retailer buys in most lines of commerce need not be extremely great in order to reach a peak in efficiency and low cost of handling. From that point on, there is no appreciable savings in cost, though the added volume per dealer has an intrinsic and sometimes intangible value to the seller, which is expressed in a reward of 1, 2, or 3 per cent additional discount as the volume increases. Such rewards, however, do not ordinarily result in injurious discrimination among competitors.

On the other hand, volume purchases may attain a size where they become disadvantageous, if not dangerous to the interests of the seller. Most manufacturers, in the past, have always sought to diversify their outlets and to avoid selling too large a share of their production to any one purchaser. To do so was to invite, sooner or later, the domination of one's business by the single large purchaser. Commercial history has shown that one of two things generally occurred: (1) The single large purchaser demanded more and more concessions; profits were reduced or vanished; the manufacturer's other customers could not compete with the large purchaser, and he lost those channels of distribution, placing him solely at the mercy of the single large purchaser; or (2) before that complete state of affairs was reached, the large-volume purchaser switched to a new source of supply and left the manufacturer high and dry. In any case, if a manufacturer permitted too much of his business to go into the hands of a single large buyer, he often invited ultimate bankruptcy and failure.

Therefore, while the business of a reasonable-volume buyer was inviting and at the same time demonstrated economic savings in cost, that volume soon reached a point where there were no further savings in cost regardless of how great the volume became; that is, the law of diminishing returns came into play. So the above dealer has more or less correctly sized up the fallacies of quantity discounts and prices. If one were to chart the cost factor in the handling of consumer goods, he would find a similarity of experience in nearly all kinds of goods: Beginning with a single article, his cost per unit would decline rapidly as quantities increased. It would soon approach a point, however, where his chart line would level off, and from there on decline imperceptibly, if at all, as the quantity unit increased in size. In many cases, the per-unit cost factor may rise as the bulk unit is increased.

It is apparent, therefore, that articles in commerce may be handled in convenient quantities, most often determined by the point at which the most efficient cost factor is attained. That point also determines the size of the bulk container or carton. From there on, however, the cost *per carton* handled does not appreciably change, regardless of whether a single carton is delivered to one purchaser or a hundred cartons are delivered at one time to another purchaser.

The law of diminishing returns may be applied to selling, advertising, retailing, and manufacturing with the same results. The assumption that greater and greater quantity discounts may be granted because as the quantity increases the cost decreases in direct proportion is frequently far from the facts. Wherever sellers operate on that theory alone, there is an ever-present possibility that the Robinson-Patman Act has been violated, because the price discriminations that result may exceed the cost savings in manufacture, sale, or delivery of the goods involved.

PRIVATE VERSUS REGULAR BRANDS

No. 34. Question. If a manufacturer sells his standard-brand merchandise under his own name at one price and sells the same goods under a buyer's private label at a lower price, and all other conditions of manufacture, sale, and delivery are the same, is this a violation of the Act?

Opinion. According to the facts as stated, the Act has been violated if the favored buyer is in competition with less-favored buyers who are injured by reason of the discrimination.

No. 35. Question. May a manufacturer discriminate in price between branded and unbranded goods?

Opinion. Solely on that basis, he may not. The mere fact that he may have placed his brand on one article and does not brand another of like grade and quality does not perceptibly change the cost of either article. The question is whether the sale of the manufacturer's products to competing customers results in giving one an unfair price advantage over the other.

No. 36. Question. Is it permissible under the Act for a seller to employ different firm names for the merchandising of his products of like grade and quality, in order to conceal his identity or the identity of the product for the purpose of discriminating in price between customers?

Opinion. Such a practice would not affect the cost of the products or result in differences in cost. It is only in accordance with differences in cost that a legal price discrimination may be made under the Act.

FUNCTIONAL DISCOUNTS

No. 37. Question. May a manufacturer quote wholesalers, retailers, and consumer cooperatives the same price?

Opinion. There is no requirement in the law for a seller to make different prices to different customers. However, the thrust of the Robinson-Patman Act is against discriminatory treatment of customers. For that reason, a seller who has organized his business primarily to sell to wholesalers, depending on them to perform sales work, warehousing, and other functions incident to the sale and distribution of the seller's products, may be considered to have engaged in discriminatory conduct if he should not make promotional allowances to his wholesaler-customers as compensation to them for the sales promotional work they have performed in promoting the sale of the seller's products. These allowances would be in addition to those made to direct-buying retailer accounts who perform no general sales promotional functions particularly directed to the specific seller's products. In this type of situation, if the seller does not make any allowances in the form of a functional discount, but charges all his customers—the direct-buying retailers and the wholesalers—the same prices, there could be a question of whether he has made proper allowances on proportionately equal terms to his different customers on the basis of their performance of different functions.

Again it is noted that the law does not require the making of different prices to different customers. Nevertheless, there remains a legal question as to whether or not the Robinson-Patman Act covers discriminatory conduct of a seller in charging the same prices to a wholesaler and to a direct-buying retailer who operate at different levels and perform varying amounts of sales promotional services to the seller. On September 27, 1961, the Bergen Drug Co., Inc., Hackensack, N.J., filed a $1,950,000 civil antitrust damage suit against Parke-Davis & Co. in the New Jersey Federal District Court to test the question of whether the Robinson-Patman Act can be used by wholesalers as a basis for securing an additional allowance for the services they perform beyond the allowances and services allowed and performed by direct-buying retailers.[30] Although the Bergen Drug Co. lawsuit has the earmarks of a new legal offensive by wholesalers against sellers who do not differentiate in price between wholesalers and direct-buying retailers, it is not the first such legal action to raise the legal question involved. In 1956, a retailer who was a customer of a toy jobber sued a toy manufacturer because the latter had sold toys at the same net price to jobbers and to retail chains.[31] The retailer alleged that neither he nor his jobber could compete with the direct-buying chains. The U.S. District Court dismissed the case on the ground that indirect-buying retailers are not customers of the manufacturer and that, therefore, no discrimination was involved, since the manufacturer had not discriminated between direct purchasers— namely, the jobbers and the chains who paid the same price. The United States Circuit Court of Appeals for the Third Circuit affirmed the lower court's decision, but solely on the ground that an indirect-buying retailer was not a customer of the manufacturer and, therefore, could not sue. In cases where the direct-buying chains have received lower prices than the wholesalers, a difference in price, of course, was involved, and different rulings have been made by the courts. In a number of these cases, the courts have held the Robinson-Patman Act would apply.[32]

No. 38. Question. Where one customer does not have storage facilities

---

[30] Bergen Drug Co. v. Parke-Davis & Co. Civil Action No. 822–61 (D.N.J.).

[31] Klein v. Lionel Corp., 138 F. Supp. 560 (D. Del. 1956).

[32] Krug v. International Telephone & Telegraph Corp., 142 F. Supp. 230 (D. N.J. 1956). Compare Chicago Sugar Co. v. American Sugar Refining Co., 176 F.2d 1 (7th Cir. 1949); Sano Petroleum Corp. v. American Oil Co., 187 F. Supp. 345 (E.D.N.Y. 1960); Secatore's Inc. v. Esso Standard Oil Co., 171 F. Supp. 665 (D. Mass. 1959).

and requires spot deliveries during the rush of the season, for which the manufacturer must produce in advance and store in order to obtain the fullest utilization of his plant capacity, while another customer orders for delivery in off-seasons, handling the storage himself and saving the manufacturer that cost, may such a saving be expressed in a price differential?

Opinion. In the first instance, the manufacturer performs the wholesaling function; in the second, the buyer performs it for himself, and he may therefore receive a price differential equal to the cost of the wholesaling function that he assumes.

No. 39. Question. A local chain-store company is retailing a product at $9.75. Absolutely the lowest price at which a local dealer can buy the same product, regardless of quantity, is $11.75, and local wholesalers must pay $10.05. Does the Act take care of this situation?

Opinion. It is necessary to trace the price complained against to its source. Then, when all the conditions are known, it may be determined whether it is the result of unlawful price discrimination or justified savings in cost to the manufacturer. Circumstances would have to be most unusual, however, to permit a manufacturer to justify selling to wholesalers at a price so much higher than the price to a chain that the chain can retail at a price lower than the wholesale price.

No. 40. Question. May a seller give our chain customers an allowance equal to the actual savings they accomplished and also give them an additional warehouse allowance?

Opinion. When chain customers have been given all the allowances they have earned, they may be given no more. If in truth and in fact the warehousing function relieves the seller of a corresponding item of cost, that is part of the savings the buyer has earned and may, therefore, be included in discounts granted to them.

No. 41. Question. Does the Act apply to the wholesale trade, or does it apply to all business, both wholesale and retail?

Opinion. The Act applies to all forms of interstate commerce, including wholesale and retail trade.

No. 42. Question. Is it legal for a manufacturer to allow a greater discount to a jobber than to a retailer, provided the jobber sells to retailers?

Opinion. It is, provided the discount can be established as a legitimate cost-saving discount.

No. 43. Question. If a manufacturer sells direct to retailers in a certain community and also sells to wholesalers in the same community, and if the direct retail accounts are in competition with purchasers of the wholesalers, must the manufacturer justify any differential in price to wholesalers by showing a saving in the cost of manufacture, cost of sale, or cost of delivery on the quantity purchases made by such wholesalers?

Opinion. A manufacturer may establish functional discounts without direct reference to costs, but there is attached to that freedom the moral and legal responsibility to see that competition is preserved at the retail point of sale. There must be no direct or indirect discrimination in price or services between wholesalers and between retailers.

No. 44. Question. A manufacturer has two published prices—a price to the retailer, and a price to the wholesaler. In territories where he has no wholesale trade, he gives the retailer the wholesaler's price, or a price between the wholesale price and the retail price. Is such a practice a violation of the Act?

Opinion. Ordinarily, no. The Act applies to discriminations that result in injury to competition or competitive customers or that result in substantial lessening of competition in lines of commerce.

No. 45. Question. Does the law permit a manufacturer or wholesaler to classify his customers into wholesalers, dealers, and consumers?

Opinion. The law neither prohibits nor requires a classification of customers.

No. 46. Question. If a wholesale buyer has an efficient sales force to merchandise my ware, is there a saving in the cost of sales and delivery that can be reflected in price?

Opinion. Efficiency or economies that are reflected in savings in cost of manufacturing, selling, or delivering to the wholesaler may be reflected in differences in prices to the wholesaler.

No. 47. Question. Manufacturer A, a full-line manufacturer, and manufacturer B, a short-line manufacturer, both in interstate commerce, sell to wholesalers, allowing the usual preferential on their respective lines. Manufacturer B allows a special price when manufacturer A takes the merchandise of B into his stock and ships it with his own merchandise to his customers. When A asks B to ship direct to A's customer, is A entitled to a better price than B gives to his own distributors?

Opinion. The law does not require B to pay anything to A or make any price differential. However, if B has established the practice of granting A an extra discount for the delivery service, then proceeds to perform the delivery service himself, he cannot justify the price differential as against his wholesale customers in competition with A.

No. 48. Question. Under the Act, may a manufacturer sell to a mail-order house or a chain store at a lower price than he sells to his wholesale customers?

Opinion. He may if there is an economic difference in cost of manufacture, sale, or delivery. If he is required to assume the wholesale function for the mail-order house or chain store, however, the lower economic difference in cost may be capable of disproof in court, and the manufacturer is in real danger of heavy damages to his retail customers (direct, or through wholesalers).

The nub of this important question is this: Is the lower price to the chain the result of provable economies to the manufacturer, resulting from the fact that the manufacturer is relieved of certain definite functions (and the cost thereof) that are not performed for the chain but are performed for the chain's competing retailers through wholesale customers of the manufacturer?

No. 49. Question. Under the Robinson-Patman Act, is a manufacturer obliged to sell merchandise of his own manufacturer to a retailer at the same price he sells to a wholesaler if the retailer buys in the same quantities as the wholesaler?

Opinion. He is not, but he may not sell to one retailer at the wholesale price and deny it to another retailer on the same terms. The Act does not prohibit a manufacturer from setting up a functional discount for his wholesale customers. Such customers perform a wholesale function in distributing to retailers, which he would otherwise have to perform and assume the cost of. There is nothing in the Act that prevents him from protecting the wholesaler in the performance of that function by giving him a price differential and refusing the same to retailers. In fact, there are conditions that might make him liable under the Act if he did not extend that protection to his wholesale customers.

No. 50. Question. Does the Robinson-Patman Act make sales of merchandise in interstate commerce by the manufacturer unlawful if a different price is charged to wholesalers from that charged to retailers when the difference in price is not being based directly on differences in cost, notwithstanding the fact that all wholesalers are treated fairly and alike and all retailers are treated fairly and alike?

Opinion. Such price differentials are not unlawful in and of themselves. To show them to be unlawful, it would be necessary to show that the discrimination resulted in injury to competitors or to others in some line of commerce. The wholesaler performs a functional service and is legally entitled to prices reflecting the cost of the performance of that function.

No. 51. Question. Wholesalers who buy 50 or more articles are given a special 15 per cent commission. Can this be continued?

Opinion. If this is a quantity discount over and above the functional discount, the legal limitations regarding price differentials would apply. If the 15 per cent commission, as you call it, exceeds the difference in cost of manufacturing, selling, or delivery between the 50-unit shipment and your next lower quantity unit, you may be liable as a result of competitive injury to your competitors or to the competitors of your customers who are not able to handle 50-unit quantities.

No. 52. Question. May a seller legally discriminate in price between a manufacturer operating branch wholesale houses, or a wholesaler operating branch houses, and a wholesaler operating only one place of business, provided the wholesaler operating only one place of business buys in quantities equal to the quantities purchased for one of the branch houses?

Opinion. To answer would require a detailed analysis of costs of selling, manufacturing, and delivery under the differing conditions. It is possible that a difference in selling cost may result without a corresponding difference or any difference in cost of manufacturing and delivering. Whatever difference results would be allowable under the Act. All three cost elements—manufacture, selling, and delivery—may be evaluated in arriving at price differentials.

No. 53. Question. May a manufacturer, in addition to his regular discount to wholesalers, allow a special discount to those who have showrooms, and another special discount to those who regularly carry a balanced stock?

Opinion. These are payments for legitimate services and facilities rendered. They are only prohibited by the Act if allowed as a subterfuge for unlawful price differentials, when no service or use of facilities is actually rendered in return; but they must be made available to all wholesalers able to meet the same requirements.

No. 54. Question. May a manufacturer sell to wholesalers and retailers at a different price for the same grade, quality, and quantity, on the theory that they are not in competition with each other?

Opinion. Price differentials made to wholesalers as a class, although they involve differences in cost of manufacturing, selling, and delivery, are primarily recognized in commerce as making due allowance for the performance of functions in the process of distribution of goods. The cost of the performance of the wholesaling function governs the determination of price differentials between wholesalers and retailers. It is not determined on the theory that they are not in competition with each other.

No. 55. Question. Some sellers are bewildered as to their position with regard to prices to jobbers and to retail stores. Is a jobber's discount prohibited as such?

Opinion. The Robinson-Patman Act does not prohibit the wholesaler's or jobber's functional discount as such.

No. 56. Question. Can a manufacturer sell a certain quantity of merchandise to a wholesaler at one price and the same quantity of merchandise to a retailer at a different price?

Opinion. He can. But he incurs a responsibility under the Act to see that competitive injury does not result, directly or indirectly, to either party. At all times, he may resort to the difference-in-cost proviso.

No. 57. Question. Can a manufacturer who sells direct to retailers as a general rule quote a different price to wholesalers and to ultimate consumers to protect functional service?

Opinion. There is nothing in the Act that prevents a seller from establishing a functional discount, either for the wholesale function or the retail function. The cost of each occupies a separate bracket in the price the consumer pays. The various functions may be performed exclusively by separate parties, or all may be performed by one party, as in the factory-direct-to-consumer system. The cost brackets—i.e., the functional discounts —allowed for the performance of each function are only indirectly related to quantity. The allowance of functional discounts should not be confused with quantity discounts or allowed in lieu thereof.

No. 58. Question. Are functional discounts optional, permissible, or mandatory under the Robinson-Patman Act? What section of the Act applies?

Opinion. They are both permissible and optional—optional to the same degree that a seller has the right to select his own customers. However, if he elects two competing channels of distribution, in one of which he delegates the wholesaling function to separate parties and in the other of which he assumes that function himself, the law makes it mandatory that he protect the parties separately performing the wholesale function for him and, through them, protect their customers, who are indirectly the customers of the manufacturer. Section 2(a) applies in that he may not directly or indirectly discriminate in price.

No. 59. Question. There are within this state, and also in other states, many hardware firms doing both a wholesale and retail business. What regulations must be observed under the Robinson-Patman Act to protect competitors of the retail departments of such combination wholesale-and-retail firms? Must buying for the wholesale department and retail department be segregated? Must the wholesaler sell to his own retail department on the same basis as he sells to competing retailers? Or does the intrastate nature of the business between the wholesale and retail departments of the same firm exempt such a transaction?

Opinion. The business done between two departments of the same firm assuredly does not of itself make the transaction an intrastate transaction and exempt it from the jurisdiction of the Act. If a wholesaler-retailer knowingly (which he must in this case) benefits from an unlawful price discrimination in the form of a wholesale functional discount, he is, of course, as guilty as the seller under the Act. There exists between a seller and a wholesaler-retailer a peculiar, confidential relationship, which the Act does not disturb. There is nothing in the Act that prohibits a seller from giving a wholesaler-retailer the wholesale functional discount on all his purchases, both those he purchases for resale to others and those he buys for retailing through his own retail outlet. This is true as long as he performs the wholesale function on all his purchases.

All the confusion can be avoided by observing one simple rule: A wholesaler-retailer's sales at *retail* should be priced on an equal basis with those of any other retailer. If he does not take advantage of his wholesale status to undersell and thus unfairly compete with retailers of the same product who have bought through him or through some other wholesale customer of the manufacturer, there is not likely to be a violation within the intent of the Act.

No. 60. Question. Can a wholesaler who buys merchandise for resale to dealers sell direct to consumers at dealer prices without violating this law?

Opinion. There are certain conditions outlined in the Act under which such transactions are illegal. Unlawful discriminations may occur under these conditions, for the Act applies whether goods are sold for resale or for use and consumption. See reply to the previous question.

No. 61. Question. Would a wholesaler be within the law if he should segregate his retail department, charging all his goods to this department at the same price he charges other retail customers?

Opinion. He would fully comply with the provisions of the Act in this manner.

PRICES FAVORING UNITED STATES GOVERNMENT AND OTHER PUBLIC BODIES

No. 62. Question. If a manufacturer sells to government, municipal, or public institutions, is he in violation of the law if he does not make the same price for the same quantity available to the wholesalers to whom he sells?

Opinion. The Attorney General of the United States has ruled that the Act does not apply to the government.

No. 63. Question. If a manufacturer sells his product to wholesalers, and also sells to government, municipal, or public institutions at a price lower than he sells to his wholesale customers to meet the price of his competitor, how does the law apply?

Opinion. The Robinson-Patman Act does not apply.

Under date of December 28, 1936, the Attorney General of the United States ruled on this question in a letter to the Secretary of War, as follows:

I have your letter of October 30, requesting my opinion concerning the application of the Robinson-Patman Act (approved June 19, 1936, c. 592, 49 Stat. 1526) to government contracts for supplies.

The statute reads, in part, as follows:

> Section 2 of the Act entitled "An Act to supplement existing laws against unlawful restraints and monopolies, and for other purposes," approved October 15, 1914, as amended (U.S.C., title 15, sec. 13), is amended to read as follows:
>
> Sec. 2.(a) That it shall be unlawful for any person engaged in commerce, in the course of such commerce, either directly or indirectly, to discriminate in price between different purchasers of commodities *of like grade and quality, where either or any of the purchases involved in such discrimination are in commerce,* where such commodities are sold for use, consumption, or resale within the United States or any Territory thereof or the District of Columbia or any insular possession or other place under the jurisdiction of the United States, and where the effect of such discrimination may be substantially to lessen competition or tend to create a monopoly in any line of commerce, *or to injure, destroy, or prevent competition with any person who either grants or knowingly receives the benefit of such discrimination, or with customers of either of them:* Provided, That nothing herein contained shall prevent differentials which make only due allowance for differences in the cost of manufacture, sale, or delivery resulting from the differing methods or quantities in which such commodities are to such purchasers sold or delivered. . . .
> (Italics supplied.)

Aside from the proviso, the above quoted portion of the statute differs from Section 2 of the Act of October 15, 1914, in no respect save as indicated by the italicized words, which did not appear in the earlier statute. The language of the proviso is different from that of the corresponding proviso in the earlier statute, but the change does not bear upon the question which you have submitted.

In my opinion of April 20, 1936, to the Secretary of War concerning contracts with motor vehicle carriers, it was pointed out that statutes regulating rates, charges, etc., in matters affecting commerce do not ordinarily apply to the Government unless it is expressly so provided; and it does not seem to have been the policy of the Congress to make such statutes applicable to the Government. As Mr. Justice Brandeis observed, in *Emergency Fleet Corporation v. Western Union Telegraph Company,* 275 U.S. 415, 425, "it may be doubted whether the prescribed rule requiring equality of treatment would ever be violated by giving to the Government preferential rates."

The Act of June 19, 1936, merely amended the Act of October 15, 1914, as above pointed out, and, in so far as I am aware, the latter Act has not been regarded heretofore as applicable to Government contracts. The practice in this respect indicates that it has been customary in the past for those dealing with the various agencies of the Federal Government to grant to them special prices on contracts for supplies. Such prices are often below the regular market for similar material supplied to the regular trade—due, perhaps to an estimated lower cost of doing business with the Government because of quantity purchases and absence of credit risk, solicitation expense, etc., although it may often be impossible to evaluate such factors with exactness.

It has been suggested that the force which would ordinarily be attributed to this practice may be weakened because of the probability that the prices named have seldom, if ever, violated the statute, even assuming its application. Perhaps this is true. It is also conceivable that if the past practice is maintained the prices hereafter named to the Government will seldom, if ever, violate the amended statute, likewise assuming its application; and this would seem to supply another reason for avoiding a construction that would make the statute applicable to the Government in violation of the apparent policy of the Congress in such matters, in the absence of any clear indication that it intended to depart from that policy in this instance.

It is therefore my opinion that the Act of October 15, 1914, as amended by the Act of June 19, 1936, is not applicable to Government contracts for supplies.

Respectfully,
HOMER CUMMINGS
Attorney General

Following the opinion of the Attorney General of the United States, clarifying the situation regarding the Robinson-Patman Act and purchases by the United States government, there was approved on May 26, 1938, Public Law No. 550, 75th Congress, to the following effect:

> *Be it enacted by the Senate and House of Representatives of the United States of America in Congress assembled,* That nothing in the Act approved June 19, 1936 (Public Law, Numbered 692, Seventy-fourth Congress, second session), known as the Robinson-Patman Antidiscrimination Act, shall apply to purchases of their supplies for their own use by schools, colleges, universities, public libraries, churches, hospitals, and charitable institutions not operated for profit.

The action of a seller in quoting different prices to different customers and in making offers to sell at such prices is not enough to bring application of the statute. There must be actual sales at different prices by the same seller to two or more actual purchasers.[33]

The word "purchaser" within the meaning of the Robinson-Patman Act is not limited in its application to buyers of his product who buy direct from the seller charged with discrimination. The Federal Trade Commission defined the word "purchaser" as it appears in subsection 2(a) in the following manner:

---

[33] U.S. v. Borden Co., 111 F. Supp. 562 (D.C. Ill. 1953); Baim & Blank v. Philco Corp., 148 F. Supp. 541 (D.C.N.Y. 1957).

A retailer who purchases respondent's goods from jobbers and wholesalers is considered by the Commission to be a "purchaser" within the meaning of the Robinson-Patman Act, as well as retailers buying direct.[34]

The Supreme Court of the United States, in the case of *Corn Products Refining Co. v. FTC*,[35] referring to the word "purchaser" appearing in subsection (e) of Section 2 of the Robinson-Patman Act, stated:

> The Statute does not require that the discrimination in favor of one purchaser against another shall be provided for in a purchase contract or be required by it. It is enough if the discrimination be made in favor of one who is a purchaser and denied to another purchaser or other purchasers of the commodity.

The sales at different prices to different purchasers to meet the requirements of the statute must be shown to have involved the sale of "commodities." In its broadest sense, the word "commodity" might possibly include items of trade other than those in tangible form—for example, advertising, insurance, brokerage service, and similar items. However, the word is ordinarily used in the commercial sense to designate any movable or tangible thing that is produced or used as the subject of barter. This is the definition for the word "commodity" used in the application of the Robinson-Patman Act.

Mr. Clayton, for the House Committee on the Judiciary Report, April 26, 1912, said:

> . . . labor is not, and ought not to be regarded as, a commodity, within the purview of antitrust laws. FTC LIBRARY COMPILATION: TRUST REPORTS AND DOCUMENTS 475, 485.

The courts have been called upon to interpret the term "commodity" as it is used in the Clayton Act, as amended by the Robinson-Patman Act. In *Fleetway, Inc. v. Public Service Interstate Transportation Company*,[36] the United States District Court for New Jersey considered a charge of violation of Section 2 of the Clayton Act through discrimination in rates by a bus operating company. There the court said:

> This section refers to "commodities" only. And although some courts have applied it to "service," claimed by attorney for the plaintiff to be in the same class as furnishing transportation, I cannot so construe the word in that manner. In my opinion, "commodities" is not applicable to transportation by busses, and consequently plaintiff is not entitled to relief under this section.

---

[34] Kraft-Phenix Cheese Co., No. 2935, FTC, 1937, 25 F.T.C. 537, 546.
[35] 324 U.S. 726, 744.
[36] 4 F. Supp. 482, 484.

On appeal, the Third Circuit in August, 1934, said:

> The section (namely, Section 2 of the Clayton Act) prevents dis-
> crimination in price between different purchasers of commodities
> which are sold for use, consumption, or resale within the United
> States, etc. This clearly refers to a commodity such as merchandise,
> and has no reference to transportation of passengers by busses, for
> discrimination in price between purchasers of commodities on account
> of differences in grade, quality, or quantity, or a discrimination which
> makes only due allowance for differences in the cost of selling or trans-
> portation is not prohibited. It would be a strange and strained con-
> struction that would apply this language to the transportation of
> passengers by busses. (72 F.2d 761, 763.)

It is interesting to note that plaintiff in the above case relied heavily on
the case of *McKinley Telephone Company v. Cumberland Telephone Company*[37] in support of its contention that bus transportation did come within
the Clayton Act. In answer to this argument, the court made the following
observation relative to the *McKinley* case at page 764:

> There the court was dealing under the state law with "the supply or
> price of any article or commodity" and, under the statute, furnishing a
> telephone service might be stretched to mean the supply of a com-
> modity, but the language of Section 2 of the Clayton Act forbids such
> construction of the word "commodity" as there used.

The Senate bill made the law applicable only to commodities "manufactured or produced and sold for use, consumption, or resale." The House
bill did not contain the words "manufactured or produced and." Thus, we
have in the existing law the language "sold for use, consumption, or resale
within the United States or any territory thereof, or the District of
Columbia, or any insular possession or other place under the jurisdiction of
the United States."

Were the Commodities Involved in the Transaction of Like Grade and Quality?

Commodities having actual, genuine physical sameness with respect to
ingredients, appearance, utility, and acceptance would be regarded as being
of like grade and quality under the Robinson-Patman Act. Commodities
having different physical characteristics tailored to an individual product
buyer's use, and not merely decorative or fanciful probably would not be
regarded as of like grade and quality under the Robinson-Patman Act.

The original Section 2 of the Clayton Act, as approved in 1914, provided

---

[37] 140 N.W. 38, 39.

that nothing therein should prevent discrimination in price on account of difference in grade or quality. The section, as amended by the Robinson-Patman Act in 1936, provides that the prohibitive discriminations in price shall apply in the sale of commodities of like grade and quality. Thus it is seen that originally a seller was permitted to defend charges that he had discriminated in price by showing that his different prices applied to commodities of different grade or quality. Section 2, as amended by the Robinson-Patman Act, imposes on the plaintiff the burden of proving, in the first instance, that the commodities involved in the alleged discriminations were of like grade and quality.

There are a few indications of what courts may do in determining the meaning of the phrase "like grade and quality." It has been held that a seller may not be charged with price discrimination for quoting a combination price for joint purchases of two items lower than the total price for both if separately bought.[38]

Commodities made of separate materials or ingredients have not been deemed of "like grade and quality" with standard items.[39]

Nominal physical differences in the appearance of some items, which do not affect their functional utility, may not exempt differentials from the reach of the Act.[40]

The Federal Trade Commission has disregarded brand names and labels as determinants of "like grade and quality" and thereby has exposed to attack the variations in a seller's product line, although some were promoted under individual wrappings with slogans aimed at distinctive markets or particular classes of purchasers.[41]

It is, of course, clear the "like grade and quality" concept is relevant solely to compare two or more items sold by one seller to his several customers, and not to measure the similarity of his goods with those of a competitor.[42]

Actual, genuine, physical differentiations tailored to an individual product buyer's use, and not merely decorative or fanciful, probably remove a case from the reach of the Robinson-Patman Act.

---

[38] Package Closure Corp. v. Sealright Co., 141 F.2d 972, 979–980 (2d Cir. 1944); cf. General Shale Products Corp. v. Struck Construction Co., 132 F.2d 425, 428 (6th Cir. 1942).
[39] Boss Manufacturing Co. v. Payne Glove Co., 71 F.2d 768 (8th Cir. 1934).
[40] Bruce's Juices v. American Can Co., 87 F. Supp. 985, 987 (S.D. Fla. 1949), aff'd, 187 F.2d 919 (5th Cir. 1951).
[41] Goodyear Tire and Rubber Company, 22 F.T.C. 232, 290 (1936); U.S. Rubber Company, 46 F.T.C. 998, 1006–8 (1950); 28 F.T.C. 1489, 1500 (1939); Page Dairy Co., No. 5974, FTC, Oct. 30, 1953, 50 F.T.C. 395; E. Edelmann & Co., No. 5770, FTC. (initial decision filed March 5, 1954).
[42] E. B. Muller & Co. v. FTC, 142 F.2d 511, 518 (6th Cir. 1944); cf. McWhirter v. Monroe Calculating Machine Co., 76 F. Supp. 456 (W.D. Mo. 1948).

Is THE PERSON CHARGED WITH THE VIOLATION OF SUBSECTION 2(a) OF THE ROBINSON-PATMAN ACT ENGAGED IN COMMERCE, AND WERE THE CHALLENGED TRANSACTIONS IN THE COURSE OF SUCH COMMERCE?

The term "commerce," as set forth in Section 1 of the Clayton Act, includes not only interstate commerce but also commerce with foreign nations and commerce within and with the District of Columbia, Territories of the United States, insular possessions, and other places under the jurisdiction of the United States. It should be stressed that this is a stationary definition applicable to the Robinson-Patman Act. Nowhere in the Constitution does the term "interstate commerce" appear. Insofar as the Robinson-Patman Act is concerned, the term "interstate commerce" has developed out of and from the definition appearing in Section 1 of the Clayton Act, as above described.

The Committee on the Judiciary, in House Report No. 2287 on H.R. 8442, the Patman Bill, 74th Congress, after making reference to the definition of the term "commerce," discussed the application of subsection 2(a) to discriminatory practices of a seller when some of his sales are entirely intrastate, but others, at different prices, are made "in the course of interstate commerce." In that connection, it was stated:[43]

> When granted by a given seller to his customers in other States, and denied to those within the State, they involve the use of that interstate commerce to the burden and injury of the latter. When granted to customers within the State and denied to those beyond, they involve conversely a direct resulting burden upon his interstate commerce with the latter. Both are within the proper and well-recognized power of Congress to suppress; and the following clause, contained in the opening portion of section 2(a):
>
> > . . . where either or any of the purchases involved in such discrimination are in commerce . . .
>
> is of first importance in extending the protections of this bill against the full evil of price discrimination, whether immediately in interstate or intrastate commerce, wherever it is of such a character as tends directly to burden or affect interstate commerce.

Today, the term "commerce" is accepted as descriptive of the conduct of trade across state lines, and that form of "commerce" has been accepted as within the exclusive jurisdiction of the Congress of the United States under the Constitution. The several state legislatures may not, therefore, legislate with respect to "interstate commerce." However, "intrastate commerce"—

---

[43] H.R. REP. No. 2287, 74th Cong., 2d Sess. 8 (1936).

the form of trade that originates and ceases wholly within the confines of a single state—is not subject to Federal regulation. It would seem that the difference between interstate and intrastate commerce should not be difficult to determine, but the line of demarcation is not always clear. It rests with the courts to determine whether a person is engaged in "commerce"— meaning "interstate commerce"—within the meaning of the Robinson-Patman Act, or whether, due to the nature and scope of his business, he has confined himself wholly to "intrastate commerce."

As pointed out earlier, before the Robinson-Patman Act can be applied to any discrimination in price practiced by a person, it must be shown not only that the person is engaged in commerce, but that the discrimination alleged has involved the charging of different prices "in the course of inter-state commerce."[44]

Anyone engaged in a trade or business involving interstate movement or any component part of an interstate movement of goods, wares, mer-chandise, or services rendered in the course of carrying on a trade across state lines is engaged in interstate commerce.

As used in the Constitution, the word "commerce" is the equivalent of the phrase "intercourse for the purposes of trade." *Carter v. Carter Coal Co.*,[45] *Pensacola Telegraph Co. v. Western Union Telegraph Co.*[46]

All interstate commerce is not sales of goods. *International Textbook Co. v. Pigg*;[47] *Atlantic Cleaners & Dyers, Inc. v. U.S.*;[48] *American Medical Ass'n v. U.S.*;[49] and *Blackwell Publishing Company*, No. 2456, FTC, (O.C.D. September 5, 1936).

New York stock quotations furnished by telegraph to subscribers in Massachusetts were held to be interstate commerce. *Western Union Tele-graph Co. v. Foster.*[50]

The transmission of news to and from various parts of the country by means of the telephone and telegraph constitutes interstate commerce within the meaning of the National Labor Relations Act and the Constitu-tion. *Associated Press v. NLRB.*[51]

Radio broadcasting conducted under a Federal license is interstate com-merce. *Fisher's Blend Station, Inc. v. State Tax Commission.*[52]

---

[44] H.R. REP. No. 2287, 74th Cong., 2d Sess. 8 (1936).
[45] 298 U.S. 238, 298 (1936).
[46] 96 U.S. 1, 9 (1878).
[47] 217 U.S. 91, 107 (1910).
[48] 286 U.S. 427, 1932.
[49] 317 U.S. 519, 1943.
[50] 297 U.S. 105 (1918).
[51] 301 U.S. 103 (1937).
[52] 297 U.S. 650 (1936).

Insurance business, when carried on across state lines, is interstate commerce. *South-Eastern Underwriters Ass'n. v. U.S.*[53]

Interstate advertising as a part of interstate selling is interstate commerce. *Sunbeam Corp. v. Wentling.*[54] See also *Manual for Attorneys,* pp. 113 and 114.

Sales of cattle in the stockyards in Chicago after shipment from other states were held to be in interstate commerce, as well as sales of prepared meats by agents of the packers after shipments to their local stores in different states. *U.S. v. Swift & Co.*[55]

> The underlying test is that the transaction as an entirety, including each part calculated to bring about the result, reaches into two or more States; and that the parties dealing with reference thereto deal from different States. . . . The purchase of cattle shipped habitually from other States to markets where defendants purchase, in the expectation that the purchase will be made by the slaughter companies, is an act of interstate commerce. *Hopkins' Case,* 171 U.S. 590, 19 Sup. Ct. 40, 43 L. Ed. 290.
>
> It is none the less interstate commerce merely because the local incidents or facilities for such purchase are to be regarded as outside the interstate character of the transaction. Thus the local commission broker, or the men who drive the cattle from the pens to the slaughter house, need not, in any survey of the transaction, be held to be within the interstate status of the transaction. With them, it is essentially the same whether the cattle come from the State in which the purchase is made, or from other States. They are aids or facilities only, and as such are merely local incidents. But the purchase of livestock thus brought habitually from other States, relates, in its larger bearings, to a transaction that had its beginning in other States. The original shipments are influenced, and to a large extent brought about, by the character of the purchase.
>
> The purchase, the shipments, and the transportation are commercially interdependent; and in any survey of the transaction, as an entirety, none could be omitted. They each go to make the transaction, and covering different States they stamp the transaction—not all its incidents, but its essential body—as a transaction in interstate commerce.
>
> Coming now to the other branch of the transaction—the sales by the defendants—a like result follows. Unquestionably, it is interstate commerce when purchasers from other States buy directly from the defendants and have the meats shipped to them by the vendors. The situs of such a transaction, both as to initiatory intercourse, and as to transportation in furtherance of the exchange, includes a State other than the one from which defendants deal.
>
> I think the same is true of meat sent to agents and sold from their

---

[53] 322 U.S. 533 (1945).
[54] 185 F.2d 903 (3rd Cir. 1950).
[55] 122 Fed. 529.

stores. The transaction in such case, in reality, is between the purchaser and the agents' principal. The agents represent the principal at the place where the exchange takes place; but the transaction, as a commercial entity, includes the principal, and includes him as dealing from his place of business. (pp. 522–533.)

The Supreme Court affirmed that decision and, in doing so, stated through the opinion of Mr. Justice Holmes that:

> . . . Commerce among the States is not a technical, legal conception, but a practical one, drawn from the course of business. When cattle are sent for sale from a place in one State, with the expectation that they will end their transit, after purchase, in another, and when in effect they do so, with only the interruption necessary to find a purchaser at the stockyards, and when this is a typical, constantly recurring course, the current thus existing is a current of commerce among the States, and the purchase of the cattle is a part and incident of such commerce. What we say is true at least of such a purchase by residents in another State from that of the seller and of the cattle. Swift & Co. v. United States, 196 U.S. 375, 398 (1905).

The intrastate transportation of passengers and their luggage between stations in the city of Chicago is "clearly a part of the stream of interstate commerce" when the passengers are making interstate railroad trips that carry them through Chicago, during the course of which they must disembark from a train at one railroad station, travel from that station to another some two blocks to two miles distant, and there board another train for the purpose of continuing their interstate journey. When persons or goods move from a point of origin in one state to a point of destination in another, the fact that a part of the journey consists of transportation by an independent agency solely within the boundaries of one state does not make that portion of the trip any less interstate in character. *The Daniel Ball*, 10 Wall. 557, 565. That portion must be viewed in its relation to the entire journey rather than in isolation. So viewed, it is an integral step in the interstate movement. *U.S. v. Yellow Cab Co.*[56]

Where commodities are bought for use beyond state lines, the sale (intrastate) is a part of interstate commerce. *U.S. v. Rock Royal Co-operative, Inc.;*[57] *Dahnke-Walker Milling Co. v. Bondurant;*[58] *Lemke v. Farmers Grain Co.;*[59] *Currin v. Wallace;*[60] *Pennsylvania R.R. v. Clark Brothers;*[61] *Pennsylvania R.R. v. Sonman Shaft Coal Co.*[62]

Likewise, intrastate leases and sales of commodities by consignees in a

---

[56] 322 U.S. 218, 228–229 (1947).
[57] 307 U.S. 533, 568–569 (1939).
[58] 257 U.S. 282 (1921).
[59] 258 U.S. 50 (1922).
[60] 306 U.S. 1 (1939).
[61] 238 U.S. 456 (June 21, 1915).
[62] 242 U.S. 120 (December 4, 1916).

particular state, after shipments of such commodities across state lines to them for such purposes, have been held to be a part of interstate commerce. In *Binderup v. Pathe Exchange, Inc.*,[63] the Supreme Court, speaking through Mr. Justice Sutherland, said:

> If the commodity were consigned directly to the lessees, the interstate character of the commerce throughout would not be disputed. Does the circumstance that in the course of the process the commodity is consigned to a local agency of the distributors, to be by that agency held until delivery to the lessee in the same State, put an end to the interstate character of the transaction and transform it into one purely intrastate? We think not. The intermediate delivery to the agency did not end and was not intended to end the movement of the commodity. It was merely halted as a convenient step in the process of getting it to its final destination. The general rule is that where transportation has acquired an interstate character "it continues at least until the load reaches the point where the parties originally intended that the movement should finally end."

It has been held that even local financing of motor vehicle purchases is an essential adjunct to and a part of interstate commerce when done by an agent of a principal acting pursuant to a unified plan of selling and financing cars shipped in interstate commerce. The Sixth Circuit Court of Appeals has stated in that connection:

> The Federal Trade Commission Act was enacted under the power of Congress to regulate interstate and foreign commerce and by its express terms (sec. 4) (15 U.S.C.A. sec. 44) deals only with such commerce. Interstate commerce includes intercourse for the purpose of trade which results in the passage of property, persons, or messages from within one State to within another State. All of those things which stimulate or decrease the flow of commerce, although not directly in its stream, are essential adjuncts thereto and the Congress has power to confer on the Federal Trade Commission their regulation (*Stafford vs. Wallace*, 258 U.S. 495, 516) . . .
>
> The sale on credit of petition's (sic) cars by its local dealers, when separately considered, may be intrastate in character but when the activities of petitioner's local agencies are weighed in the light of their relationship to the petitioner, and its financing sales of cars, it is at once apparent that there is such a close and substantial relationship to interstate commerce that the control of such activities is appropriate to its protection. Ford Motor Co. v. FTC, 120 F.2d 175, 183 (6th Cir. 1941).

That line of reasoning followed what had been stated by the Second Circuit Court of Appeals, speaking through Circuit Judge Augustus N. Hand:

---

[63] 263 U.S. 291, 309 (1923).

The contention that the Commission was without jurisdiction because GMAC was not engaged in interstate commerce is without merit. While GMAC was primarily acting as a local finance company, it was wholly owned by General Motors, and, with the Sales Corporation, acted as an agent of General Motors in a unified plan of selling and financing cars shipped in interstate commerce. Under the decision of the Supreme Court in *Federal Trade Commission vs. Education Society,* 302 U.S. 112, 120, . . . there was jurisdiction. *Cf. National Harness Manufacturers' Ass'n v. Federal Trade Commission,* 6 Cir. 268 Fed. 705, 709. General Motors Corp. v. FTC, 114 F.2d 33, 36 (2d Cir. 1940).

Judge Yankwich, in deciding the case of *United States v. Standard Oil Company of California*[64] in the District Court for the Southern District of California, held that intrastate sale of a commodity was nevertheless to be considered part of interstate commerce when the commodity involved in such sale is under the control of a seller who had originated its handling and movements in interstate commerce. There he stated:

> . . . we refer to the contention that the activities of Standard are local in character. Recent cases have obliterated the rigid distinction between intrastate and interstate activities. Activities purely local which interfere with interstate commerce come under the interdiction of the antitrust statutes. The control of a commodity originating in interstate commerce, although exercised after it comes to rest in a state, does not take it out of the purview of the Sherman or Clayton Acts, if the flow is continuous, and if the restrictions affect it. (*Mandeville Island Farms Co. vs. American Crystal Sugar Company* (1948), 68 S. Ct. at pp. 1005, 1006.) The latest decisions give effect to the broad definition of commerce contained in one of the older and leading cases on the subject:
>
> "The evidence shows that they and other defendants conspired to burden the free movement of live poultry into the metropolitan area. It may be assumed that some time after delivery of carload lots by interstate carriers to the receivers the movement of the poultry ceases to be interstate commerce. *Public Utilities Comm. vs. Landon,* 249, U.S. 236, 237, 245, 39 S. Ct. 268, 63 L. Ed. 577; *Missouri vs. Kansas Natural Gas Co.,* 265 U.S. 298, 309 44 S. Ct. 544, 68 L. Ed. 1027; *East Ohio Gas Co. vs. Tax Comm.,* 283 U.S. 465, 470, 471, 51 S. Ct. 499, 75 L. Ed. 1171. But we need not decide when interstate commerce ends and that which is intrastate begins. *The control of the handling, the sales, and the prices at the place of origin before the interstate journey begins or in the state of destination where the interstate movement ends may operate directly to restrain and monopolize interstate commerce.*"

Without detailing the distributive system used by Standard, it is

---

[64] 78 F. Supp. 850, 864, 865, 873, 874 (June 7, 1948).

evident that there is constant interstate flow of the products it produces and distributes.

The point is pressed that some of the products, such as gasoline, are supplied to California stations exclusively from California refineries. And it is argued that, so far as the California stations are concerned, their dealings in gasoline are beyond the purview of interstate commerce . . . As already shown, there is a constant flow in interstate commerce of these products and supplies. The contracts affect, and the transactions under them are in the course of, interstate commerce.

To the same effect was the holding in the case of *Gavril v. Kraft Cheese Co.*,[65] which was decided on November 27, 1941, in the District Court for the Northern District of Illinois. There, one of the considerations involved was whether driver-salesmen making intrastate sales for the Kraft Cheese Company were engaged in interstate commerce. On this question, the court, speaking through District Judge Campbell, in part stated:

> The defendant on page 13 of its original brief cites several other Acts of Congress wherein the phrase "engaged in commerce" is used and later cites cases interpreting the use of that phrase in some of those Acts. Among the other Acts of Congress which use this phrase the defendant lists the Federal Trade Commission Act, 15 U.S.C.A. sec. 41 et seq., the Clayton Act, 15 U.S.C.A. sec. 12 et seq., and the Robinson-Patman Act amending it, 15 U.S.C.A. sec. 13(a).
>
> In the case of *Federal Trade Commission vs. Kraft-Phenix Cheese Corporation,* Federal Trade Commission Complaint No. 2935 (Vol. 2 Federal Trade Regulation Service Par. 9061), the Federal Trade Commission in an opinion dismissing a proceeding against Kraft-Phenix Cheese Corporation said, among other things:
>
> "Respondent Kraft-Phenix Cheese Corporation, individually and through subsidiaries, manufactures and distributes on a nation-wide scale a line of processed cheese, package cheese and salad dressing. Respondent itself ships these products across state lines from factories to warehouses and the products are usually distributed from warehouses to retailers by truck by sales subsidiaries of respondent or independently owned jobbers and wholesalers. The distribution from the warehouses to retailers is usually within the confines of a single state, although in some cases this distribution crosses state lines. Respondent advertises its products extensively to the purchasing public and maintains a force of salesmen who contact retailers, most of whom buy Kraft products from independent jobbers. There is a continuous, uninterrupted flow and current of commerce in respondent's products from the factories to warehouses and from the warehouses over regularly established routes to retailers, whose identity is known in advance. The course of such commerce runs between, among,

---

[65] 42 F. Supp. 702.

across, and within all the states of the United States, and the District of Columbia.

"Considered in their character as interstate commerce, respondent's products, upon reaching the warehouse, do not become mixed with or a part of the general mass of property within the state in which such warehouse is located. On the contrary, such warehouses are clearing houses or distributing points, serving one function in respondent's system of making its perishable products available for sale by retailers to the ultimate consumer, the purchasing public. Respondent's advertising, its solicitation of retailers, and the facilities which it provides for the sale and distribution of its products to the retailer, are all vital and essential elements in the process of marketing these commodities . . .

"The Commission concludes that respondent, . . . is engaged in interstate commerce, and that the sales of its products to retailers are likewise made in the course of such commerce."

Kraft-Phenix Cheese Corporation was, as is disclosed by the title on the complaint filed herein, the name which the defendant in this case formerly used.

While it is quite possible that the activities of the defendant may have changed somewhat since the order of the Federal Trade Commission was entered on July 17, 1937, nevertheless, from the facts before the Court on the affidavits heretofore referred to, the Court is of the opinion that the present activities of the defendant constitute commerce within the meaning of the Fair Labor Standards Act just as the Federal Trade Commission was of the opinion that similar activities of the defendant under its former name constituted commerce under the Clayton Act and the Robinson-Patman Amendment to that Act when it describes such activities as "a continuous, uninterrupted flow and current of commerce in respondent's (defendant's) products from the factories to warehouses and from the warehouses over regularly established routes to retailers . . ."

It therefore follows that the plaintiffs in this case, being "drive-salesmen" (sic) engaged in the final phase of the interstate flow of the defendant's products (the delivery to the retailers), are engaged in commerce within the meaning of the Fair Labor Standards Act.

In the case of *Mid-Continent Petroleum Corporation v. Keen*,[66] it was held that Mid-Continent, as a producer and wholesale distributor of petroleum products, was engaged in interstate commerce in making local intrastate sales from bulk storage plants, where it maintained a sufficient supply of gasoline to meet anticipated demands of retail service stations in such localities. There Judge Riddick, speaking for the Eighth Circuit, in part stated:

    . . . obviously, the petroleum products remained in the channels of commerce until they reached the service stations. The petroleum

---

[66] 157 F.2d 310, 314 (8th Cir. 1946).

products were transported in commerce to the bulk plants with the intention on the part of Mid-Continent, in advance of transportation, that all of the products (except incidental sales) would go to certain retailers, the service stations handling Mid-Continent products. The retail service stations were the intended final destinations of all of the petroleum products. The temporary storage of the petroleum products in the tanks at Mid-Continent's bulk plants was merely "a convenient intermediate step in the process of getting them to their final destination." *Walling vs. Jacksonville Paper Co.,* 317 U.S. 564, 568–570, 63 S. Ct. 332, 87 L. Ed. 499; *Walling vs. Mutual Wholesale Food and Supply Co.,* supra (141 F.2d 331, 335, C.C.A. 8, 1944). And see *Republic Pictures Corporation vs. Kappler,* 8 Cir., 151 F.2d 543, 162 A.L.R. 228, *affirmed,* 66 S. Ct. 523; *A. H. Phillips, Inc. vs. Walling,* 1 Cir., 144 F.2d 102; *Walling vs. American Stores Co.,* 3 Cir., 133 F.2d 840.

A ruling to that effect was made by the Supreme Court of the United States, where it stated:

> Such sales are well within the jurisdictional requirements of the Act (the Robinson-Patman Act). Any other conclusion would fall short of the recognized purpose of the Robinson-Patman Act to reach the operations of large interstate businesses in competition with small local concerns. Such temporary storage of the gasoline as occurred within the Detroit area does not deprive the gasoline of its interstate character. Standard Oil Company of Indiana v. FTC, 340 U.S. 231, 232–238 (1951).

In the case of *Walling* v. *Jacksonville Paper Co.,*[67] on certiorari to the Court of Appeals for the Fifth Circuit, involving the Fair Labor Standards Act, the Supreme Court, speaking through Mr. Justice Douglas, in part stated:

> . . . The entry of the goods into the warehouse interrupts but does not necessarily terminate their interstate journey. A temporary pause in their transit does not mean that they are no longer "in commerce" within the meaning of the Act. As in the case of an agency (*cf. De Loach vs. Crowley's, Inc.,* 5 Cir., 128 F.2d 378) if the halt in the movement of the goods is a convenient intermediate step in the process of getting them to their final destinations, they remain "in commerce" until they reach those points. Then there is a practical continuity of movement of the goods until they reach the customers for whom they were intended. That is sufficient. Any other test would allow formalities to conceal the continuous nature of the interstate transit which constitutes commerce.

In *Walling v. American Stores Company,*[68] the Court of Appeals for the Third Circuit, speaking through Circuit Judge Goodrich, in substance held

[67] 317 U.S. 564, 63 S. Ct. 332, 335, 87 L. Ed. 460 (1943).
[68] 133 F.2d 840 (3rd Cir. 1943).

that where a chain-store organization's warehouses received goods from many states and supplied such goods to the organization's retail stores, and there was practical continuity of movement of goods until they reached retail stores, and maintenance of warehouses was to make continuity economical and uninterrupted, warehouse employees were engaged in "commerce" within the Fair Labor Standards Act.

In determining the question of commerce involved herein, reference is also made to the case of *Fleming v. Alterman*,[69] decided by the District Court for the Northern District of Georgia, involving the Fair Labor Standards Act, wherein that Court made an exhaustive analysis and study of many of the court decisions dealing with "commerce," and, speaking through District Judge Russell, stated in part (pp. 98, 101):

> . . . it is urged that because the goods so introduced never thereafter leave the State of Georgia the stamp of interstate commerce is thereby erased, so that all subsequent handling and dealing therein is local or internal commerce. The argument overlooks the effect of the evidence that at least a portion of such goods never really stop in the warehouse, and those which are stored do not "come to rest" but as a rule have only a short "breathing spell" until they continue to what has been in effect, and in the minds of all the parties from the beginning, their ultimate destination, the retailer or consumer. This contention also overlooks the fact that due to this, continuous and recurring, purchase-sale-transportation-unloading-delivery-resale-repurchase and so on round and round the circle during the year, the defendant at least wades in the stream of commerce if indeed he does not swim therein. . . .
>
> If the contention that wholesale grocers may remove themselves from engaging in interstate commerce by confining their sales and shipments to one State be correct, it must follow that the consequent establishment of forty-eight (48) separate trading areas, by States, and confined to State boundaries, could result without concern or interference by the national government, and this despite the great dislocation of present commerce which would result. Such is contrary to the fundamentals underlying the adoption and employment of the commerce clause for the protection and promotion of uninterrupted national commercial intercourse. . . .
>
> He who ships interstate is unquestionably engaged in commerce, and one whose business is to all practical purposes exclusively the receipt and distribution of such shipments by wholesale and in such manner as to produce a constant and continuous recurrence thereof is also so definitely enmeshed as a part thereof by the day in and day out receipt and distribution of such goods as he who ships them. Each activity is a part of the whole of commerce between the several States, and the whole includes the parts.

---

[69] 38 F. Supp. 94 (April 2, 1941).

The question of whether there is subsequent interstate shipment furnishes one test of interstate commerce, but does not supply a definite and unvarying standard which may be applied to all transactions to measure and define their inter or intrastate character. Of necessity, each transaction and business must be determined in the light of all surrounding circumstances . . .

In *Midland Oil Co. v. Sinclair Refining Co.*,[70] decided by the District Court for the Northern District of Illinois, that Court considered an action by Midland against Sinclair for damages caused by price discrimination between different purchasers of Sinclair's gasoline in violation of Section 2(a) of the Clayton Act [15 U.S.C.A. § 13(a)], and, speaking through District Judge Campbell, stated in part (p. 437):

. . . the Court is of the opinion that the defendant is engaged in interstate commerce within the meaning of the said Act both as to its less-than-tank-car-load sales as well as its tank car load sales which admittedly constitute interstate commerce. The defendant is engaged in the business of refining and selling gasoline. Its refinery is located in the State of Indiana. For its less-than-tank-car-load sales which are the transactions at issue in this case, it ships its gasoline from Indiana to various "bulk plants" which it operates in the State of Illinois. The gasoline is stored at these bulk plants until an order is received from a customer whereupon the amount of gasoline ordered is taken by truck from the bulk plant to the customer. The fact that the defendant finds it convenient to use these bulk plants in its system of distribution for less-than-tank-car-load quantities does not alter the interstate nature of its business. The defendant owns the refineries, the bulk plants and the method of delivery to the customer. The customer deals with the defendant directly. The gasoline remains the property of the defendant from the time it is refined until the time it is actually delivered to the customer. In my opinion this constitutes one direct uninterrupted flow in interstate commerce.

When intrastate commodities are physically commingled with interstate commodities and become inseparable from those to be shipped outside the state, the transactions involving any part of the total become transactions in interstate commerce. *United States v. Rock Royal Cooperative, Inc.;*[71] *Currin v. Wallace.*[72]

In those situations in which a person, partnership, or corporation has been found to be engaged in commerce, discriminations practiced by him are not subject to the Robinson-Patman Act unless *some* of the different prices charged by him involve sales and shipments of goods across state lines. In other words, subsection 2(a) does not prohibit price discrimina-

---

[70] 41 F. Supp. 436 (Sept. 15, 1941).
[71] 307 U.S. 533 (1939).
[72] 306 U.S. 1 (1939).

tions which merely *affect* commerce. Some transactions involving the challenged transactions must be *in* commerce and not merely those which *affect* interstate commerce,[73] since the Robinson-Patman Act only prohibits discriminations in price made in the course of commerce—that is, interstate commerce.

The Supreme Court of the United States has held that it is enough to show that the person charged with discrimination under the statute is engaged in commerce and that *some* of the sales made in the alleged discrimination in price were made in interstate commerce. If other sales were made either at higher or lower prices wholly in intrastate commerce, it is sufficient to bring the discrimination in price within the statute.[74]

In the *Mead's* case, it was held that, although Mead did not discriminate in interstate business but did so between customers who made intrastate purchases and those who made interstate purchases, the course of action fell within the language "in the course of such commerce" as used in subsection 2(a). In view of the ruling in the *Mead's* case, it appears that a seller should not assume that his intrastate pricing policies and practices are not subject to the Robinson-Patman Act, even where the only resulting damage is to intrastate competition. That is true because it is always probable that it will be alleged that his lower prices, which injure local competition, are subsidized, in part, by the higher prices he has charged interstate purchasers.[75]

WHAT ARE THE PROBABLE EFFECTS OF THE CHALLENGED DISCRIMINATIONS?

Discriminations prohibited by subsection 2(a) of the Robinson-Patman Act are those whose effect may be:

1. Substantially to lessen competition in any line of commerce; or,
2. To tend to create a monopoly in any line of commerce; or,
3. To injure, destroy, or prevent competition—
    (a) With any person who either grants or knowingly receives the benefit of such discrimination; or,
    (b) With customers of either of them (i.e., the grantor or grantee).

Some definition is needed for the words "may be," "substantially," and "injure," as used here. It has been made clear, through the use of the term "may be," that the statute was designed to reach discriminations "in their

---

[73] FTC v. Bunte Bros. Inc., 312 U.S. 349 (1941).
[74] See Moore v. Mead's Fine Bread Co., 348 U.S. 115 (1954). See also the discussion respecting the definition of "commerce" appearing earlier in this chapter.
[75] FTC v. Anheuser-Busch, 363 U.S. 536 (1960).

incipiency" and before harm to competition occurred. For that reason, the term "may be" has been defined to include probabilities. In other words, it has been held that the term gives the statute the reach that would permit its application to discriminations that, if continued, probably would have the effect of substantially lessening competition.[76]

This, however, obviously was not intended to mean every remote lessening of competition, for as the Supreme Court has held in *Standard Fashion Co. v. Magrane-Houston Co.*,[77] in construing the words "may be" as used in Section 3 of the Act, there is a specific requirement that such lessening must be "substantial."

Perceptibility appears to have been the measure by which the Federal Trade Commission determined "substantiality" or the lack of it in another instance when it dismissed a complaint for the reason, among others, that the showing made regarding the amount of the discriminations involved would "not appear to inflict *any perceptible* injury upon those who did not receive it."[78]

Webster's dictionary, in defining the words "substantial" and "substance," relies heavily on the idea of perceptibility. Distinguishing things that have substantiality as the opposite of illusive, imaginary, shadowy, or visionary objects. Thus, it appears that to have substance, objects must be perceptible, material, and contain demonstrated worth.

It appears that discriminations must be of such nature and scope that, under the circumstances involved, the effect flowing therefrom would be regarded as material. Otherwise, they would not be acceptable as a basis for a course of action under subsection 2(a). In other words, without these characteristics, it is not likely the discriminations would be regarded as being sufficiently substantial to probably "injure" competition.

In proceeding to determine whether a given discrimination in price probably would "injure" competitors or customers of the discriminating seller, the Commission has taken into account many factors. In doing so, it has reasoned whether, in a given set of circumstances, a discrimination of a particular kind and scope would have the proscribed effects. In other words, through reasoning the Commission has determined whether a given discrimination would "injure" others engaged in business. In a sense, then, a "rule of reason" has been applied by the Commission in determining the definition of "injure" as applied to a particular circumstance in a given case arising under subsection 2(a).

---

[76] Corn Products Refining Co. v. FTC, 324 U.S. 726, 739 (1945); *cf.* Standard Fashion Co. v. Magrane-Houston Co., 258 U.S. 346, 356, 357.

[77] 258 U.S. 346.

[78] Kraft-Phenix Cheese Corp., 25 F.T.C. 537, 544 (1937).

It has been the view of the Federal Trade Commission that a prima facie case of violation of Section 2(a) may be established by proving (1) jurisdiction, (2) the sale of goods of like grade and quality to one of two or more purchasers at discriminatory prices, and (3) the existence of circumstances under which it is reasonably apparent that there is a probability of the adverse competitive effects described in the statute. Of course, the circumstances indicating the probability of the adverse competitive effects could involve either the line of commerce in which the seller is engaged, the line of commerce in which his customers are engaged, or the line of commerce in which customers of the favored purchasers are engaged. In any case, it is the tendency and probable effect of the discriminatory prices rather than the actual results that are important, and in no case is there a definite yardstick by which the probable effects may be quantitively measured. The question in every case is whether or not, in view of the circumstances, there is a reasonable likelihood of substantial adverse competitive effects. That is the applicable standard, regardless of whether primary-line competition or secondary-line competition is involved.

Our discussion of the definitions of various words and phrases appearing in the "effects" clauses of subsection 2(a) has devoted considerable space to the definitions of such terms as "may be," "substantially," and "injure." It is the purpose of the discussion at this point to explore the requirements regarding the nature and degree of the challenged discrimination and the probable extent of injuries flowing therefrom for applicability of the law.

The majority opinion of the Supreme Court of the United States in the *Morton Salt* case[79] expressed the thought that subsection 2(a) would apply if

> . . . there is a "reasonable possibility" that competition may be adversely affected by a practice under which manufacturers and producers sell their goods to some customers substantially cheaper than they sell like goods to the competitors of these customers. This showing in itself is sufficient to justify our conclusion that the Commission's findings of injury to competition were adequately supported by evidence.[80]

Mr. Justice Jackson, with whom Mr. Justice Frankfurter joined in dissent, concurred in the result of the majority, but in doing so, stated:

> . . . the use of the word "may" was not to prohibit discriminations having "the mere possibility" of those consequences, but to reach those which would probably have the defined effect on competition.[81]

---

[79] FTC v. Morton Salt Co., 334 U.S. 37, 50 (1948).
[80] *Id.* at 50, 51.
[81] *Id.* at 57.

The Federal Trade Commission has stated:

> The words "may be" indicate neither bare possibility nor certainty, but probability to be deduced from intent or inherent character of the acts themselves . . .

The Commission further stated:

> The words "where the effect may be" are obviously used merely to indicate that it is tendency and probable effect rather than the actual results that are important . . .

The Federal Trade Commission, in its interpretation of the original Act, adopted this view and later elaborated on it in its findings in the *Staley* case.[82] The Supreme Court gave the same construction of the Robinson-Patman amendment in the *Corn Products* case.[83] There it was made clear that Section 2 does not require a finding that the discriminations in price have in fact had an adverse effect on competition in either the primary line or the secondary line of commerce; a finding of probability of such effect, determined from all of the circumstances of the case, is sufficient.

In 1922, the Commission acted in several cases on the theory that Section 2 of the original Clayton Act covered competitive injury in the secondary line of commerce, or at the customer level. In one of these cases—against the *Mennen Company*[84]—the order to cease and desist entered by the Commission was reversed by the Circuit Court of Appeals for the Second Circuit.[85] Thereafter, and until the statute was amended by the Robinson-Patman Act in 1936, the Commission was reluctant to proceed in cases where the injury to competition appeared only in the secondary line of commerce or at the customer level.

Following the passage of the Robinson-Patman Act, most of the cases brought by the Commission under subsection 2(a) involved competition in the secondary line of commerce or at the customer level, but a number of cases that have been brought were based primarily on alleged injury in the primary line of commerce or at the level of the discriminating seller. Regardless of whether the Commission in its cases has alleged injury to competitors of the discriminating seller or to some of his nonfavored customers, it has not rested its proof regarding the element of injury on a showing of injury to tradesmen in any particular line of commerce. Instead, the Commission has, in addition to alleging injury to tradesmen in a particular line of commerce, also proceeded to allege, prove, and find general injury or the probability of it to the state of competition in the line or lines of com-

[82] FTC v. Staley Mfg. Co., 324 U.S. 746 (1945).
[83] 324 U.S. 726.
[84] 4 F.T.C. 258 (1922).
[85] See Mennen Company v. FTC, 288 Fed. 774 (1923), *cert. denied*, 262 U.S. 759 (1923).

merce concerned. In other words, the cases brought by the Federal Trade Commission, as a general rule, involved a showing that the challenged discriminations gave rise to a substantial lessening of competition in a line of commerce or a tendency toward monopoly in that line of commerce.

Undoubtedly, there are many who would disagree with that assertion. Capable and respected lawyers argue and take the position that the Commission has acted in Robinson-Patman cases on the sole basis of a showing of injury to particular tradesmen. Their arguments and statements of position have been carefully studied and evaluated.

In the *Moss* case,[86] the Commission directed much of its attention to the effect of the discriminations by Moss on its competitors, but then proceeded to the conclusion the discriminatory prices "had a substantial and injurious effect upon competition."[87] In other cases where the Commission's first attention was directed to the effect of competition in the primary line, its findings have included conclusions to the effect that the discriminations involved, if continued, would destroy or prevent competition in the broad sense. In other words, in those cases where unlawful price discrimination has been found, it has been concluded there was *general injury to competition*. Like findings and conclusions have been made by the Commission in those cases where it directed its primary attention to the effect of the discriminations in the secondary line of commerce or at the customer level. For example, in the *Morton Salt* case,[88] which turned principally on the effects of Morton Salt Company's discriminations in the secondary line of commerce, the Commission found:

> . . . that the effect of the discriminations in price generally and specifically described herein may be substantially to lessen competition in the line of commerce in which the purchaser receiving the benefit of said discriminatory price is engaged and to injure, destroy, and prevent competition between those purchasers receiving the benefit of said discriminatory prices and those to whom they are denied, and may tend to create a monopoly in those purchasers receiving the benefit of said discriminatory prices in said line of commerce in the various localities or trade areas in the United States in which said favored customers and their competitors are engaged in business.[89]

The Supreme Court indicated that the Federal Trade Commission in the *Morton Salt* case was not required to go as far as it did in its proof or in its findings. In that connection, it was stated:

---

[86] Samuel H. Moss, Inc., 36 F.T.C. 640. See also Samuel H. Moss, Inc. v. FTC, 148 F.2d. 378 (1945).
[87] 36 F.T.C. at 649.
[88] 39 F.T.C. 35 (1944). See also FTC v. Morton Salt Co., 334 U.S. 37 (1948).
[89] 39 F.T.C. at 44.

We think that the language of the Act, and the legislative history just cited, show that Congress meant by using the words "discrimination in price" in Section 2 that in a case involving competitive injury between a seller's customers the Commission need only prove that a seller had charged one purchaser a higher price for like goods than he had charged one or more of the purchaser's competitors. This construction is consistent with the first sentence of Section 2(a) in which it is made unlawful "to discriminate in price between different purchasers of commodities of like grade and quality where either or any of the purchases involved in such discrimination are in commerce . . . and where the effect of such discrimination may be . . . to injure, destroy, or prevent competition with any person who either grants or knowingly receives the benefit of such discrimination or with customers of either of them . . .[90]

On January 16, 1961, the Supreme Court of the United States, in the case of *Radiant Burners, Inc. v. Peoples Gas Light and Coke Company*, held that in actions brought for triple damages arising by virtue of things forbidden under the antitrust laws, it is unnecessary to allege or prove that there has been any general injury to the competitive processes or that the public at large has suffered any economic harm. In that connection, it was stated:

> . . . to state a claim upon which relief can be granted under that section, allegations adequate to show a violation and, in a private treble damage action, that plaintiff was damaged thereby are all the law requires.[91]

The sponsors of the Act made it clear that the application of the law should not be restricted to cases in which the showing was a general injury to competitive conditions or to those situations where it was shown that competitors of the seller had been injured. In the report on the Patman bill, it was stated that the requirement in that regard had been

> too restrictive in requiring a showing of *general injury to competitive conditions* in the line of commerce concerned, whereas the more immediately important concern is in injury to the *competitor victimized* by the discrimination.[92]

In the *Anheuser-Busch* case,[93] the Federal Trade Commission's attention was directed to price discriminations that it alleged and found were aimed at the local competitors of Anheuser-Busch. Although the Commission

---

[90] 334 U.S. at 45.
[91] 364 U.S. 656. It should be noted that, although this case was based upon an alleged violation of Section 1 of the Sherman Act, it does not appear that the ruling would have been any differently stated by the Court if the action had been brought for violation of 2(a) of the Robinson-Patman Act.
[92] H.R. REP. No. 2287, 74th Cong., 2d Sess. 8 (1936).
[93] 54 F.T.C. 277.

found in that case that the effect of the discriminations involved did injure the business of specified local competitors of Anheuser-Busch, the Commission did not stop at that point, but proceeded to find and rest its case on the further finding that the practice shown was "not only one of injury to competitors, but of injury to their line of commerce."[94] The United States Court of Appeals for the Seventh Circuit held that even though the price discriminations of Anheuser-Busch were directed to and injured its local competitors and the line of commerce in which they were engaged, this was not to be condemned under subsection 2(a), since the *competing* purchasers of Anheuser-Busch were not charged different prices.[95] The Supreme Court reversed the ruling and held that it was sufficient when the proof and the findings showed injury to primary-line competition without reliance on or the presence or absence of competition among purchasers.[96] Thereupon, the Supreme Court remanded that case to the Circuit Court for further proceedings on other points the Circuit Court had not considered. On January 25, 1961, the Court of Appeals for the Seventh Circuit, in its further consideration of the case, set aside the Commission's order on the ground that the Commission had not proved Anheuser-Busch had, in fact, discriminated with the effect of injury to competition, and that it was of no moment and insufficient even if the record could be said to show that the effect of the discriminations *could* injure competition. It ruled out the element of injury and, in doing so, stated that it cannot be said that use of price discriminations

> . . . may produce these adverse results to competition any more than it can be logically maintained that a powerful drug, used under a physician's supervision to alleviate human pain, may, if misused, injure or kill a person.[97]

WHAT CONSTITUTES EVIDENCE OF INJURY TO COMPETITION?

It is no more possible to devise a list of hypothetical evidence by which a substantial lessening or prevention of competition would be found than it is to prescribe what circumstantial evidence must result in a finding of unlawful agreement, or to list the evidence that would predetermine the illegality of any and all mergers. Obviously, both the evidentiary facts and the weight to be given the facts will vary in individual cases, and the ultimate economic question of whether a discriminatory practice should be stopped must follow a careful combing for facts relevant to the particular

---

[94] 54 F.T.C. 277, 290.
[95] 265 F.2d 677, 681.
[96] 363 U.S. 536.
[97] 289 F.2d 835.

competitive setting and a careful analysis to determine the weight to be given to such facts. The best that can be provided as a guide, therefore, is an understanding of the general objectives of the law, and a general statement of the kinds of facts that should be considered in the several broad types of situations in which problems have arisen or might arise, plus, perhaps, a warning against overemphasis on any single economic theory or "ultimate test."

The general purpose and objectives of the original Section 2, and the Robinson-Patman amendment thereto, are rather clearly set out in the legislative history of these enactments and in the practical business problems that gave rise to these enactments. The original Clayton Act followed a period when large national businesses had been arising to replace smaller firms that had been marketing on local or regional scales. As we know, the primary concern at that time, and the subject of most of the legislative discussion, was injury in the primary line. In the less-complex business setting of that day, it was rather clearly recognized that discriminatory selling is a practice that accrues to the competitive advantage of the larger sellers. This seems to have been most sharply understood, and frequently demonstrated, in terms of geographical discriminations. The point most frequently mentioned was that large marketers were, by selling at different prices in different parts of the country, destroying their local and regional competitors.

Similarly, the Robinson-Patman amendment followed a period when independent retailers and wholesalers had been losing out to the chain organizations in distributing what was by then a set of largely standardized products emanating from the manufacturing segment of business. The legislative emphasis here was, as we know, on the competitive inequalities that are created among buyers when the supplier discriminates in his prices. Almost no challenge has been raised against the proposition that where sellers do grant price concessions over and above those justified by differences in their costs, it is generally the larger buyers who receive the unearned advantage. Sellers have reasons for preferring larger buyers, and for making unwarranted discriminations in favor of larger buyers, which lie outside the realm of economic justification. A large buyer's superior bargaining powers are not, of course, within the scope of an economic cost savings, nor are the variously imagined ways of spreading overhead costs among different buyers.

If we had to provide a single statement as to the economic tests of an objectionable price discrimination, we would have to say that it is a discrimination that has a substantial tendency to divide the market shares in ways different from the division that would take place if efficiency were the sole determinant of this question. This cannot mean, of course, that all small sellers should be allowed to discriminate and that their large competitors should be prohibited from discriminating. Although a primary purpose of the law was to prevent large firms from having an undue advantage over their smaller rivals, it is manifest that a firm of any size that engages in discriminatory practices would probably enjoy a substantial competitive advantage over a rival of equal size that eschewed such practices.

Summing up the adverse tendencies of discriminatory selling, then, we can say that the general tendency is to give larger sellers an advantage over smaller competing sellers and, again generally, to give larger buyers an unearned advantage over smaller competing buyers. Business efficiency, one of the primary objectives of restraints on discrimination, is in many instances substantially advanced by conveniences involving technical price discriminations that are insignificant in their adverse effects or are without even the vestige of an adverse effect. For example, as Professor Morris Adelman, Professor of Economics, Massachusetts Institute of Technology, has pointed out, discrimination in the economic sense occurs both when a seller fails to pass on cost savings and when a seller makes a price concession that is not justified by cost differences.

Under these circumstances, a variety of situations can be found where discriminations are not only harmless but, on balance, are actually beneficial to competition. Thus, as Professor J. M. Clark, Professor of Economics, Columbia University, phrased the matter some years ago, there are situations in which discriminations provide "offsetting imperfections." This does not mean that the discussion of the general economic effects and desirability of price discrimination contained in the Standard Oil (Indiana) decision[98] is in any way correct. Here the majority opinion expresses the view that as a general rule discrimination is good and wholesome for competition in the primary line, and is, perhaps, necessary to competition among sellers, although an unfortunate byproduct of such competition is that it creates inequalities in the secondary line, and that it was with this inherent contradiction that Congress consciously sought to deal in framing the Robinson-Patman Act.

In discussing the kinds of evidentiary facts that should be considered in the various types of problems that arise under Subsection 2(a), it might be well to enter a general word of caution concerning several tests and economic concepts that may have been overemphasized.

The opinion of the Court of Appeals for the Seventh Circuit in the *Minneapolis-Honeywell* case,[99] rendered July 5, 1951, serves to point up

[98] Standard Oil Co. of Indiana v. FTC, 340 U.S. 231 (1951).
[99] 44 F.T.C. 351 (1948). Decided against the Commission by the Seventh Circuit Court of Appeals 1951, 191 F.2d 786, *cert. denied,* 344 U.S. 206 (1952).

various factors considered by the Court to be of importance in determining
the probability of injury in that case. The Commission had found the req-
uisite adverse effects on competition stemmed in part from the fact that
the respondent's price discriminations had induced oil-burner manufacturers
to purchase the respondent's controls, thus diverting to the respondent trade
that otherwise would have gone to its competitors. Its finding with respect
to injury to customer competition was that the cost of controls was the
largest single item of cost going into the manufacture of oil burners. The
manufacturer getting a lower price on controls had a material advantage
over competitors in selling oil burners. Manufacturers who paid the higher
prices for controls either had to sell their burners at competitive prices, thus
reducing their profits by the amount of the discriminations, or sell their
burners at prices higher than their competitors, thus reducing their volume
of business.

The Court held that the facts relied on by the Commission to establish
injury to competition with the respondent were outweighed by the undisputed facts—

(1) that the prices charged for controls by the respondent's competitors
were generally lower than those of the respondent, and that there was no
evidence of any undercutting of its competitors' prices by Minneapolis-
Honeywell;

(2) that throughout the complaint period there existed the keenest kind
of price competition among control manufacturers;

(3) that the total business of the respondent's competitors increased, and
the three new concerns that entered the industry after 1932 enjoyed a steady
growth in sales volume;

(4) that the respondent's share of the available control business was
reduced from 73 per cent in 1937–1938 to only 60 per cent in 1950;

(5) that in 1941 the respondent lost to its competitors 53 per cent of
the control business of thirty-one customers who previously had standardized on Minneapolis-Honeywell controls; and

(6) that in the same year, 126 of the respondent's other oil-burner-
manufacturer customers also purchased competitive controls.

It further held that as far as customer competition was concerned, there
was no showing of any "causal connection" between the prices paid by the
oil-burner manufacturers for the controls and the price received by such
manufacturers for the oil burners.

As a result of the decision in *Minneapolis-Honeywell*, there seems to be
some thought that all primary-line cases must present evidence on changes
in market shares of the different competitors—and even that such evidence
will present the final test of whether there has been a substantial lessening of
competition. Actually, changes in market shares may or may not be relevant

to the question of substantial injury, and where such evidence is presented, there is an obligation to show the connection between the facts and the discrimination in question. As we know, there are many economic forces at work, some tending in the same direction as the price discrimination, some in the opposite direction. The mere fact that the price discriminator may have lost a share of the market during the period of discrimination does not absolve him, nor does the mere fact that he has increased his share of the market convict him. The ultimate question should not be whether market shares have changed, but whether they would be changed if the discriminatory practices were stopped.

There is one factual picture that should be supplied in all situations. This involves defining the market in which competition is alleged to be adversely affected and describing the competitors in this market. The approximate area of the market or the class of business affected should be stated, and the number of competitors in the market, in the trade level where the injury is alleged to take place, should be given, together with an indication of the competitors' approximate sizes. It is suggested that the sizes of the various competitors, or at least of various classes of competitors, should be shown both in terms of complete total assets and in terms of the competitors' shares in the market for the commodity in question. In all instances, moreover, account should be taken of near substitutes for the commodity in question. Similarly, it will be necessary to ascertain the point at which a price difference becomes critical in the commodity in question and at the trade level where business is alleged to be diverted. For example, in some commodities and at some trade levels, a price difference of a fraction of a per cent is sufficient to divert business, while in others, much greater price differences will not cause buyers to shift from one supplier to another.

At least three different types of primary-line problems arise under Section 2(a).

(a) First, a substantial lessening of competition may result when one seller or several sellers employ discriminatory practices to destroy the smaller competitors or to so impair the strength of the rivals that, in the long run, vigor of competition promises to become impaired. This was the type of lessening of competition alleged in the *Standard Oil* case[100] (under the Sherman Act), where it was shown that Standard ultimately took over 90 per cent of the business; it was also the allegation in the *Moss* case[101] and in the recent *General Foods* case.[102]

Following the per curiam opinion by the Second Circuit Court of Appeals

---

[100] 221 U.S. 1.
[101] 148 F.2d 378.
[102] General Foods Corp., No. 5675, FTC, 1956.

in the *Moss* case in 1945, it was frequently contended by those who looked with disfavor on the Robinson-Patman Act that a "presumption doctrine" had been developed. It was argued that this "presumption doctrine" had the effect of "shifting the burden of proof to anyone who sets two prices." This point was argued with greater vigor after the Second Circuit Court of Appeals had followed its rule of the *Moss* case in deciding the *Standard Brands* case.[103] Then it was argued that the effect of these decisions was to cast the burden of disproving injury on every seller who accorded different prices to different purchasers.

Of course, such contentions were erroneous. There has never been a presumption which shifted the burden of proof to anyone who sets two prices. Instead, facts and circumstances surrounding the setting of two prices have been used by the Federal Trade Commission and the courts as a basis for a finding of fact that the probable effect of the challenged price differential would be those proscribed by the statute. Nothing short of such a finding of fact would provide a prima facie case against one charged with the violation of subsection 2(a).

Too often it is overlooked that the Federal Trade Commission takes into account many facts and circumstances in addition to the differential in price in determining what the probable effects of the challenged discrimination may be. In many instances, the facts and circumstances considered include the following:

1. The volume of business done by each competitor in the market affected, and the volume of business done in other markets;

2. The prices charged in the different markets, an estimate of the differences in the discriminator's cost of serving the different markets, the discriminator's profit margins, the profit margins of the firms alleged to be adversely affected, and the incomes of the various competitors from activities in other lines of commerce;

3. The amount of capital that is estimated to be required for a new firm to enter and become an effective competitor in the field, together with a description of other barriers to entry into the field, such as patent restrictions, limited raw material resources, etc.;

4. The area in which there is consumer acceptance of the products of the injured seller, together with estimates of the cost and other barriers, such as sellers would have to meet in marketing and gaining consumer acceptance in other marketing areas;

5. Evidence as to the long-term level of prices and the character of the competition in markets where the discriminations do not take place.

---

[103] 189 F.2d 510, 515 (1951).

In short, the effects on competition to be questioned are the long-range effects. Although it is obvious that consumers may temporarily enjoy lower prices in the areas where discriminations take place, and the competition may appear active and vigorous, the question to be answered is whether the long-range effects will be a substantial disappearance of competitors and, presumably, a substantial lessening of competition. The statute is obviously not to be used to protect the profits or the convenience of an individual competitor or individual groups of competitors. On the other hand, it cannot be said that there will be no instance where the disappearance or the threatened disappearance of a single competitor will not constitute a substantial lessening of competition, any more than it can be said that a single merger would never be in violation of Section 7 of the Clayton Act.

(b) A substantial lessening of competition also comes about in some instances in the sense that competition between the rival sellers is restrained. Such, for example, was the result of the discriminations inherent in the marketing system of the cement manufacturers. (*Staley* case, 324 U.S. 746, and *Corn Products Refining Co.* case, 324 U.S. 726, 1945.) It was probably also a result of the marketing system in the *Glucose* cases, although the factual injury to competition found in the *Glucose* cases was in the secondary line. The injury to competition in such situations is in the immediate, short-run sense, and it involves problems of a conspiratorial or near-conspiratorial nature. Discriminations may at times underlie price-leadership phenomena where there is less element of agreement, as in the case of an industry dominated by a large seller who makes a practice of systematically meeting prices or of establishing punitive prices in reprisal for smaller sellers' independence in initiating price reductions.

The *Cement* and *Glucose* cases should provide adequate examples of the kind of evidence needed for appraising the competitive effects of a short-run nature.

(c) A third type of question concerning injuries in the primary line has arisen in the theory of the *Spark Plug* cases. The injuries sustained in the *Spark Plug* cases were suffered not only by those who purchased from the discriminating seller at higher prices than competing purchasers, but also the theory involved injuries to those engaged in the primary line, namely manufacturers and sellers of spark plugs who were in direct competition with the discriminating seller. Here it may be noted, moreover, that the Commission did not reject the theory of these cases but found that the evidence presented was sufficient to show that there was no substantial lessening of competition. The kinds of evidence presented in these cases would seem adequate for making such determinations.

As has been pointed out, most of the Commission's case experience has been in cases involving secondary-line competition, and the record of these cases should provide a wealth of demonstrations as to the kinds of evidence that will be needed in most instances. There are, however, special problems for which separate comment should be reserved.

(a) In the ordinary problem that arises, namely, where sellers simply respond to bargaining situations to favor certain buyers at the expense of others, the types of evidence needed are pretty much those outlined under (a) on page 57, except that there should be an added emphasis and explanation of the following:

1. Evidence as to the importance of the commodity in question in the total revenues of the competitors, together with evidence as to the effect the discrimination has upon these revenues. This will involve showing the resale prices of the various competitors and their profit margins on the commodity in question. Finally, there should be evidence to show in what ways and to what extent business is channeled from the unfavored to the favored buyers, and what the ultimate effect on the unfavored buyers is likely to be. Such discriminatory prices may be reflected in favored buyers' ability to make larger expenditures for sales promotion or to provide larger services, as well as in lower resale prices. Evidence as to the diversion of customers through these means should also be presented.

2. There must be evidence to show that the favored and the unfavored competitors are in actual competition, or that they would probably be in actual competition if the discrimination were not made.

3. There should also be evidence to show whether disfavored buyers may readily and reasonably become aware of their disfavored treatment, and if so, whether or not acceptable substitutes are available from other suppliers at nondiscriminatory prices.

(b) Quantity discounts must be subjected to the same type of evidence and the same ultimate tests as those outlined above, but a rule of reason must apply in determining the correctness of a seller's discount schedules and in relating these schedules to a reasonable schedule of average costs. Formal quantity discount schedules usually occur, and are most economically justified, where the buyers are numerous. In such instances, significant quantity discounts should be permitted only where there is a rather consistent relationship between costs and quantities purchased. On the other hand, there can be no insistence that sellers pass on cost savings to each and every buyer making such savings possible. Consequently, discounts that are reasonably related to the costs for the large majority of individual buyers in each discount category should generally be acceptable.

It is clear that the Robinson-Patman Act was not intended to bring about an attack on functional discounts as such, yet it is equally clear that discriminations that have the prohibited effects stated in the statute are not to be exempted on the grounds that they may be designated functional discounts. Despite these fundamentally correct legislative instructions however, functional discounts present the most difficult practical problems arising under the Act. The ultimate test that is applicable to other discriminations—i.e., whether the vigor of competition would be enhanced if the discrimination were prohibited—may not always apply. To prohibit a discrimination (discount) between wholesaler and retailer may result in nothing more than the seller's exercising his right to name exclusive dealerships by refusing to sell one or the other trade level at any price. It is far from clear that competition would be enhanced by forcing suppliers to take over further distributive functions or, conversely, to retire from distributive functions that are concurrently performed by his customers. Differences in the seller's costs of serving different trade levels are not, of course, the full guide to allowable price differences. Consequently, where problems involving functional discounts arise, the objective must be to determine whether the functional designations are based on objective criteria and whether or not there are substantial differences in the functions performed by the various trade levels.

Where these conditions are found missing, moreover, it is suggested that a deficiency of competition in the primary line will also be found and that it will be more appropriate to consider a remedy of the basic cause under the Sherman Act or Section 5 of the Federal Trade Commission Act, rather than under Section 2 of the Clayton Act, as amended.

Conclusion Regarding Injury

We have noted that evidence of injury to competition in the primary line of commerce—that is, injury to competitors of the seller charged with unlawful discrimination—is sufficient on which to base a case under subsection 2(a). Damage to competition in the primary line of commerce has been alleged in a majority of the cases arising under subsection 2(a) in which orders to cease and desist were entered. Such damage to competition has been found in a majority of all of the cases in which findings were made by the Commission.

The cases based on injury to the primary line of commerce—the line of commerce in which the discriminating seller is engaged—have not been as numerous as those that have involved injury in the secondary line of commerce—the line of commerce in which the seller's direct customers are engaged. However, the primary-line cases that have reached the courts have proved to be important milestones. The first was *E. B. Muller & Co. v. FTC*.[104] There, the respondent was charged with predatory pricing discriminations that involved the making of low prices on chicory in some markets and subsidizing those lower prices through higher prices maintained in other parts of the country. To similar effect were the cases of *Moore v. Mead's Fine Bread Co.*,[105] *Maryland Baking Co. v. FTC*,[106] and *Anheuser-Busch, Inc. v. FTC*.[107] Of course, in some instances these cases rested solely on a showing of injury to the primary line of commerce, because customers of the seller who paid different prices were not in competition with each other. That is particularly true of the *Mead* and *Anheuser-Busch* cases. In the *Mead* case, the seller made its lower price in Santa Rosa, N.M., available to all its other customers there, and in the *Anheuser-Busch* case, the seller made its lower price in St. Louis available to all its customers there. However, despite the fact that customers of the seller getting the lower prices in such areas were not in competition with other customers of the same seller in other areas, it was held to be sufficient that the seller was in competition with other sellers. Other territorial pricing cases arising under subsection 2(a) may be decided in the same way, with some showing of adverse effects on competition in the primary line of commerce, even though the seller's customers who are charged different prices are not in competition with each other and are, in fact, located in distant parts of the country from each other.

Injury to competing sellers in the primary line of commerce may arise from discriminations other than territorial price discriminations. For example, discriminations practiced in favor of certain large purchasers and not made available to others in the same or different markets may give rise to injury to sellers who are unable to compete for that business. It would be immaterial whether or not these discriminations stemmed from cumulative or volume discount plans, as were involved in the *Morton Salt* case, or from efforts to shut out smaller competing sellers, as in other Federal Trade Commission cases.[108] Likewise, price discrimination arising from

---

[104] 142 F.2d 511 (6th Cir. 1944).

[105] 348 U.S. 115 (1954).

[106] 243 F.2d 716 (4th Cir. 1957).

[107] The Commission's order in this case was set aside by the Seventh Circuit Court of Appeals (265 F.2d 677, 1959), but that decision was reversed by the U.S. Supreme Court in 1960 (363 U.S. 536). The order of the Commission was later set aside (Jan. 25, 1961) by the Circuit Court of Appeals for the Seventh Circuit (289 F.2d 835). There the Court held that the Commission had not shown that the discriminations involved were relevant to the injury sustained.

[108] Champion Spark Plug Co., No. 3977, FTC, 1953; Federal-Mogul Co., No. 5769, FTC, 1958.

functional discounts that have no reasonable relationship to differences in costs of the different functions involved may give rise to injury in the primary line of commerce sufficient to sustain a cause of action under subsection 2(a). Just as in the case of territorial price discriminations, it is immaterial whether the customers of the seller engaged in lines of commerce at different functional levels are in competition with each other.

Another type of discrimination involved in primary-line injury was manifested in the case of *Samuel H. Moss, Inc. v. FTC*, 148 F.2d 378 (2nd Cir. 1945). It was alleged and found that Moss, a manufacturer of rubber stamps, in making sales to such large users of stamps as railway companies, had engaged in unjustified price discriminations by charging different prices in sales to different customers and by making its prices in each instance just low enough to insure the elimination of competitors from the particular piece of business. It was alleged that Moss, in following that practice, had captured a major share of the total market from all its competitors and was approaching a position where it would hold a monopoly control over the price of rubber stamps. Upon a showing of this situation, the Second Circuit Court of Appeals held that the Commission had established a prima facie case, and that to successfully defend itself, Moss would have the burden of showing that particular instances of price discrimination had not resulted in injuries to specified competing sellers. Critics charged that this was a device for "shifting the burden of proof to anyone who sets two prices" and described it as the development of a doctrine of "presumptive injury." This criticism of the result in the *Moss* case cannot be accepted as valid. It should not be overlooked that it was not a case for damages arising out of injury to a private individual. As has been pointed out, in such instances the courts require that the plaintiffs must not only prove adverse effects on competition, but, also, the amount of damage sustained by the plaintiffs as a result of the alleged discriminations. In that connection, we have pointed to the decision in *Mead's Fine Bread Co. v. Moore*, 208 F.2d 777 (10th Cir. 1953).

After the Federal Trade Commission decision in the *Moss* case was affirmed, the Commission, in the matter of the *General Foods Corp.* (No. 5675, FTC), dismissed its complaint, and in doing so attempted to play down the significance of the opinion and decision of the Second Circuit Court of Appeals in the *Moss* Case. The Report of the Attorney General's National Committee to Study Antitrust Laws, which was published March 31, 1955, states (at page 162) that the Commission's *General Foods* opinion noted that the decision of the Court of Appeals in the *Moss* case furthered a principle that the Commission's attorneys had never urged upon the court. The report went on to state:

In that case, the Commission re-examined and took account of the criticism leveled at the "presumptive" doctrine of the *Moss* case.

In dismissing the complaint in the *General Foods* case, the Commission in effect held that the Commission's counsel had not presented a sufficient amount of proof relating to the lessening of competition. Hon. James M. Mead, a former chairman of the Federal Trade Commission, who remained for a time as a member of that agency, dissented from the views of the majority regarding the dismissal of the *General Foods* case. In his dissent, he stated:

> The record in this case shows that General Foods increased its share of the market and that the competitors of General Foods had a decreasing share of the market. . . . in 1939, the year immediately prior to the initiation of the deals, General Foods controlled 62.2 per cent of the national market in pectin. . . . General Foods' share of the market increased during the "deal" years to 1946, when its share was 80.5 per cent of the market. . . .
>
> Economists may differ as to what particular percentage of the national market a concern may have before it may be classified as a monopoly. A concern having 35 per cent of the market may not be a monopoly, but certainly when a concern begins to obtain over 50 per cent of the national market in any particular commodity, then such concern, because of such a share, is in the position to exert a very significant effect on the market. An area price discrimination by a concern having 35 per cent of the market may not have as great an adverse effect as a discrimination by a concern controlling 80 per cent of the market. . . .
>
> It is admitted that Government counsel did not offer in evidence in this case the scalps or the hides of the small-business competitors of General Foods. We do not have in evidence pounds of flesh or buckets of blood. We should not expect the type of evidence that Salome is said to have asked of Herod—the head of John the Baptist on a silver platter.

Regardless of the merits of the case or of its dismissal, the opinion and decision of the Commission in the *General Foods* case was regarded as significant, and for some time it was followed by its hearing examiners in their handling of similar cases. For example, as was noted in the report of the Attorney General's National Committee to Study the Antitrust Laws (page 165), the Commission's hearing examiner in the matter of *Purex Corp.* (No. 6008, FTC, April 16, 1954), carefully reasoned that the factual situation in the *Purex* case was somewhat analogous to the one in the *General Foods* case. Therefore, on the authority of the *General Foods* case, the hearing examiner proceeded to dismiss the complaint in the *Purex* case. The hearing examiner's decision in the *Purex* case was affirmed by the Federal Trade Commission on September 27, 1954. However, as we have observed in our references to the *Maryland Baking Company* case and the *Anheuser-Busch* case, in its recent decisions the Federal Trade Commission appears to be veering back into the orbit of its earlier opinion and decision in the *Moss* case.

Reference has been made to the fact that in a large number of cases that have arisen under subsection 2(a) of the Robinson-Patman Act, the damage to competition occurred to the line of commerce in which the seller's direct customers were engaged—that is, in the secondary line of commerce. As has been noted, it is immaterial in making out such a case whether the discrimination arose as a result of a direct or indirect discrimination in price. Also, it is immaterial whether the discrimination was based on territorial price discriminations, as in the *Corn Products* and *Staley* cases, or cumulative volume discounts, as in the *Morton Salt* case.

Injury to competition in the third line of commerce—the line of commerce in which the customers of the favored purchaser are engaged—is usually more difficult to show than injury to other lines of commerce, because many of the discriminations in price that would give rise to cases based on alleged injury in the third line of commerce involve the so-called functional discounts. Whether these functional discounts give rise to a reasonable probability of injury to the customers of the nonfavored purchaser is open to considerable question, even when the customer of the nonfavored purchaser is shown to have paid a much higher price for a commodity of like grade and quality to that sold by the same original seller directly to a purchaser in competition.

Injury and Orders to Cease and Desist:

In discussing the required showing of injury to sustain a case arising under subsection 2(a), it would be amiss if references were not made to the relationship of this showing to provisions in the Federal Trade Commission's cease-and-desist orders prohibiting *all* differentials in price. This has been done in cases even where there was no evidence that smaller differentials would have the injurious effects that the specifically challenged differentials were shown to have had. In other words, the courts have held that where the proof supports a finding that certain differentials in price may injuriously affect competition, the Commission's cease-and-desist order in the same case may legally prohibit other and smaller differentials, even in the absence of evidence that the smaller differentials would have the prohibitive effect. This was so held in the *Ruberoid* case,[109] where the order prohibited the seller from selling its products to any purchaser at a price higher than the price charged any other purchaser who competes with the purchaser paying the higher price in the resale of the products. However, the

---

[109] Ruberoid Co. v. FTC, 189 F.2d 893 (2nd Cir. 1951), *aff'd,* 343 U.S. 470 (1952).

Commission's cease-and-desist orders of this type have not been limited to cases where injuries were found only in the secondary line of commerce. For example, in the matter of the *Page Dairy Company*,[110] a case involving injury in the primary line, the FTC entered an order as follows:

> That the respondent, Page Dairy Company, a corporation, its officers, representatives, agents and employees, directly or through any corporate or other device, in connection with the sale of fluid milk in commerce, as "commerce" is defined in the aforesaid Clayton Act, do forthwith cease and desist from discriminating in price by selling said fluid milk of like grade and quality to any purchaser at prices lower than those granted other purchasers where respondent, in the sale of such product, is in competition with any other seller.

In recent years, many FTC cease-and-desist orders in cases arising under subsection 2(a) have contained these broad provisions, prohibiting discriminations where a relationship exists between the seller and his competitors or between his customers and their competitors.

The United States Court of Appeals for the Second Circuit on June 22, 1961, in the case of *Swanee Paper Corp. v. FTC*, reviewed and affirmed an order to cease and desist that had been entered by the Commission against Swanee for violation of subsection 2(d) of the Robinson-Patman Act. However, in doing that, the court objected to the broad and general terms in which the Commission had drawn its order to cease and desist. In that connection, the court stated:

> It is true that Swanee did not object to the order during the proceedings below and that orderly appellate review of administrative decisions usually requires that such objections be made. See *U.S. v. Tucker Truck Lines,* 344 U.S. 33 (1952). Swanee did object to the order, however, in its petition to review, and at the time this was filed, the Commission could have modified its order if it had so wished. See 15 U.S.C. Sec. 21(b). Moreover, the order as written is so broad that, under the new enforcement provisions of the Clayton Act (15 U.S.C. Sec. 21), the duty of enforcing the prohibitions of Section 2(d) as to Swanee is shifted from the Commission to the federal courts, which may in the future be forced to decide the very issues that Congress has entrusted the Commission to determine. See *FTC v. Morton Salt Co.,* 334 U.S. 37 (1948). Proper judicial administration requires that the order be modified, and we therefore hold that the order should be limited to the particular practice found to violate the statute.

The Court also stated:

> "Although the Commission's finding of a Section 2(d) violation is supported by the record, the breadth of the order issued is not justified

---

[110] No. 5974, FTC, 1953, 50 FTC 395.

by the facts. Administrative agencies have wide discretion in framing their orders and are empowered to enjoin other related unlawful acts which may occur in the future (e.g., *FTC v. Mandel Brothers, Inc.,* 359 U.S. 385 (1959)), but there must be some relation between the facts found and the breadth of the order. (*FTC v. Mandel Brothers, Inc., supra; FTC v. National Lead Co.,* 352 U.S. 419 (1957); *NLRB v. Express Pub. Co.,* 312 U.S. 426 (1941); *NLRB v. Crompton-Highland Mills, Inc.,* 337 U.S. 217 (1949).)[4] Nothing in the record here indicates flagrant or extensive violations of Section 2(d) by Swanee; the single violation found occurred in an uncertain area of the law and was discontinued before the complaint was filed. Moreover, the order is not even limited to related activities but enjoins Swanee from violating Section 2(d) in the very words of the statute. As the Supreme Court stated in *NLRB v. Express Pub. Co., supra:*

> "The mere fact that a court has found that a defendant has committed an act in violation of a statute does not justify an injunction broadly to obey the statute and thus subject the defendant to contempt proceedings if he shall at any time in the future commit some new violation unlike and unrelated to that with which he was originally charged" (*id.* at 435).

---

[4] See also 2 U.S. Cong. & Admin. News, p. 1807 (1959) where the report of the House Committee which studied the recent enforcement provision of the Clayton Act, 15 U.S.C. Sec. 21, stated that the Commission should "make a continuous effort to issue orders that are as definitive as possible" and that deficiencies in this regard may be corrected by judicial review.

The preceding footnote 4 is the Court's footnote.

The Second Circuit Court of Appeals a few months later (February 7, 1962) handed down its decision in the case of *Grand Union Company v. FTC:*

> In this case, presenting an admittedly novel application of Sec. 5 of the Federal Trade Commission Act, what we said as to the need for specificity in Commission orders in *Swanee Paper Corp. v. FTC,* supra, 2 Cir., 291 F.2d 833, 837–838, has especial significance.[20] As under the new enforcement provisions of the Clayton Act, 15 U.S.C. Sec. 21, so under Sec. 5(1) of the Federal Trade Commission Act, 15 U.S.C. Sec. 45(1), violations of the order are enforceable in civil proceedings in the federal courts. . . .
>
> . . . The arrangement attacked here has terminated, and there is nothing in the record to suggest that Grand Union intends to resume this or any related activity. We therefore hold that the order should be limited to the particular practice found to violate the statute. Swanee Paper Corp. v. FTC, supra, 2 Cir., 291 F.2d 833, 838. (The following footnote 20 is the Court's footnote.)

---

[20] Grand Union has filed a separate petition for review seeking modification of the broad terms of the order. But since this relief can be sought on the original petition, see Swanee Paper Corp. v. FTC, 2 Cir., 291 F.2d 833, we grant the Commission's motion to dismiss this second petition.

The Supreme Court of the United States, on January 15, 1962, dealt with this problem in its decision in the case of *FTC v. Henry Broch & Company*, a Section 2(c) case involving the brokerage section. There the Court, in upholding a broad order of the Commission stated almost in the words of the statute, expressed itself on the point in the following language:

> . . . The Commission has a wide discretion to formulate a remedy adequate to prevent Broch's repetition of the violation he was found to have committed. See *Jacob Siegel Co. v. Federal Trade Comm'n,* 327 U.S. 608, 611–612. We cannot say that the Commission exceeded its discretion in banning repetitions of Broch's violation in connection with transactions involving *any* seller and buyer, rather than simply forbidding recurrence of the transgression in sales between Canada and Smucker. *Federal Trade Comm'n v. Cement Institute,* 333 U.S. 683, 728–729. Compare *United States v. United States Gypsum Co.,* 340 U.S. 76, 90. . . .
>
> In considering Broch's challenge to paragraph (2) it is necessary to observe that the 1959 amendments to Sec. 11 of the Clayton Act —which substitute for the Clayton Act provisions for enforcement of administrative orders those in Sec. 5 of the Federal Trade Commission Act—do not apply to enforcement of the instant order.[5] In consequence, Broch cannot be subjected to penalties except for violation of an enforcement order yet to be entered by an appropriate Court of Appeals, to be predicated upon a determination that some particular practice of Broch violated the Commission's order. Thus Broch is not, by virtue of that order, presently acting under the risk of incurring any penalty without further administrative and judicial consideration and interpretation, despite the fact that he has already received determination of his petition for review. *Federal Trade Comm'n v. Ruberoid Co.,* 343 U.S. 470, 477–480.[6]
>
> Upon any future enforcement proceeding, the Commission and the Court of Appeals will have ready to hand interpretive tools—the employment of which we have previously sanctioned—for use in tailoring the order, in the setting of a specific asserted violation, so as to meet the legitimate needs of the case. They will be free to construe the order as designed strictly to cope with the threat of future violations identical with or like or related to the violations which Broch was found to have committed,[7] or as forbidding "no activities except those which if continued would directly aid in perpetuating the same old unlawful practices." *Federal Trade Comm'n v. Cement Institute,* 333 U.S. 683, 727. They need not—as we have already made clear— read the order as denying to Broch the benefit of statutory defenses or exceptions. . . .
>
> We do not wish to be understood, however, as holding that the generalized language of paragraph (2) would necessarily withstand scrutiny under the 1959 amendments.[10] The severity of possible penalties

prescribed by the amendments for violations of orders which have become final underlines the necessity for fashioning orders which are, at the outset, sufficiently clear and precise to avoid raising serious questions as to their meaning and application.[11] See *Labor Board v. Express Pub. Co.,* 312 U.S. 426, 435–437; *Federal Trade Comm'n v. Cement Institute,* 333 U.S. 683, 726; *Federal Trade Comm'n v. Morton Salt Co.,* 334 U.S. 37, 54. Compare *New Haven R. Co. v. Interstate Commerce Comm'n,* 200 U.S. 361, 404; *Swift & Co. v. United States,* 196 U.S. 375, 400–401.

---

[5] 38 Stat. 734, 15 U.S.C. Sec. 21, as amended July 23, 1959, Pub. L. 86–107, 73 Stat. 243. The order herein was entered by the Commission on December 10, 1957. The procedures enacted by the 1959 amendments therefore do not apply to it. See Sperry Rand Corp. v. Federal Trade Comm'n, 288 F.2d 403.

[6] The 1959 Amendments resulted from a congressional conclusion that the former Sec. 11 procedures were too cumbersome to assure effective enforcement of agency orders. It was said in the House Committee Report accompanying the 1959 amendments:

"The Clayton Act, in its present enforcement procedures, permits a person to engage in the same illegal practices three times before effective legal penalties can be applied as a result of action by the commission or board vested with jurisdiction. First, in order to issue and serve a cease-and-desist order initially, the commission or board must investigate and prove that the respondent has violated the prohibitions of the Clayton Act. No provision of the Clayton Act, however, makes the commission or board's cease-and-desist order final in the absence of an appeal by the respondent for judicial review. At the present time, the Clayton Act contains no procedure by which the commission or board may secure civil penalties for violations of its orders.

"Second, before the commission or board may obtain a court ruling that commands obedience to its cease-and-desist order, it must again investigate and prove that the respondent has violated both the order and the Clayton Act. The jurisdiction of the court of appeals, under the present provisions of Clayton Act section 11, cannot be invoked by the commission or board unless a violation of the cease-and-desist order is first shown.

"Third, enforcement of the court's order must be secured in a subsequent contempt proceeding, which requires proof that new activities of the respondent have violated the court's order. This entails a third hearing before the commission and a review thereof by the court of appeals.

"In contrast, the procedures that are contained in the Federal Trade Commission Act for enforcement of cease-and-desist orders issued thereunder are much simpler and more direct. A cease-and-desist order issued pursuant to section 5 of the Federal Trade Commission Act, as amended, becomes final upon the expiration of the time allowed for filing a petition for review, if no such petition is filed within that time." H.R. Rep. No. 580, 86th Cong., 1st Sess. 4. See also S. Rep. No. 83, 86th Cong., 1st Sess. 2–3.

[7] Cf. *Federal Trade Comm'n v. Morton Salt Co.,* 334 U.S. 37, 51–53; *Federal Trade Comm'n v. National Lead Co.,* 352 U.S. 419, 430–431. "In carrying out (its) function the Commission is not limited to prohibiting the illegal practice in the precise form in which it is found to have existed in the past. If the Commission is to attain the objectives Congress envisioned, it cannot be required to confine its roadblock to the narrow lane the transgressor has traveled; it must be allowed effectively to close all roads to the prohibited goal, so that its order may not be by-passed with impunity." *Federal Trade Comm'n v. Ruberoid Co.,* 343 U.S. 470, 473.

[10] See notes 5, 6, supra.

11 The penalties under the 1959 amendments are as follows:

"Any person who violates any order issued by the commission or board under subsection (b) of this section after such order has become final, and while such order is in effect, shall forfeit and pay to the United States a civil penalty of not more than $5,000 for each violation. . . . Each separate violation of any such order shall be a separate offense, except that in the case of a violation through continuing failure or neglect to obey a final order of the commission or board each day of continuance of such failure or neglect shall be deemed a separate offense."

(The immediately preceding footnotes 5, 6, 7, 10 and 11 are the Court's footnotes in the opinion in Broch.)

DEFENSES AVAILABLE IN CASES ARISING UNDER SUBSECTION 2(a)

Cost Defense Proviso

Provided: That nothing herein contained shall prevent differentials which make only due allowance for differences in the cost of manufacture, sale, or delivery resulting from the differing methods or quantities in which such commodities are to such purchasers sold or delivered.

Definition of Basic Terms: The first task confronting anyone who would undertake to make out a defense based on cost justification in a case arising under subsection 2(a) would be a determination of the meaning of the cost justification and how it would apply to the factual situation at hand.

In referring to the cost proviso, Congressman Utterback, who presented the Patman bill to the House of Representatives, said:

The bill assures to the mass distributor, as to everyone else, full protection in the use and rewards of efficient methods in production and distribution. . . . There is no limit to the phases of production, sale, and distribution in which such improvements may be devised and the economies, when demonstrated, may be expressed in price differentials in favor of the particular customers whose distinctive methods of purchase and delivery make them possible.[111]

The Senate received the same assurance when the Robinson bill was presented to it for its consideration. The Senate Judiciary Committee, in its report on the Robinson bill, made reference to the cost proviso in the following language:

. . . it leaves trade and industry free from any restriction or impediment to the adoption and use of more economic processes, and to the translation of appropriate shares of any savings so effected up and down the stream of distribution to the original producers and to the ultimate consumer. . . .[112]

111 80 CONG. REC. 9416 (1936).
112 S. REP. No. 1502, 74th Cong., 2d Sess. 5 (1936).

An understanding of the cost proviso is enhanced by an understanding of the key terms appearing therein. The principal term is "due allowance." That term is construed to refer to a showing that challenged price differentials were no greater than the differences in the cost involved in making the different sales to different customers at the different prices. It has been argued that "due allowance" should not be construed in every case to require full and complete justification of a price differential, but only to require "reasonable allowance" in the form of cost differences. Of course, this argument for a "rule of reason" has been accepted by the Federal Trade Commission in a few cases, particularly where the failure of the cost justification to make full and complete "due allowance" was *de minimis*. This exercise of reason in the application of the cost proviso in a limited number of cases should not be taken as a modification of the meaning of the term "due allowance." Instead, these cases should be taken as examples of situations where the Federal Trade Commission did not deem it necessary to apply the statute, even though full and complete cost justification of the challenged price differential had not been laid out.

The meaning of the phraseology "resulting from the differing methods or quantities" appearing in the cost proviso has been the focal point of much dispute. It has been argued that Congress intended this phraseology to be interpreted broadly and liberally, giving effect to the many differing methods or quantities involved in sales at different prices to different customers or classes of customers. Here again, reason has prevailed. In the consideration of this problem by the Federal Trade Commission, it has been found that the differing methods and quantities are generally ascertainable, and that cost differentials arising therefrom are determinable. These include cost differentials arising from different methods of delivery and from different distances to which deliveries are made. But cost of transportation is only one element. Other cost elements properly attributable to a particular transaction may be considered and compared or contrasted with similar cost elements in, or eliminated from, other transactions involved in the challenged price differentials. The terms "manufacture, sale, or delivery," appearing in the cost proviso, comprehended almost the entire range of industrial and commercial operating costs, but to be significant, any cost differences based on these elements must be related to "differing methods or quantities." The cost differences eligible to be taken into consideration may include direct or indirect costs, including those incurred for any given product, customer, or group of customers, when discriminations and arbitrary actions are not involved in classifying or grouping customers for cost-determining purposes.

The Robinson-Patman Act does not define the term "cost." The determination of what cost differences are, therefore, is left to the Federal Trade Commission, which has been guided by accepted rules of cost accounting. The many methods of doing business and the variations in the availability of accounting and statistical data, as well as the underlying philosophy of the Robinson-Patman Act, precluded the use of uniform methods and procedures of cost accounting for Robinson-Patman Act purposes. Actual differences in costs attributable to differing methods or differing quantities are to be taken into account in determining whether price differentials make only due allowance for differences in cost. There should be no mystery about this matter. In plain accounting terms, price differentials are permitted if they properly reflect differences in cost.

It may be, as some authorities have contended, that cost accounting is not an exact science. Nevertheless, the widely approved and widely accepted rules and methods of cost accounting, plus the simple rules of mathematics, have been and will be applied in determining whether a cost-justification defense has been made out in a case arising under subsection 2(a). Other defenses relating to competitive market practices and conditions are separate and distinct matters that will be discussed in a later section of this chapter.

In February, 1956, an advisory committee on cost-justification problems under the Robinson-Patman Act made a report to the Federal Trade Commission. In doing so, it listed and discussed the following as suggested factors to be taken into account in evaluating a cost justification defense to a charge of price discrimination arising under subsection 2(a):

(c) *Specific cost differences*

It is well to note that in some circumstances a very simple cost analysis is the best one. If the price differential is based entirely on some characteristic of the transaction whose cost can be directly measured, attention may be directed at that item of cost and at no other. An obvious example is the distinction between carload and less-than-carload freight. If a seller's regular delivered price is based on the expectation that he will normally ship in full carloads and pay freight accordingly, and if his less-than-carload price reflects the freight differential only, attention may be concentrated on the freight factor, without regard to other manufacturing, selling, or delivery costs. Another example would be the case of advertised and unadvertised products, if the price differential does not exceed the unit advertising cost. In many cases, however, price differentials are related to a complex of circumstances and their cost justification requires consideration of many, if not all, of the costs involved.

(d) *Direct and indirect costs*

Costs separately incurred for any given product, customer, or group of customers are readily assigned. These are direct costs. On the other hand, indirect costs, which are jointly incurred for two or more products, customers, or groups of customers must be allocated before total costs for any given category can be ascertained.

The importance of sound methods and procedures for assigning all costs is apparent. Although, for reasons stated heretofore, standardization is impracticable, the Committee believes a discussion of the problems involved, and some acceptable solutions thereof, may be beneficial. Basic principles, adaptable to all circumstances, are discussed in paragraphs (e), (f), and (g) below. For a more detailed discussion we attach Appendix A entitled, "Illustrative Methods and Procedures for Allocating Manufacturing and Distribution Costs." These illustrations are suggestions only, and are not intended to foreclose the use of entirely different approaches where suitable. In all cases, it is essential that the specific conditions and factors involved in the manufacturing and distribution process be fully developed before selecting methods of cost analysis.

(e) *Methods of determining amount of direct cost*

The amount of direct cost variation per unit of product may be determined by the most applicable of the following methods:

(1) *Count.* To enumerate by mechanical or other means the number of units required for a given unit of product. This includes such devices as magnetic and electric-eye counters, time clocks, and such procedures as numbering each unit or physically counting the number of units passing a given point. This also includes such methods of counting as time studies, time analyses and time cards where the unit of work is counted and recorded.

(2) *Measure.* To gauge the dimensions, quantity or volume of units used.

(3) *Weigh.* To ascertain by balance or scale the quantity or weight of units used.

(4) *Compute.* To ascertain by calculation or mathematical relationship the units used; e.g., as numbers of parts and assemblies; as quantities available for use, used and remaining.

(f) *Methods of determining amount of indirect cost*

The amount of indirect cost variation per unit of product may be determined by the most applicable of the following methods:

(1) *Statistical Analysis.* Analysis of past performance to develop apportionment basis.

(2) *Sampling.* Statistical technique of testing current performance to develop basis for apportionment.

(3) *Standard Allowance for Related Items.* Mutual dependence of cost items used as apportionment basis; e.g., apportioning cost of heat treating on the basis of standard allowance for weight or material in product.

(4) *Compute.* To ascertain by calculation or mathematical relationship the units used.

(g) *Method of determining most applicable methods of determination of direct cost or of apportionment of indirect cost*

The most applicable methods of determination of direct costs or of allocation of indirect costs should be in the order listed as follows:

(1) That method historically used by the company concerned, the result of which has periodically and routinely been evaluated and found reasonably accurate.

(2) That method historically used by the company which most closely reflects approved and accepted accounting practice.

(3) That method which theoretically appears to be the most logical and reasonable, or that which most closely approximates a satisfactory measure of benefit or activity in terms of rational analysis and can reasonably and practicably be used.

Where efforts are made to justify price differentials on the basis of differences in cost by grouping products by classes or by grouping customers by classes, the seller should proceed with great caution and care.

The Supreme Court of the United States in the case of *U.S. v. Borden Company, et al,* 370 U.S. 460, June 25, 1962, held that an effort to justify price differentials by way of cost justification by the grouping of most chain stores in one class and most independent stores in another class on the assumption that "most chain stores do purchase larger volumes . . . than do most independent stores" was invalid. In that connection, the Court observed that such effort "is like averaging one horse and one rabbit." In that connection, the Court held that:

> . . . High on the list of 'musts' in the use of the average cost of customer groupings under the proviso of Sec. 2(a) is a close resemblance of the individual members of each group on the essential point or points which determine the costs considered.

The Court with reference to its holding that the Borden Company had not shown its price differentials to be cost justified said:

> In this regard we do not find the classifications submitted by the appellees to have been shown to be of sufficient homogeneity. Certainly, the cost factors considered were not necessarily encompassed within the manner in which a customer is owned. . . .

The Court in referring back to the discussion on this point by the Advisory Committee on Cost Justification at page 8 of the 1956 Report to the Federal Trade Commission stated:

> . . . A balance is struck by the use of classes for cost justification which are composed of members of such selfsameness as to make the averaging of the cost of dealing with the group a valid and reasonable indicium of the cost of dealing with any specific group member. . . .

For the most part, commodities of like grade and quality are manufactured to be stocked, as distinguished from goods manufactured by special order of a customer. Where "run of the mill" goods are manufactured for stock, it is obvious that it would be quite difficult to establish genuine differences in cost of manufacture as between customers or classes of customers who would be buying these goods of like grade and quality out of stock. Therefore, it is in the distribution (marketing) of a product that the principal cost differences involved in making two or more sales to different customers would be most likely to be found.

It is often contended that development of reasonable, accurate distribution-cost information is either impossible or too expensive to be justified for use in Robinson-Patman Act cases. This argument appears to be groundless. During the advancement of industrialization in this country, it was argued that accurate cost accounting on production costs was not feasible, but the work of good cost accountants disproved those arguments. The science of cost accounting and particularly the advancement of the training and experience in that field are bringing out the fact that accurate cost accounting of distribution is available to those who need it and wish to avail themselves of the opportunity to use it.

Much of the belief that it is not feasible to present accurate analyses of distribution costs in Robinson-Patman Act cases stems from the infrequent success of such efforts in Robinson-Patman Act cases brought by the Federal Trade Commission. However, these arguments do not take into account that the Commission does not make public the results of investigations that terminate without formal proceedings. Therefore, available records do not show the frequency with which the cost-justification defense has been successfully offered and accepted in Robinson-Patman Act cases. It is known that it has been a factor in a large number of cases subjected to investigation by the Federal Trade Commission out of which no formal proceedings developed. In view of these circumstances, the Commission's formal proceedings are necessarily misleading as a record of the successful resort to cost-justification as a defense in price-discrimination cases under the Robinson-Patman Act. In less than a score of the formal proceedings brought by the Federal Trade Commission under subsection 2(a) has the cost-justification defense been offered. The cost defense offered was sustained in whole or in part, either by the Commission or by the others, in numerous cases. *Minneapolis-Honeywell Regulator Co., 44 F.T.C. 351 (1948); U.S. Rubber Co., 46 F.T.C. 998 (1950); B. F. Goodrich Co., No. 5677, FTC, 1954; Sylvania Elec. Products Co., No. 5728, FTC, 1954.*

The attempt to defend price discrimination through the cost defense has also been rejected in many cases. *Standard Brands, Inc., 29 F.T.C. 121 (1939), 30 F.T.C. 1117 (1940); E. B. Muller & Co., 33 F.T.C. 24*

(1941); Morton Salt Co., 39 F.T.C. 35 (1944); Standard Oil Co., 41 F.T.C. 263 (1945); Curtiss Candy Co., 44 F.T.C. 237 (1947); International Salt Co., No. 4307, FTC, 1952; Champion Spark Plug Co., No. 3977, FTC, 1953; Niehoff & Co., No. 5768, FTC, 1954.

The following questions and answers relate to the cost-justification defense.

No. 64. Question. How can one insure or determine a saving in cost of manufacture, sale, or delivery?

Opinion. A cost system is the proper method. However, given any usual combination of circumstances, cost accountants may determine cost differences within reasonable limits of accuracy.

No. 65. Question. What are some examples of "due allowances for differences in the cost resulting from the differing methods in which commodities are manufactured, sold, or delivered"?

Opinion. Presumably, this question is confined to goods of like grade and quality. Differences may arise out of market changes in raw material; changes in wage scales; elimination of functions, such as the wholesaling function, which the buyer may perform for himself; elimination of salesmen, brokers, advertising, warehousing, etc.; and differing quantities and methods of delivery.

No. 66. Question. Does the Act permit a price differential merely because the quantities purchased are different, or methods of selling are different, or methods of delivery are different, or because the seasons of the year in which they are produced are different?

Opinion. No. In every instance, a real difference in cost must be established.

No. 67. Question. Is it the intent of the Act that all purchasers shall pay the same price within very close tolerances or range, or that they shall pay identical prices?

Opinion. The Act does not require a one-price policy. It is believed, however, that price discriminations will be considerably narrowed. By and large, at any given period of commercial history, the three basic and inescapable functions of production, wholesaling, and retailing have about the same cost factor, with the great variation arising in raw material and labor costs. The Robinson-Patman Act does not seek to fix material and labor costs, or any other cost. It does, however, compel all purchasers to pay their full share of material and labor costs, as well as their proportionate share of all functional costs for the functional services that are made available to them by the seller. As a result, with functional costs averaging about the same regardless of who performs them, the enforcement of the Robinson-Patman Act will mean that prices will approach within close tolerances in many lines. Efficiency of operation will then earn its own rewards.

No. 68. Question. Where special designs of goods are made for certain companies from their own patterns or from their own molds, on what basis will it be allowable to sell to such concerns?

Opinion. The Act is not concerned, if the goods are not of like grade and quality. However, differences in grade and quality arbitrarily created to create differences in cost may be challenged. Under any other condition, price differences must not exceed the difference in cost of the various orders, and each purchase must bear its proportionate share of costs.

Congress wrote into the Robinson-Patman Act a limitation on the cost-justification defense that is frequently referred to as the "Quantity-Limit Proviso." This limitation on the cost-justification defense is important enough to justify the detailed discussion that follows.

Quantity-Limit Proviso: The text of the proviso, which appears as a part of subsection 2(a) of the Act, is to the effect—

> That the Federal Trade Commission may, after due investigation and hearing to all interested parties, fix and establish quantity limits, and revise the same as it finds necessary, as to particular commodities or classes of commodities, where it finds that available purchasers in greater quantities are so few as to render differentials on account thereof unjustly discriminatory or promotive of monopoly in any line of commerce; and the foregoing shall then not be construed to permit differentials based on differences in quantities greater than those so fixed and established.

Understanding of this important provision is enhanced by knowledge of its origin, derivation, background, and purpose.

The proviso as finally enacted found its derivation in committee amendments to the Patman bill, H.R. 8442, and the Robinson bill, S. 3154. The two bills, as originally introduced in the Congress, were identical. Mr. H. B. Teegarden, general counsel of the U.S. Wholesale Grocers Association, consulted with and assisted the authors in the drafting of the bills.

As originally introduced, the bills made no mention of the proviso in any form. Mr. Teegarden testified that he "felt satisfied at the time to rely upon differences in cost as a guarantee against abuse of the price differential," and that "as originally drawn, introduced and referred to the committee [the House Committee on the Judiciary], the bill limited price differentials only by the requirement that they be supported by differences in cost as between customers involved in the discrimination."[113]

---

[113] *Hearings on H.R. 8442, H.R. 4995, and H.R. 5062 before the House Committee on the Judiciary,* 74th Cong., 1st Sess. 222–24, 257–58 (1935).

Mr. Teegarden, in a brief he submitted to the House Judiciary Committee, stated that the principle of fixing quantity limits on a commodity rests "not upon the theory that beyond them no appreciable differences in unit costs are in actual practice likely to be found, but upon the ground that, in spite of such differences, so few buyers remain available in those large quantity brackets, that any further price differential on account thereof must in its very nature be unjustly discriminatory."[114]

This principle was first expressed in terms of the so-called "carlot" amendment. It reads as follows:

> Provided, however, That the foregoing shall not be construed to permit differentials based on differences in quantities greater than car-load lots.[115]

The following quotations show why the carlot amendment was tentatively submitted to the House Committee on the Judiciary:

> A demand was presented by important interests, including members of Congress, that a quantity limit be inserted beyond which quantity differentials should not be permitted . . . As the hearings (before the House Committee on the Judiciary) progressed, serious objections developed from the so-called heavy industries, based largely upon this provision (the carlot-quantity limit proviso), and it became apparent that, conceding the principle of quantity limits to price differentials, those limits may well vary with the character of the commodity. With some, such as certain drugs, the proper limit

---

114 *Id.* at 258. "It should be understood, however, that the fixing of such limits rests, not upon the theory that beyond them no appreciable differences in unit costs are in actual practice likely to be found; but upon the ground that, in spite of such differences, so few buyers remain available in those large quantity brackets, that any further price differential on account thereof must in its very nature be unjustly discriminatory.

"This principle has been applied by the Interstate Commerce Commission practically since its creation in refusing to permit lower freight rates for greater-than-carload shipments than for carload shipments; and such were the grounds upon which it was based, as announced by Judge Cooley, first chairman of the Interstate Commerce Commission, in *Providence Coal Co. v. Providence & Western Ry.* (1 I.C.C. 107), nearly half a century ago."

115 *Hearings on H.R. 8442, H.R. 4995, and H.R. 5062 before the House Committee on the Judiciary,* 74th Cong., 1st Sess. 237 (1935). (Letter from Noel Sargent, Economist, National Association of Manufacturers, to the Hon. Hatton W. Sumners, Chairman, Committee on the Judiciary, House of Representatives.

(Note: This excerpt is included to show the derivation of the quantity-limit proviso in H.R. 8442.)

"While it is true that differentials in price are not prohibited 'which make only due allowance for differences in cost of manufacture, sale, or delivery resulting from the differing methods or quantities in which such commodities are to such purchasers sold or delivered,' this permissible use of quantity discounts is seriously restricted in the following proviso:

" 'Provided, however, That the foregoing shall not be construed to permit differentials based on differences in quantities greater than carload lots.'

"In effect, this proviso prohibits quantity discounts in those situations where most justified. In our opinion, therefore, it is essential to call to the attention of your committee the economic justification for quantity price differentials from the standpoint of the manufacturer."

may be less than the carload lot; with others, such as building materials, coal, ore, etc., it may be greater than the carload lot.[116]

Thus, the terms of the carlot amendment, in which the principle of the present proviso was first expressed, were thought to be too rigid to be practicable. A carload would contemplate a huge quantity of the commodities of some industries, such as drugs or dyes, while in other industries, such as mining or heavy machinery, a carload would encompass a relatively small quantity. Therefore, the proviso as now written was proposed as an alternative to the carlot amendment.

The rigidity of the carlot amendment was not the only difficulty encountered by the proponents of the proviso, even though the desirability of providing for a quantity limit on commodities as a legal principle was assumed. It was impractical to establish an individual limit for separate commodities at the primary level of lawmaking, yet fear was expressed that the unrestricted delegation of this power would be such a broad grant of authority that it would be declared too indefinite to be enforceable.

Notwithstanding the difficulty of finding a satisfactory medium in which the quantity-limit principle might be expressed, and the outright opposition of opponents, the following version of the proviso was incorporated in a report submitted by Mr. Utterback from the House Committee on the Judiciary to accompany H.R. 8442, recommending passage of the bill as amended by the committee:

> Provided, however, That the Federal Trade Commission after due investigation and hearing to all interested parties, following insofar as applicable the procedure and subject to the recourse of the courts, provided in section 11 of this act, may issue an order fixing and establishing quantity limits and revising the same as it finds necessary, as to particular commodities or classes of commodities, and the foregoing shall then not be construed to permit differentials based on differences in quantities greater than those so fixed and established.[117]

When first introduced in the Senate by Senator Robinson, S. 3154, as has been stated previously, made no mention of the quantity-limit proviso. The first mention was made of any version of the proviso before the Senate was in its present form. This occurred in a report submitted by Mr. Logan from the Senate Committee on the Judiciary to accompany S. 3154, recommending passage of the bill as amended by the committee.[118]

As thus placed before the Senate, this marked the first time that the proviso, as it now appears, was ever considered by the entire membership

---

[116] *Id.* at 257–58.
[117] H.R. REP. No. 2287, 74th Cong., 2d Sess. (1936).
[118] S. REP. No. 1502, 74th Cong., 2d Sess. 6 (1936).

of either House of Congress. It can hardly be doubted, however, that the source of the proviso, as expressed in the committee amendment to S. 3154, was in the hearings held by the House Committee on the Judiciary in July 1935.[119]

The proviso in S. 3154 remained unchanged from the time of its inception in the bill by committee amendment until final enactment. It did not pass through formative stages, as it had in the companion bill in the House, due quite probably to an analysis of the problems it involved, which were developed in the prior hearings held by the House Judiciary Committee on H.R. 8442. This is not to say that the proviso did not meet with opposition in the Senate, for it did, but the form it was to take does not appear to have been strongly controverted, if at all.[120]

The present proviso was incorporated in S. 3154 as amended and passed by the Senate on April 30, 1936.

No mention of the proviso was made in the conference committee report to the Senate, other than by inclusion in the recommended bill. In the conference committee report to the House, there was included a statement of the managers of the legislation on the part of the House. This statement makes the following reference to the proviso:

> Both the House bill and the Senate amendment contained a provision permitting the Federal Trade Commission, after investigation and hearing, to fix and establish quantity limits, above which differentials based on differences in quantities are not permitted. The Senate provision contained a rule for the Commission's guidance as follows: Where it finds that available purchasers in greater quantities are so few as to render differentials on account thereof unjustly discriminatory or promotive of monopoly in any line of commerce;
>
> The House accepted the Senate provision as preferable.[121]

The primary purpose of the proviso was to prevent the tendency to monopoly its proponents feared might result from the lower prices received by a few large purchasers because of the huge quantities in which they bought.[122]

---

[119] *Hearings on H.R. 8442, H.R. 4995, and H.R. 5062 before the House Committee on the Judiciary,* 74th Cong., 1st Sess. 224 (1935).

[120] 80 Cong. Rec. 6425–35 (1936); 80 Cong. Rec. 6334–38 (1936); 80 Cong. Rec. 8418 (1936).

[121] H.R. REPT. No. 2951, 74th Cong., 2d Sess. 6 (1936).

[122] The report of the Senate Judiciary Committee contained the following comment on the quantity-limit proviso:

"This proviso . . . is designed to enable, when necessary, the determination of quantity limits as to various commodities, beyond which quantity price differentials shall not be permitted even though supported by differences in cost. It rests upon the principle that where even an admitted economy is of a character that is possible only to a very few units of overshadowing size in a particular trade or industry, it may become in their hands none-

The proviso was, therefore, specifically designed to provide a means of controlling the quantity of a commodity for which the lowest price might be charged, irrespective of cost savings that might be achieved through sale of larger quantities.

Use of Quantity-Limit Proviso: The Federal Trade Commission has invoked the quantity-limit proviso only once. That was in the matter of Federal Trade Commission File 203–1 regarding rubber tires and tubes.

The Federal Trade Commission's action in fixing a quantity limit is quasi legislative in character; it does so through a rule-making proceeding. In September, 1949, the Commission published a notice proposing a rule to fix a quantity limit of a carload of 20,000 pounds in the sale of replacement rubber tires and tubes for motor vehicles. Following a hearing before the full Commission on that proposal, the Commission on December 13, 1951, issued a rule as follows:

> The quantity limit as to replacement tires and tubes made of natural
> or synthetic rubber for use on motor vehicles as a class of commodity
> is twenty thousand (20,000) pounds ordered at one time for delivery
> at one time.

Immediately, representatives of the B. F. Goodrich Company and other large producers of tires and tubes challenged the validity of the Commission's rule by filing complaints in the U.S. District Court for the District of Columbia. In their complaints, the plaintiffs contended that the Commission's rule-making proceeding was invalid because it had not been conducted as required by the provisions of Sections 7 and 8 of the Administrative Procedure Act for the conduct of adjudicatory matters. Also, it was contended that the plaintiffs had been denied due process, and, moreover, that the Commission was without a proper factual basis for its findings and ruling in the matter. The District Court dismissed the complaints for lack of jurisdiction, and also for failure to state a claim on which relief could be granted. Appeal was taken to the United States Court of Appeals for the District of Columbia, which reversed the District Court and remanded the case to the District Court for a trial on the issue of whether the Commission had acted on a proper basis in issuing its findings and ruling.[123]

In August, 1953, a majority of the Commission (Commissioners Mead, Spingarn, and Carretta) requested the Solicitor General to seek a writ of

---

theless the food upon which monopoly feeds, a proboscis through which it saps the lifeblood of its competitors; and that in forbidding its use and foregoing its benefits the public
is but paying a willing price for its freedom from monopoly control. A similar limitation
has been applied without challenge for nearly half a century in the field of transportation,
in refusing to extend freight rate differentials beyond the car lot quantity." (S. REPT. NO.
1502, 74th Cong., 2d Sess. (1936).

[123] B. F. Goodrich Co. v. FTC, 208 F.2d 829 (1953).

certiorari from the Supreme Court. That request was based on the assertion that the District Court was correct in its ruling that the complaint should be dismissed for lack of jurisdiction, in that it was for the Commission and not for the courts to determine whether the facts justified the issuance of the rule.

The Solicitor General announced on September 30, 1953, a decision not to seek certiorari in the matter. Thereupon, the cases came on for a hearing in the District Court before a judge who had not previously been involved in consideration of the cases. That court, after considering cross-motions for summary judgment, granted the motion of the plaintiff manufacturers and held that the statutory finding expressly required by the Act of Congress as a basis for the order had not been made and, therefore, that the order should not stand.[124] The Federal Trade Commission appealed the matter to the Court of Appeals for the District of Columbia Circuit, which held that the Commission's rule was not based on factual findings but on unwarranted inference from the borrowed experience of the Interstate Commerce Commission and was, therefore, arbitrary and capricious.[125] In its opinion, the Court of Appeals stated:

> The Commission concedes that the three formal findings, upon which it said in the order of promulgation it was basing the Rule, do not include a finding that available purchasers in quantities greater than a carload are so few as to render differentials on account thereof unjustly discriminatory or promotive of monopoly. Instead of dealing directly with that question of fact in its findings, the Commission seems to have been primarily concerned with the fewness of available purchasers in annual dollar volumes greater than $600,000. Obviously, a finding concerning that does not support a rule fixing a quantity limit of one 20,000-pound carload.
>
> . . . It may be that, had the Commission not made any specific separate findings labeled as such, it could have supported the order by writing an opinion embodying the requisite finding of fact. But, when it made formal findings in separate numbered paragraphs and said it was basing its order upon them, the order must stand or fall on the basis of those findings alone.
>
> . . . Even though the Commission's accompanying Statement may have indicated its belief that available buyers in quantities greater than a carload are so few as to give it authority under the quantity-limit proviso (which appellees seriously question), the Commission did not purport to base its order on that belief. We find no satisfactory explanation of its failure to do so. When a statute provides, as this one does, that a specified finding is a prerequisite to the exercise of

---

[124] B. F. Goodrich Co. v. FTC, 134 F. Supp. 39 (1955).
[125] FTC v. B. F. Goodrich Co., 242 F.2d. 31 (1957).

power, and where formal findings are made which are said to be the basis of the power claimed, there is no justification for reliance on a later statement to support the exercise of the power.

From that decision and opinion of the Court of Appeals, no petition was filed for a writ of certiorari from the Supreme Court. The matter was thus allowed to become a closed chapter. In view of this inconclusive disposition of the only proceeding undertaken under the quantity-limit proviso, many questions remain unanswered. However, it appears that the quantity-limit proviso may be taken as a limitation on the cost justification defense. The outcome of the only proceeding under the quantity-limit proviso requires no change in that concept. Also, the authority and power of the Commission to apply the quantity-limit proviso to differentials on account of purchases which are found to be "unjustly discriminatory" or "promotive of monopoly," and where the purchases of the quantities involved are "so few" as to give rise to those effects, remain unaffected by the outcome of that proceeding.

Right of Selection of Customers: Section 2(a) contains still another proviso:

> That nothing herein contained shall prevent persons engaged in selling goods, wares, or merchandise in commerce from selecting their own customers in bona fide transactions and not in restraint of trade.

The right to "select customers" is not a new addition to the antitrust laws. The above proviso is found word for word in the old Section 2 of the Clayton Antitrust Act, from which it has been lifted bodily and carried into the Robinson-Patman Act, the whole of which replaces the old Section 2. It is a well-established principle, both in law and in practice, that a seller may select his own customers in bona fide transactions and not in restraint of trade.

The Robinson-Patman Act immeasurably enlarged the Federal government's protection of competition in commerce. In doing that, it laid down new conditions under which a seller may or may not discriminate in price, grant advertising allowances or anything of value for facilities or services furnished by a seller or buyer, or pay brokerage and commissions.

Therefore, a seller's right to select his own customers in bona fide transactions and not in restraint of trade came into renewed importance and is being subjected to more intense scrutiny than ever. It is frequently asked whether the Robinson-Patman Act changes the long-established construction of that right. Does it place any interpretation on it that was not there before? Have any of the conditions been changed? Has a seller's right to select his own customers been curtailed in any way? Do the provisions of the Act, because of their application to certain specific processes of distribution, now compel a seller to sell his goods to a buyer to whom he previously did not sell, or would not have elected to sell?

The Robinson-Patman Act does not change the import or the meaning of the proviso from what the courts have heretofore held it to mean. It only adds new impetus and importance to its consideration as far as the seller is concerned.

The proviso has been a matter of law and a part of the Clayton Act since its adoption in 1914. Its inclusion in the Act is merely giving lawful expression to a moral right that always has been considered as belonging to any party engaged in commerce. It is akin to property rights, and its inclusion as a part of the Clayton Act was no doubt for the purpose of giving warning that the provisions of the Clayton Act must not abridge reasonable rights of a man to dispose of his property as he chooses.

But the right to own property and dispose of it, the right to engage in commerce—to buy and sell goods and wares in the course of their distribution from producers to consumers—these involve the seller in certain responsibilities and provide opportunities for the seller to engage in practices that may result in injury to trade and industry. Such injury may be the result of negative action rather than positive. It may arise from a refusal to sell rather than a willingness to sell, a practice in restraint of trade rather than an encouragement of it. Therefore, the law recognizes this possibility and, in negative fashion, says in substance: "A seller shall not refuse to sell, or to select customers, where the effect restrains trade."

How may a seller, by refusing to select customers, act to restrain trade? Two illustrations will suffice. If a party has proceeded well on the way to accomplishing monopoly control of a product in demand in commerce, he may reach a point where he is able to dominate the market for that product. He may then set up restrictions on the sale of his product, which all of his customers must abide by. He refuses to sell to anyone who will not abide by his rules. The courts have held that such a practice is operating in restraint of trade. Although they do not lay down a general rule regarding his selection of customers, the courts may, on appeal, compel him to sell his product to a dealer who has sought to purchase it.

On occasions, by collusive action, tacit agreement, or mutual understanding, members of a particular industry may agree in concert to certain restrictions and policies under which they will select their customers, agreeing to sell only to certain parties and refusing to sell to others. Sooner or later, this policy operates in restraint of trade in the opinion of the court, and the interested parties' right to select their customers is encroached upon. The industry may be ordered to discontinue the restrictions and policies, and they may be ordered to sell to parties who desire to purchase their merchandise but have been refused theretofore.

Thus, a seller's right to select his own customers is upheld by the law, except when he misuses the right. In those cases, by due process of law, the courts may step in and restrain him in the interests of commerce as a whole.

The right to select customers must meet another qualification: The selection must be done in bona fide transactions. That is, a sale must be made in good faith; the transaction must be consummated and title to the goods must pass to the customers.

The final qualification is that sellers be engaged in selling goods, wares, or merchandise in commerce. The proviso in the Act is limited to those persons engaged in selling commodities. This means, not that those engaged in other kinds of occupations and business pursuits are denied the right to select their own customers, but merely that in this instance, the insurance company, the lawyer, or others who sell their services are not affected one way or the other by this Act.

In the selection of customers, a seller may set up any conditions he sees fit, as long as he does not discriminate between his customers in any manner prohibited by the Robinson-Patman Act and does not operate in restraint of trade. Just as he may deny the purchase of one part of his products to a customer while selling him other parts, he may require that a customer confine his requirements in his line to him, on pain of withdrawing his entire line from the customers; his right, within reason, to select his customers is undisputed.

The Robinson-Patman Act, therefore, neither adds to nor detracts from the previous moral and legal right of a seller to select his own customers in bona fide transactions and not in restraint of trade. He continues to be governed as he has been in the past. His previous freedom in the exercise of this right is neither enlarged nor curtailed; he is still bound by the same limits and restrictions. He must be engaged in bona fide transactions, and the result of his exercise of that right must not be to injure or restrain trade and industry. He need have no fear as long as his selection of customers is made with due regard for the rights and interests of both seller and buyer and the result is to increase and promote the socially and economically profitable exchange of articles in commerce.

No. 69. Question. May a seller select only one buyer in each city and refuse to sell to others?

Opinion. Yes. Any seller may select his customers in any manner he sees fit, so long as practices in restraint of trade are not engaged in.

No. 70. Question. Suppose a seller chooses to sell exclusively to chain stores?

Opinion. There is nothing in the Act to prohibit exercising that right.

No. 71. Question. May a manufacturer decide he will confine his sales exclusively to wholesalers and refuse to sell to anyone not a wholesaler?

Opinion. Yes.

No. 72. Question. A well-known cosmetic manufacturer has refused to sell my client any of its products. Is not this refusal a violation of the Robinson-Patman Act?

Opinion. A refusal to sell one dealer does not comprise an act in restraint of trade. The Act does not compel a seller to sell to all bidders.

No. 73. Question. Inasmuch as a manufacturer can select his customers, is it permissible for any manufacturer to decide that he will sell only to wholesalers and the large corporate chains, both on an equal basis, but will refuse to sell to a group of independent stores represented by an organization such as ours (a cooperative buying group), although the quantities and time of purchase would be approximately the same?

Opinion. A manufacturer may elect to sell to wholesalers and the large corporate chains and refuse to sell to other types and classifications of buyers, without qualification other than that his method of selection does not operate in restraint of trade as commonly defined. It is when he sells to the chains at one price and sells to you at a different price, when quantities and terms are the same, that he runs counter to the law.

No. 74. Question. In selecting customers, may differences be made in prices to customers who require different terms and conditions of sale?

Opinion. The "right to select customers" is not involved in this case. It is a case of discrimination between customers you have selected, and as such is legal if done in conformity with the Act.

Courts in many important cases have upheld the right to the selection of customers. In their decisions, they have uniformly followed the principle that a seller may refuse to sell any person for any reason satisfactory to himself so long as this is the result of his own independent judgment and not in restraint of trade or violation of law. This has been made clear by the United States Supreme Court in a long line of cases beginning with *United States v. Colgate and Co.*,[126] and continuing through *FTC v. Raymond Bros.-Clark Co.*[127] and *Times-Picayune Publishing Co. v. U.S.*[128]

In the *Times-Picayune* case, the Court declared:

> Refusals to sell, without more, do not violate the law. Though group boycotts, or concerted refusals to deal, clearly run afoul of section 1 (Sherman Act) . . . different criteria have long applied to

[126] 250 U.S. 300 (1919).
[127] 263 U.S. 565 (1924).
[128] 345 U.S. 954 (1953).

qualify the rights of an individual seller. Beginning with *United States v. Colgate and Co.* (1919) (250 U.S. 300), this Court's decisions have recognized individual refusals to sell as a general right, though "neither absolute nor exempt from regulation." *Lorain Journal Co. v. U.S.* (1951) (342 U.S. 143). If accompanied by unlawful conduct or agreement, or conceived in monopolistic purpose or market control, even individual sellers' refusals to deal have transgressed the act. *Lorain Journal Co. v. U.S.* (342 U.S. 143 (1951)), *U.S. v. Bausch and Lomb Optical Co.* (321 U.S. 707 (1944)) and *Eastman Kodak Co. v. Southern Photo Materials Co.* (273 U.S. 359 (1927)), and *U.S. v. A. Schrader's Son, Inc.* (252 U.S. 85 (1920)).

In the *Colgate* case, which serves as a pivot in the law on refusal to sell, Justice McReynolds stated:

> In the absence of any purpose to create or maintain a monopoly, the act (Sherman) does not restrict the long recognized right of a trader or manufacturer engaged in an entirely private business, freely to exercise his own independent discretion as to parties with whom he will deal; and, of course, he may announce in advance the circumstances under which he will refuse to sell.

As authority for this rule, Justice McReynolds cited *U.S. v. Trans-Missouri Freight Assn.,*[129] in which Justice Peckham commented that—

> The trader or manufacturer, on the other hand, carries on an entirely private business, and can sell to whom he pleases.

In the *Cream of Wheat* case (1915), the Circuit Court of Appeals, in affirming the right of the company to select its own customers, declared:

> We had supposed that it was elementary law that a trader could buy from whom he pleased and sell to whom he pleased, and that his selection of a buyer or seller was wholly his own concern. (*Great Atlantic and Pacific Tea Co. v. Cream of Wheat Co.,* 27 Fed. Rep. 46, 48–49.)

The factor of market control approaching conditions of a monopoly was carefully considered by the Supreme Court in the case of *Eastman Kodak Co. v. Southern Photo Materials.*[130] That factor served to distinguish that case from the *Raymond Bros.-Clark Co.* case, decided three years earlier, where the Court pointed out there was an absence of collusive action, agreements in restraint of trade, or conditions approaching market control. It is interesting to note that Justice Sanford wrote the opinion for the Court in both of those cases. In the first, the seller's right to the selection of his cus-

[129] 166 U.S. 290, 320 (1897).
[130] 273 U.S. 359 (1927).

tomer was upheld. In the second, it was held that the Eastman Kodak Co. had violated the law in refusing to sell to the Southern Photo Materials Co.

Exemption as to Perishables, Obsolescence, and Changing Conditions: The last proviso in subsection (a) specifies:

> That nothing herein contained shall prevent price changes from time to time where in response to changing conditions affecting the market for or the marketability of the goods concerned, such as but not limited to actual or imminent deterioration of perishable goods, obsolescence of seasonal goods, distress sales under courts process, or sales in good faith in discontinuance of business in the goods concerned.

Strictly construed, this proviso would appear to permit only price changes from time to time. It does not specifically exempt price discriminations. However, it is apparent from the legislative history that it was intended to provide an exemption from the general prohibition against price discriminations otherwise made unlawful by subsection 2(a). The House Judiciary Committee inserted the proviso in its present broadened form.[131] In that connection, the Judiciary Committee reported that the proviso exempts price changes "in response to changing conditions affecting the market for or the marketability of the goods concerned, such as, but not limited to, actual or imminent deterioration of perishable goods, obsolescence of seasonal goods, distress sales under court process, or sales in good faith in discontinuance of business in the goods concerned." Although it is not believed that the principal prohibitions of Section 2(a) apply in any case to such price changes, nor has such construction ever been suggested or contended for under present section 2, this specific exemption is included as an added precaution to safeguard the ready disposition of goods characterized by fluid market conditions.

Wherever anyone relies on this proviso to justify a discrimination between purchasers, the burden of proof is on him to show that the conditions designated in the proviso can be satisfied by the facts and circumstances involved in the particular case of discrimination.

The intent and purpose of the proviso is well stated in the proviso itself. It is intended to provide for continuance of the normal and economically justifiable freedom of action that will permit a seller to dispose of goods on hand where he is threatened with immediate or imminent loss as the result of changing marketing conditions, deterioration, or obsolescence of the goods themselves, or any other similar circumstance that requires the sudden and immediate movement of goods on hand to avoid losses resulting

---

[131] H.R. Rep. No. 2287, 74th Cong., 2d Sess. 11 (1936).

from conditions beyond his control. The Act gives him the legal right under such conditions to dispose of the goods at whatever price may be obtained, without regard to differences in cost or undue concern for discrimination between purchasers.

In all such cases, the burden of proof remains upon the seller to establish the necessity for such action. He must be prepared to defend himself against an accusation of unlawful discrimination by showing the justification for his act within the limitations provided by this proviso.

Wherever a seller believes that an action on his part may later result in complaint against him of unfair price discrimination in violation of the Act, he may best protect himself by preservation of all records of the transaction in question and such proof as may be at hand to show the justification for his act.

No. 75. Question. Does this proviso apply to price discriminations involved in the sale of goods manufactured for off-season sales?

Opinion. No. It applies to sales from regular stock where obsolescence, deterioration, or other conditions that arise require disposal of the particular goods. Therefore, the proviso must be regarded as referring to existing stocks of specific goods.

No. 76. Question. Does this proviso apply to the raising or lowering of prices on a line of products responsive to changes in market demand?

Opinion. No. A seller is privileged to raise or lower his prices in response to changing market conditions affecting the demand for his product, but price discriminations to accommodate changes in the market demand is another matter. The proviso does not cover that sort of thing. Any ordinary price change made in the regular course of business, in response to changes in market demand, should be made effective at the same time to all competing purchasers.

The Good-Faith Meeting of an Equally Low Price of a Competitor: Subsection (b) of Section 2 of the Robinson-Patman Act contains the following language:

> Upon proof being made, at any hearing on a complaint under this section, that there has been discrimination in price or services or facilities furnished, the burden of rebutting the prima facie case thus made by showing justification shall be upon the person charged with a violation of this section, and unless justification shall be affirmatively shown, the Commission is authorized to issue an order terminating the discrimination: *Provided, however,* That nothing herein contained shall prevent a seller rebutting the prima facie case thus made by showing that his lower price or the furnishing of services or facilities to any purchaser or purchasers was made in good faith to meet an

equally low price of a competitor, or the services or facilities furnished by a competitor.

This language serves as a substitute for a provision that appeared in Section 2 of the original Clayton Act as approved in October, 1914, to the following effect:

> That nothing herein contained shall prevent . . . discrimination in price in the same or different communities made in good faith to meet competition.

When Mr. Clayton introduced H.R. 15657 on April 14, 1914,[132] Section 2 did not contain any proviso providing for discriminations made in good faith to meet competition. The "good-faith" proviso was inserted in the bill by the Senate Judiciary Committee. The debate in the Senate on the proviso makes it clear that the proviso was for the purpose of permitting a man to meet "another's price in protecting his business in a district."[133] During the course of the debates in Congress, concern was expressed about the possibility that the proviso would seriously weaken the law.[134]

The fears that had been expressed about the possible effect of the "good faith" proviso in the Clayton Antitrust Act of 1914 proved to be well founded. In the 20-year period following the passage of the Clayton Antitrust Act of 1914, it proved to be an ineffective tool for use against destructive price discriminations. As pointed out herein, the Federal Trade Commission made many investigations and reported that the practice of price discrimination was widespread, that it was leading to the creation of monopolistic conditions, and that "The Commission has no evidence which would establish that price discrimination by chain stores has not been in

---

132 51 Cong. Rec. 6714 (1914).

133 51 Cong. Rec. 9096 (1914). See also 51 Cong. Rec. 14228 (1914).

134 "MR. CUMMINS . . . [B]ut we are not making this law to arrest the progress of monopoly in outrageous cases only. We are making it to preserve competition.

"We might just as well have said . . . that the seller can do anything that he desires or pleases to meet competition that is not in violation of the antitrust laws; if it is in violation of the antitrust law, we need no further condemnation or penalty. We have wound up this section practically by saying that the seller can do whatsoever he pleases with regard to his business, provided he does not violate the antitrust law; and yet this is one of the sections that have been proposed to strengthen the antitrust law, to add to the antitrust law, to accomplish the purpose of the antitrust law by forbidding something that is not now forbidden by the States." Id. at 14250.

"MR. STERLING . . . Passing the paragraph or proviso which permits discrimination in price because of differences in grade, quality, or quantity, or differences in cost of selling or transportation, I come to this significant provision injected by the committee, namely, the provision which permits 'discrimination in price in the same or different communities made in good faith to meet competition.' It is easy to conceive of the multitude of sins that may be covered by that broad and generous cloak . . .

"Think of it. It can always be urged against the charge of unlawful discrimination that it was done for the purpose of meeting competition. 'We found our competition charging a certain price for these goods.' We cut the price of ours, below cost even, to meet his competition. What have you got to say about it under this law?" Id. at 16115.

good faith to meet competition and there is good ground to conclude that in many cases it has been for that purpose."[135]

It was easy to see why the big chains were driving the independents out. They were getting price concessions and secret rebates far beyond anything that was justified by the suppliers' cost differences. The investigations revealed, for example, that prior to 1935 the Atlantic & Pacific Tea Company had been receiving on an annual basis $6 million in off-the-invoice discounts and another $2 million a year in brokerage fees on its purchases.

In many instances, the big buyers were demanding special price concessions and coercing small suppliers into granting special concessions with threats of putting up their own manufacturing plants. In other instances, they were playing the suppliers off against one another, forcing suppliers of nationally advertised products to meet the prices of small, exclusive suppliers who could not, in practice, market to the independent trade. It was overwhelmingly obvious that something had to be done to check this abuse of power and return the competitive contest more to a contest of efficiency.

The Federal Trade Commission, in its *Final Report on the Chain Store Investigation,*[136] stated that the Clayton Antitrust Act, as then written, permitted destructive price discriminations "when made in good faith to meet competition." The Commission reported that such "good faith" provision of the law, as then interpreted, virtually nullified the law against price discriminations, and it commented:

> A simple solution for the uncertainties and difficulties of enforcement would be to prohibit unfair and unjust discrimination in price and leave it to the enforcement agency, subject to review by the courts, to apply that principle to particular cases and situations. The soundness of and the extent to which the present provisos would constitute valid defenses would thus become a judicial and not a legislative matter.[137]

The Commission, in its report on the chain store investigation, rejected suggestions that the Sherman Antitrust Act be relied on and used to halt these destructive price discriminations.[138] Resolutions were introduced in the House of Representatives providing for an investigation of the trade practices of big-scale retail and wholesale buying and selling organiza-

---

[135] FTC, *Final Report on the Chain Store Investigation,* S. Doc. No. 4, 74th Cong., 1st Sess. 51 (1934).

[136] *Ibid.*

[137] *Id.* at 96.

[138] "While price discrimination was one of the methods used to build up the monopoly which the Supreme Court held unlawful in the Standard Oil dissolution suit, it has never been held to be a violation of the Sherman Act in and of itself." *Id.* at 65.

tions.[139] Those resolutions provided for the investigations to be made by a special committee of seven members of the House—four Democrats and three Republicans, under the chairmanship of the author.[140]

When this practice was being investigated in 1935–36, it was found that injurious price discriminations were being practiced in industry after industry.

In the light of the facts uncovered during the course of investigations of big-scale buying and selling in 1935–36, it was not difficult for one to see why the law against price discrimination had broken down. One of the main reasons was the defect in the law pointed out by the Federal Trade Commission in its report on the chain-store investigation—the provision that allowed sellers who were discriminating in price to defend on the ground that they were meeting competition in good faith. Bills were introduced in both the House and the Senate to overcome the defects in the laws against price discrimination, including the loophole that permitted discriminations "made in good faith to meet competition."[141] Neither the Robinson nor the Patman bill contained any provision similar to the "meeting competition" proviso that had been a part of the original Section 2 of the Clayton Act was inserted in the Robinson bill by Amendment. The House Judiciary Committee reported the Patman bill with a subsection identical to the present subsection (b) of Section 2, except it did not mention services or facilities. The Conference Committee rejected the Senate amendment and approved the House version, and in doing so stated:

> This language is found in existing law, and in the opinion of the conferees is one of the obstacles to enforcement of the present Clayton Act. The Senate receded, and the language is stricken. A provision relating to the question of meeting competition, intended to operate only as a rule of evidence in a proceeding before the Federal Trade Commission, is included in subsection (b).[142]

Congressman Utterback, who presented the Conference Report to the House, explained this proviso as follows:

> It is to be noted, however, that this does not set up the meeting of competition as an absolute bar to a charge of discrimination under the bill. It merely permits it to be shown in evidence. This provision is entirely procedural. It does not determine substantive rights, liabilities and duties. . . .

---

139 H.R. Res. 203 and 239, 74th Cong., 1st Sess. (1934).
140 Rep. Wright Patman (D. Texas), Chairman; Rep. Sol Bloom (D., N.Y.); Rep. Scott W. Lucas (D., Ill.); Rep. John F. Dockweiler (D., Calif.); Rep. Donald H. McLean (R., N.J.); Rep. W. Sterling Cole (R., N.Y.); Rep. Gerald J. Boileau (R., Wisc.).
141 H.R. 8442 [introduced by Rep. Wright Patman (D. Texas)], and S. 3154 [introduced by Senator Joseph Robinson (D., Ark.)], 74th Cong., 2d Sess. (1935).
142 H.R. REP No. 2951, 74th Cong. 2d Sess. 7 (1936).

This procedural provision cannot be construed as a *carte blanche* exemption to violate the bill so long as a competitor can be shown to have violated it first, nor so long as that competition cannot be met without the use of oppressive discriminations in violation of the obvious intent of the bill. . . .

If this proviso were construed to permit the showing of a competing offer as an absolute bar to liability for discrimination, then it would nullify the act entirely at the very inception of its enforcement; for in nearly every case mass buyers receive similar discriminations from competing sellers of the same product.[143]

With the need for remedial legislation so urgent,[144] the Congress acted in a manner that made its intent clear with an emphatic vote. The Robinson-Patman Act passed the House by a vote of 290 to 16, and when it was finally voted on in the Senate, it was passed without objection.

The Supreme Court of the United States, by a five-to-three decision in 1951, held that meeting a competitor's price in good faith is a complete justification for price discrimination that otherwise would be violative of subsection 2(a). That question was squarely presented and so decided in the case of *Standard Oil Co. of Indiana v. FTC*.[145]

The Court in the *Standard Oil Co.* case stated:

The proviso in Sec. 2(b), as interpreted by the Commission, would not be available when there was or might be an injury to competition at a resale level. So interpreted the proviso would have so little, if any, applicability as to be practically meaningless.[146]

That statement in the opinion of the Court, as well as observations made by Justices during the course of the oral arguments in the case, make clear the fact that the Commission failed in its presentation to satisfy the Court as to how a person charged would be able to show justification by "rebutting the prima facie case."

The Commission's findings in the *Standard Oil Co.* case were clear and to the effect that the seller had been discriminating in price, with the actual effect of substantially lessening competition and tending to create a monopoly. That fact did not rest on evidence sufficient to support an inference that the effect of the challenged discriminations was to substantially lessen competition or to tend to create a monopoly. It is clear that the latter would

---

[143] 80 CONG. REC. 9418 (1936).
[144] The House Committee Report on the need for the legislation stated: "Your Committee is of the opinion that the evidence is overwhelming that price discrimination practices exist to such an extent that the survival of independent merchants, manufacturers, and other businessmen is seriously imperiled and that remedial legislation is necessary." H.R. REP. No. 2287, 74th Cong., 2d Sess. 3 (1935).
[145] 340 U.S. 231 (1951).
[146] *Id.* at 250.

have been rebuttable as a prima facie case. More than that, it would have provided a basis for the seller arguing that it discriminated in good faith, in that there was no showing that the seller had any reason to believe that the effects of the discriminations were those proscribed by the Act. In a case resting on such probabilities, there would have been considerable opportunity for the seller charged with violation to show justification by "rebutting the prima facie case" through evidence that the inference regarding effects was not well founded, or by showing that the probability of effects, even if they should eventuate, were not foreseeable by the seller and, therefore, that the seller should be credited with having discriminated in good faith. If the Supreme Court in the *Standard Oil Co.* case had been able to see the question in that light, perhaps it could have reasoned that the good-faith defense was procedural only. Perhaps the Court could have thus reasoned without considering that Congress had done a futile thing. However, this idea was not made clear in the *Standard Oil Co.* case, and consequently the Court failed to see why Congress had written subsection 2(b) unless it was to be regarded as providing for the good-faith defense as an absolute bar to a charge of violation of subsection 2(a).

The Commission and Justice Reed, in his dissent from the opinion and decision of the Court in the *Standard Oil Co.* case, were unable to reconcile the purposes and objectives of the Act with the decision handed by the Court in the *Standard Oil Co.* case. Justice Reed in his dissent stated:

> . . . the "meeting competition" provision was separated from the other provisos, set off from the substantive provisions of Section 2(a), and relegated to the position of a proviso to the procedural subsection, Section 2(b). Unless it is believed that this change of position was fortuitous, it can be inferred that Congress meant to curtail the defense of meeting competition when it banished this proviso from the substantive division to the procedural. . . . in contrast to [the provisos of Section 2(a)], the proviso to Section 2(b) does not provide that nothing "shall prevent" a certain price practice; it provides only that "nothing shall prevent a seller rebutting a prima facie case by showing" a certain price practice—meeting a competitive price. The language thus shifts the focus of the proviso from a matter of substantive defense to a matter of proof. Mr. Justice Reed, dissenting in Standard Oil Co. of Indiana v. FTC.[147]

The net result is the holding that the discriminating seller is privileged to discriminate in price—with the effect of destroying its competitors and its customers, and with the effect of substantially lessening competition and tending to create a monopoly—as long as the seller shows that it has ac-

---

[147] 340 U.S. 231 (1951).

complished all those things in "good faith" in meeting an equally low price of a competitor.

Since it has been held the proposition that the meeting of a competitor's price in good faith is a complete justification of price discriminations otherwise violative of subsection 2(a), it is appropriate to proceed with consideration of situations to which the good faith defense may be applied.

No. 77. Question. Is the good-faith defense available in cases arising under subsections 2(c), 2(d), and 2(e) of the Robinson-Patman Act, as well as those arising under subsection 2(a)?

Opinion. No. A seller charged with a violation of subsection 2(c) may not defend his actions by showing that the alleged reduction in price in lieu of brokerage or the payment of brokerage to the buyer was made in good faith to meet an equivalent reduction or payment made by a competitor.

In a long line of cases beginning with the decision of the U.S. Circuit Court of Appeals for the Second Circuit in the case of *Biddle Purchasing Co. v. FTC*,[148] the courts have held consistently that subsection 2(c) is to be construed separately and in a different light from subsection 2(a), and cases arising under subsection 2(c) are not clothed with the defenses applicable to cases arising under subsection 2(a).[149]

The Federal Trade Commission has held that the good-faith defense cannot be applied as a substantive defense to a charge of violation of subsection 2(d).[150] On the other hand, the Commission on May 19, 1960, adopted and issued *Guides for Advertising Allowances and Other Merchandising Payments and Services; Compliance with Sections 2(d) and 2(e) of the Clayton Act, as Amended by the Robinson-Patman Act,* in which it was stated:

> A seller charged with discrimination in violation of Section 2(e) may defend his actions by showing that the services were furnished in good faith to meet an equivalent service furnished by a competitor. However, this is a very technical defense subject to important limitations. The Commission has held that the defense of meeting competition in good faith is not available to a seller charged with discrimination in violation of Section 2(d).

No. 78. Question. Is the good-faith defense to a seller charged with price discrimination in a private damage suit as well as in government proceedings?

Opinion. Yes. See Moore v. Mead Service Co., 190 F.2d 540, 542 (10th

---

[148] 30 F.T.C. 447 (1938).
[149] See also Oliver Bros. v. FTC, 102 F.2d. 763, 767; Great Atlantic & Pacific Tea Co. v. FTC, 106 F.2d. 667, 675.
[150] Henry Rosenfeld, Inc., No. 6212, FTC, 1956.

Cir. 1951); American Cooperative Serum Ass'n. v. Anchor Serum Co., 153 F.2d 907, 912 (7th Cir. 1946).

No. 79. Question. To what kind of situation in a case arising under subsection 2(a) does the good-faith defense apply?

Opinion. Section 2(b) permits a single company to sell to one customer at a lower price than it sells to another if the price is "made in good faith to meet an equally low price of a competitor." See FTC v. Cement Institute, 333 U.S. 683, 725 (1948).

No. 80. Question. If the equally low price of a competitor applies to goods that normally sell at a lower price than that normally applicable to goods offered by the person charged, because of lower grade or cost or less acceptance or different packaging, may such lower price be met in good faith?

Opinion. The usefulness of the good-faith defense in such situations is doubtful. The Federal Trade Commission, on a remand of the *Standard Oil Co.* case, held that because of such circumstances the Standard Oil Co. was not in good faith in meeting the lower price or lower cost and grade of gasoline. Consequently, the Commission held that the good-faith defense was not made out. The Court of Appeals set aside the Commission's order to cease and desist based on that reason.[151] The Supreme Court of the United States affirmed the decision of the Seventh Circuit Court of Appeals.[152]

No. 81. Question. Is it necessary for the person charged with a violation of subsection 2(a) to have knowledge in advance of a lower price of a competitor before he makes a price discrimination to meet such lower price, in order to sustain the good-faith defense?

Opinion. Yes. See Minneapolis-Honeywell Regulator Co., No. 4920, FTC, 1948, *rev'd on other grounds,* 191 F.2d 786 (7th Cir. 1951).

No. 82. Question. Does subsection 2(b) permit a seller to utilize the good-faith defense when the seller uses a sales system that consistently results in his getting more money for like goods from some customers than he does from others?

Opinion. No. See FTC v. Cement Institute, 333 U.S. 683, 725 (1948); FTC v. Staley Manufacturing Co., 324 U.S. 746, 754–755 (1945). The Act places emphasis on individual competitive situations, rather than on a general system of competition.

No. 83. Question. May a seller utilize the good-faith proviso to justify quantity or volume discounts, which he regularly grants to customers qualifying therefor on the basis of quantities they purchase, by showing that any

---

[151] Standard Oil Co. v. FTC, 233 F.2d 649 (7th Cir. 1956).
[152] FTC v. Standard Oil Co., 355 U.S. 396 (1958).

one of his purchasers could have obtained an equally low price from another seller on a like quantity?

Opinion. No. See International Salt Company, No. 4307, FTC, 1952.

No. 84. Question. Is the good-faith defense available to a seller who discriminates in price by making a lower price available to a customer so the customer can meet lower prices of his competitors?

Opinion. No. See Sun Oil Company, No. 6641, FTC, 1959; Enterprise Industries, Inc. v. Texas Co., 136 F. Supp. 420 (D.C. Conn. 1955), *rev'd on other grounds,* 240 F.2d 457 (2d Cir. 1957).

No. 85. Question. May a seller invoke the good-faith defense to justify price discriminations in order to obtain new business and new customers?

Opinion. See Standard Oil Co. of Indiana v. FTC, 340 U.S. 241, 250 (1951). On July 11, 1962, the United States Court of Appeals for the 7th Circuit in the case of Sunshine Biscuits, Inc. v. Federal Trade Commission, 306 Fed. 2d 48, held that a seller may discriminate in price as an aggressor to obtain new customers with as much impunity as in the taking of such action *to retain* old customers. The Supreme Court of the United States in the *Standard Oil Company case* apparently had made a distinction between the action of a seller *to retain* a customer and aggressive action by way of price discrimination to capture new customers from its competitors. The 7th Circuit Court of Appeals in the *Sunshine Biscuits case* in holding against the Commission on this point said:

> . . . the distinction between old and new customers is economically unsound and would defeat the purpose of the Robinson-Patman Act seems obvious. If, in situations where the Section 2(b) proviso is applicable, sellers could grant good faith competitive price reductions only to old customers in order to retain them, competition for new customers would be stifled and monopoly would be fostered. In such situations an established seller would have a monopoly of *his* customers and a seller entering the market would not be permitted to reduce his prices to compete with his established rivals unless he could do so on a basis such as cost justification. Moreover, the distinction would create a forced price discrimination between a seller's existing customers to whom he had lawfully lowered his prices under Section 2(b) and a prospective new customer. These results, we believe, are incompatible with the purpose for which the Robinson-Patman Act was enacted.

However, another court of appeals recently held that a lower price is within subsection 2(b) "only if it is used defensively to hold customers rather than to gain new ones." See also Edelmann & Co. v. FTC, 239 F.2d 1952 (7th Cir. 1956); Niehoff & Co. v. FTC, 241 F.2d 37 (7th Cir. 1957); Standard Motor Products Co. v. FTC, 265 F.2d 674, (2d Cir. 1959).

No. 86. Question. In the *Standard Oil Co.* case, the Court made frequent comments to the effect that the good-faith defense is a complete justification for price-discrimination practice in order to meet in "good faith" a *lawful* and equally low price of a competitor. What does the word "lawful" in this context mean?

Opinion. The Act makes no distinction between meeting an equally low *lawful* or *unlawful* price of a competitor. The Court in the *Standard Oil Co.* case emphasized that it considered that the good-faith proviso had been included in the Act to give a seller a "substantial right of self-defense against a price raid by a competitor."[153] Harsh action is justified at law as a measure in self-defense utilized to counter wrongful and unlawful action of another. A man can justify homicide in self-defense when he is attempting to counter wrongful bodily injury to himself. He could never defend successfully any such homicide by showing that his adversary indulged only in lawful actions.

In view of this concept of the right of self-defense, it is difficult to understand the meaning of the word "lawful" in the context in which it was used in the *Standard Oil Co.* case with reference to an equally low price of a competitor. It would seem that it would have been more appropriate to require that the seller use nondiscriminatory prices in meeting "lawful" prices of a competitor and to permit him to discriminate in price to meet unlawfully discriminatory prices in self-defense. As applied in the *Standard Oil Co.* case, the "lawful price" limitation serves to bar self-defense in those instances where the right to self-defense is most needed and to permit its use in those instances where it is least justified.

Even though it is difficult to explain how the Court came to apply the "lawful price" limitation to the good-faith defense in the *Standard Oil Co.* case, one may speculate on how that came about. Earlier, the Court had rendered its decision in the *Staley* case.[154] In that case, counsel representing the Commission was successful in convincing the Court that Staley should not be held to have acted in good faith in meeting the prices of a competitor company when the discriminatory pricing of the competitor was part and parcel of an unlawful pricing system. There was more involved than Staley's merely meeting the competitor's prices in that instance; Staley was implicated in the price-making activity that gave rise to the discriminatory pricing systems utilized by it and its competitor. Therefore, Staley was a party to the making of the unlawful discriminatory prices that it asked the Court to accept as a basis in justification of its discriminations. That the Court refused to do. However, that was in 1945. It was six years later in 1951, that

---

153 340 U.S. 231, 249.
154 FTC v. Staley Mfg. Co., 324 U.S. 746 (1945).

the Court undertook its consideration of the *Standard Oil Co.* case. We may inquire whether it recalled that its decision in 1945 against Staley's attempted good-faith defense was predicated at least in part on the fact of Staley's complicity in the making of unlawful discriminatory prices that it allegedly met. Certainly it is not clear from anything the Court said in its opinion in the *Standard Oil* Co. case that it was distinguishing that case from the Staley case on that ground. It is a sufficient ground for distinguishing the two cases, but if they should be distinguished on that ground, then the "lawful price" limitation to the good-faith defense is without a basis in the *Standard Oil Co.* case.

Undoubtedly the Court, when faced with this question in the future, will undertake to provide us with a full explanatory statement of the meaning of the word "lawful" as used in the opinion and decision in the *Standard Oil Co.* case, with reference to the meeting of an equally low price of a competitor. In the meantime, if the competitor's price is unlawfully discriminatory, other suppliers may meet it only by lowering their prices across the board. On the other hand, the small business firm doing business only in a single market at a low, nondiscriminatory, and lawful price is fair game for discriminations practiced by the multimarket operator who is privileged to discriminate as long as he is able to show that he is "meeting this low, lawful price" of a competitor. Also, in the meantime, it remains uncertain whether the person charged with discriminating in violation of subsection 2(a) has the burden of showing that the actual competitor's prices he meets were, in fact, lawful prices.[155]

No. 87. Question. What must the person charged show to sustain his claim that he was meeting an equally low price of a competitor?

Opinion. The Supreme Court in the *Staley* case[156] fully explored this question. In doing so, it recognized that a competitor's prices are not always ascertained with a great degree of accuracy. Therefore, the Court would not require the person charged to prove actually what his competitor's price was, but he would be required to prove what he had reason to believe it was and that he did use reasonable diligence in ascertaining the facts that led him to believe that his lower price was no greater than that of his competitors. The Court pointed out various means in which that could be done and various methods that would prove dangerous if relied upon for ascertaining the facts. For example, it was pointed out that the statements and reports of some customers regarding prices quoted by com-

---

[155] Balian Ice Cream Co. v. Arden Farms Co., 231 F.2d 356 (9th Cir. 1955), *cert. denied,* 350 U.S. 991; Standard Oil Co. v. Brown, 238 F.2d 54 (5th Cir. 1956). See also Mid-South Distributors, No. 5766, FTC, 1959, affirmed (5th Cir. 1961) 287 F.2d 512, *cert. denied* 368 U.S. 838 (1961).
[156] 324 U.S. 746.

petitors were not fully reliable in the *Staley* case and were held to be insufficient to establish good faith unless fully justified. In that connection, the Court pointed out that—

> The facts as stipulated were only that the discriminations were made in response to verbal information received from salesmen, brokers or intending purchasers, without supporting evidence, to the effect that in each case one or more competitors had granted or offered to grant like discriminations. It is stipulated that respondents, "believing such report to be true, has then granted similar" price discriminations. The record contains no statements by the persons making these reports and discloses no efforts by respondents to investigate or verify them, and no evidence of respondents' knowledge of their informants' character and reliability. . . .
>
> Section 2(b) does not require the seller to justify price discriminations by showing that in fact they met a competitive price. But it does place on the seller the burden of showing that the price was made in good faith to meet a competitor's. . . . We agree with the Commission that the statute at least requires the seller, who has knowingly discriminated in price, to show the existence of facts which would lead a reasonable and prudent person to believe that the granting of a lower price would in fact meet the equally low price of a competitor.[157]

SUBSECTION 2(A) RECORD OF ENFORCEMENT

Enforcement by Federal Trade Commission

Between the effective date of the Robinson-Patman Act in 1936 and May 31, 1961, the Federal Trade Commission decided 240 cases in which it had alleged a violation of subsection 2(a) of the Robinson-Patman Act. Of these, 54 cases contained charges that respondents charged in the complaints had violated other subsections of Section 2 of the Robinson-Patman Act. Of the total of 240 cases thus brought by the Federal Trade Commission, 170 resulted in orders to cease and desist and 70 in orders of dismissal. The orders to cease and desist entered by the Commission in two of the cases were set aside by the courts. These were the *Minneapolis-Honeywell* case and the *Standard Oil of Indiana* case.[158] The results left in effect 168 orders to cease and desist entered by the Commission in cases arising under subsection 2(a) in the period from June 19, 1936, to May 31, 1961.

---

[157] *Id.* at 758–60.
[158] Standard Oil Co. of Indiana v. FTC, 340 U.S. 231; Minneapolis-Honeywell v. FTC, 191 F.2d 786, *cert. denied,* 344 U.S. 206.

Of these, 14 were reviewed and affirmed by the courts.[159] Nine of these were reviewed and affirmed by the Supreme Court of the United States. Of the remaining five, which were affirmed by the Circuit Court of Appeals, certiorari was denied by the Supreme Court in two.

In Part I of Appendix A is a table of all cases in which the Commission initiated proceedings under subsection 2(a) of the Robinson-Patman Act. These tables of cases show not only the docket number and the title of the case, but citations to Federal Trade Commission decisions wherein the case may be found, the nature of the product or products involved, the date on which disposition was made of the case, and citations to the *Federal Reporter* and *Supreme Court Reporter* in each instance where court review was involved.

Enforcement by the Department of Justice

The Department of Justice has proceeded in only four cases since June 19, 1936, in which it charged a violation of subsection 2(a) of the Robinson-Patman Act. None of those cases were concluded successfully. Three of them were dismissed, and one, which was instituted in 1951, was pending as of January 1, 1962.

Litigation by Private Parties

In the first 20 years following the passage of the Robinson-Patman Act in 1936, approximately 75 private proceedings were instituted. More than half of these were decided for the defendants. Of the remainder, the courts, on appeal, sustained judgment for the plaintiffs in six cases.

In the period since 1956, a much larger number of triple-damage cases have been filed by private parties, based on allegations that the plaintiffs were injured through price-discrimination practices of the defendants. A large percentage of these cases remain pending in the courts. Many of those filed were dismissed with judgment for the defendants, and many others were settled by agreement of the parties. Records are not available, since most of these cases are not reported.[160]

---

[159] Standard Brands case, 189 F.2d 510; American Crayon case, 233 F.2d 264; Muller case, 142 F.2d 511; Corn Products case, 324 U.S. 726; Staley case, 324 U.S. 746; Moss case, 155 F.2d 1016; Cement case, 333 U.S. 683; Morton Salt case, 334 U.S. 37; Ruberoid case, 343 U.S. 470; Whitaker Cable case, 353 U.S. 938; Moog Industries case, 355 U.S. 411; Edelman case, 355 U.S. 941; Niehoff case, 355 U.S. 411; National Lead case, 352 U.S. 419.

[160] During January, 1962, an excellent informative article entitled, "Private Enforcement of the Antitrust Laws: The Robinson-Patman Experience," by Professor Richard J. Barber, Professor of Law, Southern Methodist University, appeared in the *George Washington Law Review*, Volume 30, Number 2, December, 1961. At page 196 of that article, it is shown that 111 private suits based on Robinson-Patman violations had been undertaken in the period from 1936–1961. Of that number, 85 involved violations of subsection 2(a).

Chapter III

THE BROKERAGE PROVISION OF SUBSECTION 2(c)

THE TEXT

The Text of Subsection 2(c) is as follows:

"It shall be unlawful for any person engaged in commerce, in the course of such commerce, to pay or grant, or to receive or accept, anything of value as a commission, brokerage, or other compensation, or any allowance or discount in lieu thereof, except for services rendered in connection with the sale or purchase of goods, wares, or merchandise, either to the other party to such transaction or to an agent, representative, or other intermediary therein where such intermediary is acting in fact for or in behalf, or is subject to the direct or indirect control, of any party to such transaction other than the person by whom such compensation is so granted or paid."

BACKGROUND

No. 88. Question. What is brokerage?

Opinion. Neither the processes of nature in the production of raw materials nor the methods of processing and manufacturing those raw materials into finished products lend themselves economically to an even flow from the producer to the consumer, nor is demand itself steady. Agricultural products are seasonal; extraction of raw materials lends itself to bulk methods; even consumption may be more or less seasonal, recurring, or infrequent as to the needs of any one consumer. Therefore, goods produced in quantity must be warehoused for varying periods, distributed by degrees in wholesale quantities to the retailer, and finally sold in single units to the consumer. The process requires the functions of transportation, warehousing, wholesaling, and retailing.

Advertising, packaging, and merchandising add value by making the products more easily accessible to the consumer, and they increase the total consumption of goods. In the many consecutive processes of trade and industry, the important responsibility is imposed on government to protect the best interests of those engaged in commerce and the larger interests of the people as a whole, who are dependent on the smooth flow of commerce for their daily needs.

The necessary functions in accomplishing these needs for orderly and efficient marketing of food are performed by groups of business concerns that have become more or less classified as processors, brokers, wholesalers, and retailers. Following the food manufacturers and processors, the next in the chain of food distribution are the brokers. The food brokers are looked to by the manufacturers, processors, and packers not only as a means of communicating with food buyers in terminal markets, but also as sales agents who are expected to locate and promote markets and buyers for the food items the manufacturers, processors, and packers have for sale. The brokers are of great importance to the small and independent processors of food as local sales representatives in terminal markets. Surveys have shown that, on the average, a food broker represents as many as 23 different food manufacturers and processors. He handles their sales on a small, local basis, being paid only for the goods actually sold. This fact, and the fact that a salesman employed by the broker, when calling on wholesale buyers and retailers, can be taking orders on an average for 23 manufacturers rather than just one, demonstrates the possible economy arising from a food broker's operation.

Efficiency of operation is not the only reason why food brokers are important to small and independent manufacturers, processors, and packers of food. To these, the food brokers are important links in the chain that connects them with small food buyers in terminal markets. Without the brokers, there would be no bridge over the great distances between the small manufacturers and processors on the one hand, and the small food buyers in the terminal markets on the other hand.

The function of brokerage and the payment of brokers' fees or salesmen's commissions has a distinct place in the scheme of distribution. They make an important contribution to place utility. A manufacturer or grower may have a product of better-than-average merit. His methods of production may be as efficient as any. He may be located at the crossroads of the country's transportation system. But if he does not know how to sell his goods or how to employ good salesmen or use established selling agencies, his goods remain in his warehouse. They have no commercial value.

Subsection 2(c) of the Robinson-Patman Act does not require any grower or food manufacturer to select any particular customer, any particular class of customer, or any particular means of distribution. It does not tell him how much he shall pay for selling his merchandise, nor prohibit him from waiting until buyers come to his doorstep. But if he goes out to look for those buyers, or hires some one to do it for him, he enters upon the performance of a function in distribution. He incurs a cost. He must employ a selling agency, whether it is his own or an independent one. That cost has a distinct bracket in the compilation of his selling price. All his production and sales promotion efforts are tied in with and inseparable from that particular sales cost and are of value to the purchaser who buys his merchandise.

A producer may enter into a sustained program of national advertising on his product. That advertising creates a demand. But the expenditure will avail him little if he does not prepare beforehand with a distribution set-up through which to contact the consumer and to serve him with a reasonable degree of expediency in the delivery of his merchandise. This set-up may involve the establishment of warehousing units at strategic points throughout the country. Whatever may be involved, his program is almost certain to require personal sales contact, the cost of which he must provide for in his selling price.

The sustained advertising has created a consumer acceptance of his product. It has thereby enhanced the value of his product in the hands of those who purchase it for resale. He may find some purchasers for his product without the advertising. Effective advertising may decrease his sales cost for commission and brokerage by reducing sales resistance.

But advertising alone will not do his selling job. There again, the accumulated values of all the functions he performs are distinctly dependent on and tied in with the direct selling effort. To waive the cost of the brokerage or commission to one purchaser and assess it against another represents an unfair discrimination between the purchasers.

Still another angle of the question is involved in the ethics of sellers in paying or allowing discounts in the name of brokerage to the buyer or agent of the buyer. As has been pointed out previously, brokerage or commission is a cost element included in the selling price to reimburse the seller for the cost of performing the brokerage or personal selling function— the necessary function of bringing the goods to the attention of the buyer or the buyer's agent. If it were possible in the ordinary course of commerce to sell merchandise without the seller entering on the performance of this function, no purpose would be served in setting up in the selling price a cost factor to cover the brokerage cost. The sales price of the average seller would be reduced by the amount of the otherwise anticipated cost of the function. On the other hand, if no cost factor for brokerage or commission is included in the selling price, then the allowance of a brokerage or commission to the purchaser represents an outright price concession. It must be treated, therefore, as a price discrimination in fact.

All practical experience has shown that the chief responsibility for the movement of goods rests on the shoulders of the owner of the goods. Therefore, it is the universal practice for the seller to include the complete cost of selling his goods in the selling price of his products. It is a point in law as well as in morals that a man cannot serve two masters. The Robinson-Patman Act has simply reinforced this legal concept of the relationship between an agent and his principal by making it unlawful for a seller to pay brokerage to a buyer or agent of the buyer.

The true broker serves either as a representative of the seller or as the representative of the buyer. It is ethically and practically impossible for him to serve the best interests of both the buyer and the seller in the same transaction. If he is employed by the seller to find profitable market outlets for his products, he is expected to render certain distinct services to the seller on behalf of the sale of his goods. This usually requires that he spend a reasonable amount of effort, time, and perhaps money in a search for buyers in a free and open market.

On the other hand, he may be employed by a buyer. His duties then usually involve an expenditure of effort, time, and money in search of sources of supply for the buyer. In certain phases of commerce, the interests of a buyer and seller may be identical, as the mutual relationship of a manufacturer or wholesaler and his retail customer are sometimes said to be; on the whole, however, the buyer's and seller's interests are directly opposed. The buyer seeks merchandise of the highest quality at the lowest price. The seller seeks to obtain the highest possible price for his products. The opposition of interests constitutes the heart of free and open competition.

Where both fail to function, they do so either as the result of ill-advised inertia on the part of buyer or seller or because of collusion on the part of the broker or intermediary, who ostensibly is receiving payment from one party but actually is in the employ of the other party. Where such hidden or open affiliation exists in the brokerage relationship, it borders on or invites a widespread practice of commercial bribery—an evil that has long been recognized and prohibited in many business codes of ethics, and by law in many kinds of business. For the first time, the subject of brokerage payments has been directly dealt with in Federal law in the Robinson-Patman Act.

In a free and open market, the practice of sellers' allowing brokerage to buyers or agents of buyers does not exist. When free of the coercive influence of mass buying power, discounts in lieu of brokerage are not usually accorded to buyers who deal with the seller direct, since such sales must bear their appropriate share of the seller's own selling cost.

The Practice of Paying Brokerage to Buyers

Prior to the Robinson-Patman Act, the growing concentration of wholesale-distributor buying power, particularly in the food industry, developed terrific pressure on sellers to grant discriminatory price differentials. Among the price differentials demanded was one computed on the basis of alleged savings to the seller in his cost of sales arising from the performance of services by the mass buyer (through its own employees, agents, or other intermediaries controlled by it). The big buyer was saying to sellers, in effect, "You no longer need to come to us; we come to you. We thereby save you all sales expense in transactions with us, and you should therefore pass this saving on to us in the form of a price differential."

Investigation of differentials showed that they usually were in the sum of the commissions or brokerage customarily paid by the seller to his own salesmen, agents, or brokers, and that the differential was demanded by the mass buyers on the theory that they were entitled to it because they were paying their "salesmen," agents, or brokers to perform the seller's sales function.

The trade-practice conferences conducted by the Federal Trade Commission during the period 1920 to 1932 showed that the majority of members of many important industries recognized the evil of the practice of concealed price discriminations (such as came to be prohibited by the Robinson-Patman Act), and the industries voluntarily cooperated with the Federal Trade Commission in defining and prohibiting the same as per se injurious to trade or commerce.

In a Federal Trade Commission pamphlet, *Trade Practice Conferences* (GPO 1929), published July 1, 1929, it was stated that:

> The trade practice conference affords a means through which representatives from an industry voluntarily assemble under auspices of the Commission for the purpose of considering unfair practices in their industry and collectively agreeing upon and providing for their abandonment in cooperation with and with the support of the commission. It is a procedure whereby business or industry may take the

initiative in establishing self-government of business, by business and for business through making its own rules of business conduct, resembling, in a sense, its own "law merchant," subject, of course, to sanction or acceptance by the commission.

In the course of adoption of resolutions and rules for eliminating unfair practices during the years 1920 to 1929, all the practices later prohibited by Section 2(c), (d), and (e) of the Robinson-Patman Act came to be covered by a general prohibition, which was absolute. Thus, the Oil Industry resolutions, published by the Federal Trade Commission on December 10, 1920, condemned "all forms of secret rebates and settlements" as being unfair methods of competition. The Anti-Hog Cholera Serum and Virus resolutions, published June 4, 1925, declared to be "practices unfair and injurious to the industry and to the public" the "Granting of rebates, refunds, credits, or allowing unearned discounts to purchasers of serum and virus to induce or retain patronage," as well as the "Payment of specific advertising expense in behalf of certain purchasers, and not offered to all purchasers, under like terms and conditions." By the summer of 1928, the Commission was affirmatively approving the following prohibition as a part of Group I Rules for Industries:

> *Secret Rebates*—The payment or allowances of secret rebates, refunds, credits, or unearned discounts, whether in the form of money or otherwise, or extending to certain purchasers special services or privileges not extended to all purchasers under like terms and conditions, is an unfair trade practice.

The Federal Trade Commission pamphlet above referred to includes Millwork Industry Group I Rules, published July 19, 1928; Flat Glass Industry Group I Rules, published October 15, 1928; Wood-working Machinery Industry Group I Rules, published February 11, 1929; Gypsum Industry Group I Rules, published June 10, 1929; Cut Stone Industry Group I Rules, published July 8, 1929; Barn Equipment Industry Group I Rules, published July 11, 1929, etc.

The Fertilizer Industry Group I Rules, published by the Federal Trade Commission June 12, 1929, included an equally sweeping rule (Rule II) that prohibited secret rebates and allowances "irrespective of the form they may assume" and further declared that allowances for fictitious advertising services and *sales service* violated the principle of the prohibition against secret rebates.

The Grocery Industry Group I Rules, published by the Federal Trade Commission January 16, 1929, contained the following elaboration on the typical trade-practice conference prohibition of secret rebates and allowances:

Rule I. *Whereas it is essential in the interest of the trade and the consuming public that the production and distribution of grocery products be conducted in accordance with sound principles* of economics and justice, in order to afford an *equal opportunity to all manufacturers and merchants* and to secure effective competition in serving the public: Be it

Resolved, That (1) *terms of sale shall be open* and strictly adhered to; (2) *secret rebates* or secret concession or secret allowance of *any kind are unfair methods of business;* (3) price discrimination that is uneconomic or unjustly discriminatory is an unfair method of business. [Italics added.]

Of course, prior to 1936, all responsible functioners in the food industry tried to practice these fair rules of the game, but their high hopes and good intentions were frustrated by the incessant coercive influence of mass buying power in all the market places. Recognizing the inequity of seller payments of brokerage to buyers or their intermediaries on their own purchases, the National Canners Association adopted the following resolution on January 27, 1928, and reaffirmed it by resolution on January 19, 1934:

Whereas, *the National Canners Association recognizes that the food broker* who acts strictly as the trustworthy representative of the canner whose account he has, *is an important link in the chain of distribution* and deserves full payment for such trustworthy service, therefore be it

Resolved, that the National Canners Association deplores any confusion that may exist concerning brokerage and urges that *brokerage be regarded by members of this Association only as a payment made by the canner to his own broker for services rendered* and as having no other relation to the price charged any buyer or the representative of any buyer.

The National Canners Association further urges that its members keep constantly in mind that *brokerage is an element of cost and not of price,* and that the party employing the broker, whether buyer or seller, is the one for whom the service is rendered and the one from whom he should receive compensation.

Congress had become acutely aware of this problem in 1928, particularly with reference to chain stores, and passed Senate Resolution 224 (70th Cong., 1st Sess.) directing the Federal Trade Commission to undertake a comprehensive investigation and study of chain stores, to report to the Congress on the practices leading to their growth, and to recommend additional legislation. Over a period of six years, the Commission submitted to the Congress more than 30 separate, factual studies pursuant to this resolution and a final report on its investigation was submitted on December 14, 1934. (S. Doc. No. 4, 74th Cong., 1st Sess. 1934)

In that investigation, the Commission found that it had been the persistent policy of the chain stores to seek out and demand secret, special, and unwarranted price concessions on the goods they bought, and that payments of brokerage commissions on their purchases were a favorite device employed by the chains for securing these price concessions. As an independent retail grocer (who was also a director of the National Association of Retail Grocers) put it before the House Committee of the Judiciary which conducted the hearing on the Robinson-Patman bill (H.R. 8442) in July of 1935, "For years we have suffered on account of brokerage allowance . . ."

LEGISLATIVE HISTORY

It is clear that Congress, in its consideration of the Robinson and Patman bills, arrived at a determination to include in these legislative proposals outright prohibitions against the practice of a seller paying brokerage to the buyer or to an intermediary who was serving as an agent of both the buyer and the seller. In its report on the Patman bill (H.R. 8442), the House Committee on the Judiciary noted that this subject was covered in subsection (b) in that bill, and in that connection stated:

> Section (b) deals with the abuse of the brokerage function for purposes of oppressive discrimination. The true broker serves either as representative of the seller to find him market outlets, or as representative of the buyer to find him sources of supply. In either case he discharges functions which must otherwise be performed by the parties themselves through their own selling or buying departments, with their respective attendant costs. Which method is chosen depends presumptively upon which is found more economical in the particular case; but whichever method is chosen, its cost is the necessary and natural cost of a business function which cannot be escaped. It is for this reason that, when free of the coercive influence of mass buying power, discounts in lieu of brokerage are not usually accorded to buyers who deal with the seller direct since such sales must bear instead their appropriate share of the seller's own selling cost.[161]

The public record shows indisputably that in 1936 Congress found it injurious to commerce for sellers to be allowed to pay compensation or brokerage to buyers or to buyers' representatives for their services rendered in connection with the purchase of goods by or for the account of the buyers.

The Committees on the Judiciary of both the Senate and the House of Representatives reported the evil to Congress as follows:

---

[161] H.R. REP. No. 2287, 74th Cong., 2d Sess. 14–15 (1936).

Among the prevalent modes of *discrimination* at which this bill is directed is the practice of certain large buyers to demand the allowance of brokerage direct to them upon their purchases, or its payment to an employee, agent, or corporate subsidiary whom they set up in the guise of a broker, and through whom they demand that sales to them be made. [Italics added.][162]

The legislative history of subsection 2(c) clearly shows that Congress knew that the only effective way to stamp out and prevent the practice of mass buyers coercing sellers to pay them compensation for fictitious sales services was by prohibiting sellers absolutely from paying or allowing *any* such compensation to *any* buyers or their intermediaries.

Subsection 2(c) prohibited payments of brokerage "except for services rendered in connection with the sale or purchase of goods," and the Committees' reports made it clear that this statutory exception had reference to *true* brokerage (sales) services. Thus, the reports stated:

Whether employed by the buyer in good faith to find a source of supply, or by the seller to find a market, the broker so employed discharges a sound economic function and is entitled to appropriate compensation by the one in whose interest he so serves.[163]

So, too, the Committee reports made it perfectly clear that to be effective, subsection 2(c) had to prohibit absolutely brokerage payments for fictitious sales services—services that buyers or their intermediaries are incapable of performing for sellers:

. . . But to permit its payment or allowance where no *such* service is rendered, where in fact, if a "broker," so labeled, enters the picture at all, it is one whom the buyer points out to the seller, rather than one who brings the buyer to the seller, would render the section a nullity. [Italics added.][164]

The House report clearly summarized the Committee's intent to make the prohibition absolute as follows:

Section (b) permits the payment of compensation by a seller to his broker or agent for services actually rendered in his behalf: Likewise by a buyer to his broker or agent for services in connection with the purchase of goods actually rendered in his behalf; *but it prohibits the direct or indirect payment of brokerage except for such* [i.e., true sales] *services rendered.* It prohibits its allowance by the buyer direct to the seller, or *by the seller direct to the buyer;* and it prohibits its payment by either to an agent or intermediary acting in fact for or

---

162 *Ibid.;* S. REP. No. 1502, 74th Cong., 2d Sess. (1936).
163 H.R. REP. No. 2287, 74th Cong., 2d Sess. 15 (1936).
164 *Ibid.*

in behalf, or subject to the direct or indirect control of the other. [Italics and matter in brackets added.][165]

That the prohibition was intended to apply absolutely to *all* buyers or their intermediaries, regardless whether they were chains or independents or cooperatives, is perfectly clear from the legislative history. However, it was made equally clear in the debates on the Robinson and Patman bills that the brokerage provision of the Robinson-Patman Act was not intended to prohibit legitimate functions or payments therefor. Senator Logan, the chairman of the Senate Committee on the Judiciary, in discussing this matter stated:

> Let me say in the beginning that the bill does not affect legitimate brokerage either directly or indirectly. Where the broker renders service to the buyer or to the seller the bill does not prohibit the payment of brokerage. It is not aimed at the legitimate practice of brokerage, because brokerage is necessary. The broker has a field all his own and he should not be interfered with. In order to evade the provisions of the Clayton Act, however, it was found that while direct price discrimination could not be indulged in, the buyer, if he were sufficiently powerful, could designate someone and say, "That is my broker." Perhaps it was a clerk in his office. Perhaps it was a manager of a store. Perhaps it was a subsidiary corporation organized for the purpose. However, the buyer would say to the seller, "You must sell through that man, and you must pay him a certain percentage or amount of brokerage"; and when the so-called broker or dummy broker received what was paid him, he turned it over to the buyer, and in that way a price discrimination was brought about.
>
> I undertake to say in this august body that there is not a Member of the Senate, there is not a Member of the House, who will not at once condemn a practice of that kind, which provides secret rebates under the guise of brokerage.[166]

JUDICIAL INTERPRETATION OF SUBSECTION 2(c)

Opposition to the application of the brokerage provision of the Robinson-Patman Act resulted in much early litigation reaching the Federal appellate courts.

In *Biddle Purchasing Co. v. FTC*,[167] the first adjudicated case under the brokerage provision, the court held that the prohibition against buyers or their agents receiving brokerage must be applied absolutely and uniformly without classification.

Biddle supplied a purchasing and marketing information service for

---

[165] *Ibid.*
[166] 80 CONG. REC. 6281 (1936).
[167] 96 F.2d 687 (2d Cir. 1938).

buyers, for which it collected brokerage from sellers and passed it on to its customer-buyers in the form of reduced fees. Though it acted as a buyer's agent, Biddle claimed it performed a service for sellers and was legally entitled to receive brokerage from sellers for its service. This argument was rejected, the Court pointing out that Congress prohibited payment of brokerage fees by a seller to a buyer or an intermediary of a buyer.

> Congress may have had in mind that one of the principal evils inherent in the payment of brokerage fees by the seller to the buyer directly or through an intermediary, is the fact that this practice makes it possible for the seller to discriminate in price without seeming to do so. If a price discount is given as a brokerage payment to a controlled intermediary, it may be and often is concealed from other customers of the seller. One of the main objectives of subsection 2(c) was to force price discriminations out into the open where they would be subject to the scrutiny of those interested, particularly competing buyers.[168]

It is clear that, had Biddle been allowed to act as an agent of buyers, collect brokerage from sellers, and pass all or a part back to the buyers it represented, the brokerage provision would have been nullified in practical effect. The Commission's order, which was upheld on review, served the very useful and necessary purpose of applying the law as it had to be applied if the brokerage provision was to serve the purpose Congress intended. To be sure, Biddle represented some small buyers, but the purpose of the brokerage prohibition in the Act was to stop an unfair trade practice that injured many thousands of small buyers to a substantial extent. As the court said in the Biddle case:

> Section 2(c) was clearly intended to restore equality of opportunity in business by strengthening the anti-trust laws through protecting trade and commerce against unfair practices and unlawful price discrimination.[169]

The second case of major importance under subsection 2(c) is *Oliver Bros. v. FTC*.[170] In this proceeding, as in the *Biddle* case, Oliver was cited as a purchasing agent for buyers whom it represented. The Commission charged Oliver with receiving brokerage commissions from sellers, which it credited or passed onto the buyers. Oliver asserted that it rendered a service to sellers that justified the brokerage commissions paid to it.

But the court held:

> Oliver is the agent of the buyers and not of the sellers and is paid by the buyers for the service rendered them. It collects brokerage

---

[168] *Id.* at 687, 692.
[169] *Id.* at 692.
[170] 102 F.2d 763 (4th Cir. 1939).

> commissions from the sellers on purchases made for the buyers which it credits to the accounts of the buyers or otherwise passes on to them. In furnishing the service which it has contracted to furnish the buyers, it affords to the sellers facilities for placing their goods before the buyers and obviates the necessity of their employing brokers to reach these customers; but this is a service rendered the buyers which Oliver has bound itself to render them under their subscription contracts. The benefit to the sellers is incidental to this service rendered the buyers and is not the result of a service undertaken for the benefit of the sellers.[171]

Thus, early in the judicial interpretation of the brokerage clause, it was held that a favored buyer or his intermediary cannot justify a price reduction reflecting the payment of brokerage on the assumption that he has rendered a valuable service to the seller. The "services rendered" exception in subsection 2(c) was not construed to open a loophole in the provision. If this exception were allowed to permit buyers to receive brokerage payments from sellers, the prohibition contained in the provision would be robbed of any practical effect.

However, like Biddle, Oliver represented some small buyers and used this as basis of defense. But the court found this argument without merit, saying:

> It is sufficient answer that the Act makes no distinction as to size and shows no intention to give the small any more than the great the right to receive brokerage commissions on their purchases. Because of the buying power possessed by purchasing agents, whether representing chains or independent dealers, sellers may be willing to allow them brokerage commissions and may consider such commissions earned in the sense that the sellers are thus enabled to sell goods without resorting to other sales devices; but the fact remains that the buyer who receives the brokerage allowed his purchasing agent receives an advantage, and a concealed advantage, which the buyer who purchases directly from the dealer does not receive.[172]

In carrying out the intention of Congress with respect to the brokerage provision, the court clearly had in mind the obvious fact that allowing a purchasing agent of a buyer to collect brokerage from a seller would certainly open the way for large buyers to receive such payments while their smaller competitors were denied them. Thus, in both the *Biddle* and the *Oliver* cases, the brokerage provision was construed as its language indicates—to prohibit a seller granting a commission or brokerage, or any allowance in lieu thereof, to a buyer or his agent.

Another device challenged as violative of subsection 2(c) was the billing

[171] *Id.* at 763, 766.
[172] *Id.* at 771.

of a net price that reflected what was formerly a direct brokerage payment to the buyer. During June, 1936, in the period immediately preceding the approval of the Robinson-Patman Act, a number of buyers who had been accorded preferred and discriminatory treatment by receiving brokerage payments on their purchases advised their suppliers that henceforth invoices should not reflect brokerage payments. The suppliers were instructed to prepare invoices that specified net prices. These net prices were lower than the usual prices to other buyers, but lower by the exact amount the suppliers previously had paid to the buyers as brokerage. This device was involved in the third case to reach the courts under subsection 2(c): *Great Atlantic & Pacific Tea Co. v. FTC*.[173] In this case, no intermediary was involved; A&P, the buyer, received brokerage payments by sellers through its employees.

In this case the net prices on the invoices submitted by the suppliers were lower than the usual prices by precisely the same amount allowed previously as brokerage. This change in the billing was made effective on or before June 19, 1936, the day on which President Roosevelt signed the Robinson-Patman Act.

As in the two previous cases, it was claimed that the buyer performed services for sellers that entitled it to brokerage commission.

In answering this argument, the court said:

> The question presented for our consideration is simply whether or not the vendee may be compensated for services rendered by the vendee's agent acting as agent for the vendors. It is obvious that dual representation by agents opens a wide field for fraud and oppression. Conflicting interests are always engaged when an attempt is made by buyers and sellers to arrive at a market price for commodities. We entertain no doubt that it was the intention of Congress to prevent dual representation by agents purporting to deal on behalf of both buyer and seller. For this reason paragraph (c) is framed by disjunctives. The edge of the paragraph cuts two ways, prohibiting the payment or receipt of commissions, discounts or brokerage to the adversary party by the other's agent. The phrase "except for services rendered" is employed by Congress to indicate that if there be compensation to an agent it must be for bona fide brokerage, viz., for actual services rendered to his principal by the agent. The agent cannot serve two masters, simultaneously rendering services in an arm's length transaction to both. While the phrase, "for services rendered," does not prohibit payment by the seller to his broker for bona fide brokerage services, it requires that such service be rendered by the broker to the person who has engaged him. In short, a buying and selling service cannot be combined in one person.[174]

---

173 106 F.2d 667 (3rd Cir. 1939).
174 *Id*. at 667, 674.

The court also pointed out its opinion that the so-called services rendered by the chain's buying agents to sellers were more imaginary than real. Sellers were not saved any brokerage expense by dealing with A&P; the sums they normally paid to their brokers "were not saved to them at all, but were merely translated into another form to the financial benefit of the petitioner."[175]

The court held in this case that payment of brokerage, or compensation in lieu thereof, to a buyer on his purchases is absolutely prohibited, and it rejected the argument by A&P that the brokerage provision permits the payment of brokerage to buyers on the theory that a saving of cost is involved. The court took the position that a cost saving to the seller was not involved in this case at all, and even if this were true, it would not change the result since the cost defense in subsection 2(a) cannot be read into subsection 2(c). The opinion in this case makes it clear that A&P actually received nothing more than a discriminatory price reduction, which Congress clearly intended to prohibit.

In *Webb-Crawford Co. v. FTC*,[176] three individuals were partners in a brokerage company and owned 95 per cent of the stock of Webb-Crawford Co., a wholesale distributor. The brokerage partners controlled the buying organization, and brokerage was received by them. One of the brokers, a vice-president of Webb-Crawford, did all its buying.

The court found that in essence Webb-Crawford received the brokerage commissions. "Sellers who sell to the Webb-Crawford Company cannot pay brokers' commissions to these men who in fact act for and represent the buyer in making the purchases,"[177] said the court. It did not allow mere form to submerge substance; buyers could not have controlled brokerage houses through which they collected brokerage.

The court also interpreted "except for services rendered" in the provision to prohibit any person from collecting brokerage if he has any relations whatever to the opposite party to a sale, even assuming he rendered a service. A buyer or an intermediary of a buyer cannot collect brokerage from a seller even though he renders a service to a seller, assuming such is possible. A seller's broker can collect brokerage from a seller. A buyer's broker can receive brokerage from a buyer. But a buyer's broker and his principal cannot collect brokerage from a seller. A seller's broker and his principal cannot receive brokerage from a buyer. The *Webb-Crawford* case closed an escape hatch that would have enabled powerful buyers to evade the statute.

---

[175] *Id.* at 672.
[176] 109 F.2d 268 (5th Cir. 1940).
[177] *Id.* at 268, 270.

The prohibition in the brokerage clause is absolute.

> The Congress considered the effect on commerce of the things named in subsection (c), and absolutely prohibited them. The Trade Commission is not to enter on any enquiry about their evil effect, nor whether a proceeding would be in the public interest. Its duty is to enforce the prohibition.[178]

The fifth significant case on subsection 2(c) is *Quality Bakers of America v. FTC*.[179] It also involved two buyer intermediaries owned by a large number of wholesale baking firms. One of these acted as a purchasing agent for members of an association of wholesale bakeries and provided them with various other services.

The court held:

> It can be reasonably concluded from the evidence before the Commission that the Service Company was the purchasing agent of the buyers and in that capacity dealt with the sellers. Undoubtedly the sellers received valuable benefits and advantages from the business given them by the Service Company, other than the ordinary profits on the sales. For instance, they were saved the expense incident to obtaining the business and dealing separately with numerous customers taking a large amount of merchandise. In that way and to that extent the Service Company rendered services and had contractual relationship with the sellers. For those benefits the sellers were willing to pay and did pay and, no doubt, after such a course of dealing had been established, it was considered by all parties that there was an implied agreement to pay, but it is a mistake to assume that the payments made were other than essentially commissions on the sales or to suppose that such a practice was lawful after the passage of the Robinson-Patman Act.[180]

It also decided in this case that the provision in Section 4 of the Robinson-Patman Act allowing cooperatives to return all or part of their net earnings or surplus to members, producers, or consumers "does not authorize cooperative associations to engage in the practices forbidden by Section 2(c) of the Act, nor except them from its provisions."[181]

A similar case arose in *Modern Marketing Service, Inc. v. FTC*,[182] involving an intermediary for a large number of grocery wholesalers. Modern Marketing received brokerage fees on the purchases of such wholesale buyers, who also received the benefit of such fees in the form of services performed for them by Modern Marketing.

---

178 *Id.* at 269.
179 114 F.2d 393 (1st Cir. 1940).
180 *Id.* at 393, 398.
181 *Id.* at 400.
182 149 F.2d 970 (7th Cir. 1945).

The court found that Modern Marketing Service, Inc. "was not only buyer-controlled but that it was a purchasing agent for the buyers as found by the Commission."[183] As in the previous cases involving buyer-controlled intermediaries, the Commission's order stopping the receipt of brokerage from sellers was upheld.

In *FTC v. Herzog*,[184] the buyer intermediary was a resident buyer for fur garment retailers and department stores. Here, also, the order of the Commission prohibiting an agent of a buyer from receiving brokerage from sellers was enforced by the court.

The absolute prohibition of Section 2(c) was restated in *Southgate Brokerage Co. v. FTC*.[185] In this case, the court distinguished a discrimination in price and services under Sections 2(a) and 2(d) from the receipt of illegal brokerage prohibited by Section 2(c).

Whether or not a discrimination in price is involved, Section 2(c) absolutely prohibits a buyer or his agent receiving brokerage from a seller.

> It is argued that the section is not applicable here because the receipt by the company of brokerage from the sellers results in no discrimination against buyers, since the company sells only to wholesalers, who pay the prices that they would otherwise pay if the sales were made to them through brokers. It is said that a distributor, such as the company, renders to the wholesale trade the service that a broker ordinarily performs, and that no discrimination is involved in allowing such distributor the ordinary broker's commissions. The answer is that price discrimination, which is covered by section 2(a) of the Act, 15 U.S.C.A. Sec. 13(a), is not necessary to a violation of section 2(c), quoted above, which specifically forbids the payment of brokerage by the seller to the buyer or the buyer's agent.[186]

As for the argument that the buyer rendered services to the seller for which the brokerage payment is lawful, the court said:

> We are not impressed with the argument that the company renders services to those from whom it purchases, within the meaning of the exception to subsection (c) quoted above. The services which the company proposes to show by the evidence that was excluded are services rendered to itself, as purchaser, owner and subsequent seller of the goods purchased, and not to those from whom it has purchased them. It is immaterial that those persons are benefited by the fact that the company purchases from them the goods which it subsequently resells. The crucial fact is that all of the services upon which it relies are services rendered in connection with its own purchase, ownership

---

183 *Id.* at 970, 974.
184 150 F.2d 450 (2d Cir. 1945).
185 150 F.2d 607 (4th Cir. 1945).
186 *Id.* at 607, 609.

or resale of the goods; and these services it renders, not to those from whom the goods are purchased, but to itself.[187]

Independent Grocery Alliance Distributing Co. v. FTC[188] reasserted the rule that "intermediaries acting in behalf or under the control of buyers may not receive brokerage payments upon the purchases of such buyers."[189]

All these cases established the pattern for interpreting the brokerage section. From the argument that buyer-controlled intermediaries act as brokers to the argument that buyers render a sales service to sellers for which they are entitled to brokerage, the courts rejected every effort to undermine the effectiveness of the provision.

Some of the cases involved purchasing agents for relatively small and medium-size buyers. Particularly in the grocery field, it was claimed that strict enforcement of subsection 2(c) would seriously injure, if not destroy, small retailers affiliated with buying groups. The courts wisely applied the statute without distinction or classification, and today, under strict enforcement of subsection 2(c) for over two decades, these grocery-buying groups are more prosperous than ever before. The Federal Trade Commission has found that the growth of grocery wholesaler-sponsored buying groups has been substantial, especially within the last few years. The same is true of retailer-owned cooperative groups.[190]

The most recent case of substantial significance relating to the brokerage section of the Act is *FTC v. Henry Broch & Company*.[191] This was the first subsection 2(c) case to be decided by the Supreme Court.

As we have seen, several serious legal attacks were made on the brokerage provision following its passage in 1936. When these efforts failed, there followed a period of several years when the focal point of resistance moved from the courts.

But this did not last long. The *Broch* case broke the spell. Broch was a seller's broker. Both he and his principal agreed to a 5 per cent commission. However, to arrange a sale to a large buyer who demanded a price lower than the seller was originally willing to accept, Broch and his principal agreed to reduce the brokerage paid on sales to this particular buyer to 3 per cent. Other buyers were charged the regular price, and 5 per cent brokerage was paid on these transactions.

The large buyer received the favored low price he demanded because the

---

[187] *Id.* at 610.
[188] 203 F.2d 941 (7th Cir. 1953).
[189] *Id.* at 941, 945.
[190] FTC STAFF REPORT, ECONOMIC INQUIRY INTO FOOD MARKETING, Pt. I, Chs. VI, VII (1960).
[191] 363 U.S. 166 (1960).

broker was willing to absorb half of the reduction by taking a lower brokerage on sales to this preferred buyer.

Broch was charged with violating subsection 2(c). The Commission issued an order against him for paying a part of his brokerage commission to a favored buyer.

Broch appealed on the grounds that subsection 2(c) did not apply to seller's broker. The Court of Appeals for the Seventh Circuit set aside the Commission's order, holding that "Neither the language of subsection 2(c) nor its legislative history indicates that seller's broker is covered by subsection 2(c)."[192] In a five to four decision, the Supreme Court held that subsection 2(c) was applicable. A contrary holding, the majority said, "would disregard the history which we have delineated, overturn a settled administrative practice, and approve a construction that is hostile to the statutory scheme—one that would leave a large loophole in the Act."[193]

Summarizing its understanding of the purpose and application of the brokerage provision, Mr. Justice Douglas, speaking for the Court said:

> Congress enacted the Robinson-Patman Act to prevent sellers and seller's brokers from yielding to the economic pressures of a large buying organization by granting unfair preferences in connection with the sale of goods. The form in which the buyer pressure is exerted is immaterial and proof of its existence is not required. It is rare that the motive in yielding to a buyer's demands is not the "necessity" for making the sale. An "independent" broker is not likely to be independent of the buyer's coercive bargaining power. He, like the seller, is constrained to favor the buyers with the most purchasing power. If respondent merely paid over part of his commission to the buyer, he clearly would have violated the Act. We see no distinction of substance between the two transactions. In each case, the seller and his broker make a concession to the buyer as a consequence of his economic power. In both cases the result is that the buyer has received a discriminatory price. In both cases the seller's broker reduces his usual brokerage fee to get a particular contract. There is no difference in economic effect between the seller's broker splitting his brokerage commission with the buyer and in his yielding part of the brokerage to the seller to be passed on to the buyer in the form of a lower price.
>
> We conclude that the statute clearly applies to payments or allowances by a seller's broker to the buyer, whether made directly to the buyer, or indirectly, through the seller. The allowances proscribed by subsection 2(c) are those made by "any person" which, as we have said, clearly encompass a seller's broker. The respondent was a necessary party to the price reduction granted the buyer. His yielding

---

[192] 261 F.2d 725 (7th Cir. 1958).
[193] 363 U.S. 166.

of part of his brokerage to be passed on to the buyer was a sine qua non of the price reduction.[194]

The Supreme Court found what is perfectly obvious—that if a seller's broker is permitted to reduce his brokerage on a sale to a favored buyer, allowing that buyer to receive a discriminatory price reduction, the purpose and effectiveness of the entire Act would be frustrated. If a seller's agent is permitted to do indirectly what the seller cannot do under the Act, the law is reduced to an absurdity. "The powerful buyer who demands a price concession is concerned only with getting it. He does not care whether it comes from the seller, the seller's broker, or both."[195]

Other recent cases of some importance have held that the "meeting competition" defense in subsection 2(b) is not applicable to brokerage violations under subsection 2(c),[196] and that the brokerage provision does not prohibit a seller from ceasing to employ brokers, adopting direct selling methods, and giving a lower price to a buyer.[197]

At the Commission level, it has been held in the *Thomasville Chair Company* case[198] that the prohibition in subsection 2(c) applies to a seller diverting his employee salesmen's commissions to favored buyers just the same as it applies to brokerage commissions. The Commission in this case pointed out that subsection 2(c) covers in the words of the statute "anything of value as a commission, brokerage, or other compensation, or any allowance or discount in lieu thereof."[199]

The paying or granting of brokerage or allowance to an intermediary acting in fact for, on behalf of, or subject to the direct or indirect control of a person other than the one making the payment is prohibited. Likewise, the receiving or accepting of any such brokerage or allowance is prohibited. The prohibition does not depend on any showing that any part of the brokerage or allowance was passed along by the intermediary to the buyer or that the buyer secured any benefit or competitive advantage therefrom.[200]

Any contract that would provide for payments of brokerage or allowances violative of subsection 2(c) cannot be enforced at law.[201]

The United States Court of Appeals for the 5th Circuit on August 14,

---

194 *Ibid.*
195 *Ibid.*
196 FTC v. Washington Fish & Oyster Company, F.2d (9th Cir. 1960), 282 F.2d 595.
197 Robinson v. Stanley Home Products, Inc., F.2d, 174 F. Supp. 414, June 29, 1959 (1st Cir. 1959).
198 No. 7273, FTC, August 12, 1960.
199 *Ibid.*
200 Fitch v. Kentucky-Tennessee Light & Power Co., 136 F.2d. 12 (1943).
201 Merchandise Service Corp. v. Libby, 40 N.E.2d 835 (1942); Pittsburgh Plate Glass Co. v. Jarrett, 42 F. Supp. 723 (D.C. Ga. 1942).

1962, reviewed the *Thomasville Chair Company* case (Thomasville Chair Company v. Federal Trade Commission, 306 F. 2d 541, 5th Cir.). It set aside the Commission's order to cease and desist and in doing so it stated:

> . . . We conclude, therefore, that unless the classification of customers by Thomasville Chair Company was justified by differences in the cost to Thomasville 'of manufacture, sales, or delivery, resulting from the different methods of quantities in which such commodities are . . . sold or delivered,' (Section 2(a)), then it would be open for the commission to infer that the payment by Thomasville of less than the full commission to the salesmen for sales to the 'J' customers, combined with a reduction in price of the commodities to the 'J' customers constituted the granting of an allowance or discount in lieu of commissions, prohibited by Section 2(c).
>
> It thus became necessary for the commission to permit a full scale inquiry into the propriety of the maintenance by Thomasville Chair Company of the 'J' list of customers based upon the differentials permitted under Section 2(a) of the Act, and also a full inquiry as to whether the company's long standing contract with its salesmen under which they receive a smaller commission for sales to this list of customers, could be legally justified. If it could, then there is no violation of Section 2(c).

Thus, the Court of Appeals for the 5th Circuit for the first time has injected into a Section 2(c) case the cost difference heretofore thought applicable only in Section 2(a) cases. In other respects the opinion and decision of the Court of Appeals for the 5th Circuit is perplexing, and not in accordance with decisions by courts in previous cases. It is hoped that the Supreme Court of the United States will review the *Thomasville Chair* case and clarify this situation.

ATTACKS ON SUBSECTION 2(C)

Attacks Through the Courts

As we pointed out earlier in this chapter, the brokerage provision, subsection 2(c), was challenged sharply shortly after it went into effect. First, it was challenged in the *Biddle* case[202] and then in the *Great Atlantic & Pacific Tea Company* case.[203] In these cases, it was contended that if subsection 2(c) should be interpreted as a per se prohibition against the payment of brokerage without the requirement of a showing of adverse effects on competition, then it should be held to be unconstitutional. The courts in both the Second Circuit and Third Circuit rejected that contention and

---

[202] 96 F.2d. 687 (2nd Cir. 1938).
[203] 106 F.2d. 667 (3rd Cir. 1939), *cert. denied*, 308 U.S. 625.

held that subsection 2(c) is a separate substantive provision of law and is constitutional, and that it does no violence to the constitutional rights of parties. In the *Great Atlantic & Pacific Tea Company* case, the Third Circuit Court of Appeals said:

> The practice of paying brokerage, or sums in lieu of brokerage, to buyers or their agents by sellers was found by Congress to be an unfair trade practice resulting in damage to commerce. Paragraph (c) prohibits such practice.[204]

Other attacks in the courts on the brokerage provision were disposed of similarly.

Attacks Through Efforts to Amend the Law

During the 83rd Congress, bills were introduced at the request of opponents of subsection 2(c) that would have in large part nullified the effectiveness of this subsection. These bills were S. 2604 and H.R. 7198. Ostensibly, they were proposals for exemptions of voluntaries and cooperatives from the absolute prohibition in subsection 2(c) against receipt of brokerage by buyers who were purchasing for their own account. Representatives of groups of small-business firms and representations of the National Council of Farmer Cooperatives opposed the proposals to emasculate subsection 2(c). On February 4, 1954, with reference to these legislative proposals, the National Council of Farmer Cooperatives wrote to the chairman of the Senate Committee on the Judiciary as follows:

> The National Council of Farmer Cooperatives is unqualifiedly opposed to any legislation which will in any manner weaken the present Robinson-Patman Act, and strongly urges the adoption of legislation which will prohibit any harmful discriminatory practices.
>
> The Council represents some 5,000 separate marketing and purchasing associations serving about 2,600,000 farm families throughout the country. These associations are in the practical business of marketing every type of agricultural commodity and purchasing from production supplies of all kinds for their farmer patrons. The interest of these people in the Robinson-Patman Act does not arise from adherence to some particular economic or legal theory. They are motivated by the belief that it is for the best interest of our total economy to preserve a competitive business climate in which fair play shall continue to be the controlling rule and where competition can compete, but not to the point of destroying the opportunity to compete.
>
> We respectfully urge that none of the bills before your Committee, which directly, or in effect, affect the Robinson-Patman Act, he acted upon until there have been public hearings thereon with full opportu-

---

[204] 106 F.2d. 667, 678.

nity for all interested persons and organizations to present their views. We would appreciate receiving notice of any such hearings which may be scheduled.

This determined opposition to the proposals for weakening subsection 2(c) prevailed, and Congress failed to act on the proposals. Thus, the subsection was left intact.

Additional Attempts to Influence the Courts Against Subsection 2(c)

The Attorney General's National Committee to Study the Antitrust Laws made its report on March 31, 1955. It was extremely critical of subsection 2(c). Authors of the report acknowledged that copies of it were sent to all Federal judges who are charged with the responsibility of deciding cases arising under the Robinson-Patman Act. In that report, "advice" was provided on how the courts in future cases arising under subsection 2(c) should interpret that provision of the law. In that connection, the Attorney General's Committee stated that prior court interpretations had—

> . . . left subsection 2(c) a highly restrictive provision, sharply limiting the types of distributive functionaries who could qualify under its legal tests.
> At the same time, courts ascribed to a forbidden "brokerage" legal consequences more absolute than those attending discriminations in price under subsection 2(a).[205]

The Attorney General's Committee, in its further advice and recommendation to the courts, stated:

> The Committee considers the prevailing interpretations of the "brokerage" clause at odds with broader antitrust objectives.
> . . . fundamentally, the Committee disapproves the present disparity in the statutory consequences which attach to economically equivalent business practices. Today, "direct" or "indirect" price discriminations under subsection 2(a) do not transgress the law unless they cause adverse market effects and unless unjustifiable under one of the defensive provisos. In contrast, "brokerage" concessions . . . are illegal per se.
> We therefore favor reconciliation of Sections 2(c), (d), and (e) with the remainder of the Act. . . . Consequently, the statutory policy governing brokerage as well as allowances or services should be harmonized with the overall standards controlling the remainder of the Act.[206]

The Attorney General's Committee not only made suggestions and recommendations on how subsection 2(c) should be reinterpreted, but pro-

---

[205] ATTY. GEN. NAT'L COMM. ANTITRUST REP. 188 (1955).
[206] *Id.* at 190–192.

ceeded to recommend new legislation if necessary to effectuate the results it favored.

Subsection 2(c) has withstood all the attacks made on it through publications, the courts, and otherwise. In ten cases, the courts have reviewed these attacks and rejected them. In no case has a court sustained the contentions that subsection 2(c) does violence to the constitutional rights of parties. Likewise, the courts have continued to strengthen and clarify the original interpretations of the subsection. One of its critics has written:

> Surprisingly enough, it is the only section as to which no important question of interpretation still remains unsettled.[207]

Enforcement of Subsection 2(c)

The Federal Trade Commission enforcement of subsection 2(c) has been marked with frequency of cases and with a record of success. From June 19, 1936, through May 31, 1961, the FTC filed 278 formal charges of violations of subsection 2(c). At the conclusion of proceedings on those charges, it issued 246 orders to cease and desist. Except for the so-called "Candy cases," which involved charges under 2(c) and multiple counts, only three other charges were dismissed by the Commission. Ten of the cases in which the Commission issued cease-and-desist orders were appealed to the courts, and in all those cases, the findings, conclusions, and orders of the Commission were sustained. The enforcement of no other provision of the Federal antitrust laws enjoys such a remarkable record. Indeed, it is unlikely that any statute of national scope and of such importance as this provision of law has been so unanimously upheld by the courts.

A complete listing of all cases arising under subsection 2(c) and instituted by the Federal Trade Commission in the period from June 19, 1936, through May 31, 1961, appears in Appendix A, Part II.

---

[207] Cyrus Austin, Price Discrimination 106 (1959).

Chapter IV

ADVERTISING ALLOWANCES AND THE
FURNISHING OF SERVICES AND FACILITIES
PROHIBITED BY SUBSECTIONS 2(d) AND 2(e)

THE PROVISIONS OF SUBSECTIONS 2(D) AND 2(E)

These subsections of Section 2 of the Robinson-Patman Act deal with discrimination in the payment for or the furnishing of advertising or other merchandising services or facilities. When such indirect discriminations become part and parcel of price discriminations in all other respects and meet the standards required for the making out of a case under subsection 2(a), they can, of course, be challenged under that subsection of the Robinson-Patman Act. But under subsections 2(d) and 2(e), the discriminations in allowances and services are declared unlawful and prohibited without regard to resulting injurious effect on competition. They cannot be made the subject of affirmative defenses, such as the cost defenses available in cases arising under subsection 2(a). The text of these two subsections is as follows:

> (d) That it shall be unlawful for any person engaged in commerce to pay or contract for the payment of anything of value to or for the benefit of a customer of such person in the course of such commerce as compensation or in consideration for any services or facilities furnished by or through such customer in connection with the processing, handling, sale or offering for sale of any products or commodities manufactured, sold, or offered for sale by such person, unless such payment or consideration is available on proportionally equal terms to all other customers competing in the distribution of such products or commodities.

(e) That it shall be unlawful for any person to discriminate in favor of one purchaser against another purchaser or purchasers of a commodity bought for resale, with or without processing, by contracting to furnish or furnishing, or by contributing to the furnishing of, any services or facilities connected with the processing, handling, sale, or offering for sale of such commodity so purchased upon terms not accorded to all purchasers on proportionally equal terms.

BACKGROUND OF SUBSECTIONS 2(D) AND 2(E)

Advertising is recognized by the Robinson-Patman Act as a distinct business function contributing to the distribution of goods. It is an important aid to selling, although it is not an inescapable element of cost as are the costs of production, wholesaling, and retailing. Advertising, which is the stimulation of demand and the publication of the availability and merits of a product, may be employed at the option of the seller.

There is abundant evidence that advertising performs a valuable economic function in commerce. It has grown to a major industry and has attracted to its fold some of the best brains and intelligence in the nation. It makes possible the daily newspapers, the magazines, television, and radio. To advertising belongs a major share of the credit for the phenomenal growth of many industries and for the reduction of prices of many articles now considered essential which, without volume production, would be out of reach of the average income. Nothing in the Robinson-Patman Act discourages or hinders advertising.

Advertising performs two functions of value to the consumer, to the worker who produces the goods, and to business generally. The first is that it creates what is known as consumer acceptance of a product. Establishing an identifiable brand or name in connection with a product, it creates and fosters a favorable reputation. Consumers come to ask for the product by name, because the name has become associated in their minds with the character of the goods. A standard of value is thus established; the consumer buys more freely, because the brand gives him a degree of protection and an assurance of uniformity. The cost of repeat sales is reduced. In the long run, the cost of distribution of the product is lowered when a good product is well advertised. The producer, the distributor, and the public are the beneficiaries.

In performing its second important function, that of increasing consumption, advertising makes a distinct contribution to economic welfare. Advertising that limits itself to the fixation of a brand or name in the consumer's consciousness may have no further economic function than those mentioned above. But advertising that strives to encourage a greater use of an article in commerce, whether a brand or a commodity generally, serves best the interest of all. It induces desire where desire did not previously exist. It stimulates production to meet the demand thus created. It makes sales where they would not otherwise have existed. And as production and consumption are increased, the standards of living rise.

Legislation that hampers the freedom or restricts the methods by which advertising may fully function operates to the detriment of the public interest. The Robinson-Patman Act aids advertising to perform its economic function by requiring advertising allowances to be used for advertising. Its effect is to prevent the diversion of funds intended and duly provided for advertising.

In recent years, budgets set up by manufacturers for advertising their products to the consumer have been increasingly diverted to meet mass demands for additional discounts and concealed forms of rebates. Buying monopolies, in the form of great concentrations of buying power in the hands of a few buyers, bring pressure to bear that it has been almost impossible for an individual seller to resist. The misuse of such power has been fittingly stated in a memorable decision of the Supreme Court of the State of Ohio (March 27, 1891) in which the Court said: "Experience has shown that it is not wise to trust human cupidity where it has the opportunity to aggrandize itself at the expense of others. The claim of having cheapened the price to the consumer is the usual pretext on which monopolies are defended."

A prevalent attitude among mass buyers, as shown by testimony before Congressional committees, is that anyone else in the same position with his job to protect would use that bargaining power in the same manner as they use it. Their duties have included securing from manufacturers the utmost obtainable in extra rebates and allowances, as tangible evidence of their ability as buyers. One of the important extras thus obtained as a price concession, and thereby diverted from its rightful function of promoting a wider acceptance of the manufacturer's goods, is the fund that the manufacturer sets up for advertising.

When funds properly apportioned to advertising are diverted to satisfy the demands of mass buyers for secret price concessions, advertising and everyone connected with it suffers immeasurably, even though the mass buyers themselves claim to be, and often are, large advertisers. As retailers, they would have to be large advertisers anyway, whether or not they dried up manufacturers' product advertising by diverting those funds.

As an indicator of the extent of such diversion, consider some of the testimony introduced in the Congressional investigation of the buying practices of chains. The evidence before that committee shows that one large chain alone received over $6 million in one year in advertising allowances from manufacturers of branded goods. Officials of the company and of some of the manufacturers who appeared before the committee fell back on the timeworn argument that these allowances were given for services rendered in advertising the manufacturers' products. Arguments were advanced to show how many stores the chain controlled, the types of windows and interiors available for advertising, the close control of the chain's store personnel, the advantages of distribution in one fell swoop through thousands of retail outlets, and the fact that the makers' brands would be on display in the stores, in the windows, and in the local newspaper advertisements of this chain.

Some 300 manufacturers made over $6 million of "advertising" concessions to this chain. Advertising allowances were made similarly to many other large buyers under similar demands.

Had this $6 million been spent in advertising the manufacturers' products, in addition to the chain's own expenditures for advertising, there might be little complaint. But in answer to the charge that the fund was not intended for advertising, but was a subterfuge for an inequitable price concession that competitors did not enjoy, no manufacturer could say that he had thought it worthwhile to check to see if he had received any advertising in return. Several manufacturers testified that the expense of reporting back and keeping a check on the chain was too great and involved too much detail. They accepted the honesty and integrity of the chain buyer's declared intent as assurance, and waived the necessity of accounting for the allowances.

There might be some substance to the claim that the manufacturers received advertising in full for their $6 million. In that connection, representatives of that large chain testified, in part, as follows: "Our arrangement with General Foods provides for a flat allowance of $30,000 a month." A member of the Special Investigating Committee of the House of Representatives, in exploring the matter, asked:

> From General Foods you received 5 per cent, and that was somewhere around $360,000; and $350,000 is your advertising allowance from Standard Brands. Is that right?

To that inquiry the representative of the chain responded: "That is right."[208]

Despite the fact that a large part of the merchandise advertised by that chain-store organization consisted of the chain's own private brands and

---

[208] *Hearings pursuant to H. Res. 203 and 239 before the House Special Investigating Committee,* 74th Cong., 1st Sess. 431, 440 (1935).

unbranded food stuffs, such as fruits and vegetables, it was uncertain whether the sellers in those instances would have been successful in defending these allowances under the cost-justification proviso if they had been challenged as unlawful price discriminations under the Act. Therefore, the conclusion developed that Congress should give special attention to correcting situations of this kind, which operated to the injury of small business firms throughout the country. It was for that reason that Congress acted to prohibit instances where large buyers receive tremendous amounts as advertising allowances and the small competitors of such buyers receive nothing in the form of allowances. The result was the enactment of subsections 2(d) and 2(e), which require "proportionalization" of such allowances to large and small buyers.

In the course of the study by the Special Investigating Committee of the House of Representatives into the trade practices involved in large-scale buying and selling, it was developed that sellers of branded goods had set up pricing structures providing for a certain percentage or amount as an advertising allowance to buyers for advertising regular brands. In the case of sales made to coercive mass purchasers, the seller in effect turned the money over to the buyer for the purpose of advertising the seller's brands. The buyer used it in substantial part to advertise his own private brands and a great variety of unbranded foodstuffs; in reality, he did not spend his own money for advertising, or else he did not spend the manufacturer's allowance intended for advertising.

LEGISLATIVE HISTORY

It is clear from the legislative history of these two subsections of the Robinson-Patman Act that it was the intent of the Congress to outlaw special discounts and rebates, which we have referred to in the section of this chapter dealing with the background of subsections 2(d) and 2(e), without requiring a showing that they amounted to or were used to effectuate discriminations in prices having the effect in each specific instance of injuring competition, as is required to make out a case under subsection 2(a).

The purpose of subsection 2(d) and 2(e) were explained to the House and the Senate in substantially the same terms. The House report on the proposed legislation on those legislative proposals included the following statement:

> Still another favored medium for the granting of oppressive discriminations is found in the practice of large buyer customers to demand, and of their sellers to grant, special allowances in purported payment of advertising and other sales-promotional services, which

the customer agrees to render with reference to the seller's products, or sometimes with reference to his business generally. Such an allowance becomes unjust when the service is not rendered as agreed and paid for, or when, if rendered, the payment is grossly in excess of its value, or when in any case the customer is deriving from it equal benefit to his own business and is thus enabled to shift to his vendor substantial portions of his own advertising cost, while his smaller competitor, unable to command such allowances, cannot do so.[209]

The Chairman of the House Conferees, who presented the conference report, in explaining subsections 2(d) and 2(e) stated:

> The bill prohibits the seller from paying the customer for services or facilities furnished by the latter in connection with the seller's goods, unless such payment is available on proportionally equal terms to all other competing customers. The existing evil at which this part of the bill is aimed is, of course, the grant of discriminations under the guise of payments for advertising and promotional services which, whether or not the services are actually rendered as agreed, results in an advantage to the customer so favored as compared with others who have to bear the cost of such services themselves. The prohibitions of the bill, however, are made intentionally broader than this one sphere, in order to prevent evasion in resort to others by which the same purpose might be accomplished, and it prohibits payment for such services or facilities, whether furnished "in connection with the processing, handling, sale, or offering for sale" of the products concerned.
>
> The bill also prohibits the seller from furnishing services or facilities to the purchaser in connection with the processing, handling, or sale of the commodities concerned unless they are accorded to all purchasers on proportionally equal terms. Again the last phrase has reference to the several purchasers' equipment and ability to satisfy the terms upon which the offer is made, or the services or facilities furnished to any other purchaser.
>
> There are many ways in which advertising, sales, and other services and facilities may be either furnished or paid for by the seller upon terms that will at once satisfy the requirements of the bill concerning equitable treatment of all customers, and at the same time satisfy the legitimate business needs of both the seller and the purchaser.[210]

DISCUSSION OF THE PROVISIONS
OF SUBSECTIONS 2(D) AND 2(E)

These subsections apply to a seller of products in interstate commerce if he either pays for services or facilities furnished by his customers in con-

---

[209] H.R. REP. No. 2287, 74th Congress, 2d Sess. 15, 16 (1936). See also S. REP. No. 1502, 74th Congress, 2d. Sess. (1936).
[210] 80 CONG. REC. 9415–9418 (1936).

nection with the distribution of his products, or furnishes such services or facilities to his customers. These sections have been interpreted and applied by the Federal Trade Commission and the courts as being independent of subsection 2(a), in that any discrimination in the payment for or the furnishing of services or facilities is unlawful without regard to the standards or measurements applying to discriminations prohibited by subsection 2(a). In other words, as the United States Circuit Court of Appeals for the Seventh Circuit pointed out in a case arising under subsection 2(d),[211] under this subsection we have a rigid definition of acts constituting unlawfulness. The *fact* of paying or contracting for the payment of services or facilities referred to is proscribed, subject to the exception contained in the clause, unless such payments or the furnishing of services or facilities to all competing purchasers are extended on *proportionally equal terms.*

Earlier, the United States Circuit Court of Appeals for the Seventh Circuit ruled to the same effect in the *Corn Products Refining Co.*[212] case, a case arising under subsection 2(e). With respect to that subsection, it stated:

> This paragraph does not require even probability of adverse effect upon competition as does Section 2(a). We think it is satisfied by proof of special services rendered one purchaser not rendered to similar competing purchasers engaged in the same business and using the commodity for the same purpose.

There is no requirement that the moving party in cases arising under these subsections prove that the action of the seller resulted in injurious effects on competitors or competition. Likewise, the person charged cannot defend by showing that the discriminations involved were cost justified or otherwise justified by the affirmative defenses available under subsection 2(a).

DEFINITION OF TERMS

Here we shall undertake to define some of the terms used in these sections. In doing so, frequent reference and use will be made of language and explanations provided by the Federal Trade Commission in a statement it released May 19, 1960, entitled, "Guides for Advertising Allowances and Other Merchandising Payments and Services; Compliance with Sections 2(d) and 2(e) of the Clayton Act, as Amended by the Robinson-Patman Act."

---

[211] See State Wholesale Grocers v. Great Atlantic & Pacific Tea Co., 258 F.2d 831 (7th Cir. 1958), *cert. denied,* 358 U.S. 947.
[212] Corn Products Refining Co. v. FTC, 144 F.2d 211, 219, *aff'd,* 324 U.S. 726 (1945).

No. 89. Question. Who is a seller?

Opinion. "Seller" includes anyone who sells products for resale, with or without further processing.

No. 90. Question. Who is a customer?

Opinion. A "customer" is someone who buys directly from the seller or his agent or broker. Sometimes someone who purchases from the buyer may have such a relationship with the seller that the law also makes him a customer of the seller.

No. 91. Question. Who is a purchaser?

Opinion. The Federal Trade Commission, in regard to *Kraft-Phenix Cheese Co.,* No. 2935, FTC, 1937, 25 F.T.C. 537, 546, made the finding that:

> A retailer who purchases respondent's goods from jobbers and wholesalers is considered by the Commission to be a "purchaser" within the meaning of the Robinson-Patman Act, as well as retailers buying direct.

The Supreme Court of the United States in the case of *Corn Products Refining Co. v. FTC* (324 U.S. 726, 744), in referring to the word "purchaser" appearing in subsection (e) of Section 2 of the Robinson-Patman Act, stated:

> The statute does not require that the discrimination in favor of one purchaser against another shall be provided for in a purchase contract or be required by it. It is enough if the discrimination be made in favor of one who is a purchaser and denied to another purchaser or other purchasers of the commodity.

No. 92. Question. What is interstate commerce?

Opinion. "Interstate commerce" cannot be defined in a few words. Chapter II discussed at length situations where courts have made determinations regarding interstate commerce and what constitutes "commerce" within the meaning of the Robinson-Patman Act, and pointed out that before subsection 2(a) can be applied to a person charged with price discriminations, it must be shown that the person is engaged in interstate commerce. Subsection 2(d) specifically is limited in its application to payments made to a customer with whom the seller deals in the course of interstate commerce. Subsection 2(e) does not contain that limitation. The apparent inconsistencies in subsection (d) and (e) regarding "commerce" have been erased, and both have been considered broad enough to cover all the situations as long as it can be shown that the goods purchased by "either or any" of the competing customers were sold in interstate commerce. All that need be shown is that the seller charged, *in the course of interstate commerce,* did the things prohibited by subsections 2(d) and 2(e). For example, the

United States Circuit Court of Appeals for the Second Circuit, in dealing with this question in the *Elizabeth Arden* case,[213] stated:

> We agreed with Elizabeth Arden Sales Corporation v. Gus Blass Co., 150 F.(2d) 988, 991–993 (C.C.A. 8; cert. den. December 3, 1945), in rejecting petitioners' contention that Section 2(e) is unconstitutional because of the omission of the words "engaged in commerce" (i.e., interstate commerce), found in other subsection of Section 2. The fact that the purpose of Congress in enacting the Robinson-Patman Act was patently to exercise its well-recognized constitutional power to regulate interstate commerce, and the clear interrelation of (d) and (e), serve to show that the omission was inadvertent.

The Supreme Court in the *Corn Products* case[214] held that:

> And finally it is said that the Commission was without jurisdiction because the dextrose sold by petitioners to Curtiss was not found to have been sold in interstate commerce; that if the section is construed to apply to such transactions, it would be unconstitutional; and that in any case there is no showing that the transactions complained of, although not themselves in interstate commerce, have in any way affected such commerce. But the effect upon the commerce is amply shown by the interstate and national character of the Curtiss Company's business; by petitioners' advertising for Curtiss, which was itself frequently in interstate commerce, amounting to $750,000; and by Curtiss's own admission that it competed in the sale of its candy in interstate commerce, with all manufacturers of one cent and five cent bars of candy. Moreover some of petitioners' sales to other companies, to whom these allowances were not accorded, were made in interstate commerce; thus there was a discrimination against sales in interstate commerce, well within the power of the Commission to remedy.

These interpretations by the courts demonstrated the applicability of subsection 2(d) where any of the competing customers received discriminatory payments for services or facilities and, in turn, resold some of such goods in interstate commerce. Also, where the discriminations in services furnished are involved, in cases arising under subsection 2(e), it is sufficient to support the charge if it is shown that one or more of the purchasers either bought from the person charged in interstate commerce or, as in the case of Curtiss Candy Co. in the *Corn Products* case, utilized the furnishing of such services in resales in interstate commerce.

No. 93. Question. What are services or facilities?

Opinion. This term has not been exactly defined by the statute or in decisions. The following are merely examples; the law also covers other services and facilities.

---

213 Elizabeth Arden, Inc. v. FTC, 156 F.2d 132.
214 Corn Products Refining Co. v. FTC, 324 U.S. 726, 744–745.

(a) The following have been held to be services or facilities covered by the law where the seller has paid the buyer for furnishing them:

> Any kind of advertising
> Handbills
> Window and floor displays
> Special sales or promotional efforts for which "push money" is paid
>   to clerks, salesmen, and other employees of the customers
> Demonstrators and demonstrations
> Collecting of orders from individual stores
> Furnishing complete distribution of seller's line

(b) Here are some examples that have been held to be services or facilities covered by the law when the seller furnished them to a customer:

> Any kind of advertising
> Catalogs
> Demonstrators
> Display and storage cabinets
> Display materials
> Special packaging or package sizes
> Warehouse facilities
> Accepting returns for credit
> Prizes or merchandise for conducting promotional contests

What must a seller do when he engages in the payment for or the furnishing of services or facilities to customers or purchasers? First, the seller must determine whether the payment for services or facilities or the furnishing of services or facilities is in connection with the distribution of products he is offering for sale. If he should determine that such a connection is involved, then the seller should make payments for services or facilities or furnish services or facilities under a plan that meets several requirements. Although this plan need not be written or formal, this may be advisable, particularly if there are many competing customers to be considered or if the plan is at all complex.

Requirements to Make Out Cases Under 2(d) and 2(e)

Briefly, the requirements are:

(a) The payments or services under the plan must be available on a proportionally equal basis to all competing customers.

(b) The seller should take some action to inform all his customers who compete with any participating customer that the promotion is available.

(c) The plan must either allow all types of competing customers to participate or provide some other means of participation for those who cannot use the basic plan.

(d) The seller and customer should have a clear understanding about the exact terms of the offer and the conditions on which payments will be made for services and facilities furnished.

Proportionally Equal Terms

No. 94. Question. What is meant by the phrase "proportionally equal terms?"

Opinion. The payment or services under the plan must be made available to competing customers on proportionally equal terms. This means that payments or services must be proportionalized on some basis that is fair to all customers who compete. No single way to proportionalize is prescribed by law. Generally, this can best be done by basing the payments made or the services furnished on the dollar volume or on the quantity of goods purchased during a specified time. However, the payments made or services furnished are not required to be proportionalized on a dollar-volume basis. Such basis does not stand alone. Any properly measurable basis is acceptable if it is not artificially tailored into proportionally equal terms by fitting it into some imaginary basis or standard that never, in fact, existed.[215] It will be recalled that in the *Blass* case, Arden gave the words of the phrase their common, elementary mathematical meaning of a proportion (equal ratios) and hypothesized a proportion in which the two ratios were equal, not to a *given* ratio, but to a ratio of $\frac{900}{1}$ that it had determined for itself.

The intent of Congress on the meaning of the phrase "proportionally equal terms" is indicated in the record of the legislative history of the Robinson-Patman Act. For example, in the House report on the Patman bill, there appears the following explanation of the phrase:

> The phrase "proportionally equal terms" is designed to prevent the limitation of such allowances to single customers on the ground that they alone can furnish the services or facilities or other consideration in the quantities specified. Where a competitor can furnish them in less quantity, but of the same relative value, he seems entitled, and this clause is designed to accord him, the right to a similar allowance commensurate with those facilities. To illustrate: Where, as was revealed in the hearings earlier referred to in this report, a manufacturer grants to a particular chain distributor an advertising allowance of a stated amount per month per store in which the former's goods are sold, a competing customer with a smaller number of stores, but equally able to furnish the same service per store, and under conditions of the

---

[215] Elizabeth Arden v. Gus Blass, 150 F.2d. 993, 994

same value to the seller, would be entitled to a similar allowance on that basis.[216]

Example: A seller may properly offer to pay a specified part (say 50 per cent) of the cost of local newspaper advertising up to an amount equal to a set percentage (such as 5 per cent) of the dollar volume of purchasing during a specified time.

Example: A seller may not select one or a few customers to receive special allowances to promote his product, because of their special reputation, without making those allowances available on proportionally equal terms to other customers who compete with them.

Example: A seller's plan may not provide an allowance on the basis of rates that are graduated with the amount of goods purchased—as, for instance, 1 per cent of the first $1,000 purchases per month, 2 per cent of second $1,000 per month, and 3 per cent of all over that.

The leading case dealing with the meaning of the phrase "proportionally equal terms" was the Federal Trade Commission proceeding in the matter of *Elizabeth Arden, Inc.*[217] In that case, the Commission found that Elizabeth Arden had violated subsection 2(e) by having "failed to accord to competing purchasers . . . services or facilities on proportionally equal terms or upon any terms whatever." In that connection, the Commission found that:

> The furnishing of a service or facility which cannot be proportionalized for the benefit of competing purchasers or, in the alternative, the failure or refusal to proportionalize the terms upon which services or facilities are granted, so as to make it reasonably possible for competing purchasers to avail themselves of such services and facilities if they desire to do so, constitutes a failure to accord such services or facilities upon proportionally equal terms. The phrase "upon terms not accorded to all purchasers upon proportionally equal terms" contemplates the proportionalization of the terms, and this necessarily includes the proportionalization of the service or facility as well. The statute does not permit a seller to so tailor his terms as to favor a particular customer or group of customers and automatically exclude all the rest of his customers. This is what respondent has done.[218]

On appeal, the United States Court of Appeals for the Second Circuit affirmed the findings and order of the Commission.[219] In doing this, the Second Circuit Court cited with approval the decision and opinion by the

[216] H.R. Rep. No. 2287, 74th Cong., 2d Sess. 16 (1936). See also S. Rep. No. 1502, 74th Cong., 2d Sess. (1936), which contains a similar explanation of this phrase "proportionally equal terms."
[217] 39 F.T.C. 288 (1944).
[218] *Id.* at 302.
[219] Elizabeth Arden, Inc. v. FTC, 156 F.2d 132 (1946), *cert. denied,* 331 U.S. 806 (1947).

Eighth Circuit Court of Appeals in the *Gus Blass* case.[220] In the *Gus Blass* case, the Eighth Circuit Court of Appeals, with reference to Arden's arrangements for payment of demonstrator services, stated that:

> Its amount was arrived at by personal negotiation and individual agreement. There was no arrangement or provision for graduating it to the amount of goods purchased during any given period. Nor was it based upon any other guiding factor, such as a difference in the character of the stores and the type of facilities afforded for handling appellant's products, if that could have been made to constitute a valid legal distinction.[221]

The Second Circuit Court of Appeals, in the *Elizabeth Arden* case, unqualifiedly gave its approval and support, not only to the Commission's findings in that case, but also to the analysis, opinion, and decision of the Eighth Circuit Court of Appeals in the *Gus Blass* case. Therefore, it is interesting to note that the Commission's findings in its *Elizabeth Arden* case included the following statement:

> The Commission is of the opinion that the statute affords the seller a free election in the first instance as to what services or facilities, if any, he will provide to purchasers of his products; but having elected to furnish a particular service or facility to a particular purchaser or purchasers, he thereby assumes the obligation of according similar services to all competing purchasers to the extent required by the statute. The furnishing of a service or facility which cannot be proportionalized for the benefit of competing purchasers or, in the alternative, the failure or refusal to proportionalize the terms upon which services or facilities are granted, so as to make it reasonably possible for competing purchasers to avail themselves of such services or facilities if they desire to do so, constitutes a failure to accord such services or facilities upon proportionally equal terms. The phrase "upon terms not accorded to all purchasers on proportionally equal terms" contemplates the proportionalization of the terms, and this necessarily includes the proportionalization of the service or facility as well.[222]

The opinions and decisions in these cases held to acceptable standards approved by the courts for determining the meaning of the phrase "proportionally equal terms." However, the Federal Trade Commission retreated from these standards at the request of representatives of parties charged with violations of subsections 2(d) and 2(e) and, as a result, relaxed its enforcement of those subsections. This relaxation stemmed from

---

[220] Elizabeth Arden Sales Corp. v. Gus Blass, 150 F.2d. 993, 998 (1945), *cert. denied,* 326 U.S. 773 (1945).
[221] *Id.* at 994.
[222] 39 F.T.C. 288 (1944).

a Trade Practice Conference, which ended with the Commission pronouncing that any method or plan that is found to be *"suitable"* or *"equitable"* (whatever those terms mean in law in this context) could be regarded as forming a basis for showing that discriminations had been made on proportionately equal terms within the meaning of subsections 2(d) and 2(e).[223]

Subsequently, discriminations through payment and furnishing of advertising allowances, services, and facilities became rampant in many industries, particularly in the food industry. One net result has been that the FTC has instituted a large number of proceedings charging parties with violations of subsections 2(d) and 2(e). In view of these developments, it will be interesting to note whether the Commission will reaffirm the position it gained in the *Elizabeth Arden* case in 1945 or attempt to have the court redefine the law out of the morass of meanings possibly attributable to the words "suitable" and "equitable."

To Make Available or Accorded

No. 95. Question. What is meant by the word "available" in subsection 2(d) and the word "accorded" in subsection 2(e)?

Opinion. Subsection 2(d) requires that no seller shall make a payment for a cooperative merchandising service or facility to a customer unless the payment is "available" on proportionately equal terms to all other customers competing in the distribution of the product. Subsection 2(e) provides that the services or facilities furnished by the seller to purchasers of the commodity must be *accorded* on proportionately equal terms to all purchasers of the product. In both instances, the words must be interpreted as requiring that a seller pay or furnish the benefits in cooperative merchandising where requested by the customers or purchasers after the seller has openly and actually made it known that the benefits would be available. The seller should take some action to inform all his customers competing with any participating customer that the plan is available. He can do this by any means he chooses, including letter, telegram, notice on invoices, salesmen, brokers, etc. However, if a seller wants to be able to show later that he did make an offer to a certain customer, he is in a better position to do so if he made it in writing.

No. 96. Question. How can it be determined whether any plan covers all competing customers?

---

[223] See FTC, OFFICIAL REPORT OF PROCEEDINGS AND RULES PROMULGATED BY THE F.T.C. *In the Matter of Hearing for Establishing Trade Practice Rules Relating to Cosmetics and Toilet Preparation Industry,* Docket No. TPC 1947.

Opinion. The plan must allow all types of competing customers to participate. It must not be tailored to satisfy the needs of a favored customer or class, but must be suitable and usable under reasonable terms by all competing customers. This may require offering all customers more than one way to participate in the plan. The seller cannot eliminate some competing customers, either expressly or by the way the plan operates. Where the seller has alternative promotional plans, his customers must be given the opportunity to choose among the plans.

Example: A seller offers a plan for cooperative advertising on radio, television, or in a newspaper. Some of his customers who compete with those who receive the allowance are too small to use the offer. He must offer them some usable and proportional alternative, such as advertising in a neighborhood paper, handbills, etc.

Example: The seller's plan provides for furnishing demonstrators to large department store customers. He must provide usable alternatives to his customers who run other types of stores and compete with these customers but cannot use demonstrators. The alternatives might be services of equivalent value that the competing customers could use, or payments of like value for advertising or displays furnished by the customers.

Example: A seller of appliances makes his plan available only to customers purchasing at least some minimum number of his appliances in a single order or a stated period. If this requirement is beyond the reach of some customers competing with those participating in the promotion, it may be illegal.

Example: A seller should not refuse advertising allowances to those who advertise the seller's products at prices below a given figure, where this may be a means of fixing prices illegally.

In an effort to accord services or facilities to all purchasers of the seller's product, the seller should undertake to develop plans under which the purchasers of his product will be made aware not only of the availability of the services or facilities, but of what steps may be taken in order to secure the benefits under the plan. In some instances, these benefits are accorded to purchasers through wholesalers and jobbers. In other instances, knowledge of the availability of the benefits can be made known through national advertising, which would instruct the purchasers on ways and means of securing the benefits to be accorded under the plans operated by the seller.

The Second Circuit Court of Appeals, in the case of *Atalanta Trading Corporation v. FTC*,[224] referring to a question of whether an allowance for advertising had been made "available," said that "Nothing in the Robinson-

---

[224] 258 F.2d 365 (1958).

Patman Act imposes upon a supplier an affirmative duty to sell to all potential customers," and held that Atalanta had not violated subsection 2(d). In that connection, the court further stated:

> The mere showing that an allowance could not be offered to another competing purchaser is not the equivalent of proof that there, in fact, existed another such purchaser who was not offered the allowance.[225]

In other words, the court, in effect, held that Atalanta need only "negotiate" the offer of allowance for advertising to those with whom it was "negotiating" sales.

DEFENSES AVAILABLE AND NOT AVAILABLE TO THOSE CHARGED WITH VIOLATIONS OF SUBSECTIONS 2(D) AND 2(E)

Earlier, we pointed out that subsections 2(d) and 2(e) are subject to construction independent of the construction of 2(a) of the Robinson-Patman Act. This independent construction by the Commission and the courts has served to create and define offenses therefor that are independent of and separate from actions offensive to the provisions of subsection 2(a). Each of the subsections 2(d) and 2(e) is directed against discriminatory treatment of purchasers engaged in the resale of the seller's goods. In this respect, they seem to partake of one aspect of action against which subsection 2(a) is directed—namely, discriminatory treatment of purchasers—but there the similarity of the nature of the offense under the separate sections ends.

Discussed at length in Chapter II is the fact that subsection 2(a) prohibits discrimination in price only where the effect may be injury to competition. Subsections 2(d) and 2(e) prohibit a discriminatory treatment in the payments for or the furnishing of services or facilities when bought for resale, irrespective of whether or not injury to competition may result. Moreover, the cost-justification defense available to persons charged with violation of subsection 2(a) is not available to violators of subsection 2(d) and 2(e). On June 8, 1959, the Supreme Court of the United States, in the case of *FTC v. Simplicity Pattern Co.*,[226] unanimously rejected arguments that the cost-justification defense should be available to a violator of subsection 2(e), and that it should be held that competitive injury must be shown in order to make out a prima facie case under subsection 2(e). In that connection, the Court, in its footnote 18, stated:

---

[225] *Id.* at 372.
[226] 360 U.S. 55 (1959).

While both of these questions have been presented to us in terms of the "justification" clause of Section (b), we are equally convinced that the competitive injury and cost-differential clauses of Section 2(a) cannot be read directly into Section (e). *Elizabeth Arden, Inc.*, v. *Federal Trade Comm'n, supra,* note 10; *Corn Products Refining Co.* v. *Federal Trade Comm'n, supra,* note 10; *Great Atlantic & Pacific Tea Co.* v. *Federal Trade Comm'n, supra,* note 10. It is true that, in reference to the cost-differential clause, we have said, "Time and again there was recognition in Congress of a freedom to adopt and pass on to buyers the benefits of more economical processes." *Automatic Canteen Co.* v. *Federal Trade Comm'n, supra,* 346 U.S., at 72. But the contexts of the statements referred to show that the benefits were to be made available in *price* differentials or not at all. See, *e.g.,* 80 Cong. Rec. 8106–8107, 8111–8112, 8114, 8127–8128, 8137, 9415; H.R. Rep. No. 2287, 74th Cong., 2d Sess. See also notes 12 and 13, *supra.*

The question regarding the availability of the good-faith defense (provided for in subsection 2(b)) to persons charged with violations of subsection 2(d) or 2(e) has been discussed in a number of cases. In one of the earliest cases in which this question was discussed, one of the ablest of the Federal Trade Commission's hearing examiners rejected the argument that the good-faith defense was available to persons charged with violations of subsections 2(d) and 2(e).[227] In sustaining the hearing examiner in the *Rosenfeld* case, the Commission stated:

It is our conclusion that advertising allowances are not within the ambit of the statutory language and that Section 2(b) cannot constitute a substantive defense to a charge of violation of Section 2(d) of the amended Clayton Act.[228]

The Commission reaffirmed this position at its earliest opportunity. In the *Filbert* case, the Commission explicitly affirmed a ruling to the same effect that had been made by a hearing examiner. In so doing, the Commission stated that "Section 2(b) is not available as a defense to a charge of violation of Section 2(d) of the Clayton Act."[229]

It should be pointed out, however, that the good-faith proviso of subsection 2(b) expressly refers to the availability of the good-faith defense in cases where the *furnishing of services and facilities* are involved. The Commission held, therefore, that subsection 2(b) expressly preserves the good-faith defense in cases arising under subsection 2(e).

The Commission's most explicit statement on the subject was provided

---

[227] See Carpel Frosted Foods, Inc., 48 F.T.C. 581, 599 (1951); Henry Rosenfeld, Inc., 52 F.T.C. 1535, 1550, 1552 (1956).
[228] *Id.* at 1552.
[229] See J. H. Filbert, Inc., No. 6467, FTC, Sept. 19, 1957, 54 F.T.C. 359.

in the *Exquisite Form Brassiere* case.[230] There the Commission once again pointed out the "obvious difference between a seller furnishing a service or facility and his providing only the remuneration for the many distinctive promotional activities of his customers." The distinction, said the Commission, "can readily be seen by reference to this Commission's decisions."[231] The Commission concluded,

> Since the specific language of Section 2(b) refers only to practices covered by Sections (a) and (e) we must therefore reject the argument that the subsection must also logically apply to Section 2(d).

The Federal Trade Commission followed the same view when it decided the *Shulton* case (F.T.C. Dkt No. 7721 July 1961). There the Commission again ruled that the good-faith defense was not available to charges of a violation of subsection 2(d). In that connection, the Commission stated:

> Respondent has also taken exception to the hearing examiner's ruling denying its request for leave to adduce evidence that payments for services and facilities to one of its customers had been made in good faith to meet payments and allowances granted that customer by a competitor. This ruling is consistent with the views expressed by the Commission in the matters of *Henry Rosenfeld, Inc.,* and *Exquisite Form Brassiere, Inc.,* wherein we held that the meeting competition defense set forth in the Section 2(b) proviso is not available as a matter of law to a respondent charged with violating Section 2(d).

Commissioners Kern and Elman dissented from the Commission's decision in that case.

In its published *Guides for Advertising Allowances and Other Merchandising Payments and Services; Compliance with Sections 2(d) and 2(e) of the Clayton Act, as Amended by the Robinson-Patman Act,* adopted May 19, 1960, the Commission, regarding the availability of the cost-justification defense and the defense of meeting competition in good faith, made the following statement:

> It is no defense to a charge of unlawful discrimination in the payment of an allowance or the furnishing of a service for a seller to show that such payment, service, or facility, could be justified through savings in the cost of manufacture, sale or delivery.
>
> A seller charged with discrimination in violation of Section 2(e) may defend his actions by showing that the services were furnished in good faith to meet an equivalent service furnished by a competitor.

---

[230] Exquisite Form Brassiere, Inc., No. 6966, FTC, Oct. 31, 1960.
[231] E.g., see P. Lorillard Co. v. Federal Trade Commission, 267 F.2d 439 (3rd Cir. 1959) cert. den. 80 S. Ct. 293 (1960); Swanee Paper Corp., CCH Trade Reg. Rep. Par. 28, 212 (Dkt. 6927, 1959). [Footnote by the Commission.]

However, this is a very technical defense subject to important limitations. The Commission has held that the defense of meeting competition in good faith is not available to a seller charged with discrimination in violation of section 2(d).

The consistent position of the Commission that the good-faith meeting of competition is not a defense in cases arising under subsection 2(d) was rejected by the United States Court of Appeals for the District of Columbia Circuit in the *Exquisite Form Brassiere* case in a decision handed down November 22, 1961. (Exquisite Form Brassiere, Inc. v. Federal Trade Commission, 301 F. 2d 499, D.C. Cir. 1961, Cert. Den., 369 U.S. 888, 1962). The Court was unanimous in holding that the good-faith defense is available to those charged with a violation of subsection 2(d). Judge Prettyman, who wrote the Court's opinion, made a detailed analysis of the question in issue and how the Court arrived at its disposition of the matter. In the opinion, it was pointed out that the Robinson bill, which was incorporated into the Robinson-Patman Act, as it passed the Senate on April 30, 1936, included subsection (d)—

> . . . making it unlawful to pay anything to a customer as compensation "for any services or facilities furnished by or through such customer" unless offered to all competing customers; (2) a separate subsection making unlawful any discrimination in discounts, rebates, allowances, or advertising service charges; and (3) the meet-competition defense applied to "the furnishing of services or facilities to any purchaser." The bill then contained no Subsection (e) or any equivalent thereof. Thus there can be no doubt whatsoever that, so far as the Senate was concerned, the proviso in Subsection (b) applied to discriminations in compensation or allowances made to customers for services or facilities furnished by them, as now provided in Subsection (d); there was nothing else in the bill for this language to apply to. The bill thus passed went to the House.
>
> In the meantime, on March 31, 1936, the House bill (H.R. 8442) had been reported (H.R. Rep. 2287). As thus reported, it contained Subsection (d), Subsection (e), and a subsection which contained a meet-competition defense in respect to price discrimination only, saying nothing about services or facilities. On June 2nd the House ordered its bill printed, with the Senate bill substituted as its text. Thus the bill as it passed the Senate became H.R. 8442 on the calendar of the House. The House committee proposed its own bill as an amendment. Then the committee offered amendments to this amendment. One such amendment thus offered and adopted on the floor was to change the subsection dealing with the burden of proof and the meet-competition defense to read as Subsection (b) now reads. The sole explanation made to the House in respect to it was this one sentence: "It simply allows a seller to meet not only competition in price of other competitors but also competition in services and facilities furnished." Thus,

so far as the House is concerned, it clearly appears that the Members understood the defense permitted by the subsection they were enacting applied to competition in 'services and facilities furnished'; no limiting words as to manner of furnishing and no differences drawn on that score. As Senators had foretold, the final statute was written in conference and was enacted as we now have it. Since the subsection now (b) was the same in both Senate and House bills, nothing happened to it in conference.

Among Judge Prettyman's concluding remarks were the following statements:

> The examiner was of the view that "It is now well settled that the good faith meeting of competition defense set forth in Section 2(b) is not applicable to Section 2(d)." He cited *F.T.C.* v. *Simplicity Pattern Co.,* 360 U.S. 55 (1959). The Commission was of the same view, but agrees in its brief here that no court has yet passed directly on this question. We do not find in the *Simplicity Pattern* case the holding or the reasoning which the Commission deems dispositive in principle in the case at bar. The Court was there concerned with a violation of Subsection (e), and the questions were whether absence of competition precluded a violation of that section; and whether lack of competitive injury likewise precluded violation. The case did not concern the problem we have here. It dealt with neither Subsection (d) nor the meet-competition defense. Apparently the Commission told the Supreme Court in its brief that this question was not in that case. . . .

> We have discussed at such great length the problem posed in this case because of the great weight we attach to the view of the Commission in respect to the meaning of the statute it is charged with enforcing.[11] We would not lightly reject that view. We reject it now only because upon the most careful consideration we are of firm conviction that view is untenable.

> [11] See Skidmore v. Swift & Co., 323 U.S. 134, 139–140 (1944).

> [The immediately preceding footnote 11 is the Court's footnote in the opinion in *Exquisite Form Brassiere* case.]

In the meantime, Shulton, Inc., petitioned the United States Court of Appeals for the Seventh Circuit to review the Commission's order to cease and desist in that case.

The Supreme Court of the United States was requested to review the decision of the Circuit Court of Appeals for the District of Columbia in the *Exquisite Form Brassiere* case. It denied that petition for certiorari on May 21, 1962, 369 U.S. 888, 1962.

In the meantime, the Seventh Circuit Court of Appeals on May 10, 1962, set aside the Commission's order to cease and desist in the *Shulton* case, 305 Fed. 2d 36, 7th Cir., 1962. In doing so, the Court stated:

> . . . At that time, no court of appeals had ruled on this question. Since then, on November 22, 1961, the U.S. Court of Appeals for the Dis-

trict of Columbia Circuit has decided Appeal No. 16123, *Exquisite Form Brassiere, Inc., a corporation, Petitioner* v. *Federal Trade Commission, Respondent,* 301 F. 2d 499, D.C. Cir., 1961, wherein the Court held:

> The point of general interest upon this appeal is whether a defense of meeting competition in good faith, described in the proviso in Subsection (b) of the statute, is available in response to a charge of violating Subsection (d). All parties seem to agree that the defense thus described is available in response to charges under Subsections (a) [discrimination in price] and (e) [discrimination in furnishing services or facilities]. Is it available to a person charged under Subsection (d)? . . . The parties agree that no court has yet passed directly on this question. . . . The critical words used in the proviso are 'the furnishing of services or facilities to any purchaser.' These are the words which appear in Subsection (e). The words in Subsection (d) are 'to pay . . . *to* . . . a customer . . . *as compensation* . . . for any services or facilities *furnished by* . . . such customer.' (Emphasis added.) While 'services or facilities' are the subject of both subsections, in the one case (e) the vendor furnishes them *to* the customer; in the other they are furnished *by* the customer and the vendor reimburses him. So that, if careful note is taken of the difference between Subsections (d) and (e), and if Subsection (b) is read quite literally, the language of the statute appears to support the view of the Commission. That is, read thus the statute says that a person can meet competition by directly supplying some but not all customers with services and facilities with which to promote sales, but he cannot meet competition by reimbursing some but not all of his customers for services or facilities they procure in the first place. We think this is an unrealistic reading of the statute.

> We agree with this reasoning. The Subsection (b) defense was available to petitioner . . .

These decisions of the Circuit Court of Appeals for the District of Columbia in the *Exquisite Form Brassiere* case and of the Seventh Circuit Court of Appeals in the *Shulton* case remain as the rule of law on this point since the Supreme Court of the United States denied certiorari in the *Exquisite Form Brassiere* case on May 21, 1962. It is my view that this result does not accord with the intent of Congress. It seemed clear to me that Congress did not intend that parties charged with violations of Subsection 2(d) should be allowed to defend those violations successfully by showing that they were meeting the competition based on similar conduct of competing sellers.

RECORD OF ENFORCEMENT OF
SUBSECTIONS 2(D) AND 2(E)

Except for the recently stepped-up activity of the Federal Trade Commission in the enforcement of subsections 2(d) and 2(e), relatively few proceedings were undertaken to enforce the subsections in past years. Of course, in the late 1940's more than 30 proceedings were instituted in which candy manufacturing firms were charged not only with discriminating in price in violation of subsection 2(a), but also, in separate counts in the same proceedings, with violations of subsections 2(d) and 2(e). These cases became known as the "candy cases." Complaints in all were dismissed in September, 1949.

From June 19, 1936, through May 31, 1961, the Federal Trade Commission filed 180 formal charges under subsection 2(d). These 180 formal charges included 34 charges of violations of subsection 2(d) in the "candy cases." Of the 180 charges, 47 were dismissed; 34 of the 47 dismissals involved the so-called "candy cases."

As pointed out earlier in this chapter, few cases had been subjected to judicial interpretation regarding the meaning of subsection 2(d). One Federal Trade Commission case arising under subsection 2(d) to reach the courts was that of the *Atalanta Trading Corporation*.[232] Another charge arising under subsection 2(d) that was subjected to judicial review by the Seventh Circuit Court of Appeals is the matter commonly referred to as the *Woman's Day* case.[233] As noted earlier, the Federal Trade Commission order in the *Atalanta* case was set aside. The Seventh Circuit Court of Appeals upheld the cause of action for the plaintiff in the *Woman's Day* case. Only a few cases arising under subsection 2(d) have been contested before the Federal Trade Commission and, therefore, subjected to adjudication by it. Two of these were the *Rosenfeld* case[234] and the *Exquisite Form* case.[235]

During the period from June 19, 1936, through May 31, 1961, the Federal Trade Commission filed only 65 formal charges of violation of subsection 2(e), of which 33 were included in the so-called "candy cases." Those 33 charges and 10 others were dismissed, leaving in effect 22 orders to cease and desist under charges arising under subsection 2(e). Of these,

[232] Atalanta Trading Corp. v. FTC, 258 F.2d 365 (2d Cir. 1958).
[233] State Wholesale Grocers v. Great Atlantic & Pacific Tea Co., 258 F.2d 831 (7th Circuit 1958), *cert. denied*, 358 U.S. 947.
[234] 52 F.T.C. 1535 (1956).
[235] No. 6966, FTC, Oct. 31, 1960.

three were reviewed by the courts[236] and the orders of the Commission were sustained. Likewise, the plaintiff in a triple-damage case arising under subsection 2(c) prevailed in the *Gus Blass* case.[237]

Tables containing a complete listing of all Federal Trade Commission cases arising under subsections 2(d) and 2(e) in the period from June 19, 1936, through May 31, 1961, appear in Appendix A, Part III.

---

[236] Corn Products Refining Co. v. FTC, 324 U.S. 726; Elizabeth Arden, Inc. v. FTC, 156 F.2d 132, *cert. denied,* 331 U.S. 806; FTC v. Simplicity Pattern Co., 360 U.S. 55 (1959).
[237] Elizabeth Arden v. Gus Blass, 150 F.2d. 993.

Chapter V

SUBSECTION 2(f)—THE BUYER'S LIABILITY

TEXT

That it shall be unlawful for any person engaged in commerce, in the course of such commerce, knowingly to induce or receive a discrimination in price which is prohibited by this section.

BACKGROUND

Earlier in our discussion of subsection 2(a) in Chapter II, it was pointed out that the principal purpose of the Robinson-Patman Act was to provide an equality of opportunity, not only among sellers in the vending of their merchandise, but also among buyers engaged in the purchasing of merchandise for resale. It was realized that if that equality of opportunity was to be achieved, something would have to be done to prevent chain stores and other large buyers from using their volume purchasing power to induce and coerce preferential price treatment and thereby gain unearned competitive advantages.

The problem that the 74th Congress faced in 1935–36 was a desperate one, involving the coercion of smaller sellers by mass buyers to secure preferential prices, terms, and services.

The Federal Trade Commission made its investigation of chain stores and reported that, should the trend of the preceding 20 years continue with respect to chain-store merchandising, we would have a condition in some lines that few would dispute as being monopolistic. It based that conclusion on the evidence it had compiled regarding special discounts, allowances, concessions, pseudo brokerage allowances induced and knowingly

148

received by buyers of large chain-store organizations from many smaller and weaker firms engaged in the selling side of the market.

The Commission pointed out that the theory of the resolution under which the investigation was conducted was that chain-store merchandising had developed or was developing to a point where it threatened to monopolize the field of retail distribution and thus end the existence of the independent retailer.

The Commission also discussed the difficulties it had experienced in its attempt to enforce the provision of Section 2 of the Clayton Act.[238]

It drew attention to the fact that its attempts to prevent price discrimination in favor of chain-store purchasers as against purchasers of similar quantities (acting for pools or cooperative associations or individual stores) were fruitless.

In conclusion, the Commission not only considered what legislation, if any, should be enacted for the purpose of regulating and controlling chain store distribution,[239] but it proceeded to make recommendations for the strengthening of the antidiscrimination features of the Clayton Antitrust Act.

The Commission's official report of 1935 to the Congress had also analyzed the concessions of various kinds forced on smaller sellers by large distributors and pointed out the unwholesome effects traceable to them. It traced the rapid growth of chain organizations in the retail food field and the corresponding drop in the number of independent retail merchants and the reduced volume of business carried on by them.

The serious problem presented was vividly revealed by the evidence collected and considered by the Patman Committee in the House of Representatives, which dealt mainly with the discriminatory benefits extended to chain stores by manufacturers to the detriment of smaller distributors.[240]

---

[238] 38 Stat. 730 (1914): "Sec. 2. That it shall be unlawful for any person engaged in commerce, in the course of such commerce, either directly or indirectly, to discriminate in price between different purchasers of commodities, which commodities are sold or any Territory thereof or the District of Columbia or any insular possession or other place under the jurisdiction of the United States, where the effect of such discrimination may be to substantially lessen competition or tend to create a monopoly in any line of commerce; PROVIDED, That nothing herein contained shall prevent discrimination in price between purchasers of commodities on account of differences in the grade, quality, or quantity of the commodity sold, or that makes only due allowance for differences in the cost of selling or transportation, or discrimination in price in the same or different communities made in good faith to meet competition; AND PROVIDED FURTHER, That nothing herein contained shall prevent persons engaged in selling goods, wares, or merchandise in commerce from selecting their own customers in bona fide transactions and not in restraint of trade."

[239] S. Res. 224, 70th Cong., 1st Sess. (1928).

[240] Typical of comments appearing in the *Record* on that matter are the following:

"His weapon (that of the chain buyer) is *huge buying power,* by the manipulation of which he threatens manufacturers and others with financial stringency or even bankruptcy

The report of that Committee traced the rapid growth of chain-store organizations in the retail food field and confirmed the Federal Trade Commission's findings that manufacturers and other sellers were granting discriminatory price concessions and trade advantages to favored buyers.[241]

The influence of mass buying power is felt in the buying of advertising space to the same extent that it is felt in the buying of goods. In the newspaper field, pressure is brought by large users of advertising space for reduced rates, and there is a constant threat that advertising will be concentrated in the paper that yields the most to that mass pressure. It has been charged that the steady disappearance of worthy newspapers in smaller cities is caused by this tendency of outside advertisers to concentrate their advertising effort in a single medium in the community, and that the same concentration of control of advertising funds will cause similar difficulties in the magazine field.

In nearly all the smaller cities throughout the country, there have existed side by side at least two daily or weekly newspapers of opposing political faith, between them insuring complete discussion of important questions of the day. Local merchants usually advertised impartially in both. When chains expanded their outlets into these smaller cities, they continued that policy for a while. As their competition was felt, local independents found themselves less able to maintain their advertising, and the declining revenue often eventually forced a merger or disappearance of one paper.

The absentee chain was not particularly concerned with the resulting effect on the social and political life of the community, or with the economic advantage to the city of two newspapers of opposing faith. Chains prefer to see only one newspaper in a community because it reduces their advertising problem.

So as the chain became more firmly entrenched and both product ad-

---

if they refuse him the prices and terms he demands." [Mr. Patman, 79 CONG. REC. 9078 (1935).]

"Mr. Logan. . . . I might say that the bill is not aimed exclusively at chain stores. It applies to all large units which control *great purchasing power* and may so use it as to destroy competition and create monopoly." [80 CONG. REC. 3117 (1936).]

". . . The bill is designed to accomplish what so far the Clayton Act has done in an impotent manner, namely, to protect the independent merchant, the public, which he serves, *and the manufacturer from whom he buys,* from exploitation by his monopolistic competitor." [Mr. Ekwall. 80 CONG. REC. 3599 (1936).]

"What are the objectives of this bill? Mr. Chairman, there has grown up in this country a policy in business that a few rich, powerful organizations by reason of their size and *their ability to coerce and intimidate manufacturers* have forced those manufacturers to give them their goods at a lower price than they give to the independent merchants under the same and similar circumstances and for the same quantities of goods. . . ." [Mr. Patman. 80 CONG. REC. 8111 (1936). Emphasis supplied throughout.]

241 See H.R. REP. NO. 273, 74th Congress, 2d Sess., on American Retail Federation and Big Scale Buying and Selling.

vertising and local retail advertising diminished, the need for advertising diminished as far as the chain was concerned. Newspapers of lesser circulation often were dropped; distribution became more and more restricted to the products on display; private-brand and no-brand merchandising grew apace. From it all, the public suffered from the lack of dependable standards and the curtailment of newspapers.

Our theme here, however, is to show how newspapers and advertising itself is being subjected, like manufacturers, to the squeezing-out process exerted by concentrated control of mass buying power. The Act is definitely aimed at ending the misuse of this concentration of power; it prohibits unfair price discrimination by limiting differentials between competing customers of a seller to the actual differences in cost of manufacturing, selling, or delivery arising out of differing quantities or methods.

From this background, it is clear that the basic legislative purpose of subsection 2(f) was to prevent large buyers from using their economic power to force monopolistic price, service, or facility concessions.

Legislative History

Neither the Patman bill (H.R. 8442, 74th Congress) nor the Robinson bill (S. 3154, 74th Congress) contain a section comparable to that contained in the existing subsection 2(f) of the Robinson-Patman Act.

Congressman Mapes introduced two bills in the first session of the 74th Congress, one on January 29, 1935,[242] incorporating the Federal Trade Commission's original recommended changes in Section 2 of the Clayton Act, and the second on January 30, 1935,[243] embodying that and certain other recommendations of the Commission as contained in its final report.

Commencing on July 10, 1935, the House Judiciary Committee held hearings on three bills—the two bills introduced by Mr. Mapes and the Patman bill (H.R. 8442)—and only the Patman bill was seriously discussed. The purpose of the Patman bill was to remedy certain alleged discriminatory practices in the merchandising of groceries. It was given wide publicity as an anti-chain store bill. During the course of these hearings it was made clear that the purpose and thrust of the Patman bill was to prevent chains from receiving special discounts, concessions, unreasonable quantity discounts, dummy brokerage, pseudo advertising allowances—in general, to prevent the use of large buying power to extract concessions and differentials not warranted by any actual saving to the manufacturer. How-

---

[242] H.R. 4995, 74th Cong., 1st Sess. (1935).
[243] H.R. 5062, 74th Cong., 1st Sess. (1935).

ever, both the Patman and the Robinson bills were reported to the House and the Senate without the language that now appears in subsection 2(f).

On April 24 (calendar date, April 29), 1936, Senator Copeland introduced an amendment to S. 3154 that prohibited a purchaser from inducing or receiving a discrimination in price "or terms of sale." The late Charles Wesley Dunn, Esq., who served for many years as the general counsel of the Grocery Manufacturers of America, Inc., announced on various occasions that he prepared the language introduced by Senator Copeland as an amendment to the Robinson bill which became subsection 2(f) of the Robinson-Patman Act.[244]

The managers on the part of the House, in presenting the conference report of the Robinson and Patman bills, stated:

> Subsection (f) makes it unlawful for any person engaged in commerce knowingly to induce or receive a discrimination in price which is prohibited by this section. This subsection was not contained in the House bill, but is the same as subsection (f) in the Senate amendment, except that the words "or terms of sale" are eliminated to harmonize with subsection (a).[245]

In further explanation of subsection 2(f), Congressman Utterback, the chairman of the managers on the part of the House, stated:

> The closing paragraph of the Clayton Act amendment, for which section 1 of this bill provides, makes equally liable the person who knowingly induces or receives a discrimination in price prohibited by the amendment. This affords a valuable support to the manufacturer in his efforts to abide by the intent and purpose of the bill. It makes it easier for him to resist the demand for sacrificial price cuts coming from mass buyer customers, since it enables him to charge them with knowledge of the illegality of the discount, and equal liability for it, by informing them that it is in excess of any differential which his difference in cost would justify as compared with his other customers.
>
> This paragraph makes the buyer liable for knowingly inducing or receiving any discrimination in price which is unlawful under the first paragraph of the amendment. That applies both to direct and indirect discrimination; and where, for example, there is discrimination in terms of sale, or in allowances connected or related to the contract of sale, of such a character as to constitute or effect an indirect discrimination in price, the liability for knowingly inducing or receiving such discrimination or allowance is clearly provided for under the later paragraph above referred to.[246]

---

[244] See Robinson-Patman Act Symposium, *Proceedings Before Section on the Food, Drug and Cosmetic Law, New York State Bar Assn.* 61 (1946).
[245] H.R. REP. No. 2951, 74th Cong., 2d Sess. (1936).
[246] 80 CONG. REC. 9419 (1936).

The acts and practices provided by subsections 2(c), 2(d), and 2(e) are not actionable in proceedings against buyers in cases brought under subsection 2(f). Subsection 2(f) is not needed for action against buyers accepting illegal brokerage because subsection 2(c) contains its own express prohibition against such acts and practices. However, it does appear that it was due to legislative oversight that subsection 2(f) was not made to apply with respect to buyers for their participation in violations of subsections 2(d) and 2(e). Mr. Dunn, the self-acknowledged authority of the language of subsection 2(f), has explained it as follows:

> . . . This is a serious defect, in its practical conception; and it invites a prompt remedial amendment of section 2(f). *But it is mitigated to the important extent Section 2(d) and (e) actually reach a direct or indirect price discrimination.* This defect in section 2(f) is of immediate interest to me, because I wrote the draft of it; and the explanation of its limited application is this. When the amendment of section 2 was before Congress, Senator Copeland introduced an additional bill for its revision, which I wrote. This bill amended that section, from the standpoint of price discrimination alone; it contained the provisions now in section 2(f); Senator Copeland added them to the Robinson bill, on the floor; they eventually became section 2(f), in the enacted Patman bill; and in passing that bill *Congress overlooked the fact that section 2(f) should reach any violation of section 2(d) and (e).* (Emphasis supplied.)[247]

Support is found for this view in the statement on the bill as made by the chairman of the House conferees when, in reference to subsection 2(f), he reported to the House as follows:

> This paragraph makes the buyer liable for knowingly inducing or receiving *any discrimination in price which is unlawful under the first paragraph of the amendment.*[248]

ADJUDICATORY INTERPRETATIONS OF SUBSECTION 2(F)

It was not until July, 1953, that a final decision was rendered by the Supreme Court of the United States in the principal case to reach the courts for a determination of the meaning of subsection 2(f). That was the case of *Automatic Canteen Company v. FTC,*[249] frequently referred to as the *Automatic Canteen* case. Prior to the decision of the Supreme Court in the *Automatic Canteen* case, the Federal Trade Commission had entered

---

[247] See Robinson-Patman Act Symposium, *"Proceedings Before Section on the Food, Drug and Cosmetic Law, New York State Bar Assn.* 61 (1946).
[248] 80 CONG. REC. 9419 (1936).
[249] 346 U.S. 61.

orders in only 11 cases arising under subsection 2(f).[250] Eight of these 11 cases were settled without contest; consequently, no interpretations of the law developed from them. Two of the remaining three cases—the *Curtiss Candy Co.* and *Atlantic City Wholesale Drug Co.* cases—were fully tried in proceedings before the Federal Trade Commission. The third case—that involving the E. J. Brach & Sons—was settled for the most part through an admission of material allegations of the complaint, and the trial of the case was limited to some insignificant issues. None of those 11 cases went to court.

The most important of these cases litigated before the Federal Trade Commission prior to the decision by the Supreme Court in the *Automatic Canteen* case was the *Curtiss Candy Co.* case, which raised issues under subsections 2(a), (d), and (f) and Section 3 of the Robinson-Patman Act. A full cost justification was presented and disposed of under subsection 2(a) of the Act.

The Commission found that the respondent had knowingly induced and received discriminatory prices on its purchases of corn syrup from several corn-syrup manufacturers. The interrelations and chain-reaction character of Robinson-Patman Act proceedings are well illustrated in the relationship of the *Curtiss* case to the *Corn Products Refining Company* proceedings and the *A. E. Staley Manufacturing Company* proceedings.[251]

In these two latter cases, the Commission was sustained in its attempt to order manufacturers to cease and desist from granting discriminations in the sale and distribution of glucose, dextrose, and similar products. These cases are of immediate interest in connection with the *Curtiss* proceedings, for this candy company was the principal buyer from Corn Products and

---

[250] The 11 orders filed under Section 2(f) before the Supreme Court decision of July 10, 1953, are:

(1) Pittsburgh Plate Glass Co., No. 3154, FTC (O.C.D. Oct. 30, 1937), 25 F.T.C. 1228.
(2) Golf Ball Mfg. Ass'n., No. 3161, FTC (O.C.D. Feb. 25, 1938), 26 F.T.C. 824.
(3) American Oil Co., No. 3843, FTC (O.C.D. Sept. 9, 1939), 29 F.T.C. 857.
(4) Miami Wholesale Drug Corp., No. 3377, FTC (O.C.D. Feb. 9, 1939), 28 F.T.C. 485.
(5) A. S. Aloe Company, No. 3820, FTC (O.C.D. Dec. 15, 1941), 34 F.T.C. 363.
(6) Atlantic City Wholesale Drug Co., No. 4957, FTC (O.C.D. June 14, 1944), 38 F.T.C. 631.
(7) E. J. Brach & Sons, No. 4548, FTC (O.C.D. Dec. 21, 1944), 39 F.T.C. 535.
(8) Associated Merchandising Corp., No. 5027, FTC (O.C.D. May 8, 1945), 40 F.T.C. 578.
(9) Curtiss Candy Co., Nos. 4556 & 4673, FTC (O.C.D. Nov. 12, 1947), 44 F.T.C. 237 (*modified* Oct. 15, 1951).
(10) National Tea Co., No. 5648, FTC (O.C.D. May 15, 1950), 46 F.T.C. 829, *modified* May 8, 1951, 47 F.T.C. 1314.
(11) Atlas Supply Co., No. 5794, FTC (O.C.D. July 19, 1951), 38 F.T.C. 53.

[251] Corn Products Refining Co. v. FTC, 324 U.S. 726, 65 Sup. Ct. 961, 89 L. Ed. 1320 (1945); FTC v. A. E. Staley Mfg. Co., 324 U.S. 746, 65 Sup. Ct. 971, 89 L. Ed. 1338 (1945).

A. E. Staley Companies. Moreover, the Automatic Canteen Company was also charged with inducing and receiving discriminatory prices in its purchases from the Curtiss Candy Company.

THE AUTOMATIC CANTEEN DECISION—ITS EFFECT ON THE COMMISSION'S ENFORCEMENT OF SUBSECTION 2(F)

The Supreme Court decision in the *Automatic Canteen* case[252] focused attention on subsection 2(f) and its enforcement against buyers.

The Automatic Canteen Company was a dominant firm in the sale of confectionary products through vending machines. As such, its operations were divided into two parts—the developing and leasing of vending machines to distributors, and the purchase of confectionary products for resale to distributors, who sold to the public through some 230,000 automatic vending machines.

The original Federal Trade Commission complaint was in two counts. Count II charged violation of subsection 2(f) of the Robinson-Patman Act through knowingly inducing and receiving price discriminations in the purchase of confectionary products, while Count I charged a violation of Section 3 of the Act. The company appealed both counts, and the Circuit Court sustained the Federal Trade Commission.[253] The Automatic Canteen Company accepted the decision on Count I, but took Count II to the Supreme Court. It is with Count II that we are concerned here.

According to the Commission's finding, Automatic Canteen Company knowingly induced and knowingly received prices that were from 1.2 per cent to 33 per cent lower than those paid by its competitors. These differentials were obtained from about 80 of its 115 suppliers.[254] The differentials were obtained in three different ways: (1) by informing the supplier of the prices and terms of sale that would be acceptable; (2) by refusing to buy unless the price was reduced below prices at which a particular supplier sold the same merchandise to others; and (3) by trying to convince the supplier that savings would accrue in selling to Automatic Canteen.

Since the buyer (Automatic Canteen Co.) knew that it was being favored over other buyers, the Commission held that a prima facie case of violation under section 2(f) was established. The Commission's theory

---

[252] Automatic Canteen Co. v. FTC, 346 U.S. 61 (1953), *vacating order of Seventh Circuit,* 194 F.2d 433 (7th Cir. 1952).

[253] *Ibid.*

[254] Answer to Respondent's Motion to Dismiss, *In re* Automatic Canteen Co. of America, No. 4933; FTC filed Dec. 7, 1945; reply brief filed April 25, 1946; argued on Nov. 6, 1947, before Commission by Attorney Austin H. Forkner; decision on December 6, 1947.

was that this placed on the buyer the burden of justifying the differential on the basis of any one of the various provisos in Section 2(a) or 2(b) (e.g., savings in cost).

The buyer contended, however, that the Commission had not proved that the buyer *knowingly* induced price reductions that were greater than the cost savings in selling to it. The dispute then centered around the question of who (the Federal Trade Commission or the buyer) must introduce evidence as to the buyer's knowledge of the relative size of the cost savings and the price differentials.[255] Thus, the case did *not* hinge on whether or not the prices received by the buyer were cost justified, but rather, on the question of who had the burden of showing cost justification or the lack of it.

The Supreme Court did not give an opinion as to whether the prices received by the Automatic Canteen Company were cost justified, but did decide the type of evidence that the Commission would have to submit to support a cease-and-desist order. The word "knowingly" in 2(f) was interpreted in such a way as to make an important distinction between cases involving buyers as against sellers.

The Court held that to establish a prima facie case against the buyer, the Federal Trade Commission would have to show that the buyer not only knew that there was a price differential, but also knew—or reasonably should have known—that the available defenses, such as the cost proviso, were not applicable. In the words of the Court,

> We therefore conclude that a buyer is not liable under 2(f) if the lower prices he induces are either within one of the seller's defenses such as the cost justification or not known by him not to be within one of those defenses. . . .
>
> As we have noted earlier, the precise issue in the case before us is the burden of introducing evidence—a separate issue, though of course related to the substantive prohibition. . . .[256]
>
> Assuming, as we have found, that there is no substantive violation if the buyer did not know that the prices it induced or received were not cost-justified, we must in this case determine whether proof that the buyer knew that the price was lower is sufficient to shift the burden of introducing evidence to the buyer. . . .[257]
>
> . . . the Commission asks us to hold that a prima facie case under section 2(f), is made out with a showing of the prima facie case of section 2(a) violation "plus the additional element of having induced

---

[255] The dispute might, in other cases, involve the question of the buyer's knowledge of the applicability of any of the other provisos. Since the Automatic Canteen Company defense was primarily concerned with the cost proviso, that proviso was given major emphasis in the Supreme Court's decision. See also cost aspects of that proceeding analyzed by Herbert F. Taggart, *Cost Justification* (1959), pp. 518–26.

[256] 346 U.S. 61, 74.

[257] *Id.* at 74, 75.

or received such discrimination with knowledge of the facts which made it violative of Section 2(a)."[258]

The Commission need only to show, to establish its prima facie case, that the buyer knew that the methods by which he was served and quantities in which he purchased were the same as in the case of his competitor. If the methods or quantities differ, the Commission must only show that such differences could not give rise to sufficient savings in the cost of manufacture, sale or delivery to justify the price differential, and that the buyer, knowing these were the only differences, should have known that they could not give rise to sufficient cost savings.[259]

Implications of Supreme Court Decision

There are several important implications in the Supreme Court's decision in the Automatic Canteen Company case. In the dissenting opinion, Justice Douglas stated: "The Court's construction not only required the Commission to show that the price discriminations were not justified; it also makes the Commission prove what lay in the buyer's mind."[260]

This all adds up to the requirement that the Commission, or any other party electing to proceed against a buyer for violation of subsection 2(f), in order to prevail must not only show that the buyer knowingly received the benefits of price discriminations, and that the effect of these discriminations was injurious to competition; in addition, it must also show that the discrimination was not justified under any of the defensive provisos in subsections 2(a) and 2(b), and that the buyer knew or should have known that no such defense would have been available to the seller if the seller had been proceeded against under subsection 2(a). The effect of this interpretation of the law is a definite weakening of the enforcement against buyers by the Federal Trade Commission under subsection 2(f) of the Act. Four pending cases against buyers were quickly dismissed on the authority of *Automatic Canteen,* either for defective pleading or on account of insufficient evidence as to the buyer's knowledge of the illegality of the prices received.[261]

These cases were dismissed because the evidence supporting the complaint was not apparently adequate to prove "the degree of knowledge on

---

[258] *Id.* at 76.
[259] *Id.* at 80.
[260] *Id.* at 85.
[261] (1) Initial decision in *Crown Zellerbach Corp.,* No. 5421, FTC, July 8, 1953, sustained by F.T.C. Feb. 9, 1955; (2) *Safeway Stores, Inc.,* No. 5990, FTC, July 27, 1953; (3) *Kroger Co.,* No. 5991, FTC, Sept. 8, 1953; (4) *Sylvania Electric Products, Inc.* and *Philco Corp.,* No. 5728, FTC, initial decision (Dec. 9, 1953) dismissed by Commission (Sept. 23, 1954).

the part of the respondent" required by the Supreme Court decision in the
Canteen case. It should be recalled that in the *Crown Zellerbach* case, ex-
tensive hearings had been held before the Supreme Court's decision in the
Automatic Canteen case.[262]

From the Supreme Court decision in the *Automatic Canteen* case in
1953 to September 1, 1958, the Commission issued only two cease-and-
desist orders based on charges of violation of subsection 2(f). One of these
was issued as a consent order against a manufacturer who sold gasoline
at a discount for use in taxicabs. The taxicab companies diverted their
gasoline to the general retail market.[263] In August, 1958, another consent
order was issued against a group of distributors of automobile supplies.[264]

However, recently there has been a resurgence of enforcement activity
under this section, especially directed at jobbers of automotive products and
their group buying organizations.[265]

The record shows that only 13 orders have been issued by the Federal
Trade Commission under subsection 2(f) since the decision of the Supreme
Court in the *Automatic Canteen* case (August 10, 1953). Nine of these
orders were the result of consent agreements, and 11 had to do with the sale
of automotive parts and accessories.[266]

Of the remaining non-consent orders, the record shows that four groups

---

[262] Cost aspects of that proceeding were analyzed by Herbert F. Taggart, *Cost Justification*
(1959), pp. 518–26.
[263] Shell Oil Co., No. 6698, FTC, April 2, 1958.
[264] Warehouse Distributors, Inc., No. 6837, FTC, Aug. 14, 1958.
[265] See fn. 264 on 2(f) charges now involved in pending cases; docket Nos. 7365, 7492,
7590, 7592, 8039, and 8069 cited in fn. 269.
[266] List of all orders entered under Subsection 2(f) of the Clayton Act, as amended by the
Robinson-Patman Act, involving charges that respondents unlawfully and knowingly induced or received a discrimination in price, which is prohibited by subsection 2(f), after
August 10, 1953:

 (1) Shell Oil Co., No. 6698, FTC (O.C.D., April 2, 1958). Also on Subsection 2(a);
     54 F.T.C.D. 1274, consent.
 (2) Warehouse Distributors, Inc., No. 6837, FTC (O.C.D. Aug. 14, 1958—consent).
 (3) Midwest Warehouse Distributors, Inc., No. 6888, FTC (O.C.D. Sept. 24, 1958—con-
     sent).
 (4) Hunt-Marquardt, Inc., No. 6765, FTC (O.C.D. Dec. 23, 1958—consent).
 (5) D & N Auto Parts Company, No. 5767, FTC (O.C.D. Feb. 24, 1959, *aff'd* 5th Cir.
     1961), *petition for cert. filed* May 24, 1961.
 (6) Borden-Aicklen Auto Supply Co. Inc., No. 5766, FTC (O.C.D. Feb. 24, 1959, *aff'd*,
     5th Cir., Feb. 23, 1961).
 (7) American Motor Specialties Co., No. 5724, FTC (O.C.D. March 12, 1959). 2d Cir.,
     May 5, 1960, cert. *denied,* November 2, 1960.
 (8) Allbrights, No. 6890, FTC (O.C.D. March 27, 1959—consent).
 (9) Automotive Supply Company, No. 7142, FTC (O.C.D. August 28, 1959—consent).
(10) Automotive Southwest, Inc., No. 7687, FTC (O.C.D. Sept. 8, 1960—consent).
(11) Southwestern Distributors, Inc., No. 7686, FTC (O.C.D. Sept. 14, 1960—consent).
(12) Alhambra Motor Parts, No. 6889, FTC (O.C.D. Oct. 28, 1960. *Petition for review
     filed,* 9th Cir., Jan. 4, 1961, now pending).
(13) March of Toys, Inc., No. 7070, FTC (O.C.D. Aug. 26, 1960—consent).

of respondents have tried to reverse the orders of the Commission by appeals to the courts. The American Motor Specialties Co. lost its appeal for a writ of certiorari from an adverse decision of the Second Circuit Court of Appeals (November 2, 1960). The proceedings against the Alhambra Motor Parts Co. (No. 6889) is now pending for review before the Ninth Circuit Court of Appeals (filed January 4, 1961).

Both of the proceedings against the D & N Auto Parts Company (No. 5767) and the Borden-Aicklen Auto Supply Co. (No. 5766) were tried as a consolidated proceeding before the Commission and now have a petition pending for a writ of certiorari from the decision of the Fifth Circuit Court of Appeals (filed May 24, 1961).[267]

The Mid-South Distributors Case

The recent decision in the *Mid-South Distributors* case before the United States Court of Appeals for the Fifth Circuit may hold out some hope for the Federal Trade Commission in overcoming the effect of the *Automatic Canteen* decision. This is typical of the group-buying orders entered by the Commission recently. This group-buying case involved automotive parts, accessories, and supplies with a membership corporation. The petitioners were two cooperative buying groups, Mid-South Distributors and Cotton States, Inc., and twenty-three jobbers who were members of Mid-South and Cotton States.

These corporate groups were organized for the purpose of inducing and receiving lower prices on automotive merchandise than would otherwise be obtainable by most of the member jobbers acting individually. They were granted volume rebates based on the aggregate purchases of all group members. The question on appeal to the Fifth Circuit was whether the counsel in support of the complaint had met the burden of proof required by subsection 2(f) as interpreted by the Supreme Court in the *Automatic Canteen* case.

In its decision (February 23, 1961), the Fifth Circuit considered several issues or requirements under this *Automatic Canteen* case decision. After answering the questions adversely on whether the petitioners were exempt under the law as a cooperative and as to whether there was jurisdiction on interstate purchases, the court took up the question of whether a record of required injury and knowledge had been established.

---

[267] Mid-South Distributors & Cotton States, Inc., No. 17860 5th Cir., filed May 24, 1961. The Fifth Circuit Court of Appeals handed down its decision on February 23, 1961. In doing so, it expressly ruled that this buying group was not exempt as a cooperative under Section 4 from the violation of subsection 2(f).

The court concluded that all persons must know "constructively or actually that price discriminations which injure are prohibited," and that ignorance of this fact was no defense.

Further, on the question as to whether the buyers in that case knew or had reason to know that the prices received could not be justified on a cost basis, the court stated that there were "inferences of buyer knowledge of seller non-justification," and that the buyer knew that the procedure used represented no real savings in cost to the seller. The court held that the government's burden of proof was satisfied by showing price differentials of a kind that would cause or would be likely to cause injury to competitors.

Another typical group-buying case that has been adjudicated in the Second Circuit Court of Appeals is the *American Motor Specialties* case.[268] Respondents appealed from the Commission's order to cease and desist for violating the provisions of subsection 2(f) of the Clayton Act. There were 19 petitioners, of whom 17 firms were engaged in jobbing automotive replacement parts in the New York area. Two buying groups were organized with the 17 member firms for the purpose of persuading manufacturers to give them increased rebates on their gross purchases.

In its decision on May 5, 1960, the court ruled against the petitioners in respect to their claims that the Commission had not (1) proved there was an adverse effect on competition, and (2) established that the petitioner knowingly induced or received these discriminatory prices.

The Court also pointed out (1) that the Commission already made a' finding of injury in the cases of three manufacturers who were selling to these petitioners under this arrangement. In reference to point number (2), the Court ruled that the proof in the record was sufficient under the standards outlined in *Automatic Canteen*. The Court ruled that they were charged with notice that their price differentials could not be justified on the basis of cost.

Perhaps more meaningful and definitive law will be developed in the six remaining and pending proceedings on subsection 2(f) before the Federal Trade Commission.[269]

---

[268] American Motor Specialties Co., No. 5724, FTC (O.C.D. Mar. 12, 1959, *aff'd*, 2d Cir., May 5, 1960, *cert. denied*, 2d Cir., November 7, 1960).

[269] These pending cases are:

(1) American Metal Products Company, No. 7365, FTC. Complaint issued Jan. 30, 1959, on subsection 2(a) and (f) of Clayton Act.

(2) Fred Meyer, Inc., No. 7492, FTC. Complaint issued May 21, 1959, on subsection 2(f) of Clayton Act and F.T.C. Act.

(3) Automotive Jobbers, Inc., No. 7590, FTC. Complaint issued October 17, 1959.

(4) Ark-La-Tex Warehouse Distributors, Inc., No. 7592, FTC. Complaint issued Oct. 1, 1959.

(5) National Parts Warehouse, No. 8039, FTC. Complaint issued Nov. 18, 1960.

(6) Sears, Roebuck & Co., No. 8069, FTC. Complaint issued March 17, 1961.

THE BUYERS' LIABILITIES UNDER SECTION 5 OF
THE FEDERAL TRADE COMMISSION ACT FOR
INDUCING DISCRIMINATORY TREATMENT

Questions have arisen as to whether knowing inducement or receipt of discriminatory allowances and services, prohibited by subsections 2(d) and 2(e) of the Robinson-Patman Act, make the buyers liable therefore under Section 5 of the Federal Trade Commission Act. A question of this kind was presented to the Federal Trade Commission in the matter of the *Grand Union Company*.[270] The Commission has issued several complaints charging large retail chains with inducing and receiving payments from various sellers for advertising services, in violation of Section 5 of the Federal Trade Commission Act (unfair trade practice). Violation of the Robinson-Patman Act was not alleged, although separate complaints were issued against the sellers charging subsection 2(d) violations.

The question put to the Circuit Court of Appeals for the Second Circuit in the *Grand Union* case was whether the knowing inducement or receipt of a discriminatory advertising allowance, which is prohibited by subsection 2(d) of the Clayton Act, constitutes an unfair trade practice under Section 5 of the Federal Trade Commission Act. The respondent company argued that the Commission's authority was limited in Section 5 to illegal practices previously condemned by the antitrust laws.

After reviewing the legislative history of the Robinson-Patman Act, and particularly subsection 2(f), the Commission ruled against the respondents on this point in the following language:

> . . . In view of the clear purpose of the bill, a more plausible argument, advanced by counsel supporting the complaint, is that Congress intended to include the knowing inducement or receipt of a disproportionate allowance within the purview of Section 2(f) and that its failure to do so was the result of an oversight. [See Dunn, "Section 2(d) and (e)," New York State Bar Association, Robinson-Patman Act Symposium 55, 61 (1946).]

Respondents also claimed that there was no evidence that it or its officials knew that payments being made by their suppliers were not available to its competitors on proportionally equal terms. The Commission disposed of this argument and referred to respondent's active solicitation and extensive negotiations with these suppliers, and pressure exerted on the suppliers by respondent.

It is significant that the hearing examiner in his decision took into consideration the legislative record showing that the omission in subsection

---

[270] Grand Union Co., No. 6973 (O.C.D. August 12, 1960). FTC Act. Section 5.

2(f) with respect to inducing a subsection 2(d) or 2(e) violation was inadvertent. He stated as follows:

> . . . Such evidence as does exist suggests that the omission of a provision in the Clayton Act with respect to inducing a Section 2(d) violation, similar to that contained in Section 2(f) with respect to inducing a Section 2(a) violation, was inadvertent rather than deliberate since at the stage when section 2(f) was added to the Act the fate of Section 2(d) and (e) was uncertain. Even if this evidence be disregarded as not constituting reliable legislative history, certainly there is no evidence of a deliberate intention on the part of Congress to exclude such conduct from the category of illegality. Such an intention cannot be inferred from the mere failure to include such conduct in Section 2(f) or from the failure to include an equivalent provision in the Clayton Act with respect to the knowing inducement of a 2(d) type of violation.

The Federal Trade Commission's opinion and decision in the *Grand Union* case was handed down on August 12, 1960. It was a four-to-one decision, with Commissioner Tait dissenting. This case has gained considerably more recognition than the usual case, because under Section 5 of the Federal Trade Commission Act, the Commission has now entered an order prohibiting a large buyer, in this instance the Grand Union Company, from inducing or knowingly receiving payments from suppliers whose products it advertised when those suppliers were not extending similar payments to competing buyers on proportionately equal terms. As found by the Commission, Grand Union in that case had rented a spectacular electric signboard on Broadway in New York City and induced various of its suppliers to take advertising time on it. Twenty-eight of the 80 sellers who bought time for advertising on that sign from Grand Union were its suppliers, and each paid Grand Union $1,000 per month for the advertising of their products on the sign. Resulting benefits to Grand Union amounted to some $64,000, and $14,000 or more in cash in return for special store displays of certain suppliers' products.

The Commission noted in its opinion and decision that the specific terms of the language of the Robinson-Patman Act were not violated by Grand Union in this instance. However, the Commission concluded that the course of conduct participated in by Grand Union was contrary to the public policy of the Robinson-Patman Act. That conclusion was reached on the basis of the reasoning that the Robinson-Patman Act prohibits actions that are against public policy because of their adverse effects on competition and the tendency to create monopolies. Therefore, the Commission held that a course of conduct against public policy because of such reasoning amounted to a violation of Section 5 of the Federal Trade Commission

Act, which prohibits unfair methods of competition having a dangerous tendency unduly to hinder competition or to create monopolies. To this, Commissioner Tait dissented. He said that to accept this ruling would be tantamount to holding that the Commission's authority "is so broad that it can declare unlawful any practice which it believes contrary to the 'spirit' of the antitrust laws . . ." Obviously, Commissioner Tait considered that the standard thus relied on by the Commission was too vague an approach to the law, which he condemned as "too much sail and too little anchor."

In the *Grand Union* case, the Federal Trade Commission for the first time held that a buyer's knowing inducement of discriminatory advertising allowances prohibited by subsection 2(d) constitutes an unfair trade practice proscribed by Section 5 of the Federal Trade Commission Act. The obverse of the *Grand Union* case is illustrated by the *Swanee Paper Corp.* case (No. 6972, FTC, March 22, 1960). This 2(d) case is important for another reason as well: The Commission's opinion establishes that, when a seller grants discriminatory benefits, the intervention of a third-party intermediary between the seller and the favored buyer does not defeat the application of the statute. The principle of the *Grand Union* case was applied in the *American News Co.* case No. 7396, FTC, January 10, 1961). American and its wholly owned subsidiary, the Union News Company, were ordered to cease and desist from knowingly inducing illegal allowances from publishers and distributors of magazines, comics, and paperback books. The Commission had previously accepted consent agreements with 28 publishers and distributors[271] who had been charged with violating subsection 2(d) in making payment to American and Union. The books and periodicals published or distributed by these respondents include virtually every nationally distributed popular magazine. These orders became effective at the same time as the *American News Co.* order.

The Court of Appeals for the District of Columbia Circuit on June 14, 1962, in the case of *Giant Food, Inc.* v. *Federal Trade Commission*, 307 F. 2d 184, D.C. Cir., 1962, reviewed and affirmed a cease and desist order of the Commission which held that Giant had violated Section 5 of the

---

[271] No. 7384, FTC—Select Magazines, Inc., and the following publisher-owners: McCall Corp.; The Popular Science Publishing Co., Inc.; The Reader's Digest Assn., Inc.; Meredith Publishing Co.; Street & Smith Publications, Inc.; and Time, Inc.; No. 7385—The Curtis Publishing Co. and two wholly-owned subsidiaries: Curtis Circulation Co. and The American Home Magazine Corp.; No. 7386—Cowles Magazines, Inc.; No. 7387—Esquire, Inc.; No. 7388—New Yorker Magazine, Inc.; No. 7389—Newsweek, Inc.; No. 7390—United States News Publishing Corp.; No. 7391—The Hearst Corp.; No. 7392—McFadden Publications, Inc.; No. 7393—Fawcett Publications, Inc.; No. 7394—Triangle Publications, Inc.; No. 7611—The New American Library of World Literature, Inc. and its national distributor, Independent News Co.; No. 7612— Dell Publishing Co., Inc.; No. 7613—Bantam Books, Inc.; No. 7614—National Comics Publications, Inc. and a subsidiary, Independent News Co.; No. 7615—Pocket Books, Inc., and a subsidiary, Affiliated Publishers, Inc.

Federal Trade Commission Act through inducing and accepting payments from its suppliers which were not in accord with the provisions of Subsection 2(d) of the Robinson-Patman Act. In disposing of the petition of Giant to set aside the Commission's order the Court said:

> On this appeal, Giant's first argument is that it did not violate Sec. 5 of the Federal Trade Commission Act by inducing and accepting the above mentioned payments from its suppliers. The heart of Giant's argument in this respect is that Sec. 2(d) of the Clayton Act, as amended by the Robinson-Patman Act, only makes it unlawful for a seller to make discriminatory payments of the type involved here; with respect to a buyer, that section is silent. From this interpretation read in conjunction with Sec. 2(f) of the Act, where the buyer is covered by the general prohibition against a knowing inducement or receipt of a discrimination in price, Giant would have us conclude that the Commission is powerless to proscribe Giant's conduct under the broad language of Sec. 5 of the Federal Trade Commission Act. We do not agree.

By this approach, the Commission quickly and effectively has moved against illegal industry-wide practices. The Commission has used this technique of proceeding simultaneously against both the donor and the recipient of illegal merchandising allowances or services in a number of industries, including groceries,[272] pipe and plumbing fixtures,[273] and toys.[274]

---

[272] In a complaint issued April 19, 1960, Benner Tea Company was charged with inducing subsection 2(d) violations (No. 7866). The following suppliers of Benner Tea were charged with violation of subsection 2(d): Penick & Ford, Ltd., Inc. (No. 8118); Midwest Biscuit Co. (No. 7868); Kerr Glass Manufacturing Corp. (No. 8096); The Herst-Allen Co. (No. 7867); Dennis Chicken Products Co., Inc. (No. 8091); Chun King Sales, Inc. (No. 8093); Ball Brothers Co., Inc. (No. 8092); J. A. Folger & Co. (No. 8094); S. C. Johnson & Son., Inc. (No. 8177); Michigan Fruit Canners, Inc. (No. 8095); Paxton and Gallagher Co. (No. 8176); The Quaker Oats Co. (No. 8119) and the Aluminum Company of America (No. 8175).

A similar pattern was displayed in a Section 5 charge against J. Weingarten, Inc., a southwestern food chain and eight of its suppliers. These suppliers included Ipswich Hosiery Co., Nestle Lemur Co., Lanolin Plus, Max Factor, Inc., Shulton, Inc., Shreveport Macaroni Co., and Yakima Fruit & Cold Storage Co. (Nos. 7715–7722).

[273] American Radiator and Standard Sanitary Corp. were charged with violating Section 5 by inducing illegal allowances (No. 7835). Grantors of allowances were charged with violating subsection 2(d): Anniston Foundry Co. (No. 8031); Nibco, Inc. (No. 8074); Tyler Pipe & Foundry Co. (No. 8123); Grabler Manufacturing Co. Inc. (No. 7838); and Bridgeport Brass Co., Inc. (No. 7842).

[274] Six toy wholesaler buying groups and their wholesaler members were charged with violation of Section 5: Santa's Official Toy Preview, Inc. (No. 8231); Santa's Playthings, Inc. (No. 8259); Billy & Ruth Promotion, Inc. (No. 8240); United Variety Wholesalers (No. 8255); Individual Catalogues, Inc. (No. 7971) and ATD Catalogs, Inc. (No. 8100).

Twenty-seven toy manufacturers were charged with participation in one or more of those programs: Ideal Toy Corp. (No. 7979); Emenee Industries, Inc. (No. 7974); Transogram Co., Inc. (No. 7978); Parker Brothers, Inc. (No. 7976); Bilnor Corp. (No. 7975); American Machine & Foundry Co. (No. 7977); Wolverine Supply and Manufacturing Co. (No. 7972); Knickerbocker Toy Co., Inc. (No. 8101); Alexander Miner Sales Corp. (No. 8102); Remco Industries, Inc. (No. 8103); A. C. Gilbert Co. (No. 8104); Revell, Inc. (No.

LEGISLATIVE PROPOSALS TO REMEDY EXISTING
DEFECTS IN SUBSECTION 2(F)

On January 3, 1961, the Patman bill, H.R. 124, was introduced in the House of Representatives to remedy defects that had become apparent in subsection 2(f).

As will be seen from what has been stated previously, a further clarification is needed in the statute to fix the responsibility as to who has the burden of proof on various requirements under subsection 2(f). To provide this clarification, and thus to effectuate the original legislative purpose of this section, is the purpose of H.R. 124 relating to subsection 2(f).

The text of H.R. 124 is as follows:

> That it shall be unlawful for any person engaged in commerce, in the course of such commerce, to receive, directly or indirectly, a price, payment, allowance, service or facility prohibited by subsections (a), (d), or (e) of this section where such person knows, should know, or has reason to believe that such price, payment, allowance, service or facility is prohibited by such subsections.

H.R. 124 was duly referred to the Committee of the Judiciary of the House of Representatives for consideration and report. No hearings or report have been had on that proposal.

The United States Court of Appeals for the Second Circuit was petitioned to review and set aside the Commission's orders to cease and desist in the *Grand Union* case[275] and in the *American News Company* case.[276] The Court decided these cases on February 7, 1962 (*Grand Union Company* v. *Federal Trade Commission,* 300 F. 2d 92, and *American News Company* v. *Federal Trade Commission,* 300 F. 2d 104, 2d Cir. 1962, Cert. Den. in *American News Company* case, 371 U.S. 824, Oct. 8, 1962), and in doing so affirmed the Commission's orders to cease and desist in both cases. Judge Moore, in his dissenting opinion in the *Grand Union* case, stated:

> Regardless of half-hearted disclaimer, the Commission and the majority in supporting its decision are actually rewriting either section 2(d) or 2(f). They are either adding to 2(d), in substance, the words

---

8224); Aurora Plastics Corp. (No. 8225); Kohner Bros. Inc. (No. 8226); Mattel, Inc. (No. 8227); The Porter Chemical Co. (No. 8228); Multiple Products Co. (No. 8229); Halsam Products Co. (No. 8230); Horsman Dolls, Inc. (No. 8241); Tonka Toys, Inc. (No. 8242); Fisher-Price Toys, Inc. (No. 8243); Radio Steel & Mfg. Co. (No. 8244); Wen-Mac Corp. (No. 8245); The Hubley Manufacturing Co. (No. 8254); Milton Bradley Co. (No. 8256); Hamilton Steel Products, Inc. (No. 8257); and Hassen Bros., Inc. (No. 8258).

275 The Grand Union Company v. FTC, No. 26553, 2d Cir. (argued October 10, 1961, decided February 7, 1962; 300 F.2d 92).

276 American News Company & Union News Company v. FTC, No. 26857, 2d Cir. (argued October 10, 1961, decided February 7, 1962).

'and it shall also be unlawful for any such person to receive such benefits' or they are deleting from 2(f) the words 'discrimination in price which is prohibited by this section' and substituting the words 'any of the benefits set forth in 2(d) above.' As Commissioner Tait so directly says in his clarion dissent, the decision 'in effect, legislates a new antitrust prohibition.'

Referring to the Commission's decision, Professor Handler, who has long been an astute analyst of developments in the antitrust field, has said: 'The plain implication of the opinion is that the Commission, whenever it discovers limitations in legislative language which cannot be overcome by the liberal processes of statutory construction, can utilize the convenient vagueness of the concept of 'unfair methods of competition' as an independent source of power 'to supply what Congress has studiously omitted.'

In the majority opinion, it was stated:

. . . We do not agree that the Commission's opinion here represents an attempt to 'supply what Congress has studiously omitted.'

The majority concluded that:

The Commission's decision here is entirely consistent with the basic purpose and policy of Section 5 of the Federal Trade Commission Act. That section did not define 'unfair competition'; the concept was left flexible, so that the Commission could apply the broad Congressional standard to the myriad fact situations which would arise. The Act was intended to give the Commission the power to 'hit at every trade practice, then existing or thereafter contrived, which restrained competition or might lead to such restraint if not stopped in its incipient stages.' *F.T.C.* v. *Cement Institute, Inc., supra,* 333 U.S. 683, 693. Activity which 'runs counter to the public policy declared in the Sherman and Clayton Acts' is an unfair method of competition. . . .

Petitioner further contends that the Commission must prove injury to competition as an element of the Section 5 violation. We disagree. Section 2(d) defines an offense which is illegal *per se. F.T.C.* v. *Simplicity Pattern Co.,* 360 U.S. 55. There is no reason why this rule should not apply to the buyer as well as to the seller. Congress has made no such distinction. . . .

Chapter VI

SOME DISCRIMINATIONS ARE CRIMINAL OFFENSES— THE BORAH-VAN NUYS AMENDMENT

TEXT

The Borah–Van Nuys Amendment was added to the Robinson-Patman Act as Section 3 of that law. Its provisions are:

It shall be unlawful for any person engaged in commerce, in the course of such commerce, to be a party to, or assist in, any transaction of sale, or contract to sell, which discriminates to his knowledge against competitors of the purchaser, in that, any discount, rebate, allowance, or advertising service charge is granted to the purchaser over and above any discount, rebate, allowance, or advertising service charge available at the time of such transaction to said competitors in respect of a sale of goods of like grade, quality, and quantity; to sell, or contract to sell, goods in any part of the United States at prices lower than those exacted by said person elsewhere in the United States for the purpose of destroying competition, or eliminating a competitor in such part of the United States; or, to sell, or contract to sell, goods at unreasonably low prices for the purpose of destroying competition or eliminating a competitor.

Any person violating any of the provisions of this section shall, upon conviction thereof, be fined not more than $5,000 or imprisoned not more than one year, or both.

EXPLANATION OF THE AMENDMENT

Section 3 of the Robinson-Patman Act prohibits three kinds of trade practices: (a) general price discriminations, (b) geographical price dis-

167

criminations, and (c) selling "at unreasonably low prices for the purpose of destroying competition or eliminating a competitor."

This Section contains the operative and penal provisions of what was originally the Borah–Van Nuys bill (S. 4171). The first clause applies to discriminations in discounts, rebates, allowances, or advertising service charges between purchasers of goods of like quantity, grade, and quality. The second clause forbids the sale of goods by a party in one part of the United States at prices lower than exacted by that party in another part of the United States for the purpose of destroying competition, or eliminating a competitor at the point, or in the section in which the price reduction is made. The last clause prohibits the sale of goods at unreasonably low prices for the purpose of destroying competition or eliminating a competitor.

The Section does not conflict in any way with the provisions of the Act which were contained in the original Robinson-Patman Bill. It opens up a second line of approach to the regulation and control of acts in restraint of trade or tending to destroy competition. Its application to forms of illegal price discrimination, and, therefore, to effective enforcement, are not as specific as contained in other Robinson-Patman provisions. It applies only to discriminations as between purchasers of like quantities, and like quantities of goods of like grade and quality. Proof of knowledge is also required, and by reason of this fact penalties may be avoided by altering the size of orders.

However, if a buyer or seller should knowingly be drawn into a discrimination under the conditions specified in this section, he may not offer in defense that the discrimination was warranted by a difference in cost, or that it was justified under the other exemptions provided in the Robinson-Patman section.

In order to establish a guilty motive in the sale of goods at lower prices in one part of the country than in another, or at unreasonably low prices for the purpose of destroying a competitor or competition, proof of such a purpose on the part of the party charged with the violation is required. The burden of proof in such instances is on the government enforcing agency. Although it may be difficult to prove the purpose required by the Act, yet it is established by prior court decisions that purpose may be *inferred* from actions, conduct, and the character implied to them by all the connecting facts and circumstances. If loss-leader sales were used for the purpose of destroying localized competition, or if a jury and a court were convinced that they were used for this purpose, the seller using them would be liable to the penalties.

LEGISLATIVE HISTORY

In the hearings before the Committees on the Judiciary in the Senate and the House, in the reports of such committees on the Robinson and Patman bills, and in the conference report on the bills, very little was said or recorded about the Borah–Van Nuys Amendment. The brief statement in the conference report to the House on the Patman bill was to the following effect:

> Subsection (h) of the Senate amendment, which was not contained in the House bill, was accepted by the House conferees, and, except for the paragraph relating to cooperatives, separately treated in section 4 below, appears in the conference report as section 3 of the bill itself. It contains the operative and penal provisions of what was originally the Borah–Van Nuys bill (S. 4171). While they overlap in some respects, they are in no way inconsistent with the provisions of the Clayton Act amendment provided for in section 1. Section 3 authorizes nothing which that amendment prohibits, and takes nothing from it. On the contrary, where only civil remedies and liabilities attach to violations of the amendment provided in section 1, section 3 sets up special prohibitions as to the particular offenses therein described and attaches to them also the criminal penalties therein provided.
>
> Section 3 also makes it possible for the person subjected to a discrimination prohibited therein to cause the offender to be prosecuted in the Federal court of the district in which such violation is committed.[277]

Neither Senator Borah nor Senator Van Nuys made clear whether it was their intention to have their amendment apply as an amendment to the Clayton Antitrust law and thereby be embraced as a part of the "antitrust laws."

When the conference report was being considered in the House, Representative Miller, a House conferee supporting the bill, made the following statements:

> The penalty of triple damages is the old law. In other words, we made no change in that particular provision of the Clayton Act. Section 3, which the gentleman from New York talks about, is the Borah–Van Nuys amendment, and that is the criminal section of this bill. The first part of the bill has nothing to do with criminal offenses. It deals primarily, in my opinion, with the authority of the Federal Trade Commission to regulate and enforce the provisions of section 2 of the Clayton Act, as amended. Section 3 in the bill is placed in an effort to make the criminal offense apply only to that particular section, and I believe that is a reasonable construction, if you will look at the bill. . . .

---

[277] H.R. REP. No. 2951, 74th Cong., 2d Sess. 8 (1936).

Mr. Hancock of New York. Is it not perfectly clear that any vendor who discriminates in price between purchasers is guilty of a crime and is also subject to triple damages to anyone who claims to be aggrieved?

Mr. Miller: That is true, but the criminal part is included in section 3 and section 3 only.

Mr. Hancock of New York. But it is part of the same act?

Mr. Miller. Of course it is, but it is not a part of the Clayton Act as amended by section 2. It ought to be, as far as that is concerned, if a seller willfully discriminates.[278]

* * *

Mr. Hancock of New York. If a vendor is found guilty of discrimination as provided in this bill, is he subject to the aggrieved party for damages or has he committed a crime and subjected himself to penalty?

Mr. Celler. If he violates the Borah–Van Nuys provision or the other provision of the bill he is subject to penalties of a criminal nature and has committed an offense.

Mr. Hancock of New York. Would he also be liable for triple damages?

Mr. Celler. And he would also have to respond in triple damages under the provisions of the Clayton Act. Anyone aggrieved can sue.[279]

Congressman Celler, who thus participated in the debate on that occasion, is serving as chairman of the House Committee on the Judiciary in the 87th Congress, as he has for the terms of several previous Congresses. That Committee is the legislative committee of the House having jurisdiction over the Clayton Act, the Robinson-Patman Act, and amendments thereto. It would seem that the legislative history of the Robinson-Patman Act and the Borah-Van Nuys Amendment provides support for the argument presented by Mr. Celler on the occasion referred to, because both Sections 2 and 3 of the Robinson-Patman Act deal with and prohibit certain types of price discriminations. In view of that fact, questions inevitably follow as to why suits for triple damages for price discrimination under Section 2 should not be allowed when the discriminating practice is of the same kind condemned by Section 3 of the Robinson-Patman Act.

Senator Borah made clear that his purpose in offering the Borah-Van Nuys Amendment was merely to inhibit conduct as a matter of law "without intervention of the discriminatory power of the Federal Trade Commission or other bureaus." He said, "That, it seems to us, should be prohibited as a matter of law, and that there need not be any discrimination laid anywhere with reference to the execution of that kind of law."

---

[278] 80 Cong. Rec. 9421 (1936).
[279] Id. at 9420.

During the discussion of the conference report in the Senate, Senator Vandenberg stated:

> Mr. President, I should like to ask the Senator from Indiana one or two questions about the conference report.
>
> The fact has been called to my attention that section 3 of the bill, as agreed upon in conference, makes certain discriminations punishable by fine and also subject to treble damages, while similar discriminations under section 2(b) would be subject to rebuttal by showing, for instance, that a reduced price was made in good faith to meet an equally low price of a competitor. In other words, it is asserted to me that the defense allowed under section 2(b) is not permitted under section 3, although the act or the offense would be the same.[280]

In reply, Senator Van Nuys, one of the Senate conferees, did not contest the statement about civil and criminal penalties, but instead addressed his remarks to the contention concerning the defense:

> I think the Senator is mistaken there. The proviso to which he refers is simply a rule of evidence rather than a part of the substantive law. If a prima-facie case is made against an alleged unfair practice, the respondent may rebut the prima facie (sic) case by showing that his lower prices were made in good faith to meet the prices of a competitor. That is a rule of evidence rather than substantive law.[281]

Congressman Utterbach, the chairman of the managers of the House conferees on the Robinson and Patman bills, in remarking on the point as to whether the Borah–Van Nuys Amendment amended the Clayton Act, stated:

> Section 3 of the bill sets aside certain practices therein described and attaches to their commission the criminal penalties of fine and imprisonment therein provided. It does not affect the scope or operation of the prohibitions or limitations laid down by the *Clayton Act amendment provided for in section 1*. It authorizes nothing therein prohibited. It detracts nothing from them. Most of the acts which it does prohibit lie also within the prohibitions of that amendment. In that sphere this section merely attaches to them its criminal penalties in addition to the civil liabilities and remedies already provided by the Clayton Act. [Emphasis added.][282]

These conclusions drawn from the legislative history of the Robinson-Patman Act and the Borah–Van Nuys Amendment were echoed by one of the authors (Patman) some 14 years later in testimony before the antitrust subcommittee of the House Committee on the Judiciary, when he said:

---

[280] *Id.* at 9903.
[281] *Id.* at 9903.
[282] *Id.* at 9419.

. . . it happens that section 3, the criminal section of the Robinson-Patman Act, was not, under the terms of that act, made an amendment to the Clayton Act. Moreover, section 3 of the Robinson-Patman Act has never been added to the list of laws designated as "antitrust laws" in section 1 of the Clayton Act.[283]

ENFORCEMENT

It has been pointed out that Section 3 of the Robinson-Patman Act contains three clearly defined subsections. The first of those is general discriminations. It condemns every "knowing" participant in any discriminatory sale or arrangement. It thus makes liable not only the parties to a contract of sale and purchase, but any other party connected with negotiations resulting in a transaction that proves to be discriminatory, whether in fact performed or not. This provision, however, contains limitations not attaching to the prohibitions contained in subsection 2(a) of the Act. For example, it penalizes concessions that are in no way "available" to disfavored parties. Also, it is limited to transactions "of like quantity." However, this provision is not subject to the limitations attaching to the provisions of subsection 2(a) requiring a showing of adverse effect on competition. Neither are actions under this provision defendable on a showing of cost justification or on the grounds of "good faith meeting of competition," as are actions arising under subsection 2(a).

The second provision of Section 3 makes illegal predatory practices involving destructive discriminations utilized for the purpose of destroying competition.

The third provision prohibits sales at "unreasonably low price" when made for the purpose of destroying competition or eliminating a competitor.

Despite the care that was taken in providing for the clear purposes of the Section, the Department of Justice, as the agency charged with the responsibility for the enforcement of that provision of the law, has done little to enforce it. It is common knowledge that in the past the Department of Justice has not enforced and has had little sympathy for Section 3 of the Robinson-Patman Act as a criminal law against predatory pricing practices.

Indeed, the group who formulated the majority view for the report of the Attorney General's Committee To Study the Antitrust Laws in 1955 approved the failure of the Department of Justice to enforce Section 3 of the Robinson-Patman Act. That report acknowledged that:

---

[283] *Hearing on H.R. 7905, before the Antitrust Subcommittee of the House Committee on the Judiciary,* 81st Cong., 2d Sess., ser. 14, pt. 5, at 48 (1950).

Although Congress authorized the Department of Justice and local United States attorneys to enforce Section 3, public enforcement organs have largely forsaken this law.

The Government's reluctance to enforce Section 3 has relegated its enforcement to private treble damage litigants.[284]

The Attorney General's Committee went further. It recommended the repeal of Section 3 of the Robinson-Patman Act as "dangerous surplusage."[285]

During the first 20 years following the enactment of Section 3, the Department of Justice brought three cases that involved charges of violation of this Section.[286] All three cases were dismissed. The Section 3 charges involved in the *Petroleum Institute* case and in the *Borden* case were voluntarily dismissed on the motion of the United States government. The charge in the *Bowman* case resulted in acquittal following the government's motion for dismissal in the *Borden* case.

In a fairly recent case,[287] where the Department of Justice pressed for prosecution of a violation of Section 3, the defendant plead guilty and was assessed a fine of $25,000.

Following the disposition of that case, the Department of Justice proceeded, in a somewhat similar situation, against the practice of area price discrimination. One count in a 15-count indictment against National Dairy Products Corporation charged a violation of Section 3. This indictment was returned by a Grand Jury sitting at Kansas City, Missouri, in 1959–1960. Early in 1961, the United States District Court dismissed the count that charged a violation of Section 3, holding that the Section was unconstitutional because, in the Court's view, it was too vague and uncertain.

The fact that the government instituted so few actions to enforce Section 3 relegated its enforcement largely to private treble-damage litigants. These private litigants picked up the torch, but with little success. Although plaintiffs prevailed in some of these cases,[288] the courts apparently assumed, but did not expressly pass upon the constitutionality of Section 3. This is probably due to the fact that the litigants in those cases did not directly and squarely present issues on that point. One aspect of Section 3 that has been clearly and authoritatively interpreted and disposed of by the Supreme Court is the question of whether proceedings brought by private litigants

---

[284] ATT'Y GEN. NAT'L COMM. ANTITRUST REP. 199 (1955).
[285] *Id.* at 201.
[286] U.S. v. American Petroleum Institute, Civ. No. 8524, D.D.C. 1940; U.S. v. Bowman Dairy Co., 48 Cr. 361; U.S. v. Borden Co., 48 Cr. 362 (N.D. Ill. 1949).
[287] U.S. v. Fairmont Foods, Inc. (U.S. District Court, Mid-district of Michigan, 1958).
[288] Moore v. Mead, 348 U.S. 115 (1954); F & A Ice Cream Co. v. Arden Farms, 98 F. Supp. 180 (S.D. Col. 1951). *Compare* dicta in Bruce's Juices v. American Can Co., 330 U.S. 743, 750 (1947).

on the ground that private remedies are afforded by Sections 4 and 16 of the Clayton Act may be based on the violation of Section 3 of the Robinson-Patman Act. The Supreme Court, by a five-to-four decision on January 20, 1958, decided in each of two cases[289] that Section 3 of the Robinson-Patman Act is not available to private litigants in civil treble-damage cases because it is not to be considered as embraced by the "antitrust laws."

In its opinion in the *Nashville Milk Company* case, the Supreme Court held that:

> The Robinson-Patman Act, consisting of four sections, convincingly shows on its face that Section 3 does not amend the Clayton Act, but stands on its own footing and carries its own sanctions. . . .
>
> The important thing to note is that this section, in contrast to Section 1 of the Robinson-Patman Act, does not on its face amend the Clayton Act. Further, Section 3 contains only penal sanctions for violation of its provisions; in the absence of a clear expression of congressional intent to the contrary, these sanctions should under familiar principles be considered exclusive, rather than supplemented by civil sanctions of a distinct statute. See *D. R. Wilder Mfg. Co.* v. *Corn Products Refining Co.,* 236 U.S. 165, 174–175.

To that ruling there was sharp dissent by Mr. Justice Douglas, with whom the Chief Justice, Mr. Justice Black, and Mr. Justice Brennan concurred. In their dissent they stated:

> The treble damage provision of the Clayton Act was written into the law so as to provide incentives for private as well as governmental patrol of the antitrust field. Not a word in the legislative history of the Robinson-Patman Act suggests that this special remedy was to be denied to Section 3 actions and granted to those under Section 2. The fair intendment seems to have been that Section 3 was to be added to the body of "antitrust laws." The mechanical device used was an amendment to one section of the Clayton Act.
>
> In resolving all ambiguities against the grant of vitality to Section 3, we forget that the treble damage technique for law enforcement was designed as an effective, if not the most effective, method of deterring violators of the Act. . . .
>
> As the Court notes, it appears that the Department of Justice has never enforced the criminal provisions of Section 3 of the Robinson-Patman Act. Because of the Court's holding that Section 3 is not available in civil actions to private parties, the statute has in effect been repealed. It is apparent that the opponents of the Robinson-Patman Act have eventually managed to achieve in this Court what they could not do in Congress.

In Congress, there was prompt reaction to the decision of the Court in the *Nashville Milk Co.* case. On January 23, 1958, three days following the

---

[289] Nashville Milk Co. v. Carnation Co., 355 U.S. 373; Safeway Stores, Inc. v. Vance, 355 U.S. 389.

five-to-four decision in the *Nashville Milk* case, Senator John Sparkman, chairman of the Senate Small Business Committee, and Congressman Wright Patman, chairman of the House Small Business Committee, introduced companion bills in the 85th Congress that provided that Section 1 of the Clayton Act should be amended so that there would be no question about Section 3 of the Robinson-Patman Act being embraced as a part of the antitrust laws. These bills were referred to the Committees on the Judiciary, as are all proposed amendments to the antitrust laws. No action was taken. At the beginning of the 86th Congress, in January, 1959, similar bills were introduced for the same purpose, but no action was taken on them.

In addition, the chairman of the House Small Business Committee introduced H.R. 10235 in the 86th Congress. That bill would have amended the Federal Trade Commission Act by adding to that law a new section that would have contained, with some modifications, the provisions appearing in the existing Section 3 of the Robinson-Patman Act. A provision was added, making it clear that persons injured by things prohibited by this new section would have the right to sue for treble damages for the injuries sustained. That bill was referred to the House Committee on Interstate and Foreign Commerce, since that is the committee having jurisdiction over legislation concerning the Federal Trade Commission. Hearings were held on the bill on June 16 and 17, 1960, but due to the fact that it was so near the end of the term of the 86th Congress, no report was made by the Committee on the bill.

At the opening of the 87th Congress, the chairman of the House Small Business Committee introduced a substantially changed version of H.R. 10235 of the 86th Congress. The new bill, H.R. 127, would amend the Federal Trade Commission Act by adding a section prohibiting sales of commodities at "unreasonably low prices" if the seller is charging higher or different prices for the same product in other parts of the country. The bill was subjected to serious consideration by the House Committee on Interstate and Foreign Commerce and by the enforcement agencies of the Federal government.

In the meantime, negotiations were undertaken between representatives of the Antitrust Division of the United States Department of Justice and attorneys representing the big electrical companies that had been convicted of a violation of the Sherman Act for unlawfully fixing prices on electrical products. These negotiations were for the purpose of working out consent decrees in civil actions growing out of the criminal cases in which the electrical companies had been convicted. Persistent reports were to the

effect that representatives of the Department of Justice were insisting that
the consent decrees in the civil actions contain a provision that would prohibit the electric companies from making sales of any product in any part
of the country at "unreasonably low prices," but that the General Electric
Company and some of the other big electric companies were objecting
strenuously to the inclusion of such a provision.

Chapter VII

COOPERATIVES AND POOL BUYING AND SELLING

Section 4 of the Robinson-Patman Act was included to provide an assurance to cooperative associations that they may return to their members net earnings or surplus resulting from their trade operations in proportion to their purchases or sales.

TEXT

Nothing in this Act shall prevent a cooperative association from returning to its members, producers, or consumers the whole, or any part of, the net earnings or surplus resulting from its trading operations, in proportion to their purchases or sales from, to, or through the association.

LEGISLATIVE HISTORY

The conference report made by the House of Representatives on the Robinson and Patman bills[290] contained the following reference to and explanation of Section 4 to amend the Clayton Act:

Substantially this same provision is found in the House bill as sub-section (g), and in the Senate amendment as a part of subsection (h). However, the words "or a cooperative wholesale association from re-turning to its constituent retail members," which appeared following the word "consumers" in the Senate amendment, have been elimi-nated. As so modified, this section serves to safeguard producer and consumer cooperatives against any charge of violation of the act based on their distribution of earnings or surplus among their members on a

---

[290] H.R. REP. No. 2951, 74th Cong., 2d Sess. (1936).

patronage basis. While the bill contains elsewhere no provisions, express or implied, to the contrary, this section is included as a precautionary reservation to protect and encourage the cooperative movement. Whether functioning as buyers or sellers, cooperatives also share under the bill the guaranties of equal treatment and equal opportunity which it seeks to accord to trade and commerce generally.

BACKGROUND AND POLICY

It has never been the policy of the Federal government to restrict the activities of industrial workers, farmers, or other producers and consumers who cooperate and organize for the purpose of obtaining fair and reasonable prices for the products of their labor. Consumers are free to set up consumer cooperatives for the purpose of effecting savings in the cost of the goods they buy.

The public policy providing for antitrust exemption for industrial workers, farmers, or other producers has been expressed in Section 6 of the Clayton Antitrust Act.[291] The provisions of that Section are as follows:

> That the labor of a human being is not a commodity or article of commerce. Nothing contained in the antitrust laws shall be construed to forbid the existence and operation of labor, agricultural, or horticultural organizations, instituted for the purposes of mutual help, and not having capital stock or conducted for profits, or to forbid or restrain individual members of such organizations from lawfully carrying out the legitimate objects thereof; nor shall such organizations, or the members thereof, be held or construed to be illegal combinations or conspiracies in restraint of trade under the antitrust laws.

On February 18, 1922, the Capper-Volstead Act became law.[292] The Capper-Volstead Act broadened the Clayton Act exemption from antitrust laws with respect to agricultural cooperatives. It included cooperatives with capital stock and specified that they may act together in associations, corporate or otherwise, in collectively processing, preparing for market, handling, and marketing in interstate and foreign commerce the products of persons so engaged, and that they and their members may make contracts and agreements to effect such purposes. Only in Section 2 of that law was there placed a limitation on the collective actions of such associations and their members for the purposes indicated. The limitations were to the effect that they were not to monopolize or restrain trade in interstate or foreign commerce to such an extent that the price of any agricultural product is unduly enhanced by reason thereof.

[291] 15 U.S.C.A. § 17 (1958 Ed.).
[292] 7 U.S.C. 291.

Appropriation bills usually contain special provisos for further protection of producer cooperatives, with language to the following effect:

> That no part of this appropriation shall be expended for the prosecution of any organization or individual for entering into any combination or agreement having in view the increasing of wages, shortening of hours or bettering the conditions of labor, or for any act done in furtherance thereof, not in itself unlawful:
>
> Provided further, That no part of this appropriation shall be expended for the prosecution of producers of farm products and associations of farmers who cooperate and organize in an effort to and for the purpose to obtain and maintain a fair and reasonable price for their products.

We have noted the special provision set forth in Section 4 of the Robinson-Patman Act for cooperatives. However, it must be understood that the scope of such a provision is quite limited.

In their business activities as buyers or sellers, cooperative associations are extended no special dispensations or exemptions under the Act. They must conform to its provisions in the same manner as any other party or firm engaged in commerce under the jurisdiction of the laws of the United States. This applies whether the cooperative organizations consist of consumers, farmers, retailers, wholesalers, or other forms of cooperative associations. If, as a single unit or entity, they engage in buying and selling, they are governed the same as any other business entity.

They must recognize and abide by the same prohibitions and limitations set up by the Act. They receive the same competitive advantages. They may buy on the same differential of economically sound savings in cost that any business or corporate unit enjoys. They may receive the advantages in lower prices that the economies of their set-up or form of doing business entitles them to obtain. They are subject to the same penalties for violation as any other party or firm.

The only special dispensation they receive is the fact that the previously mentioned clauses in the appropriation laws prohibit the expenditure of funds appropriated by enforcement of the antitrust laws for the purpose of prosecuting farmer and laborer organizations. Though they may be exempt from prosecution by Federal authorities, they still remain liable to the civil-suit-and-damages clause of the Robinson-Patman Act.

The Act does not prohibit the formation of voluntary chains of independently owned retail stores or wholesaler organizations. It does not prevent retailers from organizing their own wholesaling unit, nor does it legislate against the practice of wholesalers in setting up their own chain of retail outlets wherever they may choose to do so. There is nothing in the

Act, however, that exempts any of these types of organizations from the provisions or limitations of the antitrust laws as a whole.

Moreover, the Act does not accord them any special privileges or dispensations. They must govern their commercial transactions in relation to the provisions of the Act in the same manner that any other form of business enterprise is required to do. Under the Act, they are entitled to receive the benefit of whatever economies of operation their type of organization is able to effect. Wherever they are discriminated against beyond the limitations set up by the Act, they have the usual recourse, in all its phases, that the Act affords as their protection against unfair discrimination. They likewise are subject to the penalties that the Act provides for violation of its provisions.

Whether their membership consists of consumers, producers, retailers, wholesalers, or manufacturers, the Act imposes no limitation on cooperatives that is not placed on others performing similar production or distribution functions. Cooperative retailers, for example, who buy in wholesale quantities comparable to the volume purchases of chains, and with the same economy of methods, are entitled to the same scale of discounts and proportionally equal allowances for services or facilities. To whatever extent quantities, methods, and value of services and facilities vary, they are entitled to consideration in proportion to the differences in cost or values involved. There is nothing in the Act, however, that *requires* a seller to make any discrimination between classes of purchasers. Its provisions apply only when a seller, of his own free will or by coercive influence, makes a discrimination in favor of a particular purchaser.

A cooperative cannot compel a seller, under the Act, to sell to it on the ground that he is selling to a competing chain. That is a seller's choice. But if he is selling to both he must treat them alike, and any concessions to one must be conceded to the other on proportionally equal terms.

Some indications of the limited scope of the exemption provided cooperatives by Section 4 of the Robinson-Patman Act are found in the records of a number of proceedings that which have been instituted by the Federal Trade Commission and other enforcement agencies. The records of these proceedings make clear that Section 4 of the Robinson-Patman Act provides no exemption for cooperatives from the application of any provision of the antitrust laws other than the exemptions set forth in the Robinson-Patman Act itself. Moreover, it is quite clear that exemption from the application of the provisions of the Robinson-Patman Act is only with respect to the distribution of net earnings and surplus to members of the cooperatives. The exemption has nothing whatsoever to do with discriminations practiced either in the purchase of merchandise or in the sale of it by cooperatives.

Among the proceedings that have been instituted by the Federal Trade Commission against cooperatives for violations of the Robinson-Patman Act are several involving wholesalers and jobbers of automotive parts who join themselves together to engage in group and cooperative buying effort. In Chapter V, footnote 266 we have listed 11 such proceedings (all except items 1 and 13). Other proceedings of that kind are cited in footnotes 267, 268, and 269.

These proceedings have involved charges against each of a number of buying corporations that were formed by a group of wholesalers and jobbers engaged in the sale and distribution of automotive parts and supplies. Each of these groups was charged with having endorsed or knowingly received unjustified price discriminations prohibited by subsection 2(a) of the Robinson-Patman Act.

As has been pointed out in Chapter V, orders to cease and desist have been entered by the Federal Trade Commission in a number of these proceedings. Reference has been made to the fact that the order of the Commission in the case of the *American Motor Specialties Company* was affirmed by the United States Circuit Court of Appeals for the Second Circuit on May 5, 1960, and that the Supreme Court of the United States denied certiorari on November 2, 1960. A number of other similar cases have reached or are on their way to the courts of appeals for review and decision.

Of course, in Chapter III, we have pointed out that subsection 2(c) has been invoked in the *Biddle* and *Oliver* cases against the action of cooperative buying groups for the acceptance and receipt of brokerage payments prohibited by provisions of subsection 2(c) of the Robinson-Patman Act. As was noted, the orders of the Federal Trade Commission to cease and desist in those cases were sustained by the court.

The Federal Trade Commission issued a complaint against the Central Arkansas Milk Producers Association.[293] In that complaint, the Commission alleged that the respondent association and its members were engaged in price-fixing agreements in violation of Section 5 of the Federal Trade Commission Act in the sale of dairy products at discriminatory prices in violation of subsection 2(a) of the Robinson-Patman Act. Earlier, the Supreme Court of the United States, in the case of *United States v. Maryland and Virginia Milk Producers Association, Inc.* (362 U.S. 458, May 2, 1960), had held that a cooperative association of dairy

---

[293] No. 8391, FTC, issued May 5, 1961, date for answering specified as July 18, 1961.

farmers, organized under and pursuant to the terms of the Capper-Volstead Act, were not exempt from the antimerger provisions of Section 7 of the Clayton Antitrust Act.[294] Previously, the Supreme Court had ruled that neither the provisions of Section 6 of the Clayton Antitrust Act nor the provisions of the Capper-Volstead Act exempt from the applications of the antitrust laws agreements in restraint of trade made by and between members of the Capper-Volstead Act Association and other bodies who were not producers.[295]

QUESTIONS AND OPINIONS

No. 97. Question. Are consumer cooperatives exempt under the price and discrimination sections of the Act?

Opinion. Consumer cooperatives are not exempted. They are treated the same as any other type of business enterprise or entity.

No. 98. Question. When the bill was written and passed, was it intended to make it of assistance to cooperatives?

Opinion. It was not intended to help nor to harm cooperatives. The bill was intended to protect and assist all forms of enterprise in securing equal treatment in trade and commerce. It prohibits discriminations between any form of business entity exceeding the economic difference in costs or value of services and facilities rendered.

No. 99. Question. Are cooperatives entitled to special prices?

Opinion. The Act does not require that a seller make any discrimination between purchasers, whether they are cooperatives or others. It only provides the limitations beyond which the seller may not go, if he elects to discriminate in favor of one purchaser or class of purchasers.

No. 100. Question. Will the Robinson-Patman Act prevent a cooperative from paying or distributing to its members the net earnings or surplus resulting from its trading operations?

Opinion. A special provision, Section 4 of the Act, removes all question of the right of cooperatives to distribute their earnings to their membership in proportion to their purchases or sales from, to, or through the association. Of course, their earnings must be legally acquired, like the earnings of any other concern.

No. 101. Question. What effect will the Act have on cooperative buying organizations? Will it be lawful for a wholesaler to belong to such an organization and participate in brokerage allowances to the organization in

---

[294] 15 U.S.C. 18.
[295] See U.S. vs Borden Co. 308 U.S. 188; see also F.T.C. Docket 6074 in the Matter of Florida Citrus Mutual et al., O.C.D. May 6, 1957.

accordance with the volume of his purchases made through the organization?

Opinion. The Act specifically prohibits payment of brokerage or other compensation by a seller to a buyer or any agent under the direct or indirect control of the purchaser. This precludes the payment of brokerage on the mere basis that the buyer has rendered a service to the seller by buying his merchandise. In the mere transaction of buying and selling, no particular service is rendered by the buyer to the seller that is not balanced by a similar valuable service rendered in exchange by the seller to the buyer. On such mutual grounds, the wholesaler's buying organization is not entitled to collect brokerage from sellers. But any earnings that a wholesaler cooperative may legally receive under the Act may be distributed to members in proportion to their purchases through the organization.

No. 102. Question. Under this law, can a manufacturer sell direct to an individual, collect direct from him, and give him a discount because he is a member of a group of buyers?

Opinion. He may not do so on the basis of the mere fact that the individual is a member of a group-buying organization. In the above question, that is the only condition implied. There is no savings in cost mentioned, nor is it implied that any savings in cost is effected.

No. 103. Question. We are contemplating organizing our local retailers into a cooperative buying group. Can we operate within the scope of the Robinson-Patman Act?

Opinion. Yes. In event of discriminations made by sellers between their various purchasers, you must receive similar treatment to the extent of the savings and economies that your type of operation and methods make possible.

No. 104. Question. May a seller make members of buying groups certain lower prices because they are members?

Opinion. Not on that basis alone. Two of his customers may be in competition with each other. One is a member of a buying group, the other is not. Each requires the same service; there is no difference in its cost. Therefore, a discrimination in price may not be made in favor of one just because he happens to be a member of a buying organization.

No. 105. Question. Can organizations and cooperative group-buying agencies continue to function and obtain brokerage allowances and payments from sellers?

Opinion. This is made very difficult under the Act. Discrimination on the part of sellers who sell to such agencies must not result. There must be more involved than the mutual, self-balancing services in sales transactions between buyers and sellers. If sellers confine their entire distribution through group-buying organizations of this type and do not discriminate between groups or group members in excess of the limitations provided by the Act, then it is likely that it is possible to function legally in the manner stated. However, this method of operating must continue to bear close scrutiny. Each set-up and each transaction must stand on its own feet.

No. 106. Question. Would a wholesaler controlling retail outlets be permitted to give a special rebate to these outlets and not to uncontrolled outlets?

Opinion. Not on that sole ground alone. An economic difference in cost must be demonstrated.

No. 107. Question. Can a cooperative buying group that has been getting a quantity discount continue to earn it?

Opinion. Yes, if that discount is earned within the limitations and provisions of the Robinson-Patman Act. It must render services and savings to the seller that justify him in making a price differential in its favor.

No. 108. Question. We give one buying syndicate a specific discount in return for a specific service rendered to us, but refuse it to other buying syndicates that cannot render that service. Is this permissible?

Opinion. It is permissible, if it comes within the legal limitations set up in the Act. For your own protection, you should be able at any time to prove that the specific service rendered to you by the first syndicate is worth the difference in price, and that the second syndicate cannot render that service. Fortify yourself with proof.

No. 109. Question. We have a special working arrangement with head-quarters buying organizations whereby even though the members take only one case at a time, they qualify for the maximum quantity discount. Can we continue?

Opinion. Under the Act, discriminations between purchasers cannot be made on the sole basis of membership in a buying organization. The economic differences in cost must still govern.

No. 110. Question. May a manufacturer quote wholesalers, retailers, and consumer cooperatives the same price on similar purchases of like grade, quality, and quantity, under similar conditions of delivery and service?

Opinion. Yes. However, discriminations between this type of purchaser and other types of purchasers may be justified on differences in cost.

No. 111. Question. We have a farm organization in this county that contemplates pooling their business and placing it with firms for cash discounts below the price offered to the public as a whole. Will this be a violation of the law?

Opinion. There is nothing in the Act that prohibits the organization of farmer consumer cooperatives and their securing of the advantages in price that they may be able to obtain by reason of the economies of their set-up. However, the Robinson-Patman Act applies to any illegal discriminations by which the organization may benefit, just as it applies in the case of other types of purchasers. The organization is likewise protected by the Act, in that no other purchasers may obtain illegal price discriminations that are unfair, or injurious to the farm cooperative.

No. 112. Question. Is it proper and legal to organize a corporation among members of a Federal Farm Bureau for the sale of electric appliances and other merchandise?

Opinion. This is not prohibited in any manner by the Act. After it is organized, however, it must govern its buying practices in accordance with the provisions of the Act. No party, firm, or corporation engaged regularly in interstate commerce is exempted. There is nothing in the Act that prevents a cooperative organization from paying its earnings or savings over to its membership in proportion to their sales or purchases through the organization.

CONCLUSION

No provision of the Robinson-Patman Act increases the liabilities of cooperatives under provisions of other antitrust laws. The only application of the Robinson-Patman Act to cooperatives would be based on either the sale at unjustified discriminatory prices or the knowing receipt of unjustified price discriminations. Of course, prohibitions against the payment or receipt of illegitimate brokerage violative of subsection 2(c), the payment for advertising allowances violative of subsection 2(d), or the furnishing of services and facilities violative of subsection 2(e) would apply to cooperatives.

Chapter VIII

HOW THE ROBINSON-PATMAN ACT IS ENFORCED

PROVISIONS FOR ENFORCEMENT

The Federal Trade Commission and the Department of Justice are the Federal government agencies entrusted with concurrent authority to enforce Section 2 of the Clayton Act as amended by the Robinson-Patman Act.[296] The authority given to the Federal Trade Commission to enforce the provisions of Section 2 of the Robinson-Patman Act is provided for in Section 11 of the Clayton Act.[297] The authority for the United States Department of Justice to enforce those provisions is provided by Section 15 of the Clayton Act.[298] In addition, the Department of Justice is empowered to institute criminal proceedings in the United States District Courts for violation of Section 3 (the Borah-Van Nuys amendment) of the Robinson-Patman Act.[299]

Section 4 of the Clayton Act provides that any person who shall be injured in his business or property by reason of anything forbidden in the antitrust laws may sue therefor in any district court of the United States in the district in which the defendant resides or is found or has an agent, without respect to the amount in controversy, and shall recover threefold the damages by him sustained, and the cost of suit, including a reasonable attorney's fee.[300]

Section 16 of the Clayton Act[301] provides that private parties shall be

---

[296] 15 U.S.C. 13.
[297] 15 U.S.C. 22.
[298] 15 U.S.C. 26.
[299] 15 U.S.C. 13a.
[300] 15 U.S.C. 15.
[301] 15 U.S.C. 27.

entitled to sue for and have injunctive relief in any court of the United States having jurisdiction over the parties against threatened loss or damage by a violation of the antitrust laws.

Section 2 of the Clayton Act as amended by the Robinson-Patman Act is, of course, a provision of the "antitrust laws."

FEDERAL TRADE COMMISSION

Voluntary Compliance

The Federal Trade Commission expends a considerable amount of its resources and efforts to inform businessmen and their representatives about the requirements of the law and thereby promote voluntary compliance. This is done in several ways, which are discussed below in question-and-answer form.

No. 113. Question. Does the Federal Trade Commission render advisory opinions concerning trade problems?

Opinion. No. However, the Commission is anxious to be of assistance and will provide representatives of an industry beset with unfair trade practices with opportunities for conferences and with assistance for promulgating statements of what are unfair practices.

No. 114. Question. Does the Federal Trade Commission issue guides to help businessmen understand their obligations under the law?

Opinion. Yes. In Chapter IV, we discussed at length the action of the Federal Trade Commission in adopting and releasing on May 19, 1960, a statement of *Guides for Advertising Allowances and Other Merchandising Payments and Services; Compliance with Sections 2(d) and 2(e) of the Clayton Act, as Amended By the Robinson-Patman Act.*

No. 115. Question. Are Federal Trade Commission "Guides" binding on the FTC or the courts?

Opinion. No. The "Guides" are only interpretations of the law, although it is presumed that the law thus interpreted by the FTC in the "Guides" will be so interpreted by the Commission in cases decided by it. It must be understood that interpretations of the law issued by the Commission are not binding on the courts, which are free to provide different interpretations. However, interpretations by the courts are usually in line with those provided by the Commission.

No. 116. Question. Does the Federal Trade Commission promulgate and publish trade-practice rules in the form of statements of what trade practices in a given industry are unfair?

Opinion. Yes. The Commission has a Bureau of Trade Practice Conferences and Industry Guides in which there is a division that is devoted to holding conferences with representatives of industry and preparing and issuing statements of trade-practice rules. When trade-practice rules applicable to a particular industry are prepared and issued, they are not binding, but are merely interpretative of what the Commission considers to be the requirements of the law.

No. 117. Question. Where trade-practice rules have been promulgated, does an FTC complaint usually refer to such rules?

Opinion. No.

No. 118. Question. Do the rules constitute a clarifying factor in answering questions about the legality or desirability of trade practices in an industry?

Opinion. Yes.

No. 119. Question. When a company violates its industry's trade-practice rules, is it charged by the FTC with breaking the rules, or with a violation of the statute?

Opinion. When the Commission proceeds, it proceeds under a complaint in which it is charged that the person proceeded against has violated the laws administered by the Commission. It is not alleged that the person has violated trade-practice rules.

Investigations

Persons having information or knowledge regarding a violation of the Robinson-Patman Act may write to the Federal Trade Commission, Washington, D.C., giving the information indicating any such violation. It is the policy of the Federal Trade Commission not to divulge the name of the person giving such information.

Once the Federal Trade Commission has had submitted to it an application from any person to the effect that any other person is engaged in violating the Robinson-Patman Act, the Commission ordinarily dockets the matter and undertakes an investigation to determine whether it should proceed against the person charged. The ensuing investigation is made by sending investigators into the field for interviews and examination of documentary materials, through written questionnaires, or through the use of both methods. When the person alleged to be in violation is first contacted, he is advised about the nature of the charges and the duty and authority of the Commission to investigate. Customarily, the person being investigated is informed regarding his obligation to furnish information as requested. At this point, such a person frequently expresses his desire to know what information he is required to furnish under the law and what his rights are regarding the matter. Quite often, these questions and problems prompt the person charged to consult an attorney for advice. In order to be of assistance to such a person and his attorney, the author has included in Appendix B a statement of the Federal Trade Commission's rules, statement of policy, organization, and procedures. It will be seen through reference to that material that anything more than elementary questions should be answered by an attorney employed to study the particular situation and provide legal advice. However, efforts will be made here to answer a few of the basic questions having possible application to Robinson-Patman Act cases arising in proceedings instituted by the Federal Trade Commission. These are stated below in question-and-answer form.

No. 120. Question. Can the Federal Trade Commission force business-men to turn over information that can be used to prosecute them for illegal business activity?

Opinion. Yes. The law provides that the Commission or its duly authorized agent or agents at all reasonable times shall have, for the purpose of examination, access to and the right to copy any documentary evidence of any corporation being investigated or proceeded against, and that the Commission has the power to require by subpoena the attendance and testimony of witnesses and the production of evidence relating to any matter under investigation.

No. 121. Question. Can the Federal Trade Commission require corporations to furnish information as to their organization, business conduct, and practices?

Opinion. Yes. The Commission has the power to investigate from time to time and to gather and compile information concerning the organization, business conduct, practices, and management of any corporation engaged in commerce, and its relationship to other corporations, individuals, associations, and partnerships.

No. 122. Question. Is there any penalty for refusal of a businessman to give information to the Federal Trade Commission or to permit an examination of documents?

Opinion. Yes. Section 10 of the Federal Trade Commission Act provides that any person who shall neglect or refuse to attend and testify, or to answer any lawful inquiry, or to produce documentary evidence if it is in his power to do so, in obedience to the subpoena or lawful requirements of the Commission, shall be guilty of an offense and, upon conviction thereof by a court of competent jurisdiction, shall be punished by a fine of not less than $1,000 nor more than $5,000, or by imprisonment of not more than one year, or by both fine and imprisonment. In addition, the

Commission is authorized to seek the aid of the district courts of the United States for compliance with subpoenas and other lawful requirements of the Commission for information from businessmen.

No. 123. Question. Is there a penalty for failure to file Federal Trade Commission "special report" orders on time, or for falsely answering any of the questions therein?

Opinion. If any corporation required by the Commission to file any annual or special report shall fail so to do within the time fixed by the Commission, and such failure shall continue for 30 days after notice of such default, the corporation shall forfeit to the United States the sum of $100 for each and every day of the continuance of such failure.

Formal Complaints

When the Commission shall have reason to believe that any person is violating or has violated any of the provisions of the Robinson-Patman Act, the law provides that it shall issue and serve on such person a complaint stating the Commission's charges and containing a notice of a hearing, showing a day and place fixed at least 30 days after the serving of the complaint. At the hearing, the person complained of has a right to appear and show cause why an order should not be entered by the Commission requiring such person to cease and desist from the violation of the law charged in the complaint.

No. 124. Question. By whom is the hearing held?

Opinion. The hearing is held before a hearing examiner, who receives evidence into a record of the case. When the taking of the evidence is completed, the hearing examiner makes the initial decision in the case, either dismissing the complaint or issuing an order to cease and desist.

No. 125. Question. May circumstantial evidence be used in formal FTC proceedings to establish violation of the Robinson-Patman Act?

Opinion. Yes. However, most of the evidence received in such cases consists of direct testimony about the discriminatory practices involved and documentary evidence which shows what the facts are.

No. 126. Question. Is an FTC hearing examiner permitted to seal evidence so that it may not be used against the respondent in private suits for treble damages?

Opinion. In some special situations, evidence relating to particular trade secrets, such as formulas, and, in some instances, certain evidence about costs of a particular firm may be sealed and made available only to the hearing, the examiner, the Commission, and the courts for consideration of the case. This is not to say that the evidence is sealed so that it may not be used against the respondent in private damage suits. On the contrary, it is sealed to protect secrets of the respondent in the conduct of his business, not to protect him from his liability under the law.

No. 127. Question. May the Federal Trade Commission remand proceedings of a case to the hearing examiner for the taking of further testimony because, in the opinion of the Commission, the records as constituted need to be supplemented by additional material?

Opinion. Yes.

No. 128. Question. Is it required that the findings and conclusions of the Federal Trade Commission be supported by substantial evidence viewed from the record as a whole?

Opinion. Yes. However, if there is substantial evidence to support the findings and conclusions of the Commission, then the courts will not substitute their judgment for the judgment of the Commission. This is true even though the courts would perhaps have decided the case in a different way if they had been called on to decide it in the first instance.

No. 129. Question. Is the Federal Trade Commission empowered to enter a temporary cease-and-desist order against a firm once the Commission has concluded that a prima facie showing has been made?

Opinion. No. Under existing law, the Commission is empowered to issue a cease-and-desist order only after a complaint trial of all the issues. In some instances where the issues are somewhat complex, the trials continue for a period of years. A number of cases have been in trial for periods ranging up to eight years. In the meantime, the practices against which the proceedings are directed may be continued. During the 87th Congress, bills were introduced that would empower the Commission to enter cease-and-desist orders against the practices pending the conclusion of the trials of these prolonged cases.

No. 130. Question. At what point may a decision of a hearing examiner and the Federal Trade Commission be appealed, stayed, or docketed for review?

Opinion. Under the Commission's rules of practice, the decision by the hearing examiner is described as an "initial decision." That becomes the decision of the Commission 30 days after service on the parties unless a petition or review is filed within 15 days for review by the Commission. Any party to a proceeding may file a petition for review within the time prescribed. Once the matter is before the Commission for its review of the initial decision of the hearing examiner, the Commission reviews those questions presented to it and, on the completion of its review, either approves, modifies, or sets aside the initial decision of the hearing examiner.

In the event that the action by the Commission results in approval of a cease-and-desist order against the respondent, the Commission's action may be reviewed by a United States Circuit Court of Appeals if petition is filed in such court within the time provided by the rules of the court. Ordinarily, the courts in reviewing action by the Commission and the issuance of a cease-and-desist order will consider only matters that have been raised before and considered by the Commission.

No. 131. Question. Does the Commission settle proceedings under its formal complaints by consent of the parties charged?

Opinion. Yes. Amendments to the Commission's rules of practice, which became effective July 21, 1961, provide that if the person charged in the formal complaint with violation of law replies within ten days, stating that he is willing to have the proceeding disposed of by entry of an order in substantially the form of the proposed order set forth in the complaint, then negotiations may be undertaken for that purpose. The rules provide that, except for good cause shown, the consent settlement must be negotiated within 30 days, at the conclusion of which the formal complaint will be issued and made public along with the provisions of the consent order to cease and desist. If the negotiations are not completed within the time allowed, then the Commission issues its formal complaint without such consent order. The new rules of the Commission contain a statement to the following effect: "After a complaint is issued, the consent order procedure will not be available."

No. 132. Question. Does the public have an opportunity to object to a proposed FTC consent order before it becomes final?

Opinion. No. Under the new consent-order procedure of the Commission, it does not appear that either the negotiations or the provisions of a consent order to cease and desist will be known to others than the respondent and the representatives of the Commission until it is approved and issued. At that stage, it is considered to be final. A situation similar to this applied to the consent decrees negotiated by the Antitrust Division of the United States Department of Justice prior to June 29, 1961. In other words, until that date, consent decrees negotiated for the disposition of cases arising under the Sherman Antitrust Act were not made known to the public until approved by a court and made public, at which stage they were final. However, on June 29, 1961, the Attorney General of the United States announced the establishment of a new policy: Each proposed consent judgment shall be filed in court or otherwise made available on request to interested persons, as well as to the defendants, as early as feasible, but at least 30 days prior to the approval of the proposed decree by the court. Bills have been introduced in the Congress that would require 30 days of public notice regarding the provisions of proposed consent decrees and proposed orders to cease and desist prior to the entry of such proposed judgments by the courts and proposed orders to cease and desist by the Federal Trade Commission. Of course, if such proposed legislation should be enacted, then orders to cease and desist would be made public before being made final, as is now required by the Attorney General for proposed consent decrees.

No. 133. Question. Can a consent order be changed?

Opinion. Ordinarily, a consent order cannot be modified except by consent of the Federal government and the parties that consented to its entry. However, in some cases consent decrees and consent orders to cease and desist have contained provisions that they may be modified when the public interest requires it.

No. 134. Question. Are cease-and-desist orders entered by the Federal Trade Commission valid when expressed only in the broad and general language of the law?

Opinion. Ordinarily, a cease and desist order should be phrased to apply to the acts or practices to which it is directed, and not to other acts or practices. However, courts have held that the Federal Trade Commission has a wide discretion to formulate a remedy in the form of a cease-and-desist order adequate to prevent repetition of violations of law it has found to exist. Moreover, the Commission is authorized to take into account all relevant facts that would indicate the likelihood that the respondents in a particular case would resume the prohibited practices or related practices unless the order to cease and desist should be phrased to prohibit the continuation or utilization of related injurious and unlawful practices. See, for example, *Federal Trade Commission v. Henry Broch & Company,* 363 U.S. 166, decided January 15, 1962, which is cited and discussed in Chapter II of this volume.

DEPARTMENT OF JUSTICE

We have noted that the Department of Justice has the authority to enforce Section 2 of the Clayton Act as amended by the Robinson-Patman Act. In this respect, its authority is concurrent with that of the Federal Trade Commission. Additionally, the Department of Justice has authority to enforce Section 3 of the Robinson-Patman Act as one of the Federal criminal laws. Here, of course, the United States Attorneys, acting under the direction of the Attorney General, are the only parties with such authority, since the Federal Trade Commission has no authority to enforce Federal criminal laws.

The Department of Justice has acted in very few instances since January 19, 1936, to enforce provisions of the Robinson-Patman Act. It considers the Federal Trade Commission more experienced in that area and has left the enforcement of that law almost entirely to the Commission. It has undertaken a few criminal proceedings under Section 3 of the Robinson-Patman Act, but has succeeded in securing conviction in only one of those cases. In view of this record, it is not believed that the facts warrant detailed discussion of the proceedings applicable to Robinson-Patman Act cases in United States district courts in proceedings instituted by the Department of Justice.

PRIVATE LITIGATION

We have pointed out the provisions of Section 4 of the Clayton Act for private parties to sue for threefold the damages sustained by reason of anything forbidden by the Robinson-Patman Act, and the provisions of Section 16 of the Clayton Act providing for suits by private persons, firms, and corporations for injunctions against threatened loss or damage by reason of violations of the Robinson-Patman Act. Many triple-damage suits have been filed by private parties pursuant to Section 4 of the Clayton Act, but a large percentage of these suits have been settled by agreements out of court, with no record being made of the evidence or of the amounts paid in the form of damages because in such situations the suits are withdrawn. However, some of the suits have been decided by the courts, and damages have been awarded to the injured parties.[302]

CONCLUSION

In each of the chapters in which we discussed Sections 2(a), 2(c), 2(e), and 2(f), we have included some brief references to the record of enforce-

---

[302] Moore v. Mead, 348 U.S. 115 (1954); Elizabeth Arden Sales Corp. v. Gus Blass Co., 150 F.2d 988 (1945); Bruces Juices, Inc. v. American Can Co., 87 F. Supp. 985, aff'd, 187 F.2d. 919, 190 F.2d 73; State Wholesale Grocers v. Great Atlantic & Pacific Tea Co., 258 F.2d. 831; American Cooperative Serum Assn. v. Anchor Serum Co., 153 F.2d 907; Interborough News Co. v. Curtis Publishing Co., 10 F.R.D. 330 (D.C.N.Y. 1950); Allgair v. Glenmore Distilleries Co., 91 F. Supp. 93 (D.C.N.Y. 1950); Avon Publishing Co. v. American News Co., 122 F. Supp. 660 (D.C.N.Y. 1954); Freedman v. Philadelphia Terminals Auction Co., 145 F. Supp. 820 (D.C. Pa. 1956).
NOTE: An exclusive informative article entitled, "Private Enforcement of the Antitrust Laws: The Robinson-Patman Experience," by Professor Richard J. Barber, Professor of Law, Southern Methodist University, appeared in the George Washington Law Review, Volume 30, Number 2, December, 1961. At page 196 of that article, it is shown that 111 private suits had been undertaken based on Robinson-Patman violations in the period from 1936–1961. Of that number, 85 involved violations of subsection 2(a).

ment of each such subsection and referred to the fact that in Appendix A there is a complete listing of all cases instituted by the Federal Trade Commission in the period from June 19, 1936 to May 3, 1961, under the provisions of the Robinson-Patman Act.

are a complete listing of all cases determined by the Federal Trade Commission in the period from June 19, 1936 to April 1, 1957, under the provisions of the Robinson-Patman Act.

Chapter IX

THE SUPPORTERS AND OPPONENTS OF THE ACT

THE SUPPORTERS OF THE ACT

Representatives of large groups of small business firms communicated
with members of Congress in 1935 and 1936 about the practice of price
discrimination. They complained that the practice was rampant and that
if new legislation were not enacted to curb price discriminations, small
business firms would be destroyed and competition substantially lessened.
Representatives of the groups of small business firms did much to prompt
the Congress to give favorable consideration to the Robinson and Patman
bills. In the winter of 1935–1936, these representatives made trips to Washington to meet and discuss with Members of Congress the need for legislation against destructive price discriminations. On March 6, 1936, there
was a tremendous mass meeting of the representatives of small business
firms in Constitution Hall, Washington, D.C., to consider what steps could
be taken to get before Congress factual information necessary to convince
Congress of the need for the Robinson-Patman Act. Resolutions were
adopted, and evidence was collected and presented to the Congress and to
the President of the United States. With the need for remedial legislation
so urgent, Congress acted not only in a manner to make its intent clear, but
also with a clear and one-sided decision that demonstrated unqualified determination to curb unfair price discriminations. The Robinson-Patman
Act passed the House, as we have stated, by a vote of 290 to 16, and when
finally voted on in the Senate it was passed without objection.

A few of the facts relating to the passage of the Robinson-Patman Act
have been cited to demonstrate that in effect the whole 74th Congress accepted its responsibility and met one of the really serious problems of the

day when it strengthened the laws against destructive price discrimination.

This action by the Congress was hailed with elation by the small business community and by responsible citizens and businessmen in other segments of our economy.

As the years have passed, representatives of groups of small business firms, public officials, political scientists, economists, representatives of agricultural interests, and representatives of labor organizations have expressed themselves as opposed to the practice of price discrimination, and an overwhelming majority of them openly expressed their opposition to proposals that were made by opponents of the Robinson-Patman Act to weaken that law.

For example, when it appeared that the Attorney General's National Committee to Study the Antitrust Laws was likely to write a report critical of the Robinson-Patman Act, it was informed in no uncertain terms that a strong Robinson-Patman Act is necessary to preserve our free and competitive private-enterprise system. On December 16, 1953, the following national trade associations filed a jointly subscribed statement of their views with the Attorney General's National Committee to Study the Antitrust Laws:

> National Association of Retail Grocers
> National Association of Retail Druggists
> National Congress of Petroleum Retailers, Inc.
> National Association of Independent Tire Dealers, Inc.
> United Fresh Fruit & Vegetable Association
> National Food Brokers Association
> National Candy Wholesalers Association, Inc.
> U.S. Wholesaler Grocers' Association, Inc.

This statement said:

> Constitutional freedom—equality of opportunity—of the people to engage in trade or business, is the essential concern of the national antitrust policy. . . .
>
> The *several* provisions of the Robinson-Patman Act *are indispensable* to the protection of the opportunity of business rivals to obtain commodities of like grade and quality, on equal terms. They *deter* continual and persistent price discrimination practices which unfairly favor one rival over the others. In particular, they aim to prevent a big nation-wide operator which is so disposed to use its sheer economic and financial size and power to crush its local competitors by continually getting its supplies on discriminatory terms, and at the ultimate expense of farmers, labor and the consumer. . . .
>
> No one of the independents, large or small—no tire dealer, no grocer, no druggist, no gasoline dealer, or other such businessman can hope to succeed in his contest with a competitor which continuously

gets the goods it sells at a substantially lower price not economically justifiable. What chance, what opportunity has he successfully to compete with a competitor which continually and unfairly buys the same goods as he, but 5%, 10%, 20%, etc., cheaper? What chance has a man of equal physical ability to win a 100 yard race against a man who always has a 15 yard handicap at the start? Or, to win a prize fight with an opponent who has horseshoes concealed in his gloves?

By prohibiting unfair price advantages, the Robinson-Patman Act of 1936, in our opinion, is the Magna Carta of free, independent business enterprise in America. . . .

The facts of the legislative history of the Robinson-Patman Act of 1936, its administration and enforcement, prove beyond any reasonable doubt that *all* of the provisions of that Act are a consistent, integral part of, and have marked the greatest advance in the effectuation of the national antitrust policy and in the realization by the American people of their constitutional freedom to engage in trade or business. [Italics added.]

Shortly thereafter, an organization representing many agricultural interests wrote to the chairman of the Senate Committee on the Judiciary, as follows:

A number of bills have been introduced in Congress which tend to weaken and even destroy the Robinson-Patman Act and have as their purpose the legalizing of discriminatory practices.

The Robinson-Patman Act fosters and protects a competitive economy by preserving *equality of opportunity for every business to the benefit of all segments of our nation,* including the consuming public.

Special price concessions and allowances and other discriminatory practices of all kinds are detrimental to our economy.

The National Council of Farmer Cooperatives is unqualifiedly opposed to any legislation which will in any manner weaken the present Robinson-Patman Act, and strongly urges the adoption of legislation which will prohibit any harmful discriminatory practices.

The Council represents some 5,000 separate marketing and purchasing associations serving about 2,600,000 farm families throughout the country. These associations are in the practical business of marketing every type of agricultural commodity and purchasing from production supplies of all kinds for their farmer patrons. *The interest of these people in the Robinson-Patman Act does not arise from adherence to some particular economic or legal theory. They are motivated by the belief that it is for the best interest of our total economy to preserve a competitive business climate in which fair play shall continue* to be the controlling rule and *where competition can compete, but not to the point of destroying the opportunity to compete.*

We respectfully urge that none of the bills before your Committee, which directly, or in effect, affect the Robinson-Patman Act, be acted upon until there have been public hearings thereon with full opportunity for all interested persons and organizations to present their views. We would appreciate receiving notice of any such hearings which may be scheduled.

In 1955, the representative of organizations representing millions of laborers, in testimony before the House Small Business Committee, stated:

> We recommend, Mr. Chairman, that all our energies be mobilized, both within Congress and without, to enact your fortifying amendment to the Robinson-Patman Act in the 2d session of the 84th Congress.[303]

At that time, another witness, who represented over 800,000 members of the International Association of Machinists, made clear that those he represented should be regarded as small businessmen, and stated:

> We have testified on many occasions both before this committee and other congressional committees in support of the Robinson-Patman Act, Sherman Antitrust Act, and also the Clayton Act.
>
> I want to restate here today that it is still our position that those acts must be protected. They must be improved upon and we are prepared to support amendments in the 84th Congress to carry this out.[304]

A representative of growers, shippers, and distributors of fresh fruits and vegetables made clear that business firms in that segment of our economy consider the Robinson-Patman Act indispensable. In his testimony, he stated:

> I am appearing here as counsel for the United Fresh Fruit & Vegetable Association, a nonprofit, nonmarketing nationwide association of growers, shippers, and wholesale distributors of fresh fruits and vegetables. The headquarters of the association are at 777 14th Street, N.W., Washington, D.C.
>
> My purpose in appearing at these hearings is to show (1) that the Robinson-Patman Act is as necessary today as when it was originally enacted for the preservation of competition and the regulation of discriminatory pricing practices, and (2) that to amend its provisions as suggested by the Attorney General's Committee would be extremely damaging to our entire economy.
>
> The issue to be considered by this committee and to be decided by the Congress is whether or not to amend the Robinson-Patman Act to exempt certain categories of business practice from the application of the restrictions in the statute. The report of the Attorney General's committee on antitrust laws has recommended certain changes. It is my contention that some of these changes would not be in the best interests of business in general, particularly with reference to the small employers in the produce industry.[305]

---

[303] Hearings on Price Discrimination, the Robinson-Patman Act and Related Matters before the House Small Business Committee, 84th Cong., 1st Sess., pt. I, at 592 (1955).
[304] Ibid.
[305] Id. at 597.

A witness representing the National Farmers Union, an organization of approximately 700,000 farm families, testified as follows:

> The Robinson-Patman Act has been referred to as the Magna Carta of small business. We consider it the Magna Carta of agriculture also. The farmer must have competition in the market place. If he has to deal with giant monopolies either in buying or selling, he perforce becomes an economic slave.[306]

A representative of organizations having millions of persons as members and representing the interests of consumers presented testimony vigorously supporting the Robinson-Patman Act.[307]

A leading professor of law in one of our largest universities, after protracted study of price discrimination, the Robinson-Patman Act, and criticisms of that law, testified that it was his considered judgment that the Robinson-Patman Act promoted price competition.[308] That man was not only a teacher of law, but he had served as a public official in the enforcement of the antitrust laws for a number of years. Other lawyers who had served as public officials in the enforcement of antitrust laws testified to the same effect.[309] Professors who are teaching economics and political science in a number of our leading universities, and who have given study to other problems created by the practice of price discrimination, testified to a similar effect.[310]

A report submitted by the Federal Trade Commission to the chairman of the Select Committee on Small Business, United States Senate, February 21, 1952, contained the following statement:

> Among unfair business practices, price discrimination most directly denies to small business an equal opportunity to live and grow on the basis of efficiency. Such opportunity is the very essence of the competitive economic system which our antitrust laws seek to preserve, maintain, and restore.
>
> That small business has survived or even grown despite price discrimination is of no relevancy when offered as evidence that price discrimination is not destructive of small business. What is relevant, but what must remain unknown until price discrimination is eliminated, is how successful small business can be when their large rivals cannot exercise their monopolistic power to grant and receive price discriminations. Small business is entitled to the opportunity of showing what it can do in the absence of the crippling handicap of discriminatory prices. Continued enforcement of the Robinson-Patman Act will insure that small business is granted that opportunity.

---

306 *Id.* at 54.
307 *Id.* at 472–474.
308 *Id.* at 66–67.
309 *Id.* at 3–31; 264–285; 725–742; 743–783; 842–884.
310 *Id.* at 615–672; 692–701; 785–792; 939–942.

When large sellers are not permitted to discriminate in price between purchasers located in different communities in order to smother a small seller operating in only one of them, or to discriminate between large and small buyers competing in the same community to stifle the small buyer, the most effective kind of competition will result—the kind of competition which forces sellers to lower prices generally in order to sell at all as they would have to do if in fact they were dealing in the kind of market which makes a market price in the only real meaning of that term. To permit sellers to substantially lessen competition through price discriminations promotes monopolistic conditions.

Price discrimination has been a weapon of sellers who have some degree of monopoly power and can be effectively employed only by those who have such power. It is equally true that price discriminations are granted only when doing so will contribute to the maintenance or enhancement of that monopoly power or when this same power, in some degree, resides in those to whom the discriminations are granted. It is with respect to the use of monopoly power on the part of the buyer that the Commission has observed some of the most damaging effects to small buyers.[311] [Emphasis supplied.]

On April 7, 1961, the Hon. Lee Loevinger, the Assistant Attorney General of the United States, who currently heads the Antitrust Division of the Department of Justice, addressed the antitrust section of the American Bar Association in Washington, D.C. On that occasion, he paid high tribute to our Federal legislation directed against destructive and discriminatory pricing. He emphasized that these laws, such as the Robinson-Patman Act, are necessary, and, to use his words, "are quite consistent with free and vigorous competition in a civilized society."

On November 4, 1960, President Kennedy—then a candidate for the Presidency—in writing to representatives of small business firms with reference to our antitrust laws, which, of course, include the Robinson-Patman Act, made clear that he is opposed to trade practices carried on according to the laws of the jungle. He said that we need to take effective steps of strengthening our historic policy of preventing monopoly and providing a business climate favorable to growth and prosperity of small and independent business.

On August 30, 1960, in the course of a session of the American Bar Association antitrust section regarding the role of the Robinson-Patman Act in the antitrust scheme of things, the Hon. Earl W. Kintner—then Chairman of the Federal Trade Commission—in addressing several hundred of the leading members of the American Bar Association with reference to the action by the Congress in passing the Robinson-Patman Act, said it was necessary to keep competition in distribution clear of abuses of economic

---

[311] STAFF OF SENATE SELECT COMM. ON SMALL BUSINESS, 82D CONG., 2D SESS., MONOPOLISTIC PRACTICES AND SMALL BUSINESS (Comm. Print 1952).

power. On October 10, 1960, he addressed the grocery manufacturers representatives in New York City. The theme of his address was "What the Robinson-Patman Requirements Mean to You." In that connection, he said:

> By aggressive but fair affirmative action to enforce the existing laws against discriminatory pricing and discriminatory promotional allowances the Federal Trade Commission can strengthen the hand of those who already wish to avoid unfair special deals and would prefer only a fair opportunity for their products to compete on the merits.

On June 19, 1961, the Hon. Paul Rand Dixon, chairman of the Federal Trade Commission, addressed the midyear meeting of the Grocery Manufacturers of America, Inc. Speaking about our laws designed to promote a free and competitive economy, he said:

> As I have said, the function of the Federal Trade Commission is to help industry grow within the framework of our competitive economic system. The Commission does this, primarily, by enforcing several statutes, principally the Federal Trade Commission Act and the Clayton Antitrust Act, as amended by the Robinson-Patman Act. . . .
>
> Because today, June 19, 1961, is the 25th anniversary of the passage of the Robinson-Patman Act on June 19, 1936, I should like to believe that your regard for this statute is so high that you deliberately planned this meeting on its birthday to accord it the praise which it so richly deserves.
>
> In any event, I salute the Robinson-Patman Act, wish it many happy returns of the day, and pledge myself to do all that I lawfully can to assist it in becoming what it was designed to be—the charter of freedom for businessmen, both large and small, to operate in a competitive economy.

On June 19, 1951, the 15th anniversary of the Robinson-Patman Act, and on June 19, 1961, the Silver Anniversary of the Robinson-Patman Act, that law was commemorated on the floor of the House of Representatives of the United States through addresses by members of Congress and in messages from representatives of large organizations of business firms, which were presented for inclusion in the *Congressional Record*. These addresses and messages paid great tribute to the Robinson-Patman Act and what it has done for the preservation of our free and competitive enterprise system.[312]

OPPONENTS OF THE ACT

Support for the passage of the Robinson-Patman Act outside of the Congress was not unanimous, and its enforcement has not been without

---

[312] See Vol. 107, pt. 8, CONG. REC. 9950–58 (daily ed. June 19, 1961).

opposition. From the date on which the Robinson and Patman bills were introduced in the Congress, opposition was expressed to those legislative proposals by representatives of firms that practiced price discrimination and wanted to be left free to discriminate as they chose. Representatives of the large buyers who had received the benefit of unjustified discriminations also opposed the enactment of the Robinson and Patman bills into law; they wanted their firms to be left free to receive competitive advantages not enjoyed by their competitors. Opposition from these quarters did not cease when these legislative proposals were enacted into law.

The Federal Trade Commission, with the tools provided it by the Congress through the Robinson-Patman Act, undertook its laborious task of eliminating destructive price discriminations. It met with considerable success.[313] Opposition to this success arose, grew, and stiffened. It took the form of arguments by representatives of firms accused and found to be discriminating in price, and by others, that price discriminations were evidence of competition and should not be interfered with. It was argued that the Robinson-Patman Act was a law against "effective competition." This argument was not only made to the Federal Trade Commission in briefs in the cases that were being litigated, but it was repeated in law review articles. However, the Federal Trade Commission continued its enforcement activities. One of its notable cases was that in which it challenged price-discrimination practices in the Portland cement industry.[314] The Commission was successful in that proceeding, and that success prompted representatives of the firms that had been found to be discriminating in price to ask Congress to legalize their price-discriminating methods and systems. Elaborate lobbying activities were undertaken in support of that request.[315] Arguments were made to the Congress in the course of these lobbying activities to the effect that price discrimination was evidence of effective competition,[316] and they

---

[313] See Corn Products Refining Co. v. FTC, 324 U.S. 726; FTC v. Staley Mfg. Co., 324 U.S. 746; FTC v. Morton Salt Co., 334 U.S. 37.

[314] Cement Institute, No. 3167, FTC, 19377; 333 U.S. 683.

[315] House Select Comm. on Small Business, *Price Discrimination and the Robinson-Patman Act*, H.R. REP. No. 2966, 84th Cong., 2d Sess. 11–38, 73–126, & Appendix A, 229–47 (1956).

See also Lathan, *The Politics of Basing Point Legislation*, 15 LAW & CONTEMP. PROB. 272 (1950). This report was reprinted in the record of the *"Hearings on Price Discrimination, before the House Select Committee on Small Business,* 84th Cong., 1st Sess. 541–79 (1955). See also Simon, *The Case Against the Federal Trade Commission*, 19 U. CHI. L. REV. 297 (1951), and answers to that attack on the FTC, Wallace and Douglas, *Antitrust Policies and the New Attack on the Federal Trade Commission*, 19 U. CHI. L. REV. 684 (1952). Additional materials relating to that matter may be found in H.R. REP. No. 2966, 84th Cong., 2d Sess. 35, 36 (1956).

[316] For articles relating to that matter, see Adelman, *Effective Competition and the Antitrust Laws*, 61 HARV. L. REV. 1289 (1948); Burns, *If You Are In Business You Are Probably Guilty*, 28 BARRON'S WEEKLY 5 (1948); Clark, *Toward a Concept of Workable Com-*

were persuasive in that instance; Congress passed a bill that would have had the effect of legalizing some of these price-discrimination systems and methods.[317] That bill was vetoed by the President of the United States during June, 1950.

Failure to secure approval of legislation that would have legalized many types of price discrimination prompted representatives of firms using these price discrimination practices to "re-educate" not only the leaders of the American public regarding what should be considered as "competitive" and what should be considered as "monopolistic" practices, but also to "help the courts understand the problem." Arguments in support of this program were set forth in articles, books, and speeches that were expected to come to the attention of government officials, legislators, and judges. The crux of these articles was to the effect that price discrimination and other practices previously found to be monopolistic by the Congress were, in fact, "competitive," and that laws directed specifically against such practices are laws inconsistent with an antimonopolistic policy for free and unfettered competition.

These plans and programs, along with the writings that followed, gave rise to a new body of literature regarding the laws against price discrimination. Arguments appeared in many writings describing antitrust laws prohibiting price discriminations as being inconsistent, if not in conflict, with our basic antitrust law, the Sherman Act of 1890.[318]

In the meantime, the courts took note of these writings. A number of opinions and decisions appeared, in which it was noted that in many of these writings "experts" had contended that the Robinson-Patman Act was basically inconsistent with the Sherman Antitrust Act because it interfered with price discriminations that were said by these experts to reflect vigorous competition. The Supreme Court of the United States in the case of

---

petition, 30 AM. ECON. REV. 241 (1940); Hilder, *The Attack Upon Delivered Price Systems,* 14 GEO. WASH. L. REV. (1948); Kittelle & Lamb, *The Implied Conspiracy Doctrine and Delivered Pricing,* 15 LAW & CONTEMP. PROB. 227 (1950); Mason, *Current Status of the Monopoly Problem in the United States,* 62 HARV. L. REV. 1265 (1949); Mason, *Let's Stop Kicking Business Around,* American Magazine May 1948; McAllister, *Price Control by Law in the United States,* 4 LAW & CONTEMP. PROB. 273 (1937); Oppenheim, *Federal Antitrust Legislation: Guideposts to a Revised Antitrust Policy,* 50 MICH. L. REV. 1139–1244 (1952); Simon, *Price Discrimination to Meet Competition,* U. ILL. L. FORUM 575, 581–83 (1950); Smith, *Effective Competition: Hypothesis for Modernizing the Antitrust Laws,* 26 N.Y.U.L. REV. 405 (1951).

317 S. 1008, 81st Cong., 2d Sess. (1950).

318 See also a speech made in the House of Representatives of the United States regarding this subject entitled "The Effect of Lobbyists' Propaganda on Our Supreme Court," 103 CONG. REC. 14758–67 (daily ed. Aug. 27, 1957). See also how reliance on those articles by the Supreme Court of the United States was carried over and borrowed by the judges of other Federal courts for their use as a basis for their decisions in cases against the application of laws prohibiting price discrimination. Standard Oil Co. v. Brown, 238 F.2d 54, 57 (5th Cir. 1956).

Standard Oil Co. of Indiana v. FTC reflected a leaning to this view.[319]

The Supreme Court and other courts give indications in their opinions in a number of other cases arising under the Robinson-Patman Act that the members of the courts were beginning to read these law review articles and other writings that strongly criticized the Robinson-Patman Act and added to the "new body of economic literature" by arguing that price discrimination was a form of price competition that should not be interfered with by the Robinson-Patman Act and other laws directed against the practice of price discrimination. As the evidence of the influence of these writings grew, the government and other plaintiffs in cases directed against the practice of destructive price discriminations lost out, and the courts decided the cases in favor of those who were practicing price discriminations.

Through our research we learned that once it became apparent that the Supreme Court of the United States had paid attention to and relied on arguments contained in law review articles, books, and other works of law writers without inquiring into the background of the authors, the supply of such propaganda multiplied. The increase in the supply of arguments in law review articles brought an increase in their influence upon some members of the Court. An example of that is in the opinion in the case of the *Automatic Canteen Co. of America v. FTC*.[320] In that case, Justice Frankfurter included citations to six law review articles—one of them to notes written by the editors of the *Harvard Law Review*. Other citations were to articles written by advocates in causes that were served by that decision.

It is not possible for us to appraise the extent and the significance of the damage that has been done by virtue of the fact that the report of the Attorney General's National Committee to Study the Antitrust Laws has been accepted and relied on by the Supreme Court of the United States as an authority in deciding the more important antitrust cases. One thing we do know: The Supreme Court, in relying on that report, has accepted as an authority a collection of arguments compiled by a group of which some members have opposed our public policy against monopoly and monopolistic practices. It was the announced determination of that group to formulate future antitrust policy. It is clear that a part of its plan to effect that result was to re-educate the Supreme Court and the public into believing that cer-

---

[319] 340 U.S. 231 (1951). Prominent in the reasoning of the Court and important to its decision in that case in favor of the Standard Oil Company of Indiana was the Court's reasoning that the Robinson-Patman Act, the antitrust law under which that case had been brought, was inconsistent with the Sherman Antitrust Act. In that connection it cited an authority. In a footnote at page 249 appears the following: "It has been suggested that, in theory, the Robinson-Patman Act as a whole is inconsistent with the Sherman and Clayton Acts. See Adelman, Effective Competition and the Antitrust Laws, HARV. L. REV. 1289, 1327–1350."

[320] 346 U.S. 61.

tain monopolistic practices, including the practice of price discrimination, are merely competitive, and that our antitrust laws that were designed to curb those practices are, therefore, anticompetitive.

The House Small Business Committee in the 84th Congress held extensive hearings concerning the report of the Attorney General's National Committee to Study the Antitrust Laws. On the basis of those hearings, the committee submitted to the House of Representatives *House Report No. 2966* on December 19, 1956. Appearing at pages 219 to 228 are the committee's findings regarding the report of the Attorney General's National Committee to Study the Antitrust Laws.

It is fortunate that the committee was able to investigate, hold hearings, and issue a report dealing with this important matter. That report was made available to each of the judges of the Federal judiciary to whom the Attorney General of the United States had sent a copy of the report of the Attorney General's National Committee to Study the Antitrust Laws.

In the years that have followed, there have been growing indications that the courts are becoming more aware of the fallacies in the arguments about the economic significance of the practice of price discrimination. They are evidencing less readiness to accept the "new body of economic literature" conjured up and presented to them by opponents of the Robinson-Patman Act and by advocates of the destructive practices of price discrimination without regard to the needs or dictates of a sound public policy.

In recent years, the courts have shown a tendency to read and study the detailed records on which Congress acted and which show the effects of the practice of destructive price discrimination. As they have done that, the courts have found that they cannot escape the conclusion reached by the Federal Trade Commission that—

> Price discrimination has been a weapon of sellers who have some degree of monopoly power and can be effectively employed only by those who have such power. . . .

and by the conclusion of the House Committee on the Judiciary in 1956 to the effect that—

> Price discriminations favoring preferred buyers present a danger to the competitive enterprise system which is inconsistent with the policy of the price discriminaton statute. Firms can abuse their superior market position and engage in discriminatory practices that eliminate small suppliers and small retailers from the competitive scene.[321]

Professor Holbrook Working, Associate Director, Food Research Institute, Stanford University, testified in 1955 regarding some of the argu-

---

[321] H.R. REP. No. 2202, 84th Cong., 2d Sess. (1956).

ments that have been advanced by the advocates for the practice of price discrimination. He pointed out that it was a fallacy for them to argue that we can expect nondiscriminatory pricing only in a state of theoretically perfect competition—a state of competition impossible to achieve. In that connection, he rejected the notion that price discrimination is objectionable only under conditions of pure and perfect competition. He added, as a corollary, his opinion that under departures from the pure and perfect state, discrimination remains presumptively objectionable, "with the burden of proof on those who would argue that price discrimination is harmless under particular conditions.[322] He explained his position with these words:

> Consider why the theory of perfect competition was constructed. Its purpose was to analyze the effects of competition under conditions which are somewhat artificially simplified for purposes of analysis but which were supposed to fairly well approximate actual or attainable conditions in a considerable part of the economy. The results of this analysis were to show that competition of the sort considered had desirable results. Among those results that were considered desirable are some that depend directly on absence of price discrimination. The belief that price discrimination tends to be objectionable runs as a thread through all the history of economic thought on the effects of competition. Any implication that economists have held only that price discrimination was objectionable under the peculiar and special conditions of perfect competition, and under those conditions only, is untrue.[323]

The economic cause of discrimination is fairly obvious. The seller can increase his profits to the extent that he can tailor his price schedule to fit the highest price each buyer is willing to pay. The economic effect, however, is not so easily evaluated. Defenders of price discrimination focus on the relatively small hurt to the few resulting from an antidiscrimination policy, while neglecting the really significant harm to the whole market, and indirectly to the economy at large, arising from discriminatory prices.

In conclusion, it is clear that Members of Congress and other public officials are faced with the problem of weighing those arguments for and against the practice of price discrimination. Congress has done that in the past on the basis of an abundance of factual information and has found that the effects of price discrimination are substantially to lessen competition and to tend to create monopolies. In other words, Congress has found the practice of price discrimination to be anticompetitive—and it has done so on each occasion when it studied the details of the factual information about the practice of price discrimination. These legislative findings have

---

[322] *Hearings on Price Discrimination Before the House Select Committee on Small Business,* 84th Cong., 1st Sess., pt. I, at 631 (1955).
[323] *Ibid.*

been made despite arguments by the advocates of price discrimination that it is a form of competition and that the Robinson-Patman Act and other similar legislation are antidiscriminatory. Reaffirmation by the Congress of its earlier findings on these matters would help to make more effective our antitrust legislation against price discrimination.

Chapter X

FUTURE OUTLOOK FOR THE ACT

CURRENT PRICE-DISCRIMINATION PROBLEMS

In Chapter II, in the discussion of the good-faith defense of meeting an equally low price in cases arising under subsection 2(a), it was pointed out that efforts were made to remedy some of the defects in the law through new legislation. As was noted, some of these efforts took the form of bills to make the good-faith defense absolute in all cases except those where the effect of the price discriminations involved would be to substantially lessen competition or tend to create a monopoly. The principal bills directed to that end were H.R. 11 in the House of Representatives and S. 11 in the Senate.

We noted that small business and many of the friends of small business were asking for relief from destructive price discriminations. They appeared before a number of congressional committees and testified in support of legislation such as was proposed by H.R. 11 and S. 11. In some of their appearances, they stated that among the many things small business wished from the Congress, and particularly in the field of antimonopoly legislation, was legislation to strengthen the law against price discrimination. They said that there are many things that small business needed and wanted, and that there were several pieces of legislation which they strongly recommended, including tax relief. But they said that (just to make things simple) they wanted the Congress to pass promptly the legislation provided for in H.R. 11 and S. 11 (84th Cong.; 85th Cong.; 86th Cong.; and 87th Cong.).

When no legislation developed out of these efforts to strengthen the Robinson-Patman Act against the practice of price discrimination, there appeared to be an upsurge in the use of the practice. Many complaints poured in to the Small Business Committees of the Senate and the House about large, multiple-market sellers using the practice of price discrimination with the effect of eliminating competition.

In the meantime, small business firms victimized by these price discriminations have struggled to protect themselves to the extent provided under existing law. A small wholesale baking firm doing business in Santa Rosa, New Mexico, found that a large competitor doing business at locations in several states, including Santa Rosa, was selling bread at discriminatory prices and at prices at levels below cost in Santa Rosa, with damaging results to the small baker in that community. The small business firm brought suit, not only under subsection (a) of Section 2 of the Robinson-Patman Act, but also under Section 3 of the Robinson-Patman Act. The latter section of the law makes it unlawful for a seller to sell at unreasonably low prices. In that instance, the small firm was successful, and its success was sustained by the Supreme Court of the United States in 1954.[324] However, further efforts by other small business firms to utilize Section 3 of the Robinson-Patman Act have met with failure.

On January 20, 1958, the Supreme Court of the United States, by a five-to-four decision, held that Section 3 of the Robinson-Patman Act is available only for criminal prosecutions by the U.S. Department of Justice, and, therefore, cannot be utilized by small business firms in private litigation for damages or for injunctions.[325] The reasoning underlying the Court's decisions in these cases was that Section 3 of the Robinson-Patman Act is not a part of the Federal antitrust laws. Immediately, the chairman of the House Small Business Committee introduced H.R. 10243 (85th Congress), which would have redefined the term "antitrust laws" appearing in Section 1 of the Clayton Act to include Section 3 of the Robinson-Patman Act. No action was taken on that proposal.

Before the conclusion of the 85th Congress, the rising tide of complaints from small business firms about price discriminations prompted the House Small Business Committee to create a special subcommittee to look into the matter. That special subcommittee held hearings regarding small-business problems stemming from price discrimination practices in the distribution of dairy products. The subcommittee has continued its activities in the 86th Congress and has made two reports to the House of Representatives on its investigations and hearings.[326] In these reports, the subcommittee made find-

---

[324] Moore v. Mead's Fine Bread Co.
[325] Nashville Milk Co. v. Carnation Co., 355 U.S. 373; Safeway Stores v. Vance, 355 U.S. 389.
[326] H.R. Rep. No. 2713, 85th Cong., 2d Sess. (1958); H.R. Rep. No. 714, 86th Cong., 2d Sess. (1958).

ings that small and independent processors and distributors of dairy products had been providing a substantial amount of price competition at low,
nondiscriminatory prices. The large, competing, multimarket processors
and distributors met that competition by selling at discriminatory prices in
various markets and, in some instances, by making sales at prices apparently below cost. The subcommittee concluded that these discriminatory
pricing practices of the large processors and distributors threatened the continued existence of large numbers of small and independent processors and
distributors of dairy products.

Subcommittee No. 5 of the House Small Business Committee, in the
85th Congress and again in the 86th Congress made investigations and
studies of price discrimination practices in the distribution of various food
items. In the course of those investigations and studies, a large amount of
testimony and other evidence was received to the effect that price discrimination practices in the sale and distribution of food is widespread.
Representatives of small and independent food distributors testified that the
large corporate food retailers were inducing and receiving the benefits of
the price discriminations with devastating effects on their small and independent competitors.

An abundance of testimony and other evidence was presented to
Congressional committees showing that the price-discrimination practices
continued unabated and with devastating effects.[327]

The Federal Trade Commission noted in 1958, with reference to the
food industry, that "There have developed tendencies to concentration of
economic power, to collusive price action, and to unfair competitive methods." In that connection, Hon. John W. Gwynne, then chairman of the
Federal Trade Commission, in announcing that the Federal Trade Commission would study the situation, stated: "We want to know why the industry
is getting so tough for the smaller operator. . . . The trend seems to be to
eliminate the small man entirely."

Hearings conducted by a special subcommittee of the House Small Business Committee regarding small-business problems arising from price-
discrimination practices in the dairy industry developed a large volume of

---

[327] *Hearing Pursuant to S.Res. 57 on S. 11 before the Subcommittee on Antitrust and
Monopoly of the Senate Committee on the Judiciary,* "To Amend Section 2 of the Clayton
Act" 85th Cong., 1st Sess. 962, 1074–66, 1077–79 (1957); *Hearings on H.R. 11, H.R. 2611,
H.R. 2690, H.R. 2850, H.R. 9487, H.R. 89, H.R. 1840, H.R. 2577, & H.R. 8395, before
the Antitrust Subcommittee of the House Committee on the Judiciary,* "To Amend Sections
2 and 3 of the Clayton Act," 84th Cong., 2d Sess. 223, 282–296, 341–351 (1956); *Hearings
on Price Discrimination before the House Select Committee on Small Business,* 84th Cong.,
1st Sess. 11–55 (1955); *Hearings Regarding Problems in Food Distribution before Subcommittee No. 5 of the House Select Committee on Small Business,* 86th Cong., 1st Sess.
130, 284–301, 308, 321–322, 348–349, 385–386 (1959).

evidence showing that, in many areas, multiple-market operators were continuing to make sales at prices below cost to eliminate small business firms. On May 14, 1960, a representative of small business complained to members of the House that one firm was selling dairy products in Kentucky at unreasonably low prices, and in that connection stated:

> The unreasonably low price at which these products are being sold would seem to be for the sole purpose of destroying competition, especially independent dairies such as ourselves. This can be very easily done by a large national concern who operate in many different geographical localities and are able to finance and subsidize a price war against small dairies who sell in competition. . . .
>
> By using these unfair competitive practices they would in effect force us out of business within 30 to 60 days. Therefore, the urgency for action is of the utmost importance. We ask that you help us eliminate these unfair practices as quickly as possible.

These charges by representatives of small firms were similar to complaints received from representatives of other small firms doing business in other parts of the country. In some of the areas where nationwide distributors gained monopoly control of prices, the public was found to be paying higher prices than those that prevailed before competition was eliminated.

Information of this kind prompted the House Small Business Committee and its subcommittees to conclude that price discrimination and other related trade practices were being pursued with deleterious effects on competition, and that the survival and growth of small and independent business, as well as of our competitive enterprise system, call for vigorous and effective enforcement of existing laws against price discrimination and for a strengthening of those laws.[328]

PROPOSALS FOR AMENDING THE PRICE-DISCRIMINATION LAW

Members of Congress, mindful of the upswing of the practice of price discrimination, introduced a number of legislative proposals designed to strengthen Federal legislation against the practice. Those legislative proposals were not enacted into law.[329]

The first of the bills, introduced in the House of Representatives at the beginning of the 86th Congress (H.R. 11), was designed to plug up the loophole in the Robinson-Patman Act made by the decision of the Supreme Court of the United States in 1951 in the case of *Standard Oil Co. of Indiana v. FTC,* 340 U.S. 231. Another, H.R. 1233, 87th Congress, would have empowered the Federal Trade Commission to enter temporary cease-and-

---

[328] H. REPT. No. 2231, 86th Cong., 2d Sess. 69 (1960); H. REPT. No. 2234, 86th Cong., 2d Sess. 15–16 (1960); H. REPT. No. 2235, 86th Cong., 2d Sess. 167–71 (1960).
[329] The bills referred to include the following: H.R. 11, H.R. 124, H.R. 125, H.R. 1233, and H.R. 127, 87th Congress.

desist orders where it would be in the public interest to do so, pending the resolution of long-drawn-out litigation against price-discrimination practices. H.R. 127, 87th Congress, would have amended the Federal Trade Commission Act by adding a new section containing the substantive law now appearing in Section 3 of the Robinson-Patman Act and, in that connection, providing that the small business firms victimized through violations of the substantive provisions would have been entitled to proceed with private litigation for damages and for injunctions.

It is readily apparent from the foregoing examples of discriminations that Congress is faced again with and troubled by a problem not unlike the problem it faced and acted on in 1914 and again in 1936—that is, the problem of price discriminations that have the effect of substantially lessening competition and tending to create monopolies. Incident to this problem facing the Congress is the question of whether we want monopoly in this country, even when it results from acts and practices carried on in good faith. Also to be considered are the arguments of those who use the practice of price discrimination—arguments to the effect that price discrimination is a form of vigorous competition and should not be interfered with or prohibited by law.

As carried on in many sections of the country and in many industries today, price discrimination appears no different in its effects from the price discrimination practiced by the Standard Oil Trust in earlier years. The effects have been shown to substantially lessen competition and to tend to create monopolies.

From all these circumstances, it appears likely that the public, Congress, and the Federal law-enforcement officials are becoming more mindful of the need for the Robinson-Patman Act, and that they will act to utilize and strengthen it as an effective measure against destructive price discrimination.

Quite recently, one of the most caustic critics of the Robinson-Patman Act wrote a book entitled *The Price Discrimination Law,* in which he paid a compliment to the Robinson-Patman Act in the following language:

> There is strong reason to believe that the statute has afforded effective protection against the price-cutting activities of predatory would-be monopolists and that it has substantially reduced the discriminatory advantages in price enjoyed by large buyers.[330]

In view of this appraisal of the Act by an outstanding writer who previously voiced opposition to the Robinson-Patman Act, and in view of the present strong factual showing of need for the Act, it is concluded that the future outlook is for preservation and strengthening of the law against price discrimination.

---

[330] C. D. Edwards, The Price Discrimination Law 622 (1959).

APPENDIX A

PART I

SECTION 2(A) OF THE CLAYTON ACT

(15 U.S.C. 13)

List of cases arising under section 2(a) of the Clayton Act, as amended by Robinson-Patman Act, involving charges that respondents discriminated in price between their various customers in such a manner as to substantially lessen competition or tend to create a monopoly.

Citations to FTC decisions and to court actions	FTC docket No.	Title of case, reference to product involved, and date and nature of disposition of case
22 F.T.C. 232; 92 F. (2d) 677; 304 U.S. 257; 101 F. (2d) 620.	2116	The Goodyear Tire & Rubber Company. Tires. O.C.D. Mar. 5, 1936. Order set aside by C.C.A. 6, Nov. 5, 1937. C.C.A. reversed by Supreme Court May 16, 1938. Order set aside by C.C.A. 6, Feb. 16, 1939
25 F.T.C. 57.	2650	Menasha Wooden Ware Corp., et al. Butter tubs. O.C.D. June 8, 1937.
25 F.T.C. 537.	2935	Kraft-Phenix Cheese Corp. Cheese. O.C.D. July 17, 1937.
25 F.T.C. 548.	2937	Bird & Son, Inc., et al. Floor covering. O.C.D. July 17, 1937.
25 F.T.C. 555.	3020	Hollywood Hat Co., Inc. Millinery. O.C.D. July 17, 1937.

Citations to FTC decisions and to court actions	FTC docket No.	Title of case, reference to product involved, and date and nature of disposition of case
25 F.T.C. 1116.................	3050	Christmas Club. Bank books. O.C.D. Sept. 30, 1937.
25 F.T.C. 1209.................	2936	Shefford Cheese Co., Inc. Cheese. O.C.D. Oct. 30, 1937.
25 F.T.C. 1228.................	3154	Pittsburgh Plate Glass Co., et al. Glass. O.C.D. Oct. 30, 1937.
26 F.T.C. 296..................	3263	Agricultural Laboratories. Nitrogen fixing bacteria. O.C.D. Jan. 12, 1938.
26 F.T.C. 303..................	3264	Hansen Inoculator Co., Inc. Inoculants. O.C.D. Jan. 12, 1938.
26 F.T.C. 312..................	3265	The Urbana Laboratories. Nitrogen fixing bacteria. O.C.D. Jan. 12, 1938.
26 F.T.C. 320..................	3266	The Nitragin Co. Nitrogen fixing bacteria. O.C.D. Jan. 12, 1938.
26 F.T.C. 666..................	3299	H. C. Brill Co., Inc. Bakers supplies. O.C.D. Feb. 10, 1938.
26 F.T.C. 824..................	3161	Golf Ball Mfg. Ass'n., et al. Golf balls. O.C.D. Feb. 25, 1938.
27 F.T.C. 377..................	3305	United Fence Manufacturers Ass'n., et al. Snow fence. O.C.D. July 13, 1938.
27 F.T.C. 982..................	3386	Master Lock Co. Locks. O.C.D. Sept. 1, 1938.
28 F.T.C. 169..................	3232	American Optical Co., et al. Optical goods. O.C.D. Jan. 21, 1939.
28 F.T.C. 186..................	3233	Bausch & Lomb Optical Co., et al. Optical goods. O.C.D. Jan. 21, 1939.
28 F.T.C. 1489.................	3685	U.S. Rubber Co., et al. Tires, etc. O.C.D. Apr. 25, 1939.
29 F.T.C. 121; 46 F.T.C. 1485; 47 F.T.C. 1836; 189 F. 2d 510.	2986	Standard Brands, Inc., et al. Yeast. O.C.D. June 15, 1939.
29 F.T.C. 678..................	3844	The Williams & Wilkins Co. Medical books. O.C.D. Aug. 23, 1939.
29 F.T.C. 727..................	3840	Simmons Co. Beds. O.C.D. Aug. 25, 1939.

Citations to FTC decisions and to court actions	FTC docket No.	Title of case, reference to product involved, and date and nature of disposition of case
29 F.T.C. 857.	3843	American Oil Co. Gasoline. O.C.D. Sept. 9, 1939.
30 F.T.C. 1384.	3799	Piel Brothers Starch Co. Corn products. O.C.D. Dec. 15, 1939.
30 F.T.C. 115.	2756	Nutrine Candy Company. Candy. O.C.D. Dec. 19, 1939.
30 F.T.C. 139.	3889	National Numbering Machine Co., Inc. Typographic numbering machine. O.C.D. Dec. 19, 1939.
30 F.T.C. 268.	3740	Metz Bros. Baking Co. Bread. O.C.D. Dec. 28, 1939.
30 F.T.C. 971.	3381	Curtice Brothers Company. Food products. O.C.D. Apr. 15, 1940.
30 F.T.C. 1117.	2986	Standard Brands, Inc., et al. Yeast. O.C.D. May 1, 1940.
30 F.T.C. 1209.	2987	Anheuser-Busch, Inc. Yeast. O.C.D. May 11, 1940.
30 F.T.C. 1393.	3962	Continental Baking Co. Bread. Dismissed May 31, 1940.
31 F.T.C. 986.	3798	Anheuser-Busch Co. Corn products. O.C.D. Sept. 25, 1940.
31 F.T.C. 1494.	3802	Penick & Ford, Ltd., Inc. Corn products. O.C.D. Nov. 29, 1940.
32 F.T.C. 60.	3804	Union Starch & Refining Co., et al. Corn syrup. O.C.D. Dec. 11, 1940.
32 F.T.C. 1635.	3669	General Baking Co. Baking products. Dismissed Dec. 13, 1940.
32 F.T.C. 1636.	2972	Bourjois, Inc., et al. Cosmetics. Dismissed Dec. 27, 1940.
32 F.T.C. 306; 49 F.T.C. 1799; 233 F. 2d 264.	4142	The American Crayon Co. Crayons, etc. O.C.D. Dec. 31, 1940.
32 F.T.C. 315; 5 S & D 676[1].	4143	Binney & Smith Co. Crayons, etc. O.C.D. Dec. 31, 1940.
32 F.T.C. 512.	4344	Vonnegut Hardware Co. Self-releasing fire exist. O.C.D. Jan. 23, 1941.

[1] Not reported in Federal Reporter.

Citations to FTC decisions and to court actions	FTC docket No.	Title of case, reference to product involved, and date and nature of disposition of case
32 F.T.C. 901...................	3805	American Maize Products Co. Corn products. O.C.D. Mar. 15, 1941.
32 F.T.C. 1116..................	3801	The Hubinger Co. Corn products. O.C.D. Apr. 3, 1941.
32 F.T.C. 1652..................	2951	United States Quarry Tile Co. Tile. Dismissed May 28, 1941.
32 F.T.C. 1652..................	3546	Superior Ceramic Corp. Tile. Dismissed May 28, 1941.
32 F.T.C. 1654..................	3549	C. Pardee Works, et al. Tile. Dismissed May 28, 1941.
32 F.T.C. 1653..................	3548	Mosaic Tile Co. Tile. Dismissed May 28, 1941.
32 F.T.C. 1654..................	3550	Wenozel Tile Co. Tile. Dismissed May 28, 1941.
32 F.T.C. 1655..................	3551	Wheeling Tile Co. Tile. Dismissed May 28, 1941.
32 F.T.C. 1655..................	3552	Architectural Tiling Co. Tile. Dismissed May 28, 1941.
32 F.T.C. 1656..................	3553	National Tile Co. Tile. Dismissed May 28, 1941.
33 F.T.C. 24; 38 F.T.C. 868; 142 F. (2d) 511.	3224	E. B. Muller & Co., et al. Chicory. O.C.D. June 11, 1941. Affirmed by CCA 6, Apr. 13, 1944.
33 F.T.C. 684...................	3903	National Grain Yeast Corporation. Yeast. O.C.D. July 16, 1941.
33 F.T.C. 791...................	4367	Republic Yeast Corporation. Yeast. O.C.D. July 18, 1941.
33 F.T.C. 812...................	3646	The C. F. Sauer Company. Salad dressing. O.C.D. July 31, 1941.
33 F.T.C. 1372..................	3926	Federal Yeast Corporation. Yeast. O.C.D. Sept. 22, 1941.
33 F.T.C. 1633..................	3373	Merck & Co., Inc. Chemicals. Dismissing decision July 9, 1941.
33 F.T.C. 1636..................	3330	U.S. Hoffman Machinery Corp. Pressing machines. Decision dismissing Sept. 19, 1941.

Citations to FTC decisions and to court actions	FTC docket No.	Title of case, reference to product involved, and date and nature of disposition of case
33 F.T.C. 1638.................	4103	Globe-Union, Inc. Radio parts. Decision dismissing Apr. 23, 1941.
34 F.T.C. 472...................	4571	Life Savers Corporation. Candy. O.C.D. Dec. 23, 1941.
34 F.T.C. 850; 39 F.T.C. 664; 40 F.T.C. 892.	3633	Corn Products Refining Co., et al. Byproducts of corn. O.C.D. Mar. 16, 1942. Appealed: C.C.A. 144 F. (2d) 212. Supreme Court 324 U.S. 726.
34 F.T.C. 879...................	3800	Clinton Co. & Clinton Sales Co. Byproducts of corn. O.C.D. Mar. 17, 1942.
34 F.T.C. 1362; 36 F.T.C. 1126; 39 F.T.C. 677; 40 F.T.C. 906; 135 F. (2d) 453; 144 F. (2d) 221; 324 U.S. 746.	3803	A. E. Staley Mfg. Company. Corn products. O.C.D. June 10, 1942. Remanded to Commission by C.C.A. 7, May 10, 1943. Order set aside by C.C.A. 7, July 6, 1944. C.C.A. reversed by Supreme Court, Apr. 23, 1945.
34 F.T.C. 1537.................	4725	Kimble Glass Co. Glass tubing, etc. Dismissed Mar. 9, 1942.
36 F.T.C. 25...................	3965	The Sherwin-Williams Co., et al. Paint products. O.C.D. Jan. 8, 1943.
36 F.T.C. 640; 40 F.T.C. 885; 42 F.T.C. 921; 148 F. (2d) 378; 155 F. (2d) 1016.	4405	Samuel H. Moss, Inc. Rubber stamps. O.C.D. May 1, 1943. Affirmed and enforcement granted by C.C.A. 2, Mar. 29, 1945. Petition to modify denied by C.C.A. 2, June 19, 1946.
37 F.T.C. 87; 40 F.T.C. 869; 43 F.T.C. 1101; 44 F.T.C. 1460; 45 F.T.C. 1063; 157 F. (2d) 533; 333 U.S. 683.	3167	Cement Institute, et al. Portland cement. O.C.D. July 17, 1943. Order set aside by C.C.A. 7, Sept. 20, 1946. C.C.A. reversed by Supreme Court, Apr. 26, 1948.
37 F.T.C. 345...................	4915	Dentists Supply Company of New York. Artificial teeth. O.C.D. Aug. 17, 1943.
37 F.T.C. 669...................	4506	Callaway Mills. Bedspreads. Dismissed Sept. 10, 1943.
37 F.T.C. 670...................	4744	Tennessee Tufting Co. Bedspreads, etc. Dismissed Sept. 10, 1943.

Citations to FTC decisions and to court actions	FTC docket No.	Title of case, reference to product involved, and date and nature of disposition of case
37 F.T.C. 670...................	4149	Continental Baking Co. Baking products. Dismissed Oct. 18, 1943.
38 F.T.C. 213; 50 F.T.C. 932......	5013	National Biscuit Co. Baking products. O.C.D. Feb. 23, 1944.
38 F.T.C. 463...................	5049	American Art Clay Co. Crayons, etc. O.C.D. May 12, 1944.
39 F.T.C. 35; 40 F.T.C. 388; 43 F.T.C. 1223; 44 F.T.C. 1499; 45 F.T.C. 328; 162 F. (2d) 949; 334 U.S. 37.	4319	Morton Salt Co. Salt. O.C.D. July 28, 1944. Modified Apr. 14, 1945. Set aside by CCA 7, May 27, 1947. C.C.A. reversed by Supreme Court May 3, 1948.
39 F.T.C. 86....................	5151	Caradine Hat Co. Hats. O.C.D. Aug. 16, 1944.
40 F.T.C. 690...................	4883	Booth Fisheries Corporation. O.C.D. June 29, 1945.
41 F.T.C. 244...................	5172	John B. Stetson. Hats. O.C.D. Oct. 8, 1945.
41 F.T.C. 263; 43 F.T.C. 56; 45 F.T.C. 1091; 47 F.T.C. 1766; 49 F.T.C. 923; 338 U.S. 865; 233 F. (2d) 649; 172 F. (2d) 210; 340 U.S. 231.	4389	Standard Oil Company (Indiana). Gasoline. O.C.D. Oct. 9, 1945. Modified Aug. 9, 1946. Affirmed and modified by C.C.A. 7, Mar. 11, 1949. Remanded to Commission by Supreme Court Jan. 8, 1951.
42 F.T.C. 36....................	5155	Ferro Enamel Corp., et al. Porcelain enamel. O.C.D. Feb. 26, 1946.
43 F.T.C. 480...................	5436	Draper Corporation. Bobbins, shuttles, looms. O.C.D. May 5, 1947.
44 F.T.C. 199...................	5048	Unity Stamp Company, Inc. Rubber stamps. O.C.D. Oct. 23, 1947.
44 F.T.C. 237; 48 F.T.C. 161......	4556	Curtiss Candy Co. (Also 2d, e, f, 3). Candy products. O.C.D. Nov. 12, 1947. Modified Aug. 15, 1951.
44 F.T.C. 351; 48 F.T.C. 1691; 49 F.T.C. 1695; 191 F. (2d) 786; 344 U.S. 206.	4920	Minneapolis-Honeywell Regulator Co. (Also 3 and 5). Automatic temperature controls. O.C.D. Jan. 14, 1948. See 2(a) of order dismissed by C.C.A. 7, July 5, 1951. Secs. 3 and 5 affirmed by C.C.A. 7, Sept. 18, 1951.

Citations to FTC decisions and to court actions	FTC docket No.	Title of case, reference to product involved, and date and nature of disposition of case
		Certiorari denied by Supreme Court, Dec. 22, 1952.
44 F.T.C. 1021..................	4677	Walter M. Johnson Candy Co.
		Candy bars and other candy products.
		O.C.D. June 8, 1948.
45 F.T.C. 670..................	3091	Cast Iron Soil Pipe Association, et al.
		Pipe.
		Dismissed July 30, 1948.
45 F.T.C. 136..................	5446	Jacques Kreisler Mfg. Co., et al.
		Jewelry.
		O.C.D. Aug. 11, 1948.
45 F.T.C. 723..................	3886	General Motors Corp. & A-C Spark Plug Co.
		Spark plugs and accessories.
		Dismissed Nov. 12, 1948.
		Reissued under Docket No. 5620.
46 F.T.C. 1015..................	4971	Hood Rubber Company, Inc.
		Rubber footwear.
		Dismissed July 8, 1949.
46 F.T.C. 75....................	5516	Krengel Mfg. Co., Inc., et al.
		Rubber stamps.
		O.C.D. July 15, 1949.
46 F.T.C. 100..................	5517	Adolph Gottsche, Inc., et al.
		Rubber stamps.
		O.C.D. Aug. 16, 1949.
46 F.T.C. 1041, 1061[2]...........	5544	Wayne Candies, Inc.
	5545	Melster Candies, Inc.
	5546	Ludens Candies, Inc.
	5546	D. L. Clark
	5548	Williamson Candy Co.
	5549	Bunte Brothers, Inc.
	5550	Sperry Candy Co.
	5552	Switzer's Licorice Co.
	5553	William Wrigley, Jr., Co.
	5596	Clayton A. Minter, et al.
	5597	Town Talk, Inc.
	5598	D. Goldenberg, Inc.
	5599	Cream O Specialty Labs. Co., Inc.
	5600	Euclid Candy Company, Inc.
	5601	Mason, Au & Magenheimer Confectionery Mfg. Co.
	5602	Sweets Company of America, Inc.
	5603	Kerr's Butterscotch, Inc.
	5604	Delicia Chocolate & Candy Mfg. Co., et al.
	5605	New England Confectionery Company
	5606	Charles N. Miller Co., et al.
	5607	F. B. Washburn Candy Corp.
	5608	American Chicle Company.
	5609	Planters Nut & Chocolate Co.
	5610	George Ziegler Company.

[2] Candy cases dismissed Sept. 23, 1949: (also cited under secs. 2(d) and 2(e) and, with some exceptions 2(c)).

Citations to FTC decisions and to court actions	FTC docket No.	Title of case, reference to product involved, and date and nature of disposition of case
	5611	Euclid Candy Company of Ill., Inc.
	5612	Dante Candy Company.
	5613	Fred W. Amend Company.
	5614	Shotwell Mfg. Co.
	5615	Kimball Candy Co.
	5616	M. J. Holloway & Co.
	5617	Universal Match Corp.
	5618	Hollywood Brand, Inc.
	5619	Paul F. Beich Company.
46 F.T.C. 149 and 1069..........	5526	E. I. du Pont de Nemours & Co., Inc. Degreasing solvent. Dismissed Oct. 18, 1949.
46 F.T.C. 1087..................	4841	Van Camp Sea Food Co., Inc. Seafood. Dismissed Nov. 22, 1949.
46 F.T.C. 379; 47 F.T.C. 1838; 48 F.T.C. 1699; 48 F.T.C. 1771; 189 F (2d) 893; 191 F (2d) 294; 343 U.S. 470.	5017	The Ruberoid Co. Asbestos & Asphalt roofing. O.C.D. Jan. 20, 1950. Affirmed by C.C.A., June 4, 1951.
46 F.T.C. 632...................	5579	F. & V. Manufacturing Co., Inc. Watch bands and attachments. O.C.D. Mar. 14, 1950.
46 F.T.C. 998...................	4972	U.S. Rubber Company. Footwear. O.C.D. June 30, 1950.
47 F.T.C. 169...................	5701	Horlicks Corporation (also 3). Malted milk products. Dismissed as to sec. 2a. O.C.D. Sept. 19, 1950, as to sec. 3.
47 F.T.C. 587...................	5502	Corn Products Refining Co. Corn products. O.C.D. Nov. 20, 1950.
47 F.T.C. 221, and 1030..........	5670	Ideal Cement Co. (Colo. Portland Div.). Cement. O.C.D. Sept. 28, 1950. Modified findings Mar. 8, 1951.
47 F.T.C. 839...................	5696	Central Soya Company, Inc. Animal feed. O.C.D. Jan. 11, 1951.
47 F.T.C. 1292..................	5671	Monolith Portland Midwest Co. Cement. O.C.D. May 4, 1951.
48 F.T.C. 861...................	5899	Houghton-Mifflin Company (also sec. 5).
48 F.T.C. 861...................	5900	Little, Brown & Co., Inc. (also sec. 5).
48 F.T.C. 861...................	5901	Random House, Inc. (also sec. 5).
48 F.T.C. 861...................	5902	Simon & Schuster, Inc. (also sec. 5). Books. Price discount charge dismissed Mar. 12, 1952.
48 F.T.C. 861...................	5960	Houghton-Mifflin Company.
48 F.T.C. 869...................	5961	Little, Brown & Co., Inc.
48 F.T.C. 878...................	5962	Random House, Inc.

Citations to FTC decisions and to court actions	FTC docket No.	Title of case, reference to product involved, and date and nature of disposition of case
48 F.T.C. 886....................	5963	Simon & Schuster, Inc. Books. O.C.D. Mar. 13, 1952.
49 F.T.C. 37....................	5640	Florida Citrus Canners Cooperative. Canned fruit juices. O.C.D. July 14, 1952.
49 F.T.C. 87....................	5971	Kentucky Chemical Industries, Inc. Animal feed products. O.C.D. Aug. 13, 1952.
49 F.T.C. 99....................	5972	Ubike Milling Company. Animal feed products. O.C.D. Aug. 13, 1952.
49 F.T.C. 108....................	5973	Early and Daniel Company. Animal feed products. O.C.D. Aug. 13, 1952.
49 F.T.C. 138....................	4307	International Salt Co., et al. Salt. O.C.D. Aug. 22, 1952.
49 F.T.C. 476....................	5969	Benrus Watch Company. Watches. O.C.D. Nov. 7, 1952.
49 F.T.C. 983....................	6039	Western Grain Company. Animal feeds. O.C.D. Jan. 27, 1953.
49 F.T.C. 1562....................	2973	Richard Hudnut, et al (also 2e). Cosmetics. Dismissed Jan. 9, 1953.
49 F.T.C. 1041....................	4878	Chain Institute, et al (also 5). Chains. sec. 2(a) dismissed Feb. 16, 1953. O.C.D. Feb. 16, 1953. CCA 8, pending.
49 F.T.C. 791; 352 U.S. 419 (1957).	5253	National Lead Co., et al (also 5). Lead pigments. O.C.D. Jan. 12, 1953.
49 F.T.C. 1161....................	5771	Namsco. Inc. Automotive parts. O.C.D. Mar. 17, 1953.
49 F.T.C. 1463....................	6061	Jacobs Manufacturing Co. Industrial chucks. O.C.D. June 30, 1953.
50 F.T.C. 54....................	5620	General Motors Corp., et al. (also 2d, 3, and 5). Auto accessories including spark plugs. O.C.D. July 10, 1953.
50 F.T.C. 73....................	5624	Electric Auto-Lite Co. Spark plugs. O.C.D. July 10, 1953.

Citations to FTC decisions and to court actions	FTC docket No.	Title of case, reference to product involved, and date and nature of disposition of case
50 F.T.C. 30....................	3977	Champion Spark Plug Company. Spark plugs. O.C.D. July 10, 1953.
50 F.T.C. 133...................	6042	American Biltrite Rubber Co., Inc. Shoe findings. O.C.D. Aug. 5, 1953.
50 F.T.C. 138...................	6043	B. F. Goodrich Co. Shoe findings. O.C.D. Aug. 5, 1953.
50 F.T.C. 143...................	6044	Goodyear Tire & Rubber Co., Inc. Shoe findings.
50 F.T.C. 149...................	6045	O'Sullivan Rubber Corp. Shoe findings. O.C.D. July 29, 1953.
50 F.T.C. 379...................	5828	Holtite Manufacturing Co., et al. Shoe findings. O.C.D. Oct. 30, 1953.
50 F.T.C. 395...................	5974	Page Dairy Co. Milk. O.C.D. Oct. 30, 1953.
50 F.T.C. 494...................	5585	Lever Brothers Company. Soap. Dismissed Dec. 16, 1953.
50 F.T.C. 513...................	5586	Procter & Gamble Distributing Company, et al. Soap. Dismissed Dec. 16, 1953.
50 F.T.C. 525...................	5587	Colgate-Palmolive-Peet Company. Soap. Dismissed Dec. 16, 1953.
50 F.T.C. 885...................	5675	General Foods Corporation. Pectin products. Dismissed Apr. 13, 1954.
50 F.T.C. 622...................	5677	B. F. Goodrich Company. Canvas and rubber footwear. Dismissed Jan. 22, 1954.
50 F.T.C. 994...................	6152	Aeration Processes, Inc., et al. Food products—aerated. O.C.D. June 16, 1954.
51 F.T.C. 51....................	6198	Frank F. Taylor Company. Baby strollers. O.C.D. July 29, 1954.
51 F.T.C. 282...................	5728	Sylvania Electric Products, Inc., et al. Radio tubes. Dismissed Sept. 23, 1954.
51 F.T.C. 100...................	6008	Purex Corporation, Ltd. Chemicals—bleaches. Dismissed Sept. 15, 1954.
51 F.T.C. 405...................	6199	Argus Cameras, Inc. Cameras. Dismissed Oct. 30, 1954.

Citations to FTC decisions and to court actions	FTC docket No.	Title of case, reference to product involved, and date and nature of disposition of case
51 F.T.C. 958; 239 F. 2d 253 (1956); 353 U.S. 938.	5722	Whitaker Cable Corporation. Automobile accessories. O.C.D. Apr. 29, 1955.
51 F.T.C. 931; 238 F. 2d 43 (1956); 355 U.S. 411.	5723	Moog Industries, Inc. Automobile accessories. O.C.D. Apr. 29, 1955.
51 F.T.C. 978; 239 F. 2d 152 (1956); 355 U.S. 941.	5770	E. Edelman & Company. Automobile accessories. O.C.D. Apr. 29, 1955.
51 F.T.C. 1195	5720	Bohn Aluminum & Brass Corporation, et al. Automobile accessories. Dismissed May 20, 1955.
51 F.T.C. 1114; 241 F. 2d 37; 355 U.S. 411, 741 (1958).	5768	C. E. Niehoff & Co. Automobile accessories. O.C.D. May 17, 1955.
52 F.T.C. 169	5897	Doubleday & Company, Inc. Books. O.C.D. Aug. 31, 1955.
52 F.T.C. 1017	5898	Harper & Brothers. Books. O.C.D. Mar. 23, 1956.
52 F.T.C. 1155; 245 F. 2d 281	5913	P. & D. Manufacturing Co., Inc. Automobile parts. O.C.D. Apr. 26, 1956.
52 F.T.C. 1504	5989	Fruitvale Canning Company. Canned fruit. O.C.D. June 15, 1956.
52 F.T.C. 798	6018	General Foods Corporation. Food products. O.C.D. Feb. 15, 1956.
52 F.T.C. 1659	6052	P. Sorenson Manufacturing Co., Inc. Automobile parts. O.C.D. June 29, 1956.
52 F.T.C. 110	6191	Sunshine Biscuits, Inc., et al. Bakery products. O.C.D. July 29, 1955.
52 F.T.C. 1679; 243 F. 2d 716	6327	Maryland Baking Co. Ice cream cones. O.C.D. June 29, 1956.
52 F.T.C. 623	6370	Magnesium Company of America, Inc. Industrial equipment. O.C.D. Jan. 6, 1956.
52 F.T.C. 484	6383	American Brake Shoe Co. Railroad car bearings. O.C.D. Nov. 15, 1955.
52 F.T.C. 919	6480	Thomas Y. Crowell Company. Books. O.C.D. Mar. 6, 1956.
53 F.T.C. 665	6560	Stephen F. Whitman & Sons, Inc. Candy. O.C.D. Jan. 31, 1957.

Citations to FTC decisions and to court actions	FTC docket No.	Title of case, reference to product involved, and date and nature of disposition of case
53 F.T.C. 902	6699	Pittsburgh Plate Glass Company. Auto safety glass. O.C.D. Apr. 19, 1957.
53 F.T.C. 970	6654	Sealed Power Corporation. Auto parts. O.C.D. May 3, 1957.
53 F.T.C. 1038	6700	Libbey-Owens-Ford Glass Co. Auto safety glass. O.C.D. May 22, 1957.
54 F.T.C. 277	6331	Anheuser-Busch, Inc. Beer. O.C.D. Sept. 10, 1957.
54 F.T.C. 246	6639	Arkansas City Cooperative Milk Association, Inc., et al. Milk. O.C.D. Sept. 4, 1957.
54 F.T.C. 475	6747	Topps Chewing Gum, Inc. Chewing gum. O.C.D. Oct. 25, 1957.
54 F.T.C. 480	6748	Philadelphia Chewing Gum Corporation. Bubble gum. O.C.D. Oct. 25, 1957.
54 F.T.C. 563	6737	Borden Company, et al. Milk. O.C.D. Nov. 13, 1957.
54 F.T.C. 664	6743	Grove Laboratories, Inc. Drugs and hair. O.C.D. Dec. 2, 1957.
54 F.T.C. 814	5721	Standard Motor Products, Inc. Automobile parts. O.C.D. Dec. 27, 1957.
54 F.T.C. 943	6768	Amalgamated Sugar Company. Beet sugar. O.C.D. Jan. 21, 1958.
54 F.T.C. 967	6877	Allen V. Smith, Inc. Dried food products. O.C.D. Jan. 22, 1958.
54 F.T.C. 1196	6710	Black Manufacturing Company. Work clothes and sportswear. O.C.D. Mar. 20, 1958.
54 F.T.C. 1237	6372	Southern Oxygen Company. Compressed gases. O.C.D. Apr. 1, 1958.
54 F.T.C. 1274	6698	Shell Oil Company, et al. Gasoline. O.C.D. Apr. 2, 1958.
54 F.T.C. 1628	5769	Federal-Mogul-Bower Bearings, Inc. Automotive products. O.C.D. May 20, 1958.
54 F.T.C. 1816	7052	Oxford Filing Supply Company, Inc. Filing Systems. O.C.D. June 17, 1958.

Citations to FTC decisions and to court actions	FTC docket No.	Title of case, reference to product involved, and date and nature of disposition of case
54 F.T.C. 1844..................	6919	Dan Dee Pretzel & Potato Chip Company. Pretzels and potato chips. O.C.D. June 27, 1958.
55 F.T.C. 103...................	7069	Empire Plastic Corporation. Plastic toys. O.C.D. July 7, 1958.
55 F.T.C. 433...................	6987	Guaranteed Parts Co., Inc. Auto ignition parts. O.C.D. Sept. 24, 1958.
55 F.T.C. 306...................	7090	Maguire Industries, Inc. Electronic components. O.C.D. Sept. 11, 1958.
55 F.T.C. 518...................	7032	Thermoid Company. Auto replacement parts. O.C.D. Oct. 4, 1958.
55 F.T.C. 655...................	6701	Sperry Rand Corporation. Electric shavers. O.C.D. Nov. 3, 1958.
55 F.T.C. 708...................	6891	Neapco Products, Inc. Automotive products. O.C.D. Nov. 7, 1958.
55 F.T.C. 665...................	6892	Schick Incorporated, et al. Electric shavers. O.C.D. Nov. 3, 1958.
55 F.T.C. 682...................	6900	North American Philips Company, Inc. Electric shavers. O.C.D. Nov. 3, 1958.
55 F.T.C. 9551..................	6641	Sun Oil Company. Gasoline. O.C.D. Jan. 5, 1959.
55 F.T.C. 1017..................	7066	Ronson Corporation, et al. Cigarette lighters and electric shavers. O.C.D. Jan. 8, 1959.
55 F.T.C. 993...................	7072	William Freihofer Baking Co., et al. Bakery products. O.C.D. Jan. 7, 1959.
55 F.T.C. 1252..................	5872	Thompson Products, Inc. Automotive products. O.C.D. Feb. 19, 1959.
55 F.T.C. 1225..................	7215	Hudson House, Inc., et al. Foods, bakery, fountain supplies. O.C.D. Feb. 12, 1959.
55 F.T.C. 1473..................	6764	Eis Automotive Corporation. Automotive parts. O.C.D. Mar. 20, 1959.
55 F.T.C. 1578..................	7243	Market Forge Company. Auto luggage carriers. O.C.D. Mar. 27, 1959.
55 F.T.C. 1754..................	6816	Airtex Products, Inc. Auto parts. O.C.D. May 12, 1959.

Citations to FTC decisions and to court actions	FTC docket No.	Title of case, reference to product involved, and date and nature of disposition of case
55 F.T.C. 1759.................	7141	Firestone Tire & Rubber Company. Tires and tubes. O.C.D. May 12, 1959.
55 F.T.C. 1807.................	7317	Sav-A-Stop, Inc., et al. Drug proprietaries and toiletries. O.C.D. May 19, 1959.
55 F.T.C. 1991.................	7256	Alton Canning Company, Inc., et al. Canned fruits and vegetables. O.C.D. June 1, 1959.
	7447	Pangburn Company, Inc. Candy. O.C.D. July 15, 1959.
	7067	Pressman Toy Corp. Toys. O.C.D. Aug. 3, 1959.
	7150	Westinghouse Electric Corporation, et al. Electric appliances. O.C.D. Oct. 13, 1959.
	7499	Heckethorn Manufacturing & Supply Company. Auto accessories. O.C.D. Apr. 14, 1960.
	7663	Albert Ehlers, Inc. Foodstuffs. O.C.D. Apr. 27, 1960.
	7678	Elmer Candy Company, Inc. Candy. O.C.D. May 27, 1960.
	7782	General Natural Gas Corporation. Liquefied petroleum products. O.C.D. June 30, 1960.
	7422	Hat Corporation of America. Hats. O.C.D. Aug. 11, 1960.
	7495	Idaho Canning Co., Ltd. Canned corn. O.C.D. May 2, 1961.
	7565	American Ball Bearing Company, et al. Automotive bearings. O.C.D. Dec. 8, 1960.
	7667	Borg-Warner Corporation, et al. Automobile parts. O.C.D. Apr. 1961.
	7707	Perfect Equipment Corp. Auto parts and tools. O.C.D. Dec. 12, 1961.
	7727	Northeast Capital Corporation, et al. Auto accessories and parts. O.C.D. Aug. 12, 1960.
	7783	Kelly Creamery Company. Milk and dairy foods. O.C.D. Dec. 21, 1960.

Citations to FTC decisions and to court actions	FTC docket No.	Title of case, reference to product involved, and date and nature of disposition of case
	7790	Alfonso Gioia & Sons, Inc. Macaroni. O.C.D. Oct. 21, 1960.
	7807	Kolstad Canneries, Inc., et al. Canned fruits and vegetables. O.C.D. Oct. 21, 1960.
	7837	Byer-Rolnick Hat Corporation. Men's hats. O.C.D. Aug. 18, 1960.
	7840	Cutter Laboratories, Inc. Human and veterinary biological products and pharmaceutical supplies. O.C.D. Oct. 27, 1960.
	7851	Gojer, Inc. Hand cleaners, soap, cleaning products, and dispensers. O.C.D. Dec. 1, 1960.
	7994	Graham Company, Inc. Dried beans and peas. O.C.D. Jan. 12, 1961.
	8062	Faber Brothers, Inc. Sporting goods. O.C.D. Mar. 16, 1961.
	8078	Pacific-Gamble Robinson Co. Fruits, vegetables, groceries, and canned goods. O.C.D. Dec. 7, 1960.

PART II

SECTION 2(C) OF THE CLAYTON ACT

(15 U.S.C. 13)

List of cases arising under section 2(c) of the Clayton Act, as amended by Robinson-Patman Act, involving charges that respondents have paid or accepted brokerage fees which were not earned by services rendered in connection with the sale or purchase of merchandise.

Citations to FTC decisions and to court actions	FTC docket No.	Title of case, reference to product involved, and date and nature of disposition of case
25 F.T.C. 564; 26 F.T.C. 1511; 32 F.T.C. 1867; 96 F. 2d 687; 305 U.S. 634; 117 F. 2d 29.	3032	Biddle Purchasing Co., et al. Food products. O.C.D. July 17, 1937. Affirmed by C.C.A. 2, May 2, 1938. Certiorari denied by Supreme Court, Oct. 17, 1938. (Bill of particulars granted in compliance proceeding by Commission Jan. 18, 1941). Contempt of court order, June 5, 1941.
26 F.T.C. 200; 102 F. 2d 763	3088	Oliver Brothers, Inc., et al. Hardware supplies. O.C.D. Dec. 31, 1937. Affirmed by C.C.A. 4, Mar. 25, 1939.
26 F.T.C. 486; 106 F. 2d 667	3031	The Great Atlantic & Pacific Tea Co. Food products. O.C.D. Jan. 25, 1938. Affirmed by C.C.A. 3, Sept. 22, 1939.
27 F.T.C. 1099; 109 F. 2d 268	3214	The Webb Crawford Company, et al. Food products. O.C.D. Oct. 20, 1938. Affirmed by C.C.A. 5, Jan. 30, 1940.
28 F.T.C. 1429	3129	Reeves Parvin & Co., et al. Food products. O.C.D. Apr. 15, 1939.
28 F.T.C. 1507; 29 F.T.C. 1328	3218	Quality Bakers of America, et al. Bakery products. O.C.D. Apr. 27, 1939. Modified O.C.D. Nov. 15, 1939.
29 F.T.C. 922	3834	C. R. Anthony Co., et al. Women's apparel. O.C.D. Sept. 12, 1939.
30 F.T.C. 224	3765	Fruit & Produce Exchange, et al. Food products. O.C.D. Dec. 22, 1939.
30 F.T.C. 445	3916	Charles V. Herron, et al. Food products. O.C.D. Jan. 27, 1940.
30 F.T.C. 1282	3511	Mississippi Sales Co., et al. Food products. O.C.D. May 15, 1950.
31 F.T.C. 536	3739	San Pedro Fish Exchange, et al. Seafood. O.C.D. July 13, 1940.
31 F.T.C. 625	3344	Atlantic Commission Co. Food products. O.C.D. July 24, 1940.
31 F.T.C. 1084	4290	Parket T. Frey Co., et al. Food products. O.C.D. July 24, 1940.
31 F.T.C. 1286	4233	Parr Sales Co. Food products. O.C.D. Oct. 8, 1940.

Citations to FTC decisions and to court actions	FTC docket No.	Title of case, reference to product involved, and date and nature of disposition of case
31 F.T.C. 1538................	4215	Howard E. Jones & Co., et al. Food products. O.C.D. Nov. 30, 1940.
31 F.T.C. 1543................	4275	Albert W. Sisk & Son. Food products. O.C.D. Nov. 30, 1940.
31 F.T.C. 1551................	4282	Thomas Roberts & Co. Food products. O.C.D. Nov. 30, 1940.
31 F.T.C. 1557................	4283	C. F. Unruh Brokerage Co. Food products. O.C.D. Nov. 30, 1940.
31 F.T.C. 1565................	4284	C. G. Reaburn & Co. Food products. O.C.D. Nov. 30, 1940.
31 F.T.C. 1573................	4292	H. N. Ruff, et al. Food products. O.C.D. Nov. 30, 1940.
31 F.T.C. 1581................	4298	American Brokerage Co., Inc. Food products. O.C.D. Nov. 30, 1940.
31 F.T.C. 1589................	4340	William Silver & Co., et al. Food products. O.C.D. Nov. 30, 1940.
32 F.T.C. 215.................	4285	Minetree Brokerage Co., et al. Food products. O.C.D. Dec. 19, 1940.
32 F.T.C. 370.................	4294	W. E. Robinson & Co., Inc. Canned fruit and vegetables. O.C.D. Jan. 10, 1941.
32 F.T.C. 1187................	4355	Ramsdell Packing Co. Canned sardines. O.C.D. Apr. 15, 1941.
32 F.T.C. 1192................	4358	Holmes Packing Corporation. Canned sardines. O.C.D. Apr. 15, 1941.
32 F.T.C. 1192................	4357	Machiasport Canning Company. Canned sardines. O.C.D. Apr. 15, 1941.
32 F.T.C. 1192................	4359	R. J. Peacock Canning Company. Canned sardines. O.C.D. Apr. 15, 1941.
32 F.T.C. 1192................	4356	Seaboard Packing Company. Canned sardines. O.C.D. Apr. 15, 1941.
32 F.T.C. 1193................	4411	Belfast Packing Co. Canned sardines. O.C.D. Apr. 15, 1941.
32 F.T.C. 1193................	4414	Booth Fisheries Corporation. Canned sardines. O.C.D. Apr. 15, 1941.

Citations to FTC decisions and to court actions	FTC docket No.	Title of case, reference to product involved, and date and nature of disposition of case
32 F.T.C. 1193.................	4360	Jonesport Packing Company. Canned sardines. O.C.D. Apr. 15, 1941.
32 F.T.C. 1193.................	4412	North Lubec Mfg. & Canning Company. Canned sardines. O.C.D. Apr. 15, 1941.
32 F.T.C. 1193.................	4410	Royal River Packing Corporation. Canned sardines. O.C.D. Apr. 15, 1941.
32 F.T.C. 1193.................	4362	Stinson Canning Company, etc. Canned sardines. O.C.D. Apr. 15, 1941.
32 F.T.C. 1193.................	4361	Sunset Packing Company, Inc. Canned sardines. O.C.D. Apr. 15, 1941.
32 F.T.C. 1194.................	4413	Union Sardine Co. Canned sardines. O.C.D. Apr. 15, 1941.
32 F.T.C. 1642.................	4334	Clover Farm Stores Corp., et al. Food products. Dismissed Feb. 12, 1941.
33 F.T.C. 235..................	4303	George A. Bounds & Co. Canned tomatoes and sweet potatoes. O.C.D. June 13, 1941.
33 F.T.C. 377..................	4281	General Grocer Company. Food. O.C.D. June 27, 1941.
33 F.T.C. 684..................	3903	National Grain Yeast Corporation. Yeast. O.C.D. July 16, 1941.
33 F.T.C. 830..................	4276	Giant Tiger Corporation. Food products. O.C.D. July 31, 1941.
33 F.T.C. 924..................	4277	Uco Food Corporation. Food products. O.C.D. Aug. 7, 1941.
33 F.T.C. 1114.................	4486	Reed-Harlin Grocer Company, et al. Food products. O.C.D. Aug. 21, 1941.
33 F.T.C. 1182.................	4279	R. C. Williams & Co. Food products. O.C.D. Aug. 27, 1941.
33 F.T.C. 1437.................	4286	The Thomas Page Mill Company Inc., et al. Flour. O.C.D. Oct. 1, 1941.
33 F.T.C. 1580.................	4519	Niles Brokerage Company, Inc., et al. Food products. O.C.D. Oct. 22, 1941.
33 F.T.C. 1639.................	4587	D. J. Easterlin & Co. Rice. Decision dismissing Sept. 25, 1941.

Citations to FTC decisions and to court actions	FTC docket No.	Title of case, reference to product involved, and date and nature of disposition of case
34 F.T.C. 87.....................	3221	United Buyers Corporation, et al. Groceries. O.C.D. Nov. 13, 1941.
34 F.T.C. 121....................	4280	A. Krasne, Inc. Food products. O.C.D. Nov. 14, 1941.
35 F.T.C. 49.....................	4229	Harry M. Bitterman, Inc., et al. Fur garments and other commodities. O.C.D. July 8, 1942.
35 F.T.C. 59.....................	4231	Isaac S. Dickler. Furs, etc. O.C.D. July 8, 1942.
35 F.T.C. 65.....................	4240	David M. Weiss. Fur garments. O.C.D. July 8, 1942. Enforcement order by C.C.A. 2, Nov. 12, 1946.
35 F.T.C. 71; 150 F. 2d 450.......	4257	Jack Hersog & Co. Fur garments. O.C.D. July 8, 1942. Affirmed by C.C.A. 2, July 16, 1945. Enforcement order by C.C.A. 2, Nov. 12, 1946.
35 F.T.C. 77.....................	4259	Central Buying Service, Inc. Millinery and other commodities. O.C.D. July 8, 1942.
35 F.T.C. 83.....................	4299	L. W. Powers Company. Women's ready-to-wear. O.C.D. July 8, 1942.
35 F.T.C. 354....................	4249	Style & Merit Buying Service. Furs and other commodities. O.C.D. Aug. 17, 1942.
37 F.T.C. 17.....................	4796	M. J. Kellner, etc. Food products. O.C.D. July 8, 1943.
37 F.T.C. 386; 149 F. 2d 970......	3783	Modern Marketing Services, Inc., et al. Groceries and allied products. O.C.D. Sept. 8, 1943. Affirmed and enforcement granted by C.A.A. 7, June 13, 1945.
37 F.T.C. 587....................	4833	Stanley J. Remus & Co., et al. Seafood products. O.C.D. Nov. 20, 1943.
38 F.T.C. 624....................	5087	Stacy Williams Co., Inc., et al. Steel or glass containers. O.C.D. June 13, 1944.
39 F.T.C. 46.....................	5130	Austelle-Flinton Co. Food products. O.C.D. Aug. 12, 1944.
39 F.T.C. 166; 150 F. 2d 607; 326 U.S. 774.	4821	Southgate Brokerage Co., Inc. Food products. O.C.D. Sept. 12, 1944.

Citations to FTC decisions and to court actions	FTC docket No.	Title of case, reference to product involved, and date and nature of disposition of case
		Affirmed and enforcement granted by C.C.A. 4, July 19, 1945. Certiorari denied by Supreme Court, Dec. 3, 1945.
39 F.T.C. 397...................	5217	B. F. Shriver Co. Food products. O.C.D. Oct. 23, 1944.
39 F.T.C. 480...................	4823	Fraering Brokerage Co., Inc. Food products. O.C.D. Dec. 5, 1944.
39 F.T.C. 485...................	4835	Glover & Wilson. Food products. O.C.D. Dec. 5, 1944.
39 F.T.C. 489...................	4928	W. M. Meador & Co., Inc. Food products. O.C.D. Dec. 5, 1944.
39 F.T.C. 492...................	4938	H. D. Childers Co. Food products. O.C.D. Dec. 5, 1944.
39 F.T.C. 495...................	5059	Hutchings Brokerage Co. Food products. O.C.D. Dec. 5, 1944.
40 F.T.C. 126...................	5131	Funsten Co., et al. Seafood. O.C.D. Feb. 12, 1945.
40 F.T.C. 207...................	4227	Florman & Bro., A. M., et al. Millinery. O.C.D. Mar. 19, 1945.
40 F.T.C. 241...................	5129	L. P. Maggioni & Co. Seafood. O.C.D. Mar. 20, 1945.
40 F.T.C. 286...................	5197	Coast Fishing Co. Seafood. O.C.D. Mar. 26, 1945.
40 F.T.C. 314...................	5137	Marine Products Co. Seafood. O.C.D. Mar. 29, 1945.
40 F.T.C. 373...................	3955	Jasper W. Efird, et al. Department store merchandise. O.C.D. Apr. 14, 1945.
40 F.T.C. 420...................	4792	Britt-McKinney Co., et al. Food products. O.C.D. Apr. 19, 1945.
40 F.T.C. 610...................	5267	The Halfhill Co., et al. Seafood. O.C.D. May 12, 1945.
41 F.T.C. 150...................	5333	J. V. Blevins Co., Inc. Food products. O.C.D. Sept. 17, 1945.
42 F.T.C. 108...................	4547	J. T. Jarrell Co. Food products. O.C.D. Mar. 25, 1946.

Citations to FTC decisions and to court actions	FTC docket No.	Title of case, reference to product involved, and date and nature of disposition of case
42 F.T.C. 114....................	4585	G. B. Shelton Brokerage Co., et al. Crystal phosphate. O.C.D. Mar. 25, 1946.
42 F.T.C. 119....................	5228	Washington Fish & Oyster Co., Inc. Seafood. O.C.D. Mar. 25, 1946.
42 F.T.C. 125....................	5270	C. C. Waddill Co., Inc. Food products. O.C.D. Mar. 25, 1946.
42 F.T.C. 132....................	5273	Phillips Sales Co., Inc. Food products. O.C.D. Mar. 25, 1946.
42 F.T.C. 138....................	5279	Carl Rubenstein, et al. Seafood. O.C.D. Mar. 25, 1946.
42 F.T.C. 148....................	5282	Paul Pankey & Co. Food products. O.C.D. Mar. 25, 1946.
42 F.T.C. 155....................	5284	Parrott & Co., et al. Food products. O.C.D. Mar. 25, 1946.
42 F.T.C. 165....................	5285	South Coast Fisheries, Inc. Seafood. O.C.D. Mar. 25, 1946.
42 F.T.C. 173....................	5295	William R. Hill & Co. Food products. O.C.D. Mar. 25, 1946.
42 F.T.C. 180....................	5296	Southern California Fish Corp. Seafood. O.C.D. Mar. 25, 1946.
42 F.T.C. 188....................	5297	Del Mar Canning Co. Seafood. O.C.D. Mar. 25, 1946.
42 F.T.C. 196....................	5303	Hovden Food Products Corp. Seafood. O.C.D. Mar. 25, 1946.
42 F.T.C. 202....................	5365	Sebastian-Stuart Fish Co., et. al. Seafood. O.C.D. Mar. 25, 1946.
42 F.T.C. 256....................	5383	Lakeland Highlands Canning Co., Inc., et al. Food products. O.C.D. Apr. 15, 1946.
42 F.T.C. 292....................	4939	California Lima Bean Growers Ass'n. Food products. O.C.D. May 9, 1946.
42 F.T.C. 408....................	5420	Union Fishermen's Cooperative Packing Co. Canned salmon. O.C.D. June 14, 1946.
43 F.T.C. 111....................	5432	West Coast Packing Corp., et al. Seafood. O.C.D. Sept. 5, 1946.

Citations to FTC decisions and to court actions	FTC docket No.	Title of case, reference to product involved, and date and nature of disposition of case
43 F.T.C. 164..................	5404	Custom House Packing Corp., et al. Food products. O.C.D. Sept. 23, 1946.
43 F.T.C. 173..................	5428	High Seas Tuna Packing Co., Inc. Seafood. O.C.D. Oct. 2, 1946.
43 F.T.C. 190..................	5456	French Sardine Co. of California. Canned sardines. O.C.D. Oct. 7, 1946.
43 F.T.C. 232..................	5370	Robert Rosoff. Furs, fur garments. O.C.D. Oct. 30, 1946.
43 F.T.C. 297..................	4589	C. H. Robinson Co., et al. Fruits, vegetables. O.C.D. Jan. 16, 1947.
43 F.T.C. 304..................	5462	California Marine Curing & Packing Company, et al. Seafood. O.C.D. Feb. 13, 1947.
43 F.T.C. 619..................	3221	United Buyers Corp., et al. Groceries. Modified O.C.D. June 17, 1947.
44 F.T.C. 118..................	5033	Columbia River Packers Ass'n., Inc. Seafood. O.C.D. Aug. 25, 1947.
44 F.T.C. 158..................	5164	Ketchikan Packing Co., et al. Seafood. O.C.D. Sept. 3, 1947.
44 F.T.C. 285..................	5494	Jesse Cl. Stewart Co., et al. Flour. O.C.D. Nov. 28, 1947.
44 F.T.C. 340..................	5471	New England Fish Company, et al. Seafood. O.C.D. Jan. 12, 1948.
44 F.T.C. 522..................	5501	Gevertz Buying Corp., et al. Men's wear. O.C.D. Feb. 4, 1948.
44 F.T.C. 1197.................	5152	H. A. Irving Co., et al. Food products. Dismissed Mar. 23, 1948.
	5470	Nat J. Levine. Millinery and handbags. Complaint withdrawn July 21, 1948.
45 F.T.C. 145..................	5469	Advance Realty Corp., et al. Food products. O.C.D. Aug. 11, 1948.
46 F.T.C. 10...................	5628	A. J. Harris & Company, et al. Canned food. O.C.D. July 1, 1949.
46 F.T.C. 116..................	5546	Pacific Grape Products Company. Canned food. O.C.D. Sept. 14, 1949.

Citations to FTC decisions and to court actions	FTC docket No.	Title of case, reference to product involved, and date and nature of disposition of case
46 F.T.C. 404...................	5338	National Modes, Inc. Women's wearing apparel. O.C.D. Feb. 3, 1950.
46 F.T.C. 437...................	5623	The Larson Co., et al. Canned food. O.C.D. Feb. 6, 1950.
46 F.T.C. 467...................	5576	J. Richard Phillips, Jr., & Sons, Inc., et al. Canned goods. O.C.D. Feb. 8, 1950.
46 F.T.C. 967...................	5651	Philip Barr & Co., Inc., et al. Canned goods. O.C.D. June 22, 1950.
46 F.T.C. 1062..................	5544– 5549 5551 5596– 5617 and 5619	See sec. 2(a) for case names. Candy. Dismissed Sept. 23, 1949.
47 F.T.C. 557...................	5534	Bonner Packing Company. Dried fruit. O.C.D. Nov. 9, 1950.
47 F.T.C. 671...................	5658	Pan American Food Company, Inc. Dried fruit and vegetables. O.C.D. Dec. 4, 1950.
47 F.T.C. 1106..................	5815	Hesmer, Inc., & Edw. A. Mitchell. Groceries. O.C.D. Mar. 22, 1951.
47 F.T.C. 1202..................	5819	Pacific Gamble Robinson Co., et al. Groceries. O.C.D. Apr. 5, 1951.
48 F.T.C. 53....................	5794	Atlas Supply Company, et al. (also 2f and 5). Auto accessories. O.C.D. July 19, 1951.
48 F.T.C. 192...................	5880	Dekle Brokerage Co. Fruits and vegetables. O.C.D. Aug. 16, 1951.
48 F.T.C. 254...................	5879	Consolidated Companies Inc., et al. Groceries. O.C.D. Sept. 1, 1951.
48 F.T.C. 529...................	5460	The Cooter Company. Groceries. O.C.D. Dec. 13, 1951.
48 F.T.C. 581...................	5482	Carpel Frosted Foods, Inc., et al. (also 2d). Frozen foods. O.C.D. Dec. 13, 1951.
48 F.T.C. 746...................	5921	Hastings Potato Growers Ass'n. Potatoes and vegetables. O.C.D. Feb. 15, 1952.
48 F.T.C. 894; 203 F. 2d 941......	5433	Independent Grocers Alliance Distributing Co., et al.

Citations to FTC decisions and to court actions	FTC docket No.	Title of case, reference to product involved, and date and nature of disposition of case
		Groceries.
		O.C.D. Mar. 7, 1952.
48 F.T.C. 1566	5578	Richmond-Chase Company, et al.
		Canned, dried, and frozen foods.
		Dismissed Jan. 11, 1952.
49 F.T.C. 205	5643	Christian Brokerage Company, Inc., et al.
		Groceries.
		O.C.D. Sept. 8, 1952.
49 F.T.C. 1495	6073	Jan-Warren Corporation, et al.
		Frozen foods.
		O.C.D. June 30, 1953.
50 F.T.C. 248	5784	Lagomarcina-Grupe Company of Iowa, et al.
		Food products.
		O.C.D. Sept. 15, 1953.
50 F.T.C. 333	6103	S. S. Sawyer, Inc.
		Potatoes.
		O.C.D. Sept. 25, 1953.
50 F.T.C. 349	6104	Florida Planters, Inc.
		Potatoes.
		O.C.D. Oct. 6, 1953.
51 F.T.C. 83	6160	Topco Associates, Inc.
		Food products, groceries.
		O.C.D. Aug. 17, 1954.
51 F.T.C. 412	6210	K. C. Snow Crop Distributors, Inc., et al.
		Frozen food.
		O.C.D. Oct. 28, 1954.
51 F.T.C. 424	6223	Lafayette Foods, Inc.
		Frozen foods.
		O.C.D. Oct. 28, 1954.
51 F.T.C. 784	6274	Northern Brokerage Co., et al.
		Food products.
		O.C.D. Mar. 10, 1955.
51 F.T.C. 789	6254	Spada Distributing Company, Inc.
		Food products.
		O.C.D. Mar. 11, 1955.
51 F.T.C. 917	6263	Adams Brothers Produce Co.
		Food products.
		O.C.D. Apr. 21, 1955.
52 F.T.C. 230	6259	F. C. Bloxom & Company.
		Fresh fruits and vegetables.
		O.C.D. Sept. 8, 1955.
52 F.T.C. 408	6366	Union Malleable Manufacturing Company.
		Plumbing products.
		O.C.D. Sept. 23, 1955.
52 F.T.C. 699	6420	Druggists' Supply Corporation, et al.
		Drugs.
		O.C.D. Jan. 18, 1956.
52 F.T.C. 1086	6442	Yardley of London, Inc.
		Soaps and cosmetics.
		O.C.D. Apr. 19, 1956.

Citations to FTC decisions and to court actions	FTC docket No.	Title of case, reference to product involved, and date and nature of disposition of case
52 F.T.C. 1140..................	6444	Clover Farm Stores Corporation, et al. Food products. O.C.D. Apr. 24, 1956.
52 F.T.C. 1484..................	6230	Rocky Mountain Wholesale Company, et al. Candy, tobacco, sundries. O.C.D. June 7, 1956.
53 F.T.C. 493...................	6255	Florida Citrus Exchange. Citrus fruit. O.C.D. Nov. 26, 1956.
53 F.T.C. 514...................	6606	E. A. Aaron & Bros., Inc., et al. Frozen fruits and vegetables. O.C.D. Dec. 3, 1956.
53 F.T.C. 783...................	6633	Daniel H. Sobo, et al. Sugar. O.C.D. Mar. 22, 1957.
53 F.T.C. 1149..................	6725	Colonial Manufacturing Company, Inc. Food products. O.C.D. June 13, 1957.
53 F.T.C. 1160..................	6720	Haskins Canning Corporation. Sardines. O.C.D. June 19, 1957.
53 F.T.C. 1180..................	6733	Institutional Foods Company, Inc., et al. Food products. O.C.D. June 21, 1957.
54 F.T.C. 673; 261 F. 2d 725 (C.A. 7, 1958) 363 U.S. 166.	6484	Henry Broch & Co. Food products. O.C.D. Dec. 10, 1957.
54 F.T.C. 731...................	6752	Riviera Packing Company, et al. Sardines. O.C.D. Dec. 18, 1957.
54 F.T.C. 987...................	6812	Jabie Sales Company. Food products. O.C.D. Jan. 23, 1958.
54 F.T.C. 1228..................	6969	Coyner-Evans Company, Inc., et al. Fresh vegetables. O.C.D. Mar. 26, 1958.
54 F.T.C. 1374..................	6904	American Packing Company, et al. Canned salmon. O.C.D. Apr. 17, 1958.
54 F.T.C. 1379..................	6906	Queen Fisheries, Inc., et al. Canned salmon. O.C.D. Apr. 18, 1958.
54 F.T.C. 1383..................	6907	Alaska Transportation Company, et al. Canned salmon and crab meat. O.C.D. Apr. 18, 1958.
54 F.T.C. 1393..................	6905	Farwest Fishermen, Inc., et al. Canned salmon. O.C.D. Apr. 18, 1958.
54 F.T.C. 1483..................	6910	Food Mart, Inc., et al. Groceries, frozen foods. O.C.D. May 6, 1958.

Citations to FTC decisions and to court actions	FTC docket No.	Title of case, reference to product involved, and date and nature of disposition of case
54 F.T.C. 1804.................	6942	Pacific American Fisheries, Inc., et al. Canned salmon and seafood. O.C.D. June 12, 1958.
55 F.T.C. 19..................	6977	Dehn & Co., Inc., et al. Canned salmon & food products. O.C.D. July 3, 1958.
55 F.T.C. 24..................	6978	Gavin Bros., Inc., et al. Canned salmon and seafood. O.C.D. July 3, 1958.
55 F.T.C. 29..................	6979	Walter P. Shiel & Co., et al. Canned salmon and seafood. O.C.D. July 3, 1958.
55 F.T.C. 34..................	6980	McGovern & McGovern. Canned salmon and seafood. O.C.D. July 3, 1958.
55 F.T.C. 39..................	6981	Salmon & Tuna Sales Company, et al. Canned salmon and seafood. O.C.D. July 3, 1958.
55 F.T.C. 45..................	6982	Ivar Wendt. Canned salmon and seafood. O.C.D. July 3, 1958.
55 F.T.C. 49..................	7021	Ward's Cove Packing Company, et al. Seafood. O.C.D. Oct. 16, 1958.
55 F.T.C. 572.................	7099	F. A. Gosse Company, et al. Canned salmon and seafood. O.C.D. Oct. 18, 1958.
55 F.T.C. 611.................	7147	Chinook Packing Company, et al. Salmon. O.C.D. Oct. 18, 1958.
55 F.T.C. 755.................	7035	G. P. Halferty & Co., et al. Canned salmon. O.C.D. Nov. 19, 1958.
55 F.T.C. 760.................	7089	Whiz Fish Products Company, et al. Seafood. O.C.D. Nov. 19, 1958.
55 F.T.C. 769.................	7154	C. F. Buelow Company, et al. Seafood. O.C.D. Nov. 19, 1958
55 F.T.C. 852.................	7210	Point Adams Packing Co., et al. Seafood. O.C.D. Dec. 5, 1958.
55 F.T.C. 861.................	7203	Barbey Packing Corporation, et al. Salmon and seafood. O.C.D. Dec. 11, 1958.
55 F.T.C. 936.................	7209	Nelbro Packing Company. Canned salmon. O.C.D. Dec. 24, 1958.
55 F.T.C. 1202................	7200	Parks Canning Company, Inc., et al. Seafood. O.C.D. Feb. 12, 1959.

Citations to FTC decisions and to court actions	FTC docket No.	Title of case, reference to product involved, and date and nature of disposition of case
55 F.T.C. 1208	7202	P. J. Burk Packing Co., Inc., et al. Canned salmon and seafood. O.C.D. Feb. 12, 1959.
55 F.T.C. 1214	7204	E. H. Hamlin Associates. Seafood. O.C.D. Feb. 12, 1959.
55 F.T.C. 1219	7208	P. E. Harris Company, Inc. Seafood. O.C.D. Feb. 12, 1959.
55 F.T.C. 1225	7215	Hudson House, Inc., et al. Foods. O.C.D. Feb. 12, 1959.
55 F.T.C. 1235	7249	Emard Packing Co., Inc., et al. Seafood. O.C.D. Feb. 12, 1959.
55 F.T.C. 1242	7151	Puget Sound Brokerage Co. Canned salmon. O.C.D. Feb. 17, 1959.
55 F.T.C. 1321	7240	American National Growers Corporation, et al. Fruits and vegetables. O.C.D. Feb. 26, 1959.
55 F.T.C. 1416	7239	Frito Company, et al. Mexican-style food. O.C.D. Mar. 10, 1959.
55 F.T.C. 1542	7201	Independent Salmon Canneries, Inc., et al. Salmon and seafood. O.C.D. Mar. 24, 1959.
55 F.T.C. 1633	7297	Keystone Wire Cloth Company, et al. Wire cloth. O.C.D. Apr. 9, 1959.
55 F.T.C. 1766	7274	New Orleans Shrimp Company, Inc. Shrimp. O.C.D. May 12, 1959.
55 F.T.C. 1986	7423	Eastern Canners, Inc., et al. Canned fruit and vegetables. O.C.D. June 1, 1959.
	7438	F. E. Booth Company, Inc. Fruit producer. O.C.D. Aug. 4, 1959.
	7519	D. L. Piazza Co. Fruit products. O.C.D. Dec. 8, 1959.
	7520	Egan, Fickett & Co., Inc. Fruit products. O.C.D. Dec. 8, 1959.
	7566	Southern Fruit Distributors, Inc. Fruit products. O.C.D. Feb. 12, 1960.
	7562	Kadiak Fisheries Company, et al. Canned salmon. O.C.D. June 30, 1960.

Citations to FTC decisions and to court actions	FTC docket No.	Title of case, reference to product involved, and date and nature of disposition of case
	7641	Smith Grain Company, Inc., et al. Citrus fruits, sugar, grain, animal feed, phosphate. O.C.D. June 8, 1961.
	8059	Sorrells Bros. Produce Company, Inc. Foods and citrus fruits. O.C.D. effective Aug. 4, 1961.
	8128	J. A. Morgan Produce, Inc., et al. Foods and citrus fruits. O.C.D. July 19, 1961.
	8142	Meredeith Milling Company, et al. Cottonseed meal and hulls, soybean products and animal feed. O.C.D. June 15, 1961.
	7144	Haines City Citrus Growers Association, et al. Citrus fruits. O.C.D. May 19, 1961.
	7212	Venus Foods, Inc. Bakery products. O.C.D. Oct. 28, 1960. Pending in C.A. 9 C. on petition to review filed Jan. 5, 1961.
	7273	Thomasville Chair Company. Furniture. O.C.D. Mar. 15, 1961. Pending in C. A. 5 C. on petition to review filed May 25, 1961.
	7576	Shamrock Foods, Inc., et al. Canned goods and food products. O.C.D. Sept. 16, 1960.
	7807	Kolstad Canneries, Inc., et al. Canned fruits and vegetables. O.C.D. Oct. 21, 1960.
	7918	Keen Fruit Corporation. Citrus fruits. O.C.D. May 19, 1961.
	7919	Groveland Fruit Company, Inc. Citrus fruits. O.C.D. May 19, 1961.
	7922	Battaglia Fruit Company, Inc. Citrus fruits. O.C.D. May 19, 1961.
	7923	Zellwood Fruit Distributors, Inc. Citrus fruits. O.C.D. May 19, 1961.
	7924	John S. Taylor Company (Inc.). Citrus fruits. O.C.D. May 19, 1961.
	7925	Sorrells Bros. Packing Co., Inc. Citrus fruits. O.C.D. May 19, 1961.

Citations to FTC decisions and to court actions	FTC docket No.	Title of case, reference to product involved, and date and nature of disposition of case
	7926	Knowles & Company. Citrus fruits. O.C.D. May 19, 1961.
	7927	Lakeland Highlands Cooperative Association. Citrus fruits. O.C.D. May 19, 1961.
	7928	Lake Wales Citrus Growers Association, Inc. Citrus fruits. O.C.D. May 19, 1961.
	7929	Peace River Packing Company. Citrus fruits. O.C.D. May 19, 1961.
	7930	Lakeland Packing Company, Inc. Citrus fruit. O.C.D. May 19, 1961.
	7931	Marion County Citrus Company. Citrus fruits. O.C.D. May 19, 1961.
	7932	Nelson & Company, Inc. Citrus fruits. O.C.D. May 19, 1961.
	7933	Patrick Fruit Corporation. Citrus fruits. O.C.D. May 19, 1961.
	7934	Holly Hill Fruit Products, Incorporated. Citrus fruits. O.C.D. May 19, 1961.
	7935	O. D. Huff, Jr., Groves, Inc. Citrus fruits. O.C.D. May 19, 1961.
	7936	Apopka Fruit Company. Citrus fruits. O.C.D. May 19, 1961.
	7998	Adams Packing Association, Inc. Citrus fruits. O.C.D. May 19, 1961.
	7999	Alturas Packing Company, Incorporated. Citrus fruits. O.C.D. May 19, 1961.
	8000	Arvida Fruit Co., Inc. Citrus fruits. O.C.D. May 19, 1961.
	8001	Babijuice Corporation of Florida. Citrus fruits. O.C.D. May 19, 1961.

Citations to FTC decisions and to court actions	FTC docket No.	Title of case, reference to product involved, and date and nature of disposition of case
	8002	Citrapak Corporation. Citrus fruits. O.C.D. May 19, 1961.
	8003	Deerfield Groves Company, Inc. Citrus fruits. O.C.D. May 19, 1961.
	8004	Ben Hill Griffin, Inc. Citrus fruits. O.C.D. May 19, 1961.
	8005	Egan Fickett & Co., Inc., et al. Citrus fruits. O.C.D. May 19, 1961.
	8006	Smith Enterprises Incorporated, et al. Citrus fruits. O.C.D. May 19, 1961.
	8007	South Lake Apopka Citrus Growers Association. Citrus fruits. O.C.D. May 19, 1961.
	8008	Square Deal Fruit Co. Citrus fruits. O.C.D. May 19, 1961.
	8009	Chase & Company, Inc. Citrus fruits and vegetables. O.C.D. May 19, 1961.
	8010	Herman J. Heidrick & Sons. Citrus fruits. O.C.D. May 19, 1961.
	8011	Heller Brothers Packing Company, Inc. Citrus fruits. O.C.D. May 19, 1961.
	8012	Killarney Fruit Company, Inc., et al. Citrus fruits. O.C.D. May 19, 1961.
	8013	Lake Hamilton Cooperative, Inc. Citrus fruits. O.C.D. May 19, 1961.
	8014	Snively Groves, Inc. Citrus fruits and juices. O.C.D. May 19, 1961.
	8015	Osceola Fruit Distributors. Citrus fruits and juices. O.C.D. May 19, 1961.
	8016	Newbern Groves, Inc. Citrus fruits. O.C.D. May 19, 1961.
	8017	Waverly Growers Cooperative Inc. Citrus fruits. O.C.D. May 19, 1961.
	8018	Roper Growers Cooperative. Citrus fruits. O.C.D. May 19, 1961.

Citations to FTC decisions and to court actions	FTC docket No.	Title of case, reference to product involved, and date and nature of disposition of case
	8019	Nevins Fruit Company, Inc., et al. Citrus fruits. O.C.D. May 19, 1961.
	8020	Lake Alfred Packing Company. Citrus fruits. O.C.D. May 19, 1961.
	8055	National Fiorita Fruit Company. Food products, citrus fruits, and vegetables. O.C.D. Nov. 23, 1960.
	8057	Bisese & Console, Inc. Food products and citrus fruits. O.C.D. May 16, 1961.
	8063	Bruce A. Graves & Son. Food products and citrus fruits. O.C.D. Apr. 13, 1961.
	8065	J. Segari & Co., et al. Food products and citrus fruits. O.C.D. Jan. 6, 1961.
	8067	A. R. Fiorita Fruit Co. Food products and citrus fruits. O.C.D. Dec. 1, 1960.
	8090	Growers Marketing Service, Inc. Citrus fruits. O.C.D. May 19, 1961.
	8147	Di Giorgio Fruit Corporation. Citrus fruits. O.C.D. May 19, 1961.
	8148	Peoples Packing Company, Inc. Citrus fruits. O.C.D. May 19, 1961.
	8149	Indian Lake Fruit Co., Inc. Citrus fruits. O.C.D. May 19, 1961.
	8207	Russell-Ward Co., Inc. Food products and citrus fruits. O.C.D. May 17, 1961.
	8210	Pipping Packing Company, Inc. Citrus fruits. O.C.D. May 19, 1961.

PART III

SECTION 2(D) OF THE CLAYTON ACT

(15 U.S.C. 13)

List of cases arising under section 2(d) of the Clayton Act, as amended by Robinson-Patman Act, involving charges that respondents pay customers for services or facilities which are not available on proportionally equal terms to all other customers competing in the distribution of the same products or commodities.

Citations to FTC decisions and to court actions	FTC docket No.	Title of case, reference to product involved, and date and nature of disposition of case
26 F.T.C. 824	3161	Golf Ball Mfg. Ass'n, et al. Golf balls. O.C.D. Feb. 25, 1938.
28 F.T.C. 1489	3685	U.S. Rubber Co., et al. Tires, etc. O.C.D. Apr. 25, 1939.
30 F.T.C. 268	3740	Metz Bros. Baking Co. Bread. O.C.D. Dec. 28, 1939.
30 F.T.C. 971	3381	Curtice Brothers Company. Canned fruits and vegetables. O.C.D. Apr. 15, 1940.
31 F.T.C. 734	3749	Lambert Pharmacal Co. Listerine. O.C.D. Aug. 12, 1940.
32 F.T.C. 315	4143	Binney & Smith Co. Crayons. O.C.D. Dec. 31, 1940.
32 F.T.C. 306	4142	The American Crayon Co. Crayons, etc. O.C.D. Dec. 31, 1940.
33 F.T.C. 812	3646	The C. F. Sauer Company. Salad dressing. O.C.D. July 31, 1941.
34 F.T.C. 472	4571	Life Savers Corporation. Candy. O.C.D. Dec. 23, 1941.
34 F.T.C. 1530	4335	White Swan Uniforms, Inc., et al. Uniforms for women. Dismissed Dec. 4, 1941.
36 F.T.C. 477	4740	Grabosky Brothers. Tobacco. O.C.D. Apr. 6, 1943.

Citations to FTC decisions and to court actions	FTC docket No.	Title of case, reference to product involved, and date and nature of disposition of case
38 F.T.C. 307...................	5115	General Baking Co. Bakery products. O.C.D. Apr. 25, 1944.
38 F.T.C. 463...................	5049	American Art Clay Co. Educational supplies. O.C.D. May 12, 1944.
39 F.T.C. 82....................	5020	Holzbeierlein & Sons, Inc. Bakery products. O.C.D. Aug. 16, 1944.
41 F.T.C. 244...................	5172	John B. Stetson. Hats. O.C.D. Oct. 8, 1945.
44 F.T.C. 237..................	4556 & 4673	Curtiss Candy Co. (also 2a, c, f, & 3). Candy products. O.C.D. Nov. 12, 1947.
44 F.T.C. 1180..................	3912	P. Lorillard Company. Tobacco products. Dismissed Mar. 17, 1948.
44 F.T.C. 1181..................	3913	Brown & Williamson Tobacco Corp. Tobacco products. Dismissed Mar. 17, 1948.
44 F.T.C. 1182..................	3914	R. J. Reynolds Tobacco Co. Tobacco products. Dismissed Mar. 17, 1948.
44 F.T.C. 1182..................	3915	Larus & Brothers Co., Inc. Tobacco products. Dismissed Mar. 17, 1948.
44 F.T.C. 1183..................	3919	Philip Morris & Company, Ltd., Inc. Tobacco products. Dismissed Mar. 17, 1948.
44 F.T.C. 1183..................	3921	Liggett & Myers Tobacco Company, Inc. Tobacco products. Dismissed Mar. 17, 1948.
44 F.T.C. 1184..................	3922	Stephano Brothers. Tobacco products. Dismissed Mar. 17, 1948.
44 F.T.C. 1185..................	3927	American Tobacco Co. Tobacco products. Dismissed Mar. 17, 1948
45 F.T.C. 723...................	3886	General Motors Corp. & A-C Spark Plug Co. Spark plugs and accessories. Dismissed Nov. 11, 1948.
46 F.T.C. 404...................	5338	National Modes, Inc., et al. (also 2c). Women's apparel. O.C.D. Feb. 3, 1950.
46 F.T.C. 1062..................	5544– 5553, 5596– 5619	See sec. 2(a) for case names. Candy. Dismissed Sept. 23, 1949.
46 F.T.C. 1139..................	5243	N. Erlanger, Blumgart & Co. Acetate rayon fabrics. Dismissed Mar. 13, 1950.

Citations to FTC decisions and to court actions	FTC docket No.	Title of case, reference to product involved, and date and nature of disposition of case
46 F.T.C. 1170..................	5226	Celanese Corporation of America (also 22e). Rayon yarn and fabrics. Dismissed June 21, 1950.
48 F.T.C. 3....................	5865	Consolidated Cigar Corporation, et al. Cigars. O.C.D. July 31, 1951.
48 F.T.C. 161..................	4556 and 4673	Curtiss Candy Co. (also 2e and 2f). Candy. O.C.D. Nov. 12, 1947. O.C.D. Aug. 15, 1951.
48 F.T.C. 581..................	5482	Carpel Frosted Foods, Inc., et al. (also 2c). Frozen foods. O.C.D. Dec. 13, 1951.
48 F.T.C. 971..................	5830	Bulova Watch Company, Inc. Watches. O.C.D. Mar. 17, 1952.
48 F.T.C. 979..................	5836	The Gruen Watch Company. Watches. O.C.D. Mar. 17, 1952.
48 F.T.C. 990..................	5837	Elgin National Watch Company. Watches. O.C.D. Mar. 17, 1952.
49 F.T.C. 138..................	4307	International Salt Co., et al. Salt. O.C.D. Aug. 22, 1952.
49 F.T.C. 440..................	5982	American Greetings Corporation (also 2e and 5). Greeting cards. O.C.D. Oct. 23, 1952.
49 F.T.C. 1578.................	5928	Wildroot Company, Inc. Hair preparations. Dismissed June 30, 1953.
50 F.T.C. 54...................	5620	General Motors Corporation, et al. Auto accessories. O.C.D. July 10, 1953.
50 F.T.C. 494..................	5585	Lever Brothers Company. Soap. Dismissed Dec. 16, 1953.
50 F.T.C. 513..................	5596	Procter & Gamble Distributing Company, et al. Soap. Dismissed Dec. 16, 1953.
50 F.T.C. 525..................	5587	Colgate-Palmolive-Peet Company. Soap. Dismissed Dec. 16, 1953.
51 F.T.C. 89...................	5735	Kay Windsor Frocks, Inc., et al. Women's dresses. O.C.D. Aug. 18, 1954.
51 F.T.C. 405..................	6199	Argus Cameras, Inc. Cameras. Dismissed Oct. 30, 1954.

Citations to FTC decisions and to court actions	FTC docket No.	Title of case, reference to product involved, and date and nature of disposition of case
51 F.T.C. 430..................	6216	Wooster Rubber Company. Kitchen supplies, rubber, auto mats. O.C.D. Oct. 29, 1954.
51 F.T.C. 879..................	6264	Knomark Manufacturing Company, Inc. Shoe polish. O.C.D. Apr. 7, 1955.
51 F.T.C. 1229.................	6215	Jonathan Logan, Inc., et al. Women's dresses. O.C.D. May 27, 1955.
52 F.T.C. 798..................	6018	General Foods Corporation. Food products. O.C.D. Feb. 15, 1956.
52 F.T.C. 929..................	6443	Elmo, Inc. Cosmetics. O.C.D. Mar. 7, 1956.
52 F.T.C. 1064.................	6440	Hudnut Sales Company, Inc. Cosmetics. O.C.D. Apr. 4, 1956.
52 F.T.C. 1181.................	6462	Tetley Tea Company, Inc. Tea. O.C.D. Apr. 26, 1956.
52 F.T.C. 1267.................	6441	Helena Rubenstein, Inc. Cosmetics. O.C.D. May 9, 1956.
52 F.T.C. 1535.................	6212	Henry Rosenfeld, Inc., et al. Women's suits and dresses. O.C.D. June 21, 1956.
52 F.T.C. 1692.................	6469	Jos. Martinson & Co., Inc. Coffee and tea. O.C.D. June 29, 1956.
53 F.T.C. 84...................	6466	Minute Maid Corporation. Frozen foods. July 27, 1956.
53 F.T.C. 127..................	6519	Revlon, Inc. Cosmetics. O.C.D. Aug. 17, 1956.
53 F.T.C. 199..................	6569	Dolcin Corporation. Pain reliever. O.C.D. Aug. 31, 1956.
53 F.T.C. 290..................	6521	Bymart-Tintair, Inc. Hair coloring preparations. O.C.D. Sept. 25, 1956.
53 F.T.C. 294..................	6523	Johnson & Johnson. Surgical supplies. O.C.D. Sept. 27, 1956.
52 F.T.C. 403..................	6552	O'Cedar Corporation, et al. Mops, waxes, and polishes. O.C.D. Oct. 31, 1956.
53 F.T.C. 565; 258 F. 2d 365, 2d Cir. 1958, Order set aside.	6464	Atalanta Trading Corporation. Meat products. O.C.D. Dec. 20, 1956.

Citations to FTC decisions and to court actions	FTC docket No.	Title of case, reference to product involved, and date and nature of disposition of case
53 F.T.C. 574...................	6524	Anahist Co., Inc. Medicinal preparations. O.C.D. Dec. 20, 1956.
53 F.T.C. 751...................	6635	Bourjois, Inc. Cosmetics. O.C.D. Mar. 5, 1957.
53 F.T.C. 1050..................	6465	Chestnut Farms-Chevy Chase Dairy. Dairy products. O.C.D. May 21, 1957.
54 F.T.C. 321...................	6749	Leaf Brands, Inc. Candy and chewing gum. O.C.D. Sept. 13, 1957.
54 F.T.C. 335...................	6470	McCormick & Company, Inc. Spices, extracts, tea, coffee, condiments. O.C.D. Sept. 17, 1957.
54 F.T.C. 359...................	6467	J. H. Filbert, Inc. Salad dressing and oleomargerine. O.C.D. Sept. 19, 1957.
54 F.T.C. 374...................	6468	Pompeian Olive Oil Corporation. Olive oil. O.C.D. Sept. 29, 1957.
54 F.T.C. 475...................	6747	Topps Chewing Gum, Inc. Chewing gum. O.C.D. Oct. 25, 1957.
54 F.T.C. 534...................	6460	Sweets Company of America. Candy. O.C.D. Nov. 12, 1957.
54 F.T.C. 979...................	6461	Reed Candy Company. Candy. O.C.D. Jan. 28, 1958.
54 F.T.C. 1196..................	6710	Black Manufacturing Company. Work clothes and sportswear. O.C.D. Mar. 20, 1958.
54 F.T.C. 1490..................	6592	Groveton Paper Company. Paper products. O.C.D. May 7, 1958.
54 F.T.C. 1502..................	6596	General Foods Corporation. Food products. O.C.D. May 7, 1958.
54 F.T.C. 1514..................	6597	Sunshine Biscuits, Inc. Cookies—crackers. O.C.D. May 7, 1958.
54 F.T.C. 1526..................	6598	Piel Bros., Inc. Groceries—beer. O.C.D. May 7, 1958.
54 F.T.C. 1538..................	6599	Hudson Pulp & Paper Corporation. Paper napkins and towels. O.C.D. May 7, 1958.
54 F.T.C. 1550..................	6600	P. Lorillard Company. Cigarettes. O.C.D. May 7, 1958.

Citations to FTC decisions and to court actions	FTC docket No.	Title of case, reference to product involved, and date and nature of disposition of case
54 F.T.C. 1569..................	6463	Crosse & Blackwell Company. Food products. O.C.D. May 8, 1958.
54 F.T.C. 1574..................	6595	Sunkist Growers, Inc. Fresh and frozen fruit juices. O.C.D. May 8, 1958.
54 F.T.C. 1844..................	6919	Dan Dee Pretzel & Potato Chip Company. Pretzels and potato chips. O.C.D. June 6, 27, 1958.
55 F.T.C. 136..................	6925	Judson Dunaway Corporation. Household cleaning and mothproofing products. O.C.D. July 24, 1958.
55 F.T.C. 354..................	6642	Liggett & Myers Tobacco Company, Inc. Tobacco products. O.C.D. Sept. 9, 1959.
55 F.T.C. 397..................	7119	Trifari, Krussman & Fishel, Inc., et al. Costume jewelry. O.C.D. Sept. 23, 1958.
55 F.T.C. 655..................	6701	Sperry Rand Corporation. Electric shavers. O.C.D. Nov. 3, 1958.
55 F.T.C. 665..................	6892	Schick Incorporated, et al. Electric shavers. O.C.D. Nov. 2, 1958.
55 F.T.C. 731..................	7117	Longines-Wittnauer Watch Co., Inc., et al. Watch movements and parts. O.C.D. Nov. 14, 1958.
55 F.T.C. 815..................	6961	Hafner Coffee Company. Coffee. O.C.D. Dec. 3, 1958.
55 F.T.C. 852..................	7210	Point Adams Packing Co., et al. Seafood. O.C.D. Dec. 5, 1958.
55 F.T.C. 993..................	7072	William Freihofer Baking Co., et al. Bakery products. O.C.D. Jan. 7, 1959.
55 F.T.C. 1017..................	7066	Ronson Corporation, et al.— Cigarette lighters and electric shavers. O.C.D. Jan. 8, 1959.
55 F.T.C. 1065..................	7247	Jantzen, Inc. Clothing. O.C.D. Jan. 16, 1959.
55 F.T.C. 1142..................	6833	Ward Baking Company. Bakery products. O.C.D. Feb. 10, 1959.
55 F.T.C. 1391..................	7118	Keystone Mfg. Co., et al. Home movie equipment. O.C.D. Mar. 5, 1959.
55 F.T.C. 1584..................	7288	Day's Tailor—D Clothing, Inc. Men's and boys' sportswear and work clothes. O.C.D. Mar. 27, 1959.

Citations to FTC decisions and to court actions	FTC docket No.	Title of case, reference to product involved, and date and nature of disposition of case
	7395	Bayuk Cigars Incorporated. Cigars. O.C.D. Aug. 27, 1959.
	6750	Philip Morris, Inc. Cigarettes—tobacco. O.C.D. Sept. 9, 1959.
	6830	American Tobacco Company. Cigarettes—tobacco products. O.C.D. Sept. 9, 1959.
	6848	R. J. Reynolds Tobacco Company. Cigarettes—tobacco. O.C.D. Sept. 9, 1959.
	6908	Brown & Williamson Tobacco Corporation. Cigarettes, tobacco. O.C.D. Sept. 9, 1959.
	6926	General Mills, Inc. Cereals, etc. O.C.D. Sept. 9, 1959.
	7150	Westinghouse Electric Corporation, et al. Electric appliances. Oct. 13, 1959.
	6927	Swanee Paper Corporation. Paper products. O.C.D. Mar. 22, 1960.
	7493	Burlington Industries, Inc. Textiles. O.C.D. Mar. 22, 1960.
	7516	Marlun Manufacturing Company, Inc., et al. Electric broiler-rotisseries. O.C.D. Apr. 14, 1960.
	7528	Fieldcrest Mills, Inc. Textiles. O.C.D. Apr. 27, 1960.
	7651	Bercut-Richards Packing Company, Inc. Canned food products. O.C.D. Apr. 27, 1960.
	7663	Albert Ehlers, Inc. Coffee, tea, extracts, spices, and dried foods. O.C.O. Apr. 27, 1960.
	7701	Anchor Chemical Company, Inc. Chemicals for graphic arts. O.C.D. Apr. 28, 1960.
	7700	Wetter Numbering Machine Company, Inc. Typographical numbering machines. O.C.D. May 10, 1960.
	7384	Select Magazines, Inc., et al. Magazines. O.C.D. June 30, 1960.
	7385	Curtis Publishing Company, et al. Magazines and paperback books. O.C.D. June 30, 1960.

Citations to FTC decisions and to court actions	FTC docket No.	Title of case, reference to product involved, and date and nature of disposition of case
	7386	Cowles Magazines, Inc., et al. Magazines, paperback books. O.C.D. June 30, 1960.
	7387	Esquire, Inc., et al. Magazines, paperback books. O.C.D. June 30, 1960.
	7388	The New Yorker Magazine, Inc., et al. The New Yorker Magazine. O.C.D. June 30, 1960.
	7389	Newsweek, Inc., et al. Newsweek magazine. O.C.D. June 30, 1960.
	7390	United States News Publishing Corp., et al. U.S. News and World Report magazine. O.C.D. June 30, 1960.
	7391	Hearst Corporation. Magazines, paperback books. O.C.D. June 30, 1960.
	7392	MacFadden Publications, Inc. Magazines, paperback books. O.C.D. June 30, 1960.
	7393	Fawcett Publications, Inc. Magazines, paperback books. O.C.D. June 30, 1960.
	7394	Triangle Publications, Inc. Magazines. O.C.D. June 30, 1960.
	7611	New American Library of World Literature, Inc., et al. Paperback books. O.C.D. June 30, 1960.
	7612	Dell Publishing Company, Inc. Magazines, paperback books. O.C.D. June 30, 1960.
	7613	Bantam Books, Inc. Paperbacks. O.C.D. June 30, 1960.
	7614	National Comics Publications, Inc., et al. Comic magazines. O.C.D. June 30, 1960.
	7615	Pocket Books, Inc., et al. Paperbacks. O.C.D. June 30, 1960.
	7699	Lanston Industries, Inc. Typesetting, typecasting equipment. O.C.D. June 1, 1960.
	7867	Herst-Allen Company. Nonedible products for retailers. O.C.D. Aug. 31, 1960.
	6966	Exquisite Form Brassiere, Inc. Brassieres. Pending in C.A.D.C.C. on petition to review filed Dec. 21, 1960.

Citations to FTC decisions and to court actions	FTC docket No.	Title of case, reference to product involved, and date and nature of disposition of case
	7495	Idaho Canning Co., Ltd. Canned corn. O.C.D. May 2, 1961.
	7715	Ipswich Hosiery Company, Inc. Women's hosiery. O.C.D. Oct. 12, 1960.
	7790	Alfonso Gioia & Sons, Inc. Macaroni. O.C.D. Oct. 21, 1960.
	7847	Craftsman Line-Up Table Corporation. Printing equipment, tables. O.C.D. Sept. 7, 1960.
	7868	Midwest Biscuit Company. Biscuits and crackers. O.C.D. Sept. 2, 1960.
	8031	Anniston Foundry Company. Cast iron soil pipes and fittings. O.C.D. Oct. 19, 1960.
	8074	Nibco, Inc. Valves and fittings, water supply systems. O.C.D. Mar. 2, 1961.
	8091	Dennis Chicken Products Company, Inc. Chickens and turkeys. O.C.D. Dec. 21, 1960.
	8092	Ball Brothers Company, Inc. Glass containers and closure parts, and zinc products. O.C.D. Dec. 21, 1960.
	8093	Chun King Corporation. Oriental food products. O.C.D. Jan. 12, 1961.
	8096	Kerr Glass Manufacturing Corporation. Glass containers and closure parts. O.C.D. Dec. 7, 1960.
	8116	Simmons Company. Mattresses, box springs, sofa beds, and furniture. O.C.D. Mar. 3, 1961.
	8118	Penick & Ford, Ltd., Incorporated. Dessert preparatons, puddings, pie fillings, corn and maple syrup, and molasses. O.C.D. Apr. 12, 1961.
	8177	S. C. Johnson & Son, Inc. Household and automobile waxes and polishes, insecticides, and household deodorants. O.C.D. Mar. 16, 1961.
	7721	Shulton, Inc. Toilet preparations, chemical products, pharmaceutical supplies. O.C.D. July 25, 1961.

Citations to FTC decisions and to court actions	FTC docket No.	Title of case, reference to product involved, and date and nature of disposition of case
	8123	Tyler Pipe & Foundry Company. Plumbing supplies and soil pipes. O.C.D. Aug. 11, 1961.
	8293	Marcal Paper Mills, Inc. Household paper products: waxed paper, toilet tissue, napkins, towels, etc. O.C.D. June 9, 1961.
	8342	Golden Press, Inc. Children's books. O.C.D. July 7, 1961.
	8343	Grosset & Dunlap, Inc., et al. Children's books. O.C.D. July 7, 1961.

PART IV

SECTION 2(E) OF THE CLAYTON ACT

(15 U.S.C. 13)

List of cases arising under section 2(e) of the Clayton Act, as amended by Robinson-Patman Act, involving charges that respondents furnish one purchaser services or facilities not accorded to all on proportionally equal terms.

Citations to FTC decisions and to court actions	FTC docket No.	Title of case, reference to product involved, and date and nature of disposition of case
31 F.T.C. 658....................	3736	Luxor, Ltd. Toilet articles and cosmetics. O.C.D. July 31, 1940.
32 F.T.C. 1636..................	2972	Bourjois, Inc., et al. Cosmetics. Dismissed Dec. 27, 1940.
32 F.T.C. 1637..................	2975	Coty, Inc. Cosmetics. Dismissed Dec. 27, 1940.
34 F.T.C. 850; 144 F. 2d 211; 324 U.S. 726.	3633	Corn Products Refining Co., et al. Byproducts of corn. O.C.D. Mar. 16, 1942. Modified and affirmed by C.C.A. 7, July 6, 1944.

Citations to FTC decisions and to court actions	FTC docket No.	Title of case, reference to product involved, and date and nature of disposition of case
39 F.T.C. 288; 156 F. 2d 132; 331 U.S. 806.	3133	Elizabeth Arden, Inc., et al. Cosmetics. O.C.D. Oct. 3, 1944. Affirmed and enforcement granted by C.C.A. 2, June 5, 1946. Certiorari denied by Supreme Court, Apr. 14, 1947.
44 F.T.C. 237..................	4556 and 4673	Curtiss Candy Co. (also 2 a, d, f, and 3). Candy products. O.C.D. Nov. 12, 1947. Modified Aug. 15, 1951.
46 F.T.C. 1041..................	5544– 5551 5553 5596– 5619	See sec. 2(a) for cases names. Candy. Dismissed Sept. 23, 1949.
46 F.T.C. 1139..................	5243	N. Erlanger, Blumgart & Co., Inc. Acetate rayon fabrics. Dismissed Mar. 13, 1950.
46 F.T.C. 1170..................	5226	Celanese Corporation of America (also 2d). Rayon yarn and fabrics. Dismissed June 21, 1950.
47 F.T.C. 1371..................	5773	Appleton-Century-Crofts, Inc. Books. O.C.D. June 13, 1951.
49 F.T.C. 440..................	5982	American Greetings Corporation (also 2d and 5). Greeting cards, ribbons, etc. O.C.D. Oct. 23, 1952.
49 F.T.C. 1562..................	2973	Richard Hudnut, et al. (also 2a). Cosmetics. Dismissed Jan. 9, 1953.
49 F.T.C. 1563..................	2974	Elmo, Inc., et al. Cosmetics. Dismissed Jan. 9, 1953.
49 F.T.C. 1564..................	3017	Charles of the Ritz, Inc., et al. Cosmetics. Dismissed Jan. 9, 1953.
49 F.T.C. 1564..................	3039	Primrose House, Inc. Cosmetics. Dismissed Jan. 9, 1953.
49 F.T.C. 1565..................	4435	Coty, Inc. Cosmetics. Dismissed Jan. 9, 1953.
49 F.T.C. 1565..................	4436	Bourjois, Inc., et al. Cosmetics. Dismissed Jan. 9, 1953.
51 F.T.C. 430..................	6216	Wooster Rubber Company. Kitchen supplies, rubber, auto mats. O.C.D. Oct. 29, 1954.
51 F.T.C. 879..................	6264	Knomark Manufacturing Company, Inc. Shoe polish. O.C.D. Apr. 7, 1955.

Citations to FTC decisions and to court actions	FTC docket No.	Title of case, reference to product involved, and date and nature of disposition of case
52 F.T.C. 798....................	6018	General Foods Corporation. Packaged food products. O.C.D. Feb. 15, 1956.
52 F.T.C. 929....................	6443	Elmo, Inc. Cosmetics. O.C.D. May 9, 1956.
52 F.T.C. 1267...................	6441	Helena Rubenstein, Inc. Cosmetics. O.C.D. May 9, 1956.
53 F.T.C. 127....................	6519	Revlon, Inc. Cosmetics. O.C.D. Aug. 17, 1956.
53 F.T.C. 403....................	6552	O'Cedar Corporation, et al. Mops, waxes, and polishes. O.C.D. Oct. 31, 1956.
53 F.T.C. 771; 360 U.S. 55 (1959).	6221	Simplicity Pattern Company, Inc. Dress patterns. O.C.D. Mar. 13, 1957.
54 F.T.C. 114....................	6892	Schick Incorporated, et al. Electric razors. O.C.D. Nov. 2, 1958.
54 F.T.C. 1844...................	6919	Dan Dee Pretzel & Potato Chip Co. Pretzels and potato chips. O.C.D. June 27, 1958.
55 F.T.C. 1584...................	7288	Day's Tailor-D Clothing, Inc. Men's, boys' sportswear. O.C.D. Mar. 27, 1959.
	7528	Fieldcrest Mills. Linens, towels, etc. O.C.D. Apr. 27, 1960.
	6966	Exquisite Form Brassiere, Inc. Brassieres. O.C.D. Oct. 31, 1960. Pending in C.A.D.C.C. on petition to review filed Dec. 21, 1960.
	7790	Alfonso Gioia & Sons, Inc. Macaroni. O.C.D. Oct. 21, 1960.
	7851	Gojer, Inc. Hand cleaners, soap, cleaning products, and dispensers. O.C.D. Dec. 2, 1960.

PART V

SECTION 2(F) OF THE CLAYTON ACT

(15 U.S.C. 18)

List of cases arising under section 2(f) of the Clayton Act as amended by Robinson-Patman Act, involving charges that respondents unlawfully and knowingly induce or receive a discrimination in price which is prohibited by Section II of the Clayton Act.

Citations to FTC decisions and to court actions	FTC docket No.	Title of case, reference to product involved, and date and nature of disposition of case
26 F.T.C. 824..................	3161	Gold Ball Mfg., Ass'n, et al. Gold balls. O.C.D. Feb. 25, 1938.
28 F.T.C. 485..................	3377	Miami Wholesale Drug Corp., et al. Drugs. O.C.D. Feb. 9, 1939.
29 F.T.C. 857..................	3843	American Oil Co. Gasoline. O.C.D. Sept. 9, 1939.
34 F.T.C. 363..................	3820	A. S. Aloe Company. Surgical equipment. O.C.D. Dec. 15, 1941.
38 F.T.C. 631..................	4957	Atlantic City Wholesale Drug Co., et al. Drugs and cosmetics. O.C.D. June 14, 1944.
39 F.T.C. 535..................	4548	E. J. Brach & Sons. Corn products. O.C.D. Dec. 21, 1944.
40 F.T.C. 578..................	5027	Associated Merchandising Corp., et al. Dry goods. O.C.D. May 8, 1945.
44 F.T.C. 237..................	4556 and 4673	Curtiss Candy Co. (also 2 a, d, f, and 3). Corn syrup, glucoses, and other candy ingredients. O.C.D. Nov. 12, 1947. Modified Aug. 15, 1951.
46 F.T.C. 829; 47 F.T.C. 1314.....	5648	National Tea Company. Groceries. O.C.D. May 15, 1950. Modified May 8, 1951.
46 F.T.C. 861; 194 F. 2d 433; 346 U.S. 61	4933	Automatic Canteen Co. of America (also 3). Vending machines. O.C.D. June 6, 1950. Affirmed by C.C.A. 7, Mar. 10, 1952.

Citations to FTC decisions and to court actions	FTC docket No.	Title of case, reference to product involved, and date and nature of disposition of case
		Supreme Court reversed C.C.A. as to 2(f) and remanded to C.C.A. July 10, 1953, with directions to remand to Commission. C.C.A. 7 remanded to Commission Aug. 1, 1953.
48 F.T.C. 53..................	5794	Atlas Supply Company, et al. (also 2c and 5). Auto accessories. O.C.D. July 19, 1951.
50 F.T.C. 125.................	5990	Safeway Stores, Inc. Grocery chain. Dismissed July 27, 1953.
50 F.T.C. 213.................	5991	Kroger Company. Food products. Dismissed Sept. 16, 1953.
51 F.T.C. 282.................	5728	Sylvania Electric Products, Inc., et al. Radio tubes. Dismissed Sept. 23, 1954.
51 F.T.C. 733.................	5421	Crown Zellerbach Corporation, et al. Paper products. Dismissed Feb. 9, 1955.
54 F.T.C. 1274................	6698	Shell Oil Company, et al. Petroleum products. O.C.D. Apr. 2, 1958.
55 F.T.C. 188.................	6837	Warehouse Distributors, Inc., et al. Auto parts and supplies. O.C.D. Aug. 14, 1958.
55 F.T.C. 910.................	6765	Hunt-Marquardt, Inc., et al. Auto parts and supplies. O.C.D. Dec. 23, 1958.
55 F.T.C. 1279................	5766	Borden-Aicklen Auto Supply Co., Inc., et al. Auto parts and supplies. O.C.D. Feb. 24, 1959.
55 F.T.C. 1279................	5767	D. & N. Auto Parts Company, Inc., et al. Auto parts and supplies. O.C.D. Feb. 24, 1959.
55 F.T.C. 1430................	5724	American Motor Specialties Co., Inc., et al. Automotive parts. O.C.D. Mar. 12, 1959.
55 F.T.C. 1556................	6890	Allbrights, et al. Auto parts and supplies. O.C.D. Mar. 27, 1959.
	7142	Automotive Supply Company, et al. Tires and tubes. O.C.D. Aug. 28, 1959.
	7070	March of Toys, Inc., et al. Catalog of toys. O.C.D. Aug. 26, 1960.
	6889	Alhambra Motor Parts, et al. Auto accessories and parts. O.C.D. Oct. 28, 1960. Pending in CA9C on petition to review filed Jan. 4, 1961.

Citations to FTC decisions and to court actions	FTC docket No.	Title of case, reference to product involved, and date and nature of disposition of case
	7686	Southwestern Warehouse Distributors, Inc., et al. Auto accessories and parts. O.C.D. Sept. 14, 1960.
	7687	Automotive Southwest, Inc., et al. Auto accessories and parts. O.C.D. Sept. 8, 1960.

APPENDIX B

In order to expedite the disposition of adjudicatory proceedings and to generally improve its procedures governing such proceedings, the Commission has amended, revised, and redesignated its rules governing the disposition of proceedings by the entry of consent orders and its rules of practice for adjudicative proceedings.

Under the amended and revised rules, any negotiations looking toward the disposition of a matter by the entry of a consent order will be had prior to the issuance and service of the complaint, and the rules governing adjudicative proceedings will not be applicable to such negotiations. Consent order procedure will not be available after a complaint is issued. Negotiations for agreements containing consent orders will be under the supervision and control of the Commission's Office of Consent Orders, and hearing examiners will be relieved of all duties and responsibilities in connection with matters disposed of by the entry of consent orders.

The amended and revised rules of practice for adjudicative proceedings provide a limited review procedure for initial decisions of hearing examiners. Heretofore, any party to a proceeding could, as a matter of right, file a notice of intention to appeal and thereafter appeal from a hearing examiner's initial decision. Under the amended and revised rules, the Commission's review of initial decisions will be limited to those cases in which the party seeking the review first establishes, in a petition for review, that important substantive or procedural matters are involved, and cases which the Commission upon its own motion places on its own docket for review. The principal effect of the amended rule will be to eliminate appeals *which are clearly without merit* and *which are made for the sole purpose of delaying the final decision.* [Emphasis added.]

The amended and revised rules will be applicable to all proceedings in which the complaint is served subsequent to the effective date of the amended rules.

The rules are amended, revised, and redesignated to read as follows:

260

PART 3—CONSENT ORDER PROCEDURE

§3.1 *Notice of proposed adjudicative proceeding.* Where time, the nature of the proceeding and the public interest permit, the Commission may notify a person, partnership or corporation of its determination to issue its complaint charging such party with having violated one or more of the statutes administered by the Commission. Such notice shall be served in the manner provided in §4.26(a) of the Rules of Practice for Adjudicative Proceedings, and shall be accompanied by a complaint which the Commission intends to issue, together with a proposed form of order.

§3.2 *Reply.* Within ten days after service of such notice, the parties named may file a reply with the Secretary stating whether or not they are willing to have the proceeding disposed of by the entry of an order in substantially the form proposed.

If the reply is in the negative or if no reply is filed within the time provided, the complaint will be issued and served forthwith.

If the reply is in the affirmative, the files will be referred to the Office of Consent Orders, where the parties served and members of the Commission's staff may participate in the preparation and execution of an agreement containing a consent order. The parties may appear personally or be represented by an attorney of record who has entered an appearance under §4.23. *No representations on behalf of a party by other persons will be recognized.* [Emphasis added.]

§3.3 *Agreement.* Every agreement shall contain, in addition to an order, an admission of all jurisdictional facts and express waivers of further procedural steps, of the requirement that the Commission's decision contain a statement of findings of fact and conclusions of law, and of all rights to seek judicial review or to otherwise challenge or contest the validity of the order. The agreement shall also contain provisions that the complaint may be used in construing the terms of the order; that the order shall have the same force and effect and shall become final and may be altered, modified or set aside in the same manner and within the same time provided by statute for other orders; and that the agreement shall not become a part of the official record of the proceeding unless and until it is accepted by the Commission. In addition, the agreement may contain a statement that the signing thereof is for settlement purposes only and does not constitute an admission by any respondent that the law has been violated as alleged in the complaint.

§3.4 *Disposition.* (a) *Submission af agreement.* Unless for good cause shown the time is extended by the Commission, an executed agreement containing a consent order shall be submitted to the Commission within thirty days after the date on which the files are referred to the Office of Consent Orders. If an agreement is not so submitted, or if at any time it appears to the Office of Consent Orders that the execution of a satisfactory agreement is unlikely, the files shall be returned to the Commission and the complaint will be issued and served forthwith. After a complaint is issued, the consent order procedure will not be available.

(b) *Decision.* Upon receiving an agreement containing a consent order, the Commission may accept it and issue its complaint, in such form as the circumstances require, and decision, including the order agreed upon, or reject it and issue its complaint and set the matter down for adjudication in regular course. Alternatively, the Commission may take such other action as may be appropriate.

PART 4—RULES OF PRACTICE FOR ADJUDICATIVE PROCEEDINGS

Subpart A—Scope of Rules; Nature of Adjudicative Proceedings

§4.1 *Scope of the rules in this part.* The rules in this part govern procedure in adjudicative proceedings before the Federal Trade Commission. It is the policy of the Commission, that, to the extent practicable and consistent with requirements of law, such proceedings shall be conducted expeditiously. The hearing examiner and counsel for all parties shall be governed at all times by this policy, and every effort shall be made at each stage of a proceeding to avoid delay.

§4.2 *Nature of adjudicative proceedings.* Adjudicative proceedings are those formal proceedings conducted under one or more of the statutes administered by the Commission which are required by statute to be determined on the record after opportunity for an agency hearing. The term does not include other administrative proceedings such as negotiations of agreements containing consent orders; investigational hearings held prior to the commencement of formal proceedings or for the purpose of inquiring into the manner and extent of compliance with outstanding orders; trade practice conferences; proceedings for fixing quantity limits under section 2(a) of the Clayton Act (15 U.S.C. 13(a)); investigations under section 5 of the Export Trade Act (15 U.S.C. 65); or the promulgation of substantive rules and regulations, determinations of classes of products exempted from statutory requirements, the establishment of name guides, or inspections and industry counseling, under sections 4(d) and 6(a) of the Wool Products Labeling Act (15 U.S.C. 68(b) and 68(d)), sections 7, 8(b) and 8(c) of the Fur Products Labeling Act (15 U.S.C. 69(e) and 69(f)), sections 5(c) and 5(d) of the Flammable Fabrics Act (15 U.S.C. 1194), and sections 7(c), 7(d) and 12(b) of the Textile Fiber Products Identification Act (15 U.S.C. 70).

Subpart B—Complaint, Answer, Default, and Motions

§4.3 *Commencement of proceeding.* An adjudicative proceeding is commenced by the issuance and service of a complaint by the Commission.

§4.4 *Complaint.* (a) *Form.* The Commission's complaint shall contain the following:

(1) Recital of the legal authority and jurisdiction for institution of the proceeding, with specific designation of the statutory provisions alleged to have been violated;

(2) A clear and concise factual statement sufficient to inform each respondent with reasonable definiteness of the type of acts or practices alleged to be in violation of the law;

(3) Where practical, a form of order which the Commission has reason to believe should issue if the facts are found to be as alleged in the complaint;

(4) Notice of the time and place for hearing, the time to be at least thirty days after service of the complaint.

(b) *Motion for more definite statement*. If the statement in a complaint is so vague or ambiguous that a party cannot reasonably frame a responsive answer, the respondent may move for a more definite statement before filing its answer. Such a motion shall be filed within fifteen days after service of the complaint and shall point out the defects complained of and the details desired.

§4.5 *Answer*. (a) *Time for filing*. A respondent shall have thirty days after service of the complaint within which to file an answer thereto; provided, however, that the filing of a motion for a more definite statement alters this period of time as follows, unless a different time is fixed by the hearing examiner: (1) if the motion is denied, the answer shall be filed within ten days after notice of such action; (2) if the motion is granted, in whole or in part, the answer shall be filed within ten days after service of the more definite statement.

(b) *Content of Answer*. An answer shall conform to the following:

(1) *Contesting allegations of complaint*. Such answer shall contain:

(i) A concise statement of the facts constituting the ground of defense;

(ii) Specific admission, denial, or explanation of each fact alleged in the complaint or, if the respondent is without knowledge thereof, a statement to that effect.

(2) *Admitting allegations of complaint*. If the respondent elects not to contest the allegations of fact set forth in the complaint, the answer shall consist of a statement that respondent admits all material allegations to be true. Such an answer shall constitute a waiver of hearings as to facts so alleged, and an initial decision containing appropriate findings and conclusions and an appropriate order disposing of the proceeding shall be issued by the hearing examiner. In such answer, the respondent may, however, reserve the right to submit proposed findings and conclusions and the right to petition for review under §4.20.

(c) *Default*. Failure of the respondent to file answer within the time provided shall be deemed to constitute a waiver of its right to appear and to authorize the hearing examiner, without further notice to respondent, to find the facts to be as alleged in the complaint and to enter an initial decision containing such findings, appropriate conclusions and order.

§4.6 *Motions*. (a) *Presentation and disposition*. During the time a proceeding is before a hearing examiner, all motions therein, except as provided in §4.13(f), shall be addressed to and ruled upon by him, and, if in writing, shall be filed with the Secretary of the Commission. All motions addressed to the Commission shall be in writing and shall be filed with the Secretary of the Commission.

(b) *Content*. All written motions shall state the particular order, ruling, or action desired and the grounds therefor.

(c) *Answers*. Within ten days after service of any written motion, or within such longer or shorter time as may be designated by the hearing examiner or the Commission, the opposing party shall answer or be taken to have consented to the granting of the relief asked for in the motion. The moving party shall have no right to reply, except as permitted by the hearing examiner or the Commission.

(d) *Motions for extensions*. As a matter of discretion, the hearing examiner or the Commission may waive the requirements of this section as to motions for extensions of time, and may rule upon such requests *ex parte*.

(e) *Rulings on motions for dismissal*. When a motion to dismiss a complaint or for other relief is granted with the result that the proceeding before the hearing examiner is terminated, the hearing examiner shall make and file an initial decision in accordance with the provisions of §4.19. If such a motion is granted as to all charges of the complaint in regard to some, but not all, of the respondents, or is granted as to any part of the charges in regard to any or all of the respondents, the hearing examiner shall enter his ruling on the record and take it into account in his initial decision. When a motion to dismiss is made at the close of the evidence offered in support of the complaint based upon the alleged failure to establish a *prima facie* case, the hearing examiner may, if he so elects, defer ruling thereon until the close of the case for the reception of evidence.

Subpart C—Amendments and Supplemental Pleadings; Prehearing Procedure; Voluntary Intervention

§4.7 *Amendments and supplemental pleadings*. (a) *Amendments*. (1) *By leave*. If and whenever determination of a controversy on the merits will be facilitated thereby, the hearing examiner may, upon such conditions as are necessary to avoid prejudicing the public interest and the rights of the parties, allow appropriate amendments to pleadings; provided, however, that an application for amendment of a complaint may be allowed only if the amendment is reasonably within the scope of the proceeding initiated by the original complaint.

2. *Conformance to evidence*. When issues not raised by the pleadings, but reasonably within the scope of the proceeding initiated by the original complaint, are tried by express or implied consent of the parties, they shall be treated in all respects as if they had been raised in the pleadings; and such amendments of the pleadings as may be necessary to make them conform to the evidence and to raise such issues shall be allowed at any time.

(b) *Supplemental pleadings*. The hearing examiner may, upon reasonable notice and such terms as are just, permit service of a supplemental pleading setting forth transactions, occurrences, or events which have happened since the date of the pleading sought to be supplemented and which are relevant to any of the issues involved.

§4.8 *Pre-hearing conferences*. (a) The hearing examiner upon motion of any party or upon his own motion may, and, in every case where it appears probable that the hearing will extend for more than three days he shall, direct counsel for all parties to meet with him for a conference to consider:

(1) Simplification and clarification of the issues;

(2) Necessity or desirability of amendments to pleadings, subject, however, to the provisions of §4.7(a)(1);

(3) Stipulations, admissions of fact and of the contents and authenticity of documents;

(4) Expedition in the presentation of evidence, including, but not limited to, restriction of the number of expert, economic or technical witnesses; and

(5) Such other matters as may aid in the orderly disposition of the proceeding, including disclosure of the names of witnesses or furnishing for inspection or copying of non-privileged documents, papers, books or other physical exhibits, which constitute or contain evidence relevant to the subject matter involved and which are in the possession, custody or control of any party to the proceeding.

(b) Pre-hearing conferences, in the discretion of the hearing examiner, may be stenographically reported as provided in §4.14(f), but shall not be public unless all parties so agree.

(c) The hearing examiner shall enter in the record an order which recites the action taken, the amendments allowed and the agreements made at the conference; and such order shall control the subsequent course of the proceeding, unless modified at the hearing to prevent manifest injustice. If counsel for any party after proper direction fails or refuses to disclose the names of witnesses or to make available for inspection or copying non-privileged documents, papers, books or other physical exhibits, the hearing examiner, in his discretion, may also enter in the record an order providing, as appropriate:

(1) That the testimony of the witnesses whose names are not disclosed or the documents, papers, books or other physical exhibits which are not made available for inspection or copying in accordance with the direction shall not be introduced in evidence; or

(2) That counsel who fails or refuses to comply with the hearing examiner's direction in respect of any of the foregoing shall be suspended or barred from participation in the proceeding in accordance with the provisions of §4.23(e).

§4.9 *Voluntary intervention.* (a) Any individual, partnership, unincorporated association, or corporation desiring to intervene in an adjudicative proceeding shall make written application in the form of a motion setting forth the basis therefor. Such application shall have attached to it a certificate showing service thereof upon each party to the proceeding in accordance with the provisions of §4.26(b). A similar certificate shall be attached to the answer filed by any party, other than counsel in support of the complaint, showing service of such answer upon the applicant.

(b) The hearing examiner or the Commission may by order permit the intervention to such extent and upon such terms as are provided by law or as otherwise may be deemed proper.

Subpart D—Depositions; Admissions; Evidence

§4.10 *Depositions.* (a) *When, how and by whom taken.* Good cause being shown, the testimony of any witness may be taken by deposition in any proceeding, whether at issue or not. Depositions may be taken orally or upon written interrogatories before any person designated by the Commission or the hearing examiner and having power to administer oaths.

(b) *Application.* Any party desiring to take the deposition of a witness shall make application in writing to the hearing examiner, setting forth the reasons why such deposition should be taken; the time when, the place where, and the name and post office address of the person before whom the deposition is to be taken; the name and post office address of each witness; and the subject matter concerning which each witness is expected to testify.

(c) *Notice.* Such notice as the hearing examiner may order shall be given of the taking of a deposition, but this shall not be less than five days' written notice of the taking of a deposition within the United States, and not less than fifteen days' written notice when the deposition is to be taken elsewhere.

(d) *Taking and reception in evidence.* Each witness testifying upon deposition shall be duly sworn, and the adverse party shall have the right to cross-examine. The questions propounded and the answers thereto, together with all objections made, shall be reduced to writing and, in the presence of the officer before whom the deposition is taken, read to the witness, subscribed by him, and certified in the usual form by the officer. Thereafter, the officer shall forward the deposition, with three copies thereof, in an envelope under seal, endorsed with the title of the proceeding, to the hearing examiner, and, subject to appropriate rulings on such objections to the questions and answers as were noted at the time of taking the deposition or as would be valid were the witness personally present and testifying, such deposition may be read in evidence by the party taking it as against any party who was present or represented at the taking of the deposition or who had due notice thereof.

§4.11 *Admissions as to facts and documents.* (a) At any time after answer has been filed, any party may serve upon any other party a written request for the admission of the genuineness of any relevant documents described in the request, or the admission of the truth of any relevant matters of fact set forth in such documents. Copies of the documents shall be delivered with the request unless copies have already been furnished.

(b) Each requested admission shall be deemed made unless, within a period designated by the hearing examiner, not less than ten days after service thereof, or within such further time as the hearing examiner may allow, the party so served serves upon the party making the request either (1) a sworn statement denying specifically the relevant matters of which an admission is requested or setting forth in detail the reasons why he can neither truthfully admit nor deny them, or (2) written objections on the ground that some or all of the matters involved are privileged or irrelevant or that the request is otherwise improper in whole or in part, together with a copy of a request to the hearing examiner for a hearing on the objections at the earliest practicable time. Answers on matters to which such objections are made may be deferred until the objections are determined, but if written objections are made to only a part of a request, the remainder of the request shall be answered within the period designated.

(c) Admissions obtained pursuant to this procedure may be used in evidence to the same extent and subject to the same objections as other admissions.

§4.12 *Evidence*. (a) *Burden of proof*. Counsel supporting the complaint shall have the burden of proof, but the proponent of any factual proposition shall be required to sustain the burden of proof with reference thereto.

(b) *Admissibility*. Relevant, material, and reliable evidence shall be admitted. Irrelevant, immaterial, unreliable, and unduly repetitious evidence shall be excluded. Immaterial or irrelevant parts of an admissible document shall be segregated and excluded so far as practicable.

(c) *Official notice of facts*. When any decision of a hearing examiner or of the Commission rests, in whole or in part, upon the taking of official notice of a material fact not appearing in evidence of record, opportunity to disprove such noticed fact shall be granted any party making timely motion therefor.

(d) *Objections*. Objections to evidence shall timely and briefly state the grounds relied upon, but the transcript shall not include argument or debate thereon except as ordered by the presiding official. Rulings on all objections shall appear in the record.

(e) *Exceptions*. Formal exception to an adverse ruling is not required.

(f) *Record of excluded evidence*. When an objection to a question propounded to a witness is sustained, the examining attorney may make a specific offer of what he expects to prove by the answer of the witness, or the hearing examiner upon request shall receive and report the evidence in full, unless it clearly appears that the evidence is not admissible on any ground or that the witness is privileged. Similarly, rejected exhibits, adequately marked for identification, shall be retained in the record so as to be available for consideration by any reviewing authority.

Subpart E—Hearings

§4.13 *Presiding officials*. (a) *Who presides*. All hearings in adjudicative proceedings shall be presided over by a duly qualified hearing examiner or by the Commission or one or more members of the Commission sitting as hearing examiner; and the term "hearing examiner" as used in this part means and applies to such members when so sitting.

(b) *How assigned*. The presiding hearing examiner shall be designated by the Director of Hearing Examiners, who shall notify the parties of the hearing examiner designated.

(c) *Powers and duties*. Hearing examiners shall have the duty to conduct fair and impartial hearings, to take all necessary action to avoid delay in the disposition of proceedings, and to maintain order. They shall have all powers necessary to that end, including the following:

(1) To administer oaths and affirmations;

(2) To issue subpoenas;

(3) To rule upon offers of proof and receive evidence;

(4) To take or cause depositions to be taken and to determine their scope;

(5) To regulate the course of the hearings and the conduct of the parties and their counsel therein;

(6) To hold conferences for settlement, simplification of the issues, or any other proper purpose;

(7) To consider and rule upon, as justice may require, all procedural and other motions appropriate in an adversary proceeding, including motions to open defaults;

(8) To make and file initial decisions;

(9) To certify questions to the Commission for its determination; and

(10) To take any action authorized by these Rules or in conformance with the provisions of the Administrative Procedure Act (5 U.S.C. 1001 to 1011).

(d) *Substitution of hearing examiner.* In the event of substitution of a new hearing examiner for the one originally designated, any motion predicated upon such substitution shall be made within five days thereafter.

(e) *Interference.* In the performance of their adjudicative functions, hearing examiners shall not be responsible to, nor subject to the supervision or direction of, any officer, employee, or agent engaged in the performance of investigative or prosecuting functions for the Commission, and all directions by the Commission to hearing examiners concerning any adjudicative proceeding shall appear in and be made a part of the record.

(f) *Disqualification of hearing examiners.* (1) When a hearing examiner deems himself disqualified to preside in a particular proceeding, he shall withdraw therefrom by notice on the record and shall notify the Director of Hearing Examiners of such withdrawal.

(2) Whenever any party shall deem the hearing examiner for any reason to be disqualified to preside, or to continue to preside, in a particular proceeding, that party shall file with the Commission a motion to disqualify and remove such hearing examiner, such motion to be supported by affidavits setting forth the alleged grounds for disqualification. Copy of such motion shall be served by the Commission on the hearing examiner whose removal is therein sought, who shall have ten days from such service within which to reply thereto. If the hearing examiner does not disqualify himself within ten days, then the Commission shall promptly determine the validity of the grounds alleged, either directly or on the report of another hearing examiner appointed to conduct a hearing for that purpose.

§4.14 *Hearings; transcripts.* (a) *Public hearings.* All hearings in adjudicative proceedings shall be public unless otherwise ordered by the Commission.

(b) *Rights of parties.* Every party, except intervenors, shall have the right of due notice, cross-examination, presentation of evidence, objection, motion, argument, and all other rights essential to a fair hearing.

(c) *Adverse witnesses.* An adverse party, or an officer, agent, or employee thereof, and any witness who appears to be hostile, unwilling, or evasive, may be interrogated by leading questions and may also be contradicted and impeached by the party calling him.

(d) *Expedition.* Hearings shall proceed with all reasonable expedition. Unless the Commission otherwise orders upon a certificate of necessity therefor by the hearing examiner, all hearings will be held at one place and will continue without suspension until concluded. (This shall not bar overnight, week end, or holiday recesses, or other brief intervals of the sort normally involved in judicial proceedings.)

(e) *Notice.* Not less than ten days' notice of the time and place of any hearing shall be given, and in setting such hearings due regard shall be had for the public interest and the convenience and necessity of all parties, witnesses, and counsel.

(f) *Transcripts.* Hearings shall be stenographically reported and transcribed by the official reporter of the Commission under the supervision of the hearing examiner, and the original transcript shall be a part of the record and the sole official transcript. Copies of transcripts are available to respondents and to the public from the reporter at rates not to exceed the maximum rates fixed by contract between the Commission and the reporter.

(g) *Corrections of the transcript.* Corrections of the official transcript may be made only when they involve errors affecting substance and then only in the manner herein provided: Corrections ordered by the hearing examiner or agreed to in a written stipulation signed by all counsel, and approved by the hearing examiner shall be included in the record, and such stipulations, except to the extent they are capricious or without substance, shall be approved by the hearing examiner. Corrections shall not be ordered by the hearing examiner except upon notice and opportunity for the hearing of objections. Corrections so ordered or approved shall be incorporated in the record as an appendix and when so incorporated the Secretary of the Commission shall make or cause to be made the necessary physical corrections in the official transcript so that it will incorporate the changes agreed upon or ordered. In making such physical corrections, there shall be no substitution of pages, but, to the extent practicable, such corrections shall be made by running a line through the matter to be changed, but without obliteration, and writing the matter as changed immediately above. Where the correction consists of an insertion, it shall be added, by rider or interlineation, as near as may be to the text which is intended to precede and follow it.

§4.15 *Subpoenas.* (a) *Subpoenas ad testificandum.* Application for issuance of a subpoena requiring a witness to appear and testify before a designated hearing examiner at a specified place and time may be made to the hearing examiner, or to the Commission.

(b) *Subpoenas duces tecum.* Application for issuance of a subpoena requiring a witness to appear before a designated hearing examiner at a specified time and place and produce specified documents shall be made in writing to the hearing examiner or to the Commission, and shall specify as exactly as possible the documents to be produced, showing their general relevancy and reasonable scope. Any motion to limit or quash such subpoena shall be filed within ten days after date of service of the subpoena.

(c) Service. A subpoena shall be served as provided in §4.26(a).

(d) *Appeal.* An appeal to the Commission from the hearing examiner's ruling granting or denying a motion to issue, limit or quash any subpoena will be entertained by the Commission only upon a showing that the ruling complained of involves substantial rights and will materially affect the final decision and that a determination of its correctness before conclusion of the hearing will better serve the interests of justice.

§4.16 *Witnesses and fees.* (a) Witnesses at formal hearings shall be examined orally. Witnesses shall be paid the same fees and mileage as are paid witnesses in the courts of the United States.

(b) Witnesses whose depositions are taken, and the persons taking such depositions, shall severally be entitled to the same fees as are paid for like services in the courts of the United States.

(c) Witness fees and mileage, and fees for depositions, shall be paid by the party at whose instance witnesses appear.

§4.17 *Proposed findings, conclusions, and order.* At the close of the reception of evidence in an adjudicative proceeding, or within a reasonable time thereafter fixed by the hearing examiner, any party may file with the Secretary for consideration of the hearing examiner proposed findings of fact, conclusions of law, and order, together with reasons therefor and briefs in support thereof. Such proposals shall be in writing, shall be served upon all parties, and shall contain adequate references to the record and authorities relied on. The record shall show the hearing examiner's ruling on each proposed finding and conclusion, except when his order disposing of the proceeding otherwise informs the parties of the action taken by him thereon.

§4.18 *Interlocutory appeals.* Except as provided in §4.15(d) and §4.23(e), interlocutory appeals from rulings of a hearing examiner may be filed only after permission is first obtained from the Commission. Any request for such permission shall be in writing, not to exceed ten pages in length, and shall be filed within five days after notice of the ruling complained of. No such permission will be granted unless it be shown to the satisfaction of the Commission (1) that the ruling involves a novel and substantial question of law which is not controlled by prior decisions of the Commission or the courts, *and* (2) that a determination of such question could properly be made by the Commission without reference to evidentiary or other matters of record in the proceeding, *and* (3) that an immediate determination by the Commission may materially advance the ultimate termination of the proceeding and would be in furtherance of the Commission's policy to prevent unnecessary delay.

Interlocutory appeals shall be in the form of a brief, not to exceed thirty pages in length, and shall be filed within five days after notice of the ruling complained of, in the case of appeals under §4.15(d) or §4.23(e), or within five days after notice of permission to file, in the case of appeals under §4.18. Answer thereto may be filed within five days after service of the appeal brief. The appeal shall not operate to suspend the hearing unless otherwise ordered by the hearing examiner or the Commission.

Subpart F—Decision and Order

§4.19 *Initial Decision.* (a) *When filed and when effective.* Within ninety days after completion of the reception of evidence in a proceeding, or within such further time as the Commission may allow on the hearing examiner's written request, the hearing examiner shall file an initial decision which shall become the decision of the Commission thirty days after service thereof upon the parties, unless (1) within fifteen days after service of such initial decision a petition for review thereof shall be filed, or (2) within fifteen days after expiration of such fifteen-day period the Commission issues an order placing the case on its own docket for review. A copy of the initial decision shall be served upon each counsel or other representative who has appeared in the proceeding pursuant to §4.23.

(b) *Content.* An initial decision shall include a statement of (1) findings and conclusions, with the reasons or basis therefor, upon all the material issues of fact, law, or discretion presented on the record, and (2) an appropriate order. Initial decisions shall be based upon a consideration of the whole record and supported by reliable, probative and substantial evidence.

(c) *By whom made.* The initial decision in an adjudicative proceeding shall be made and filed by the hearing examiner who presided therein, except when he shall have become unavailable to the Commission.

(d) *Reopening: termination of hearing examiner's jurisdiction.* (1) At any time prior to the filing of his initial decision, a hearing examiner may reopen the proceeding for the reception of further evidence.

(2) Except for the correction of clerical errors, the jurisdiction of the hearing examiner is terminated upon the filing of his initial decision, unless and until the proceeding is remanded to him by the Commission.

§4.20 *Petition for review.* (a) *Who may file.* Any party to a proceeding may file a petition for review within the time prescribed by §4.19.

(b) *Content.* The petition for review shall concisely and plainly state (1) the questions presented for review, (2) the facts in abbreviated form, and (3) the reasons why review by the Commission is deemed to be in the public interest. Such petition shall not exceed ten pages in length.

(c) *Answer.* Within ten days after service upon the opposing party of a petition for review, such party may file in opposition thereto an answer of not exceeding ten pages.

(d) *Disposition.* A petition for review will be granted where, on examination of the record, the petition for review, and the answer, the Commission finds that the questions presented are substantial and that determination thereof by the Commission is necessary or appropriate under the law to insure a just and proper disposition of the proceeding and to protect the rights of all parties. If the petition for review is denied, the initial decision of the hearing examiner shall thereupon become the decision of the Commission. No petition for review will be denied by the Commission where, in the opinion of two or more of its members, it should be granted.

§4.21 *Commission review.* (a) Within thirty days after service of the Commission's order granting the petition for review, the petitioner may file exceptions to the initial decision and a brief in support thereof.

(b) *Exceptions.* Each exception (1) shall relate only to substantive or procedural matters presented on the record, limited to the questions stated in the petition for review; (2) shall identify the part of the initial decision to which objection is made; (3) shall specify the portions of the record relied upon; and (4) shall state the grounds for the exception, including the citation of authorities in support thereof. Any objection to a ruling, finding, or conclusion which is not made a part of the exceptions shall be deemed to have been waived. Any exception which fails to present with accuracy, brevity and clearness whatever is essential to a ready and adequate understanding of the points requiring consideration may be disregarded.

(c) *Brief.* The brief in support of the exceptions shall contain, in the order indicated, the following:

(1) A subject index of the matter in the brief, with page references, and a table of cases (alphabetically arranged), text books, statutes, and other material cited, with page references thereto;

(2) A concise statement of the case containing all that is material to the consideration of the questions presented;

(3) A specification of the assigned errors as are intended to be urged; and

(4) The argument presenting clearly the points of fact and law relied upon in support of the position taken on each question, with specific page references to the transcript and the legal or other material relied upon.

Material not included in the exceptions or brief may not be presented to the Commission in oral argument or otherwise.

(d) *Answering brief.* Within thirty days after service of the brief upon the opposing party, such party may file an answering brief which shall also contain a subject index, with page references, and a table of cases (alphabetically arranged), text books, statutes, and other material cited, with page references thereto. It shall be limited to the questions raised in the brief in support of the exceptions and shall present clearly the points of fact and law relied upon in support of the position taken on each question, with specific page references to the transcript and legal or other material relied upon.

(e) *Reply brief.* Reply briefs, not in excess of ten pages and limited to rebuttal of matter in an answering brief, will be received if filed and served within seven days after receipt of the answering brief or the day preceding the oral argument, whichever comes first. No answer to a reply brief will be permitted.

(f) *Length of briefs.* No brief in excess of sixty pages, including any appendices, shall be filed without leave of the Commission.

(g) *Oral argument.* Oral arguments will be held in cases in which the Commission grants review, unless it otherwise orders (1) upon request of any party made at the time of filing its brief, or (2) upon the Commission's own motion. Oral arguments before the Commission shall be reported stenographically unless otherwise ordered by the Commission.

§4.22 *Decision on review.* (a) Upon review of an initial decision, the Commission will consider such parts of the record as are cited or as may be necessary to resolve the issues presented; and in addition will, to the extent necessary or desirable, exercise all the powers which it could have exercised if it had made the initial decision.

(b) In rendering its decision, the Commission will adopt, modify, or set aside the findings, conclusions and order contained in the initial decision, and will include in the decision a statement of the reasons or basis for its action.

Subpart G—Miscellaneous

§4.23 *Appearances.* (a) *Qualifications.* (1) Members of the bar of a Federal court or of the highest court of any State or Territory of the United States may practice before the Commission.

(2) Any individual or member of a partnership named respondent in any proceeding before the Commission may appear on behalf of himself or of such partnership upon adequate identification. A respondent corporation or association may be represented by a *bona fide* officer thereof upon a showing of adequate authorization.

(b) *Restrictions as to former members and employees.* No former member or employee of the Commission, and no partner, employer, employee or business associate of such former member or employee, shall appear as attorney or counsel in any proceeding which was pending in any manner or form in the Commission while such former member or employee was employed on or by the Commission, unless and until the Commission determines, upon the written statement of the former member or employee and a statement from the Secretary of the Commission, that the files of the proceeding did not come to the personal attention of such former member or employee during his employment on or by the Commission, and that he did not participate personally and substantially in the proceeding. For the purposes of this section, a former member of the Commission will be conclusively presumed to have personally and substantially participated in any proceeding, the files of which were sent to his office at any time for action of any kind.

(c) *Notice of appearance.* Any attorney desiring to appear before the Commission or a hearing examiner thereof, on behalf of a respondent in a particular proceeding, shall file with the Secretary of the Commission a written notice of such appearance, which shall contain a statement of such attorney's eligibility as provided in this rule. No other application shall be required for admission to practice, and no register of attorneys shall be maintained.

(d) *Standards of conduct.* All counsel practicing before the Commission shall conform to the standards of ethical conduct required of practitioners in the courts of the United States and by the bars of which they are members.

(e) *Suspension or disbarment of attorneys.* (1) The hearing examiner shall have the authority, for good cause stated on the record, to suspend or bar, from participation in a particular proceeding, any attorney who shall refuse to comply with his directions, or who shall be guilty of disorderly conduct, dilatory tactics, or contemptuous language in the course of such proceedings. Any attorney so suspended or barred shall have the right to appeal to the Commission from such action of the hearing examiner, whereupon the Commission will review the action of the hearing examiner and take such action as it deems warranted by the circumstances.

(2) The Commission, for good cause shown, may issue an order requiring any alleged offender to show cause why he should not be suspended or disbarred from practice before the Commission. Such alleged offender shall be granted due opportunity to be heard in his own defense. Thereafter, if warranted by the facts, the Commission will issue against such offender an order of reprimand, suspension or disbarment.

§4.24 *Requirements as to form and filing of documents other than correspondence.* (a) *Filing.* All documents in proceedings before the Commission shall be addressed to and filed with the Secretary of the Commission.

(b) *Title.* Documents shall clearly show the docket number and title of the proceeding.

(c) *Copies.* Twenty copies shall be filed of a petition for review and of all briefs; ten copies of all other documents shall be filed, with the exception of reports of compliance under §4.28, in which case only two copies need be filed, and notices of appearances under §4.23, in which case only one copy need be filed.

(d) *Form.* (1) Documents, other than briefs filed with the Commission on petitions for review, shall be printed, typewritten or otherwise processed in permanent form and on good unglazed paper. The paper must not be less than eight (8) inches nor more than eight and one-half (8½) inches by not less than ten and one-half (10½) inches nor more than eleven (11) inches. The left margin must be one and one-half (1½) inches and the right margin one (1) inch. Documents must be bound on the left side. If printed, the type shall be not less than ten (10) point adequately leaded.

(2) Briefs before the Commission on review shall be printed on good unglazed paper seven (7) inches by ten (10) inches. The type shall not be less than ten (10) point adequately leaded. Citations and quotations shall not be less than ten (10) point single leaded and footnotes shall not be less than eight (8)

point single leaded. The printed line shall not exceed four and three-quarter (4¾)
inches in length.

(e) *Signature.* (1) One copy of each document filed shall be signed by an
attorney of record for the party, or, in the case of respondents not represented by
counsel, by the respondent himself, or by a partner if a partnership, or by an
officer of respondent if it is a corporation or an unincorporated association.

(2) Signing a document constitutes a representation by the signer that he has
read it, that to the best of his knowledge, information, and belief, the statements
made in it are true, and that it is not interposed for delay. If a document is not
signed or is signed with intent to defeat the purpose of this rule, it may be stricken
as sham and false and the proceeding may go forward as though the document
had not been filed.

§4.25 *Time.* (a) *Computation.* Computation of any period of time prescribed
or allowed by these rules, by order of the Commission or a hearing examiner, or
by any applicable statute, shall begin with the first business day following that
on which the act, event or development initiating such period of time shall have
occurred. When the last day of the period so computed is a Saturday, Sunday, or
national holiday, or other day on which the office of the Commission is closed, the
period shall run until the end of the next following business day. When such
period of time, with the intervening Saturdays, Sundays and national holidays
counted, is less than seven days, each of the Saturdays, Sundays and such
holidays shall be excluded from the computation. When such period of time, with
the intervening Saturdays, Sundays and national holidays counted, exceeds seven
days, each of the Saturdays, Sundays, and such holidays shall be included in the
computation.

(b) *Extensions.* For good cause shown, the hearing examiner may, in any
proceeding before him, extend any time limit prescribed or allowed by these rules
or by order of the Commission or the hearing examiner, except those governing
interlocutory appeals and initial decisions and those expressly requiring Commission action. Except as otherwise provided by law, the Commission, for good
cause shown, may extend any time limit prescribed by these rules or by order
of the Commission or a hearing examiner; provided, however, that in a proceeding
pending before a hearing examiner, the application shall first be made to him.
Applications for extensions of time shall be made by motion.

§4.26 *Service.* (a) *By the Commission.* (1) Service of complaints, orders and
other processes of the Commission may be effected as follows:

(i) *By registered mail.* A copy of the document shall be addressed to the
person, partnership, corporation or unincorporated association to be served at his
or its residence or principal office or place of business, registered, and mailed; or

(ii) *By delivery to an individual.* A copy thereof may be delivered to the
person to be served, or to a member of the partnership to be served, or to the
president, secretary, or other executive officer or a director of the corporation or
unincorporated association to be served; or

(iii) *By delivery to an address.* A copy thereof may be left at the principal office or place of business of the person, partnership, corporation or unincorporated association, or it may be left at the residence of the person or of a member of the partnership or of an executive officer or director of the corporation or unincorporated association to be served.

(2) Documents other than complaints, orders and other processes of the Commission, the service of which starts the running of prescribed periods of time provided or allowed by any of the rules in this part or by any order of the Commission or a hearing examiner for the performance of some act or the occurrence of some event or development, shall be served in the same manner as complaints, orders and other processes of the Commission, or by certified mail.

(3) All other documents may be similarly served, or they may be served by ordinary first-class mail.

(b) *By other parties.* Service of documents by parties other than the Commission shall be by delivering copies thereof as follows: Upon the Commission, by personal delivery or delivery by first-class mail to the office of the Secretary of the Commission; upon any other party, by delivery to the party. If the party is an individual or partnership, delivery shall be to such individual or a member of the partnership; if a corporation or unincorporated association, to an officer or agent authorized to accept service of process therefor. Delivery to a party other than the Commission means handing to the individual, partner, officer, or agent; leaving at his office with a person in charge thereof, or, if there is no one in charge or if the office is closed or if he has no office, leaving at his dwelling house or usual place of abode with some person of suitable age and discretion then residing therein; or sending by mail.

(c) *Proof of service.* (1) When service is by mail, registered or ordinary first-class, it is complete upon delivery of the document by the post office.

(2) When a party has appeared in a proceeding by a partner, officer, or attorney, service upon such partner, officer, or attorney of any document other than a complaint, order or other process of the Commission shall be deemed service upon the party.

(3) The return post office receipt for a document registered and mailed, or the verified return or certificate by the person serving the document by personal delivery or ordinary mail, setting forth the manner of said service, shall be proof of the service of the document.

§4.27 *Ex parte communication.* (a) In an adjudicative proceeding, no employee or agent of the Commission who performs any investigative or prosecuting function in connection with the proceeding and no party respondent in the proceeding, or agent, or counsel, or anyone acting on behalf of a party respondent, shall communicate *ex parte,* directly or indirectly, with any member of the Commission, or the hearing examiner, or any employee involved in the decisional process in such proceeding, with respect to the merits of that or a factually related proceeding.

(b) In an adjudicative proceeding, no member of the Commission, hearing examiner, or employee involved in the decisional process of such proceeding shall communicate *ex parte,* directly or indirectly, with any employee or agent of the Commission who performs any investigative or prosecuting function in connection with the proceeding, or with any party respondent in the proceeding, or agent, or counsel, or anyone acting on behalf of a party respondent, with respect to the merits of that or a factually related proceeding.

(c) In an adjudicative proceeding, if any *ex parte* communication is made to or by any member of the Commission, the hearing examiner, or employee involved in the decisional process, in violation of subsection (a) or (b) of this section, such member, hearing examiner or employee, as the case may be, shall promptly inform the Commission of the substance of such communication and the circumstances thereof.

(d) A request for information with respect to the status of an adjudicative proceeding shall not be deemed to be an *ex parte* communication prohibited by this section.

§4.28 *Reports of compliance.* In every proceeding in which the Commission has issued an order to cease and desist, each respondent named in such order shall file with the Commission, within sixty days after service thereof, a report in writing, signed by the respondent, setting forth in detail the manner and form of his compliance with the order, and shall thereafter file with the Commission such further signed, written reports of compliance as it may require. Reports of compliance shall be under oath if so requested. Where the order prohibits the use of a false advertisement of a food, drug, device, or cosmetic, which may be injurious to health because of results from its use under the conditions prescribed in the advertisement, or under such conditions as are customary or usual, or if the use of such advertisement is with intent to defraud or mislead, an interim report stating whether and how respondents intend to comply shall be filed within ten days after service of the order. Where court review of an order of the Commission is pending, respondent shall file only such reports of compliance as the court may require. Thereafter, the time for filing report of compliance shall begin to run *de novo* from the final judicial determination.

§4.29 *Reopening of proceedings.* (a) In any case where an order to cease and desist has been issued by the Commission it may, upon notice to the parties, modify or set aside, in whole or in part, its report of findings as to the facts or order in such manner as it may deem proper at any time prior to expiration of the time allowed for filing a petition for review or prior to the filing of the transcript of record in the proceeding in a United States Court of Appeals pursuant to a petition for review.

(b) In any case where an order to cease and desist issued by the Commission has become final by reason of court affirmance or expiration of the statutory period for court review without a petition for such review having been filed, the Commission may at any time after reasonable notice and opportunity for hearing as to whether changed conditions of fact or of law or the public interest so require, reopen and alter, modify or set aside, in whole or in part, its report of findings as to the facts or order therein whenever in the opinion of the Commission such action is required by said changed conditions or by the public interest.

(c) After an order dismissing a complaint has been issued, the Commission may, upon reasonable notice to the parties and opportunity for a hearing as to whether said proceeding should be reopened, issue an order reopening such proceeding whenever, in the opinion of the Commission, changed conditions of fact or of law or the public interest so require.

Promulgated as of this date in pursuance of the action of the Federal Trade Commission on June 29, 1961, effective fifteen days after publication in the Federal Register.

(Sec. 6, 38 Stat. 721; 15 U.S.C. 46)

Issued: June 29, 1961.

By direction of the Commission.

[Signed] Joseph W. Shea,
Secretary

APPENDIX C

THE ROBINSON-PATMAN ACT

Making it unlawful for any person engaged in commerce to discriminate in price or terms of sale between purchasers of commodities of like grade and quality, to prohibit the payment of brokerage or commission under certain conditions, to suppress pseudo-advertising allowances, to provide a presumptive measure of damages in certain cases and to protect the independent merchant, the public whom he serves, and the manufacturer from whom he buys, from exploitation by unfair competitors.

Approved June 19, 1936.

THE ROBINSON-PATMAN ACT

[PUBLIC—No. 692—74TH CONGRESS]

[H. R. 8442]

AN ACT

To amend section 2 of the Act entitled "An Act to supplement existing laws against unlawful restraints and monopolies, and for other purposes," approved October 15, 1914, as
amended (U. S. C., title 15, sec. 13), and for other purposes.

*Be it enacted by the Senate and House of Representatives of the United States of
America in Congress assembled,* That section 2 of the Act entitled "An Act to supplement existing laws against unlawful restraints and monopolies, and for other purposes," approved October 15, 1914, as amended (U. S. C., title 15, sec. 13), is
amended to read as follows:

"SEC. 2. (a) That it shall be unlawful for any person engaged in commerce, in
the course of such commerce, either directly or indirectly, to discriminate in price
between different purchasers of commodities of like grade and quality, where either or
any of the purchases involved in such discrimination are in commerce, where such
commodities are sold for use, consumption, or resale within the United States or any
Territory thereof or the District of Columbia or any insular possession or other place
under the jurisdiction of the United States, and where the effect of such discrimination
may be substantially to lessen competition or tend to create a monopoly in any line of
commerce, or to injure, destroy, or prevent competition with any person who either
grants or knowingly receives the benefit of such discrimination, or with customers
of either of them: *Provided,* That nothing herein contained shall prevent differentials
which make only due allowance for differences in the cost of manufacture, sale, or
delivery resulting from the differing methods or quantities in which such commodities
are to such purchasers sold or delivered: *Provided, however,* That the Federal Trade
Commission may, after due investigation and hearing to all interested parties, fix and
establish quantity limits, and revise the same as it finds necessary, as to particular
commodities or classes of commodities, where it finds that available purchasers in
greater quantities are so few as to render differentials on account thereof unjustly discriminatory or promotive of monopoly in any line of commerce; and the foregoing
shall then not be construed to permit differentials based on differences in quantities
greater than those so fixed and established: *And provided further,* That nothing
herein contained shall prevent persons engaged in selling goods, wares, or merchandise
in commerce from selecting their own customers in bona fide transactions and not in
restraint of trade: *And provided further,* That nothing herein contained shall prevent
price changes from time to time where in response to changing conditions affecting the

280

market for or the marketability of the goods concerned, such as but not limited to actual or imminent deterioration of perishable goods, obsolescence of seasonal goods, distress sales under court process, or sales in good faith in discontinuance of business in the goods concerned.

"(b) Upon proof being made, at any hearing on a complaint under this section, that there has been discrimination in price or services or facilities furnished, the burden of rebutting the prima-facie case thus made by showing justification shall be upon the person charged with a violation of this section, and unless justification shall be affirmatively shown, the Commission is authorized to issue an order terminating the discrimination: *Provided, however,* That nothing herein contained shall prevent a seller rebutting the prima-facie case thus made by showing that his lower price or the furnishing of services or facilities to any purchaser or purchasers was made in good faith to meet an equally low price of a competitor, or the services or facilities furnished by a competitor.

"(c) That it shall be unlawful for any person engaged in commerce, in the course of such commerce, to pay or grant, or to receive or accept, anything of value as a commission, brokerage, or other compensation, or any allowance or discount in lieu thereof, except for services rendered in connection with the sale or purchase of goods, wares, or merchandise, either to the other party to such transaction or to an agent, representative, or other intermediary therein where such intermediary is acting in fact for or in behalf, or is subject to the direct or indirect control, of any party to such transaction other than the person by whom such compensation is so granted or paid.

"(d) That it shall be unlawful for any person engaged in commerce to pay or contract for the payment of anything of value to or for the benefit of a customer of such person in the course of such commerce as compensation or in consideration for any services or facilities furnished by or through such customer in connection with the processing, handling, sale, or offering for sale of any products or commodities manufactured, sold, or offered for sale by such person, unless such payment or consideration is available on proportionally equal terms to all other customers competing in the distribution of such products or commodities.

"(e) That it shall be unlawful for any person to discriminate in favor of one purchaser against another purchaser or purchasers of a commodity bought for resale, with or without processing, by contracting to furnish or furnishing, or by contributing to the furnishing of, any services or facilities connected with the processing, handling, sale, or offering for sale of such commodity so purchased upon terms not accorded to all purchasers on proportionally equal terms.

"(f) That it shall be unlawful for any person engaged in commerce, in the course of such commerce, knowingly to induce or receive a discrimination in price which is prohibited by this section."

SEC. 2. That nothing herein contained shall affect rights of action arising, or litigation pending, or orders of the Federal Trade Commission issued and in effect or pending on review, based on section 2 of said Act of October 15, 1914, prior to the effective date of this amendatory Act: *Provided,* That where, prior to the effective date of this amendatory Act, the Federal Trade Commission has issued an order requiring any person to cease and desist from a violation of section 2 of said Act of October 15, 1914, and such order is pending on review or is in effect, either as issued or as affirmed or modified by a court of competent jurisdiction, and the Commission shall have reason to believe that such person has committed, used or carried on, since the effective date of this amendatory Act, or is committing, using or carrying on, any act, practice or method in violation of any of the provisions of said section 2 as amended by this Act, it may reopen such original proceeding and may issue and serve upon such person its complaint, supplementary to the original complaint, stating its charges in that respect. Thereupon the same proceedings shall be had upon such supplementary complaint as provided in section 11 of said Act of October 15, 1914. If upon such hearing the Commission shall be of the opinion that any act, practice, or method charged in said supplementary complaint has been committed, used, or carried on since the effective date of this amendatory Act, or is being committed, used or carried on, in violation of said section 2 as amended by this Act, it shall make a report in writing in which it shall state its findings as to the facts and shall issue and serve upon such person its order modifying or amending its original order to include any additional violations of law so found. Thereafter the provisions of section 11 of said Act of October 15, 1914, as to review and enforcement of orders of the Commission shall in all things apply to such modified or amended order. If upon review as provided in said section 11 the court shall set aside such modified or amended order, the original order shall not be affected thereby, but it shall be and remain in force and effect as fully and to the same extent as if such supplementary proceedings had not been taken.

SEC. 3. It shall be unlawful for any person engaged in commerce, in the course of such commerce, to be a party to, or assist in, any transaction of sale, or contract to sell, which discriminates to his knowledge against competitors of the purchaser, in that, any discount, rebate, allowance, or advertising service charge is granted to the purchaser over and above any discount, rebate, allowance, or advertising service charge available at the time of such transaction to said competitors in respect of a sale of goods of like grade, quality, and quantity; to sell, or contract to sell, goods in any part of the United States at prices lower than those exacted by said person elsewhere in the United States for the purpose of destroying competition, or eliminating a competitor in such part of the United States; or, to sell, or contract to sell, goods at unreasonably low prices for the purpose of destroying competition or eliminating a competitor.

Any person violating any of the provisions of this section shall, upon conviction thereof, be fined not more than $5,000 or imprisoned not more than one year, or both.

SEC. 4. Nothing in this Act shall prevent a cooperative association from returning to its members, producers, or consumers the whole, or any part of, the net earnings or surplus resulting from its trading operations, in proportion to their purchases or sales from, to, or through the association.

Approved, June 19, 1936.

COMMITTEE ON THE JUDICIARY
UNITED STATES SENATE

74TH CONGRESS—2ND SESSION. REPORT No. 1502

TO AMEND ANTITRUST ACT

JANUARY 16 (calendar day, FEB. 3), 1936.—Ordered to be printed

Mr. LOGAN, from the Committee on the Judiciary, submitted the following

REPORT

[To accompany S. 3154]

The Committee on the Judiciary, having had under consideration the bill (S. 3154) to amend section 2 of the act of October 15, 1914, entitled "An act to supplement existing laws against unlawful restraints and monopolies, and for other purposes," report the same back with the recommendation that the bill be amended as follows, and that, as so amended, it do pass.

Amendment: Beginning with the words "SEC. 2," in line 3, page 2, of the printed bill, strike out all thereafter, and insert, in lieu of the language stricken out, the following:

SEC. 2. (a) That it shall be unlawful for any person engaged in commerce, in the course of such commerce, either directly or indirectly, to discriminate in price or terms of sale between different purchasers of commodities of like grade and quality, where either or any of the purchases involved in such discrimination are in commerce, where such commodities are sold for use, consumption, or resale within the United States or any Territory thereof or the District of Columbia or any insular possession or other place under the jurisdiction of the United States, and where the effect of such discrimination may be substantially to lessen competition or tend to create a monopoly in any line of commerce, or to injure, destroy, or prevent competition with any person who either grants or receives the benefit of such discrimination, or with customers of either of them: *Provided,* That nothing herein contained shall prevent differentials in prices as between purchasers depending solely upon whether they purchase for resale to wholesalers, to retailers, or to consumers, or for use in further manufacture; nor differentials which make only due allowance for differences in the cost, other than brokerage, of manufacture, sale, or delivery resulting from the differing methods or quantities in which such commodities are to such purchasers sold or delivered: *Provided, however,* That the Federal Trade Commission may, after due investigation and hearing to all interested parties, fix and establish quantity limits, and revise the same as it finds necessary, as to particular commodities or classes of commodities, where it finds that available purchasers in greater quantities are so few as to render differentials on account thereof unjustly discriminatory or promotive of monopoly in any line of commerce; and the foregoing shall then not be construed to permit differentials based on differences in quantities greater than those so fixed and established: *And provided further,* That nothing herein contained shall prevent persons engaged in selling goods, wares, or merchandise in commerce from selecting their own customers in bona fide transactions and not in restraint of trade.

(b) That it shall be unlawful for any person engaged in commerce, in the course of such commerce, to pay or grant, or to receive or accept, anything of value as a commission, brokerage, or other compensation, or any allowance or discount in lieu thereof, in connection with the sale or purchase of goods, wares, or merchandise, either to the other party to such transaction, or to an agent, representative, or other intermediary therein where such intermediary is acting in fact for or in behalf, or is subject to the direct or indirect control, of any party to such transaction other than the person by whom such compensation is so granted or paid.

(c) That it shall be unlawful for any person engaged in commerce to pay or contract for the payment of anything of value to or for the benefit of a customer of such person in the course of such commerce as compensation or in consideration for any services or facilities furnished by or through such customer in connection with the processing, handling, sale, or offering for sale of any products or commodities manufactured, sold, or offered for sale by such person, unless—

(1) such payment or consideration is offered on proportionally equal terms to all other customers competing in the distribution of such products or commodities; or unless

(2) the business, identity, or interests of such customer are in no way publicly associated, by name, reference, allusion, proximity, or otherwise, with or in the furnishing of such services or facilities and the consideration paid therefor does not exceed the fair value of such services or facilities in the localities where furnished.

(d) For purposes of suit under section 4 of this Act, the measure of damages for any violation of this section shall, where the fact of damage is shown, and in the absence of proof of greater damage, be presumed to be the pecuniary amount or equivalent of the prohibited discrimination, payment, or grant involved in such violation; limited, however—

(1) Under subsections (a) and (b) above, by the volume of plaintiff's business in the goods concerned, and for the period of time concerned, in such violation;

(2) Under subsection (c) above, to the amount or share, or its pecuniary equivalent, to which plaintiff would have been entitled if the payment concerned in such violation had been made or offered in accordance with paragraph (1) of said subsection (c).

In its consideration of this bill, the committee has had the benefit not only of the diligent studies of its own members, but of the record of hearings on a similar bill (H. R. 8442) before the Committee on the Judiciary of the House of Representatives, also of the hearings before a Special Committee of the House on Investigation of the American Retail Federation, and of the report of the Federal Trade Commission on its chain-store investigation (S. Doc. No. 4, 74th Cong., 1st sess.). These have developed so fully the facts, trade and industrial, pertinent to the objects of the bill, together with representations of all interested parties for or against its specific provisions, that this committee has felt able to reach its decision without the delays of further hearings.

The Clayton Act of October 15, 1914, addresses itself in section 2, which this bill proposes to amend, to the problem of price discriminations. It represented the hope of that time, in the words of the House committee report (H. Rept. 627; 63d Cong., 2d sess.) that it would go far to bring about the desired objects of readjustment "with as few, as slight, as easy, and simple changes as the object sought will admit of."

More than 20 years' experience and observation with respect to its operation, together with new features of trade and industrial organization that have since developed, have convinced us of its shortcomings, and of the need to strengthen its provisions and fit them more perfectly to the needs of today. This your committee has striven to do, with a careful regard to the preservation of full freedom for sound and wholesome business in all its necessary and proper operations, but with a firm resolve not to permit the desire for privilege to masquerade under the claim of right. Again in the words of the earlier House report:

Nothing essential has been disturbed, nothing torn up by the roots, no parts rent asunder, which can be left in wholesome combination.

Your committee, in its deliberations, has held steadily as its guiding ideal the preservation of equal opportunity to all usefully employed in the service of distribution comportably with their ability and equipment to serve the producing and consuming public with real efficiency, and the preservation to that public of its freedom from threat of monopoly or oppression in obtaining its needs and disposing of its products.

The aptitude of the means here chosen to that end will more fully appear from the following:

ANALYSIS OF THE BILL

I. GENERAL OBJECT

The bill proposes to amend section 2 of the Clayton Act so as to suppress more effectually discriminations between customers of the same seller not supported by sound economic differences in their business position or in the cost of serving them. Such discriminations are sometimes effected directly in prices or terms of sale, and sometimes by separate allowances to favored customers for purported services or other considerations which are unjustly discriminatory in their result against other customers. The bill is accordingly drawn in four subsections, of which the first three contain substantive measures directed at the more prevalent forms of discrimination, while the fourth is designed to facilitate private remedies in damages to persons immediately and actually injured by its violations.

II. DEFINITIONS

The special definitions of section 1 of the Clayton Act will apply without repetition to the terms concerned where they appear in this bill, since it is designed to become by amendment a part of that act. Thus the term "commerce," as used herein, becomes by force of those definitions interstate and foreign commerce of the United States and commerce in and between its various possessions.

III. DISCRIMINATIONS IN PRICES AND TERMS

Section 2 (a) attacks directly the problem of discrimination in prices and terms of sale. Like present section 2 of the Clayton Act it contains a general prohibition against such discriminations, from which certain specified exceptions are then carved, thus throwing upon any who claim the benefit of those exceptions the burden of showing that their case falls within them. This feature represents no new departure. The changes lie rather in the exceptions themselves, and in the spheres of commerce to which the protection of the bill is extended.

The weakness of present section 2 lies principally in the fact that: (1) It places no limit upon differentials permissible on account of differences in quantity; and (2) it permits discriminations to meet competition, and thus tends to substitute the remedies of retaliation for those of law, with destructive consequences to the central object of the bill. Liberty to meet competition which can be met only by price cuts at the expense of customers elsewhere, is in its unmasked effect the liberty to destroy competition by selling locally below cost, a weapon progressively the more destructive in the hands of the more powerful, and most deadly to the competitor of limited resources, whatever his merit and efficiency. While the bill as now reported closes these dangerous loopholes, it leaves the fields of competition free and open to the most efficient, and thus in fact protects them the more securely against inundations of mere power and size.

Specific phrases of section 2 (a), as now reported, may be noted as follows:

One:

* * * where either or any of the purchases involved in such discrimination are in commerce * * *.

Section 2 (a) attaches to competitive relations between a given seller and his several customers, and this clause is designed to extend its scope to discriminations between interstate and intrastate customers, as well as between those purely interstate. Discriminations in excess of sound economic differences involve generally an element of loss, whether only of the necessary minimum of profits or of actual costs, that must be recouped from the business of customers not granted them. When granted by a given seller to his customers in other States, and denied to those within the State, they involve the use of that interstate commerce to the burden and injury of the latter. When granted to those within the State and denied to those beyond, they involve conversely a directly resulting burden upon interstate commerce with the latter. Both are within the proper and well-recognized power of Congress to suppress.

Two:

* * * where such commodities are sold for use, consumption, or resale within the United States or any Territory thereof or the District of Columbia or any insular possession or other place under the jurisdiction of the United States, * * *.

This clause is retained from the present act.

Three:

* * * where the effect of such discrimination may be substantially to lessen competition or tend to create a monopoly in any line of commerce, or to injure, destroy, or prevent competition with any person who either grants or receives the benefit of such discrimination, or with customers of either of them * * *.

This clause represents a recommended addition to the bill as referred to your committee. It tends to exclude from the bill otherwise harmless violations of its letter, but accomplishes a substantial broadening of a similar clause now contained in section 2 of the Clayton Act. The latter has in practice been too restrictive, in requiring a showing of general injury to competitive conditions in the line of commerce concerned; whereas the more immediately important concern is in injury to the competitor victimized by the discrimination. Only through such injuries, in fact, can the larger general injury result, and to catch the weed in the seed will keep it from coming to flower.

Four:

Provided, That nothing herein contained shall prevent differentials in prices as between purchasers depending solely upon whether they purchase for resale to wholesalers, to retailers, or to consumers, or for use in further manufacture.

Although not specifically so provided, the present section 2 of the Clayton Act also permits these differentials, since it places no limit upon quantity differentials of any kind, nor upon any differentials not affecting general competition. Since added restrictions are here imposed in these respects, a separate clause safeguarding differentials between different classes of purchasers becomes necessary. Such differentials, so long as equal treatment is required within the class, do not give rise to the competitive evils at which the bill is aimed; while to suppress them would produce an unwarranted disturbance of existing habits of trade.

Five:

* * * nor differentials which make only due allowance for differences in the cost, other than brokerage, of manufacture, sale, or delivery resulting from the differing methods or quantities in which such commodities are to such purchasers sold or delivered * * *.

In this clause the words "other than brokerage" are added by recommendation of the committee, and are required to harmonize this subsection with subsection (b) considered below, which deals directly with the question of brokerage.

This proviso is of greatest importance, for while it leaves trade and industry free from any restriction or impediment to the adoption and use of more economic processes, and to the translation of appropriate shares of any savings so effected up and down the stream of distribution to the original producer and to the ultimate consumer, it also strictly limits the use of quantity price differences to that sphere, since beyond it they become instruments of favor and privilege and weapons of competitive oppression. Certain of its constituent phrases should be further noted as follows:

(a) "* * * which makes only due allowance * * *."

This phrase is carried over from the present act, but as coupled with the remainder of the clause, is here extended to limit quantity differentials, as well as those on account of selling and transportation costs. It marks the zone within which differentials may be granted. The bill neither requires nor compels the granting of discriminations or differentials of any sort. It leaves any who wish to do so entirely free to sell to all at the same price regardless of differences in cost, or to grant any differentials not in excess of such differences. It does not require the differential, if granted, to be the arithmetical equivalent of the difference. It is sufficient that it does not exceed it.

(b) "* * * resulting from the differing methods or quantities in which such commodities are to such purchasers sold or delivered * * *."

This limits the differences in cost which may be honored in support of price differentials, to those marginal differences demonstrable as between the particular customers concerned in the discrimination. It is designed, among other things, to preclude the grant of a discrimination to a particular customer equal to the whole saving in cost resulting to the seller's entire volume of business as augmented by that customer's patronage; to preclude also differentials based on allocated or imputed, as distinguished from actual, differences in cost, representing particular facilities or departments which the favored customer may not have immediately utilized, but with which the seller cannot dispense in the general conduct of his business.

It is designed, in short, to leave the test of a permissible differential upon the question: If the more favored customer were sold in the same quantities and by the same methods of sale and delivery as the customer not so favored, how much more per unit would it actually cost the seller to do so, his other business remaining the same? The particular words "resulting from" and "to such purchasers," as here used, are deemed competent to narrow the permitted differentials to those limits, and it seems eminently fair and just that they should be so limited. No particular customer should be permitted distinctively to claim the benefit, nor required distinctively to bear the burden, of the immediate use or nonuse of facilities which the seller must maintain for his business generally.

Six:

Provided, however, That the Federal Trade Commission may, after due investigation and hearing to all interested parties, fix and establish quantity limits, and revise the same as it finds necessary, as to particular commodities or classes of commodities, where it finds that available purchasers in greater quantities are so few as to render differentials on account thereof unjustly discriminatory or promotive of monopoly in any line of commerce; and the foregoing shall then not be construed to permit differentials based on differences in quantities greater than those so fixed and established.

This proviso is added by recommendation of your committee. It is designed to enable, when necessary, the determination of quantity limits as to various commodities, beyond which quantity price differentials shall not be permitted even though supported by differences in cost. It rests upon the principle that where even an admitted economy is of a character that is possible only to a very few units of over-shadowing size in a particular trade or industry, it may become in their hands nonetheless the food upon which monopoly feeds, a proboscis through which it saps the lifeblood of its competitors; and that in forbidding its use and foregoing its benefits the public is but paying a willing price for its freedom from monopoly control. A similar limitation has been applied without challenge for nearly half a century in the field of transportation, in refusing to extend freight rate differentials beyond the car lot quantity.

To apply such a blanket limitation to quantity price differentials in the commodity field, seems at present unwarranted, since similar protection may not now be needed with reference to all commodities, nor as to some may it ever be needed, depending as it does upon such questions of fact as the distribution of business in the given line among large and small competitors, and the degree to which peculiar economies are technically possible only to those competitors of overshadowing size. The above proviso commits to the Federal Trade Commission the power to act in the premises as and when the need arises, and to act appropriately to the nature of the need, after possessing itself of all pertinent information.

Seven:

And, Provided further, That nothing herein contained shall prevent persons engaged in selling goods, wares, or merchandise in commerce from selecting their own customers in bona-fide transactions and not in restraint of trade.

This proviso is retained from the present act.

IV. BROKERAGE

In section (b) the phrases "or any allowance or discount in lieu thereof," and "either to the other party to such transaction" are added by your committee's recommendation. As so revised, this section forbids the payment or allowance of brokerage, either to the other principal party, or to an intermediary acting in fact for or under the control of the other principal party, to the purchase and sale transaction.

Among the prevalent modes of discrimination at which this bill is directed, is the practice of certain large buyers to demand the allowance of brokerage direct to them upon their purchases, or its payment to an employee, agent, or corporate subsidiary whom they set up in the guise of a broker, and through whom they demand that sales to them be made. Whether employed by the buyer in good faith to find a source of supply, or by the seller to find a market, the broker so employed discharges a sound economic function and is entitled to appropriate compensation by the one in whose interest he so serves. But to permit its payment or allowance where no such service is rendered, where in fact, if a "broker," so labeled, enters the picture at all, it is one whom the buyer points out to the seller, rather than one who brings the buyer to the seller, is but to permit the corruption of this function to the purposes of competitive discrimination. The relation of the broker to his client is a fiduciary one. To collect from a client for services rendered in the interest of a party adverse to him, is a violation of that relationship; and to protect those who deal in the streams of commerce against breaches of faith in its relations of trust, is to foster confidence in its processes and promote its wholesomeness and volume.

V. SERVICE ALLOWANCES

Still another favored medium for the granting of oppressive discriminations is found in the practice of large buyer customers to demand, and of their sellers to grant, special allowances in purported payment of advertising and other sales promotional services, which the customer agrees to render with reference to the seller's products, or sometimes with reference to his business generally. Such an allowance becomes unjust when the service is not rendered as agreed and paid for, or when, if rendered, the payment is grossly in excess of its value, or when in any case the customer is deriving from it equal benefit to his own business and is thus enabled to shift to his vendor substantial portions of his own advertising cost, while his smaller competitor, unable to command such allowances, cannot do so.

Section 2 (c) of the bill addresses this evil by prohibiting the granting of such allowances unless made available to all other customers of the seller concerned on proportionately equal terms, or unless in the rendition of such services the customer's own business is kept out of the picture. The first of these conditions is designed to rob this practice generally of its discriminatory character, and the second to leave open a legitimate field for the use of customer services as mere employees or agents in local advertising, in lieu of salaried representatives sent it from without, or of other local personnel strangers to the seller's acquaintance. The frequency with which limited advertising appropriations admit of their expenditure only in selected communities makes it important both to the seller and to the local community to preserve this freedom so long as it is properly protected against discriminatory use.

The phrase "proportionally equal terms," used in clause 1 of section (c), is designed to prevent the limitation of such allowances to single customers on the ground that they alone can furnish the services or facilities in the quantity specified. Where a competitor can furnish them in less quantity, but of the same relative value, he seems entitled, and this clause is designed to accord him, the right to a similar allowance commensurate with those facilities. To illustrate: Where, as was revealed in the hearings earlier referred to in this report, a manufacturer grants to a particular chain distributor an advertising allowance of a stated amount per month per store in which the former's goods are sold, a competing customer with a smaller number of stores, but equally able to furnish the same service per store, and under conditions of the same value to the seller, would be entitled to a similar allowance on that basis.

VI. MEASURE OF DAMAGES

Section (d) represents a revision, approved by your committee, of the corresponding part of the bill as referred. It states a presumptive rule for the measurement of damages in private suits for violation, which are authorized by section 4 of the Clayton Act. As the practices against which this bill is directed are injurious not only to the public interest, but as well to the private parties victimized by them; as, in fact, they work their public injury only through their power to damage private competitors, your committee feels strongly that every reasonable facility should be afforded the latter to enable them to recover the damages they have suffered, and thus also to induce their active vigilance in enforcing the act, relieving the Government correspondingly of the burden of its cost. Private remedies in damages for violations of antitrust law have been authorized since its first enactment; but their use has been much impeded, due partly to the speculative character of damages based on loss of business, and to the limited facilities of private parties for obtaining evidence of a kind to satisfy the narrower requirements of the common law, to which such suits were unknown.

The measure of damages provided in section (d) is the amount of the forbidden discrimination or allowance found to have been granted, limited however to the volume of the plaintiff's business in the goods concerned, or to the amount which he would have received had the allowance been granted to all on the equal basis which the bill requires. The underlying principle of the bill is the suppression of unjust discriminations, and it seems both fair and just, and in harmony with that principle, to enable those victimized by its violation to restore themselves, through the recovery of damages, to the equal position which they would have occupied had the violation not been committed. Confronting the intending violator, as it also does, with the prospect that he will be liable to restore to others in damages tomorrow the discrimination which he grants to some today, it robs such arrangements of their business advantage, and so may well be expected to serve as a wholesome and self-enforcing deterrent against violations of the principle of equal treatment which the bill as a whole exemplifies.

COMMITTEE ON THE JUDICIARY— HOUSE OF REPRESENTATIVES

74TH CONGRESS—2ND SESSION. REPORT NO. 2287

PROHIBITION OF PRICE DISCRIMINATIONS

MARCH 31, 1936.—Committed to the Committee of the Whole House on the state of the Union and ordered to be printed

Mr. UTTERBACK, from the Committee on the Judiciary, submitted the following

REPORT

[To accompany H. R. 8442]

The Committee on the Judiciary, to whom was referred the bill (H. R. 8442) which amends section 2 of the Act of October 15, 1914, entitled "An act to supplement existing law against unlawful restraints and monopolies and for other purposes," report the same back favorably to the House with amendments with the recommendation that, as so amended, it do pass.

The committee amendments are as follows:

Strike out all after the enacting clause and insert in lieu of the language stricken out, the following:

That section 2 of the Act entitled "An Act to supplement existing laws against unlawful restraints and monopolies, and for other purposes," approved October 15, 1914, as amended (U. S. C., title 15, sec. 13), is amended to read as follows:

"SEC. 2. (a) That it shall be unlawful for any person engaged in commerce, in the course of such commerce, either directly or indirectly, to discriminate in price between different purchasers of commodities of like grade and quality, where either or any of the purchases involved in such discrimination are in commerce, where such commodities are sold for use, consumption, or resale within the United States or any Territory thereof, or the District of Columbia or any insular possession or other place under the jurisdiction of the United States, and where the effect of such discrimination may be substantially to lessen competition or tend to create a monopoly in any line of commerce, or to injure, destroy, or prevent competition with any person who either grants or receives the benefit of such discrimination, or with customers of either of them; and that it shall also be unlawful for any person, whether in commerce or not, either directly or indirectly, to discriminate in price between different purchasers of commodities of like grade and quality where in any section or community and in any line of commerce such discrimination may substantially lessen competition in commerce among either sellers or buyers or their competitors or may restrain trade or tend to create a monopoly in commerce or any line thereof; all subject to the following provisions:

"(1) That nothing herein contained shall prevent or require differentials as between purchasers depending solely upon whether they purchase for resale to wholesalers, to retailers, or to consumers, or for use in further manufacture; for the purpose of such classification of customers as wholesalers or jobbers, or retailers, the character of the selling of the purchaser and not the buying shall determine the classification, and any purchaser who, directly or indirectly, through a subsidiary or affiliated concern or broker, does both a wholesale and retail business shall, irrespective of quantity purchased, be classified (1) as a wholesaler on purchases for sale to retail dealers only, not owned or controlled, directly or indirectly, by the purchaser; and (2) as a retailer on purchases for sale to consumers.

"(2) That nothing herein contained shall prevent or require differentials which make only due allowance for differences in the cost of manufacture, sale or delivery resulting from the differing methods or quantities in which such commodities are to such purchasers sold or delivered: *Provided, however,* That the Federal Trade Commission, after due investigation and hearing to all interested parties, following insofar as applicable the procedure and subject to the recourse of the courts, provided in section 11 of this Act, may issue an order fixing and establishing quantity limits and revising the same as it finds necessary, as to particular commodities or classes of commodities, and the foregoing shall then not be construed to permit differentials based on differences in quantities greater than those so fixed and established.

"(3) That nothing herein contained shall prevent price changes from time to time where in response to changing conditions affecting the market for or the marketability of the goods concerned, such as but not limited to actual or imminent deterioration of perishable goods, obsolescence of seasonal goods, distress sales under court process, or sales in good faith in discontinuance of business in the goods concerned.

"(4) That nothing herein contained shall prevent persons engaged in selling goods, wares, or merchandise in commerce from selecting their own customers in bona-fide transactions and not in restraint of trade.

"(5) That the word 'price' as used in this section 2, shall be construed to mean the amount received by the vendor after deducting actual freight or cost of other transportation, if any, allowed or defrayed by the vendor.

"(b) That it shall be unlawful for any person engaged in commerce, in the course of such commerce, to pay or grant, or to receive or accept, anything of value as a commission, brokerage, or other compensation, or any allowance or discount in lieu thereof, except for services rendered in connection with the sale or purchase of goods, wares, or merchandise, either to the other party to such transaction or to an agent, representative, or other intermediary therein where such intermediary is acting in fact for or in behalf, or is subject to the direct or indirect control, of any party to such transaction other than the person by whom such compensation is so granted or paid.

"(c) That it shall be unlawful for any person to discriminate in favor of one purchaser against another purchaser or purchasers of a commodity bought for resale, with or without processing, by contracting to furnish or furnishing, or by contributing to the furnishing of, any services or facilities connected with the processing, handling, sale, or offering for sale of such commodity so purchased upon terms not accorded to all purchasers on proportionally equal terms.

"(d) That it shall be unlawful for any person engaged in commerce to pay or contract for the payment of anything of value to or for the benefit of a customer of such person in the course of such commerce as compensation or in consideration for any services or facilities furnished by or through such customer in connection with the processing, handling, sale, or offering for sale of any products or commodities manufactured, sold, or offered for sale by such person, unless such payment or consideration is available on proportionally equal terms to all other customers competing in the distribution of such products or commodities.

"(e) Upon proof being made, at any hearing on a complaint under this section, that there has been discrimination in price, the burden of rebutting the prima-facie case thus made by showing justification shall be upon the person charged with a violation of this section, and unless justification shall be affirmatively shown, the Commission is authorized to issue an order terminating the discrimination: *Provided, however,* That nothing herein contained shall prevent a seller rebutting the prima-facie case thus made by showing that his lower price to any purchaser or purchasers was made in good faith to meet an equally low price of a competitor.

"(f) Nothing in this section shall prevent a cooperative association from returning to its members, or a cooperative wholesale association from returning to its constituent retailer members, the whole or any part of the net earnings resulting from its trading operations, in proportion to their purchases or sales from, to, or through such associations."

Amend the title so as to read:

To amend section 2 of the Act entitled "An Act to supplement existing laws against unlawful restraints and monopolies, and for other purposes," approved October 15, 1914, as amended (U. S. C., title 15, sec. 13), and for other purposes.

STATEMENT

The purpose of this proposed legislation is to restore, so far as possible, equality of opportunity in business by strengthening antitrust laws and by protecting trade and commerce against unfair trade practices and unlawful price discrimination, and also against restraint and monopoly for the better protection of consumers, workers, and independent producers, manufacturers, merchants, and other businessmen.

To accomplish its purpose, the bill amends and strengthens the Clayton Act by prohibiting discriminations in price between purchasers where such discriminations cannot be shown to be justified by differences in the cost of manufacture, sale, or delivery resulting from different methods or quantities in which such commodities are to such purchasers sold and delivered. It also prohibits brokerage allowances except for services actually rendered, and advertising and other service allowances unless such allowances or services are made available to all purchasers on proportionally equal terms. It strikes at the basing-point method of sale, which lessens competition and tends to create a monopoly.

In the consideration of this bill, your committee has also had before it H.R. 4995, H.R. 5062, and H.R. 10486, all dealing with price discrimination and related subjects. Extensive public hearings have been held, both during this and the last session of Congress. It has also had the benefit of hearings conducted by a committee of the House on the investigation of the American Retail Federation and large-scale buying and selling. Your committee has also had the results of the Federal Trade Commission's several investigations and reports, including its investigation of the chain-store problem. (S. Doc. No. 4, 74th Cong., 1st sess.) Other sources of material for study of this legislation include the N. R. A. codes, and N. R. A. code authority hearings; also, studies of independent students and economists.

Your committee is of the opinion that the evidence is overwhelming that price discrimination practices exist to such an extent that the survival of independent merchants, manufacturers, and other businessmen is seriously imperiled and that remedial legislation is necessary.

On page 24 of the Final Report of the Federal Trade Commission Report on the Chain-Store Investigation (S. Doc. No. 4, 74th Cong., 1st sess.) the following statement appears:

As shown elsewhere, the ability of the chain store to obtain its goods at lower cost than independents and of large chains to obtain goods at lower cost than small chains is an outstanding feature of the growth and development of chain-store merchandising. These lower costs have frequently found expression in the form of special discounts, concessions, or collateral privileges which were not available to smaller purchasers. * * *

A vivid idea of the enormous bargaining power embodied in chain-store purchases may be gained from the fact that the Great Atlantic & Pacific Tea Co. makes purchases of merchandise amounting to over $800,000,000 annually and other large chains make purchases in proportionate amounts.

There were interviews with 129 manufacturers in the grocery group, 76 of which admitted that preferential treatment in some form was given. Thirty-three of the manufacturers interviewed stated positively that threats and coercion had been used by chain-store companies to obtain preferential treatment.

The report continues on page 26:

There were 88 manufacturers interviewed in the drug group, 36 of which admitted that price preferences are given to chains. * * *

Of the 26 tobacco manufacturers interviewed, 16 admitted that price preferences were given by means of extra discounts, rebates, or other allowances. Where threats or coercive measures to force discounts and allowances were employed, some of the manufacturers yielded rather than risk the consequences of their failure to meet the demands of these powerful buying organizations.

The granting of preferences is not confined to any one line of industry or distribution. In entering its cease-and-desist order in the matter of Goodyear Tire & Rubber Co., Docket 2116, recently, the Federal Trade Commission in summarizing its findings of facts stated:

Pursuant to the terms of these several tire contracts between respondent (Goodyear Tire & Rubber Co.) and Sears, Roebuck & Co., respondent has sold tires to Sears, Roebuck & Co. at prices substantially lower than it sold tires of comparable grade and quality to independent retail tire dealers. This difference in sales price has averaged, on four popular sizes of tire casings, from 32 to 40 percent in 1927; from 33 to 55 percent in 1928; from 35 to 45 percent in 1929; from 36 to 46 percent in 1930; from 35 to 50 percent in 1931; from 38 to 48 percent in 1932; from 35 to 53 percent in 1933. The average gross discrimination on these four sizes for the entire period of time from May 1926 to December 1931 was approximately 40 percent. On other sizes the gross discrimination over the entire period varied from 32 to 42 percent.

The net average sales price discrimination remaining after deductions have been made from the dealer prices for discounts and allowances and transportation, over the entire period, varied from 29 to 40 percent on eight sizes of tires. The total aggregate net discrimination, after making such allowances, amounted to approximately $41,000,000, or approximately 26 percent of the net sales price to independent dealers on a volume of business comparable to the volume sold to Sears, Roebuck & Co.

The Commission further found as a fact that such discriminatory prices were not made to Sears, Roebuck & Co. in good faith to meet competition; and also that the Goodyear Tire & Rubber Co. concealed the prices and terms at which it was selling tires to Sears, Roebuck & Co. from its own sales organization and from the trade generally, and at no time did it offer to its own dealers prices on Goodyear brands of tires which were comparable to prices at which respondent was selling tires of equal or comparable quality to Sears, Roebuck & Co.

In 1932 the Economists Committee on Anti-Trust Policy made its report. This report was signed by over 125 leading American economists representing 45 American colleges and universities located in 24 States and the District of Columbia. Their statement respecting antitrust policy was published in the American Economic Review, volume 22 (1932), page 467. The statement is as follows, to wit:

The undersigned as independent students of the subject believe that the weakening of the Sherman Antitrust Act would involve consequences of a radical nature, inconsistent with the very principles of private industry. The widening and extension of the realm of public price fixing in industry and commerce resulting from such action must impose an impossible burden upon governmental agencies of control and irreparable injury to the political and social, as well as economic, interests of the whole people. Without entering in detail into the reasons for these views, we respectfully urge the adoption of an antitrust plank in the platform of the party embodying the following propositions and principles:

1. Opposition to the amendment of the existing antitrust laws in any manner that would weaken them as agencies for preserving the policy of free markets for industrial products whereby individual and small corporate enterprise may be assured unhindered opportunity

to demonstrate through efficiency, service, and low prices to the public, its right to survival in business.

2. Reaffirmation of the essential principle of fair competition in all lines of industry not given over to public price control through commissions; recognition that unless there be such public protection the policy of free markets is essential to the interests of the great mass of people—the consumers, workers, and multitudes of independent business men.

3. Rejection of the assertion made by those seeking to break down the Sherman Act, that it makes necessary the development of excessive capacity and wasteful overproduction, and the equally false assertion that this was one of the causes of the present industrial depression. On the contrary, the most competent economic opinion, as well in Europe as in this country, can be cited in support of the view that a strong contributing cause of the unparalled severity of the present depression was the greatly increased extent of monopolistic control of commodity prices which stimulated financial speculation in the security markets. There is growing doubt whether the capitalistic system, whose basic assumption is free markets and a free price system, can continue to work with an ever-widening range of prices fixed or manipulated by monopolies.

4. Recognition of the antitrust-law legislation has been frequently violated with impunity, and has been inadequately enforced throughout much of the period since its inception; this has resulted in the control of large areas of the industrial field by great combinations and by monopolistic practices having neither legal nor economic justification.

5. Pledge, for the party, of a genuine and effective enforcement of existing laws aimed to secure regulated competition, with needed publicity in large corporation affairs, and to this and such changes in administrative practices as are needed to correct well-recognized evils and to redress the injured right of citizens in their business relations.

6. Pledge of further legislation to remedy widespread evils manifestly resulting from the abuse of the corporate fiction, and from the enormous excesses of the holding-company device.

Names of Signers

Arizona: University of Arizona, E. J. Brown.

California: Mills College, Glenn E. Hoover; Occidental College, Arthur G. Coons, John Parke Young; Pomona College, George S. Burgess, Kenneth Duncan; Stanford University, M. K. Bennett, Eliot Jones, Holbrook Working; University of California (Los Angeles), J. C. Clendenin, Constantine Fannunzio, N. S. Noble, George W. Robins, Marvel N. Stockwell, Gordon S. Watkins.

Colorado: State Agricultural College, D. N. Donaldson, L. A. Moorehouse.

Connecticut: Trinity College, G. A. Kleene; Wesleyan College, Clyde Olin Fisher; Yale University, Winthrop M. Daniels, Clive Day, James Harvey Rogers.

District of Columbia: The Brookings Institution, C. O. Hardy.

Georgia: Emory University, L. E. Campbell, T. J. Canley, M. G. Evans.

Illinois: Rawleigh Foundation, H. R. Mohat, W. J. Rawleigh; University of Chicago, Paul H. Douglas, S. E. Leland, H. A. Millis, S. H. Nerlove, Henry Schultz, Jacob Viner, Chester W. Wright; University of Illinois, E. L. Bogart, David Kinley, N. A. Weston.

Indiana: Indiana State Teachers College, Waldo F. Mitchell.

Iowa: Iowa State College, A. G. Black.

Massachusetts: Amherst College, Willard L. Thorp; Massachusetts Institute of Technology, Carroll W. Doten.

Michigan: University of Michigan, H. L. Caverly, Z. C. Dickinson, M. Elliott, Howard Ellis, Max Handman, W. A. Paton, Shorey Peterson, I. L. Sharfman, Fred M. Taylor, V. P. Timoshenka, Leonard Watkins.

Minnesota: University of Minnesota, Ralph Cassady, George Filipetti, Frederick B. Garver, Alvin H. Hansen, E. A. Heilmar, Arthur W. Marget, Bruce D. Mudgett, Emerson P. Schmidt, J. Warren Stehman.

Missouri: Washington University, I. Lippincott.

New Hampshire: Dartmouth College, William A. Carter.

New Jersey: Dana College, William L. Nunn; Princeton University, J. Douglas Brown, Denzel C. Cline, Frank T. DeVyver, Frank H. Dixon, Harold W. Dodds, Frank A. Fetter, Frank W. Fetter, Leslie T. Fournier, Stanley E. Howard.

New Jersey: Princeton University, George F. Luthringer, A. M. McIsaac, George M. Modlin, Vernon Mund, James G. Smith, Raymond C. Whittlesey.

New York: Brooklyn Law School, Henry Ward Beer; University of Buffalo, Shaw Livermore, Thomas L. Norton, Charles S. Tippetts; Columbia University, James C. Bonbright, John Bates Clark, Reavis Cox; New York University, Willard E. Atkins, Lewis H. Haney, Walter E. Spahr; New York City, John Bauer, James E. Pope; Union College, W. W. Bennett.

Ohio: Ohio State University, M. B. Hammond, F. E. Held, C. C. Huntington, Virgil Willit.

Oklahoma: University of Oklahoma, Arthur B. Adams, Frederick L. Ryan.

Pennsylvania: Bucknell University, A. B. Biscoe; Haverford College, Don C. Barrett, John G. Herndon, Jr., Frank D. Watson; University of Pittsburgh, A. E. Boer, Prentice Dean, George McCabe, Francis Tyson; Swarthmore College, Robert C. Brooks, Herbert F. Fraser; Washington and Jefferson College, M. C. Watersdorf.

Texas: University of Texas, George W. Stocking.

Virginia: University of Virginia, A. J. Barlow, Abraham Berglund, E. A. Kincaid, T. R. Snavely, G. T. Staines.

Washington: University of Washington, S. J. Coon, T. S. McMahon, H. H. Preston, H. E. Smith.

West Virginia: West Virginia University, Arnold W. Johnson, Louis A. Rufener, E. H. Vickers.

Wisconsin: Lawrence College, M. M. Bober, W. A. McConagha; Public Service Commission, E. W. Morehouse; University of Wisconsin, John R. Commons.

Attention is also directed to the unequivocal pronouncement contained in the Democratic national platform of 1932 as follows:

We advocate strengthening and impartial enforcement of the antitrust laws, to prevent monopoly and unfair trade practices, and revision thereof for the better protection of labor and the small producer and distributor.

More than 20 years' experience and observation with respect to the operation of the Clayton Act, together with new methods of trade and industrial organization that have since developed, have convinced your committee of the shortcomings of existing legislation, and of the need for strengthening existing laws and of fitting them more perfectly to the methods and needs of today. This your committee has striven to do with a careful regard to the preservation of full freedom and sound and honest business methods in all its necessary and proper operations; but with a firm resolve not to permit the desire of privilege to masquerade under the claim of right. It has been our effort to disturb nothing that is essential.

Its guiding ideal is the preservation of equality of opportunity as far as possible to all who are usefully employed in the service of distribution and production, taking into consideration their ability and equipment to serve the producing and consuming public with efficiency and the protection of the public from a threat of monopoly or oppression in the production and manufacture of the things it needs and the distribution of the same fairly and honestly without employment of unfair trade practices and unlawful price discrimination.

EXISTING LAW

The basic Federal antitrust law is the Sherman Act, enacted July 2, 1890. This law was intended to preserve the competitive system as our economic order by maintaining the natural flow of trade and freedom of competition in interstate commerce. To accomplish its purposes, the act outlawed from interstate commerce any concerted industrial action in undue restraint of interstate commerce and also the misuse of such commerce to create or maintain private monopoly.

Experience established the fact that the Sherman Act alone was inadequate to accomplish its purpose and that additional legislation was required to reach and prevent unfair methods of competition. President Wilson in 1914 sent a special message to

Congress on January 20, expressing his stern opposition to monopolies and to oppressive monopolistic practices, and recommended the enactment of supplemental legislation. Consequently, and acting in accord with the President's recommendation, Congress enacted the Federal Trade Commission Act on September 26, 1914, and shortly thereafter on October 15, 1914, enacted the Clayton Act. These acts have been in effect for over 21 years. Together with the Sherman Act, they constitute the existing legislative plan at this time.

The Commission Act created the Federal Trade Commission and was designed to outlaw all unfair methods of competition from interstate commerce. The Clayton Act addressed itself, in section 2 thereof, to the problem of price discrimination by providing—

that it shall be unlawful for any person engaged in commerce in the course of such commerce either directly or indirectly to discriminate in price between different purchasers of commodities * * * where the effect of such discrimination may be to substantially lessen competition or tend to create a monopoly in any line of commerce.

This legislation represented the hope of the Congress at that time. The Clayton Act, however, contained the following provisos:

Provided, That nothing herein contained shall prevent discrimination in price between purchasers of commodities on account of differences in the grade, quality, or quantity of the commodity sold, or that makes only due allowance for differences in the cost of selling or transportation, or discrimination in price in the same or different communities made in good faith to meet competition: *And provided further,* That nothing herein contained shall prevent persons engaged in selling goods, wares, or merchandise in commerce from selecting their own customers in bona-fide transactions and not in restraint of trade.

These provisos have so materially weakened section 2 of that act, which this bill proposes to amend, as to render it inadequate, if not almost a nullity. Some of the difficulties of enforcement of this section as it stands are pointed out in the annual report of the Federal Trade Commission above referred to, at pages 63 and following.

ANALYSIS OF THE BILL

I. GENERAL OBJECT

The object of the bill briefly stated is to amend section 2 of the Clayton Act so as to suppress more effectually discriminations between customers of the same seller not supported by sound economic differences in their business positions or in the cost of serving them. Such discriminations are sometimes effected directly in prices, including terms of sale; and sometimes by separate allowances to favored customers for purported services or other considerations which are unjustly discriminatory in their result against other customers. The bill is accordingly drawn in six lettered subsections, of which the first four (a), (b), (c) and (d) contain substantive measures directed at the more prevalent forms of discrimination, while the fifth (e) and sixth (f) contain added precautionary provisions.

II. DEFINITIONS

The special definitions of section 1 of the Clayton Act will apply without repetition to the terms concerned where they appear in this bill, since it is designed to become by amendment a part of that act.

III. PRICE DISCRIMINATIONS

Section 2 (a) attacks directly the problem of price discrimination. Like present section 2 of the Clayton Act, it contains a general prohibition against such price discriminations, from which certain exceptions are then carved.

Section 2 (a) attaches to competitive relations between a given seller and his several customers. It concerns discrimination between customers of the same seller. It has nothing to do with fixing prices nor does it require the maintenance of any relationship in prices charged by a competing seller.

Discriminations in excess of sound economic differences between the customers concerned, in the treatment accorded them, involve generally an element of loss, whether only of the necessary minimum of profits or of actual costs, that must be recouped from the business of customers not granted them. When granted by a given seller to his customers in other States, and denied to those within the State, they involve the use of that interstate commerce to the burden and injury of the latter. When granted to customers within the State and denied to those beyond, they involve conversely a direct resulting burden upon his interstate commerce with the latter. Both are within the proper and well-recognized power of Congress to suppress; and the following clause, contained in the opening portion of section 2 (a):

* * * where either or any of the purchases involved in such discrimination are in commerce * * *

is of first importance in extending the protections of this bill against the full evil of price discrimination, whether immediately in interstate or intrastate commerce, wherever it is of such a character as tends directly to burden or affect interstate commerce.

The next important clause governing the jurisdictional scope of the bill is as follows:

* * * where the effect of such discrimination may be substantially to lessen competition or tend to create a monopoly in any line of commerce, or to injure, destroy, or prevent competition with any person who either grants or receives the benefit of such discrimination, or with customers of either of them. * * *

This provision accomplishes a substantial broadening of a similar clause now contained in section 2 of the Clayton Act. The existing law has in practice been too restrictive in requiring a showing of general injury to competitive conditions in the line of commerce concerned, whereas the more immediately important concern is in injury to the competitor victimized by the discrimination. Only through such injury in fact can the larger, general injury result. Through this broadening of the jurisdiction of the act, a more effective suppression of such injuries is possible and the more effective protection of the public interest at the same time is achieved.

The specific exemptions carved from section 2 (a) are more particularly explained as follows:

CLASSIFICATION OF PURCHASERS

Subparagraph (1) permits price differentials depending solely upon whether the purchaser buys "for resale to wholesalers, to retailers, or to consumers, or for use in further manufacture," and makes specific provision for the classification of customers in those several categories. This exemption is contained by implication in present section 2 of the Clayton Act, since it places no limit upon quantity differentials of any kind nor upon differentials not affecting general competition. Since added restrictions are here imposed in these respects, a separate clause safeguarding differentials between different classes of purchasers becomes necessary. Such differentials, so long as equal treatment is required within the class, do not give rise to the competitive evils at which the bill is aimed; while to suppress such differentials would produce an unwarranted disturbance of existing habits of trade.

It should be noted that there is nothing in this exemption to prevent consumers when buying cooperatively or otherwise in quantities characteristic of retailers or retailers when buying in quantities characteristic of wholesalers from being accorded the same prices as those dealers respectively so long as their prices are respectively justified within their own class on the basis of differences in cost as required by subparagraph (2) noted below.

Wholesalers frequently find it necessary to supplement existing stock by additional purchases in smaller quantities and the above exemption, subparagraph (1), permits wholesalers to be accorded wholesale prices on these smaller purchases as incident to his business without the seller having to accord them at the same time on the whole body of purchases in similar quantities on sales direct to retailers. This protects the usefulness of the wholesaler in serving retailers dependent upon him for their source of supply.

Differentials between purchasers in each classification as set forth in the above exemption must, of course, be justified by differences in cost as provided by subparagraph (2) below.

Whether retailers acting cooperatively in their purchasing activities will be classified as wholesalers or retailers will depend naturally upon whether their cooperative organization functions as a separate entity taking title and reselling it to its retailer members, or merely as representing them severally in their dealings direct with the selling source of supply, but in either case there is nothing in the bill that requires prices accorded retailers to be higher than those accorded wholesalers or vice versa.

COST DIFFERENTIALS

Subsection (2) permits:

* * * differentials which make only due allowance for differences in the cost of manufacture, sale, or delivery resulting from the differing methods or quantities in which such commodities are to such purchasers sold or delivered * * *.

This proviso is of great importance, for while it leaves trade and industry free from any restriction or impediment to the adoption and use of more economic processes of manufacture, methods of sale, and modes of delivery, wheresoever they may be employed in streams of production or distribution; it also limits the use of quantity price differentials to the sphere of actual cost differences. Otherwise, such differentials would become instruments of favor and privilege and weapons of competitive oppression.

In the above exemption the phrase "which make only due allowance," is carried over from the present act, but as coupled with the remainder of the clause, is here extended to limit quantity differentials to differences in the cost of manufacture, sale, and delivery as provided in said subsection (2). It marks the zone within which differentials may be granted.

The bill neither requires nor compels the granting of discriminations or differentials of any sort, and the words "or require" are expressly inserted in both the above subparagraphs to make that clear. It leaves any who wish to do so entirely free to sell to all at the same price regardless of differences in cost, or to grant any differentials not in excess of such differences. It does not require the differential, if granted, to be the arithmetical equivalent of the difference. It is sufficient that it does not exceed it.

The following clause from subparagraph (2) should be noted:

* * * resulting from differing methods or quantities in which such commodities are to such purchasers sold or delivered * * *.

This limits the differences in cost which may justify price differentials strictly to those actual differences traceable to the particular buyer for and against whom the discrimination is granted, to the different methods of serving them, and to the different quantities in which they buy.

But such differentials whether they arise in operating or overhead cost must, as is plainly stated in the phrase quoted above, be those resulting from the differing methods or quantities in which such commodities are to such purchasers sold or delivered.

This, in its plain meaning, permits differences in overhead where they can actually be shown as between the customers or classes of customers concerned, but it precludes differentials based on the imputation of overhead to particular customers, or the exemption of others from it, where such overhead represents facilities or activities inseparable from the seller's business as a whole and not attributable to the business of particular customers or of the particular customers concerned in the discrimination. It leaves open as a question of fact in each case whether the differences in cost urged in justification of a price differential—whether of operating or of overhead costs—is of one kind or the other. That is, whether or not it answers the above requirements as to differences resulting from differing methods or quantities in which such commodities are to such purchasers sold or delivered.

QUANTITY LIMITS

The proviso contained in subparagraph (2) permits the Federal Trade Commission to fix, as to particular commodities, quantity limits beyond which quantity price differentials shall not be permitted, even when supported by cost differences of the character authorized earlier in the paragraph. This proviso rests upon the principle that where even an admitted economy is of a character that is possible only to a very few units of overshadowing size in a particular trade or industry, it may become in their hands an instrument that lessens competition and that tends to create a monopoly; and that in forbidding its use and foregoing its benefits the public is merely insuring its freedom from monopoly control.

A similar limitation has been applied without challenge for nearly half a century in the field of transportation in refusing to extend freight-rate differentials beyond the car-lot quantity. To apply such a blanket limitation to quantity price differentials in the commodity field seems at present unwarranted, since similar protection may not now be needed with reference to all commodities, nor as to some may it ever be needed, depending as it does upon such questions of fact as the distribution of business in the given line among large and small competitors, and the degree to which peculiar economies are technically possible only to those competitors of overshadowing size. The above proviso commits to the Federal Trade Commission the power to act in the premises as and when the need arises, and to act appropriately to the nature of the need, after possessing itself of all pertinent information. It is not designed to confer upon the Commission carte blanche authority to regulate quantity discounts without rule or guide, but only to permit it to fix limits in quantities for which quantity price differentials may be granted, guided by the principle long recognized in antitrust law administration; that the economies of mere size do not justify the risk of monopoly.

MARKET PRICE CHANGES

Subparagraph (3) exempts price changes "in response to changing conditions affecting the market for or the marketability of the goods concerned, such as, but not limited to, actual or imminent deteriorations of perishable goods, obsolescence of seasonal goods, distress sales under court process or sales in good faith in discontinuance of business in the goods concerned." While it is not believed that the principal prohibitions of section 2 (a) apply in any case to such price changes, nor has such construction ever been suggested or contended for under present section 2, this specific exemption is included as an added precaution to safeguard the ready disposition of goods characterized by fluid market conditions.

SELECTION OF CUSTOMERS

Subparagraph (4) embodies an exception retained from the present act, permitting the seller to select his customers in bona-fide transactions and not in restraint of trade.

DEFINITION OF PRICE

Subparagraph (5) defines the word "price" as used in the bill in the following words:

(5) That the word "price" as used in this section 2 shall be construed to mean the amount received by the vendor after deducting actual freight or cost of other transportation, if any, allowed or defrayed by the vendor.

This paragraph defines the word "price" as used in this bill in terms of the amount realized by the seller, as distinguished from the amount paid by the buyer. The true price received by the seller being the amount left after deducting actual freight or cost of other transportation allowed or defrayed by the vendor.

An increasing number of industries in recent years have adopted what is known as the "basing point," "multiple basing point," and "delivered price" systems under which delivered prices only are quoted by manufacturers and sellers dealing in certain commodities. Under these systems, each manufacturer defrays the actual transportation costs and charges either the railroad freight from some arbitrary point or an average zone freight rate. The result is identical delivered prices at any given destination.

There are various results of these systems:

The manufacturers refuse to quote prices f.o.b. their manufacturing plants. They charge freight at the railroad rates and then often delivery is made by waterway or highway. They thus obtain the benefit of what has been spent on public works to the exclusion of purchasers and the public.

Each manufacturer ships his product beyond other "competitor's" plants, frequently throughout the country, and allows "competitors" to enter his local territory without offering any price concession to hold his own high net return area. Each maintains base prices high enough so that he may defray the cost of distant shipments. The public pays the cross-hauling bill.

Either the manufacturer who sells f.o.b. his plant charges distant customers a higher "price" than local customers when he leaves the former to pay the transportation costs, or the basing point manufacturer charges his local customers a higher "price" than distant customers when he pays freight charges to deliver goods to his distant customers and accepts from them a substantially lower net rate.

The former obtains the same monetary consideration from all alike. The latter accepts from many distant buyers a less monetary return or true price, than from local customers whom he sacrifices to join with competitors in avoiding price discrimination.

As illustrative of the way basing point methods of sale actually operate, and as affording good opportunity for study of the effects of this system, there is presented below two examples; one taken from the cement industry and one from the steel industry:

The Iowa State Highway Commission on December 5, 1929, received bids for 2,000,000 barrels of cement to be delivered at 44 different destinations in the State of Iowa, to be used in building cement highways. There were 20 bidders, consisting of 15 well-known cement manufacturing companies and 5 cement dealers. As high as 14 and as low as 6 companies submitted bids on furnishing the amount of cement designated for the 44 different destinations. Those who bid quoted identical delivered prices for each destination for which they made bids, with the exception of one company located at LaSalle, Ill., which company quoted 5 cents a barrel less than the basing point formula price on 3 bids, and quoted higher than the basing point formula price on 10 bids, ranging from 2 to 17 cents per barrel.

The first three destinations were located nearest the mill at LaSalle. The other 10 locations were on destinations in territory adjacent to the mills at Mason City and Gilmore City, Iowa. The basing point formula price used by bidders was the base price at Mason City, at that time $1.30 per barrel, plus railroad freight from Mason City to the destination where the cement was to be delivered. The companies bidding outside of the mills at Mason City were located in the following cities and towns:

Gilmore City, Des Moines, Valley Junction, and Davenport, Iowa; Dixon and LaSalle, Ill.; Buffington, Ind.; Louisville and Superior, Nebr.; Hannibal, Sugar Lake, and St. Louis, Mo.; Bonner Springs, Mildred, and Humboldt, Kans.

Regardless of the location of the mill, all bids except that of the Marquette Cement Manufacturing Co. at LaSalle, Ill., were identical and all quoted delivered prices. A check-up on this entire transaction by the Federal Trade Commission revealed the fact that each company bid exactly the same amount, except the Marquette Co. The bids were not only identical but in each instance were the exact amount of the basing point price at Mason City plus the railroad freight from Mason City to destination. The result was that no company except the Mason City Mills received the same net or true price for the cement sold at these destinations. The system therefore has resulted both in price fixing and in price discrimination. It has destroyed competition and has created in effect a cement monopoly throughout that area.

The following facts are illustrative of the results of the basing-point system in the iron and steel industry. The facts herewith submitted are contained in the November 1934 report of the Federal Trade Commission to the President, with respect to the basing-point system in the iron and steel industry. There were 61 bidders scattered throughout the entire United States, extending from the Atlantic to the Pacific Oceans, that submitted individual bids on lots 354, 355, 356, and 357 of schedule no. 2840, United States Navy drawings on July 20, 1934. The bids were lump-sum bids. For lot 354 there were 37 bidders, of whom 23 bid $4,321.28; 8 bid $4,341.29; and 1 bid $4,365.23. On lot 355 there were also 37 bidders, on which 36 bid $5,289.69; and 1 bid $5,301.57. On lot 356 there were 54 bidders, of whom 52 bid $50,079.15; 1 bid 50,087.27; and 1 bid $50,088.94. On lot 357 there were 58 bidders, of whom 55 bid $43,571.20; one bid $43,572.64; 1 bid $43,591.20; and 1 bid $43,481.38.

The names of the companies bidding, the amount of their bids on each lot number, the shipping points of the successful bidders, and the delivery points, together with items and units of each of said lots of schedule 2840, United States Navy drawings, July 20, 1934, together with Executive orders, form of bids, together with specifications and itemized form for estimates on each item for each of the said lots 354, 355, 356, and 357, are all set out in said report of the Federal Trade Commission beginning on page 45 and following.

It should be further noted that under the basing-point system as applied in the iron and steel industry, there is practically no competition, that price quotations are with very few exceptions delivered prices, and are fixed by the base price on a multiple base system rather than a single base point system and that in each instance every mill or factory or bidder receives a different net price, or true price, for a product sold at different destinations.

It should also be noted that this system of price discrimination has resulted in the building up of a practical monopoly in the iron and steel industry. In addition thereto, it should also be noted that the largest cement manufacturing corporation in the United States, to wit, the Universal Atlas Cement Co., was organized by the United States Steel Corporation which owns and controls over one-half of the iron and steel industry in the United States. With both the cement and steel industries controlled by practical monopolies and the largest operator in both the iron and steel industry and the cement industry owned and controlled by the same interests, we cannot expect real competitive conditions between the iron and steel industry and the cement industry, to say nothing of expecting competitive conditions in those industries separately.

The matter of the basing point system in both of these lines of industry has been the subject of careful study for some years by the Federal Trade Commission. The following is quoted from the report of the Federal Trade Commission to the President with respect to the basing point system in the iron and steel industry, dated November 1934:

* * * In economics, as in medicine, diagnosis is fundamental. The diagnosis which the Commission makes is that the basing-point system not only permits and encourages price fixing, but that it is price fixing.

It is price fixing so absolute that purchasing agencies of the Federal Government are reduced to a position of such helplessness that they literally place each bid in a separate capsule, shake them up, and draw one out of a hat. It is price fixing so rigid that violations of the delivered price are actually penalized at the rate of $10 per ton even on sales to the Federal Government, while fines have been assessed on sale of as little as a fraction of a ton. It is price fixing so self-centered that as the Commission pointed out in its former report, the advantages bestowed by nature on particular sections or communities have been nullified.

Not only that, but the immense sums invested by Government in improving the gifts of nature and by private industry in the faith that natural advantages and their improvements would accrue to the benefit of the buyers, fabricators, and consumers of steel as well as the producers, have been in effect largely appropriated by the producers. The basing-point system with its supporting formula in essence withholds the gifts of nature from consuming classes and monopolizes them in the hands of the producers and sellers of iron and steel. Only aims of a blindly selfish character can account for the arbitrary abnormalities and flagrant fictions which are inherent in this basing-point system.

The necessary implication of statements by leaders of the industry is that the basing-point system in steel is a price-fixing system. As an instrument of price fixing, it has the sanction of the code whose provisions make its operation more definite and certain without in any degree lessening its inequities. The inequities of the system, whether for producer, fabricator, or consumer, arise fundamentally out of this fact, that it depends upon artificial and wholly arbitrary arrangements in the making of price, rather than upon competition automatically and impersonally working out into a price accurately reflecting a balancing of supply and demand forces * * *.

Generally speaking, when a price-fixing combination is successful in raising prices, consumption will decrease. The process of holding for a fixed price in the face of decreasing consumption means reduced employment and reduced income for labor. If consumption continues to decrease, a price-fixing system calls for still higher prices in order to protect profits and thus a new cycle of reduced consumption is initiated.

It is a most significant fact that the steel industry was able to show satisfactory profits for the first 6 months of 1934 without operating to more than half its producing capacity. * * *

* * * The situation involves social and economic consequences of far-reaching and fundamental import. If the capitalistic system does not function as a competitive economy there will be increasing question whether it can or should endure. The real friends of capitalism are those who insist upon preserving its competitive character. * * *

The above quotations will be found in said Federal Trade Commission's Report on pages 35 and following, with respect to the basing-point system in the iron and steel industry, November 1934.

It would seem that the basing-point method of selling commodities clearly results in unlawful price discrimination, that it results in the lessening of competition, and that it tends to create a monopoly. In effect, this provision of the bill is designed to put an end to price discrimination through the medium of the basing-point or delivered-price system of selling commodities. It will require the use of the f. o. b. method of sale.

IV. BROKERAGE

Section (b) deals with the abuse of the brokerage function for purposes of oppressive discrimination. The true broker serves either as representative of the seller to find him market outlets, or as representative of the buyer to find him sources of supply. In either case he discharges functions which must otherwise be performed by the parties themselves through their own selling or buying departments, with their respective attendant costs. Which method is chosen depends presumptively upon which is found more economical in the particular case; but whichever method is chosen, its cost is the necessary and natural cost of a business function which cannot be escaped. It is for this reason that, when free of the coercive influence of mass buying power, discounts in lieu of brokerage are not usually accorded to buyers who deal with the seller direct since such sales must bear instead their appropriate share of the seller's own selling cost.

Among the prevalent modes of discrimination at which this bill is directed is the practice of certain large buyers to demand the allowance of brokerage direct to them upon their purchases, or its payment to an employee, agent, or corporate subsidiary whom they set up in the guise of a broker, and through whom they demand that sales to them be made. But the positions of buyer and seller are by nature adverse, and it is a contradiction in terms incompatible with his natural function for an intermediary to claim to be rendering services for the seller when he is acting in fact for or under the control of the buyer, and no seller can be expected to pay such an intermediary so controlled for such services unless compelled to do so by coercive influences in compromise of his natural interest. Whether employed by the buyer in good faith to find a source of supply, or by the seller to find a market, the broker so employed discharges a sound economic function and is entitled to appropriate compensation by the one in whose interest he so serves. But to permit its payment or allowance where no such service is rendered, where in fact, if a "broker," so labeled, enters the picture at all, it is one whom the buyer points out to the seller, rather than one who brings the buyer to the seller, would render the section a nullity. The relation of the broker to his client is a fiduciary one. To collect from a client for services rendered in the interest of a party adverse to him, is a violation of that relationship; and to protect those who deal in the streams of commerce against breaches of faith in its relations of trust, is to foster confidence in its processes and promote its wholesomeness and volume.

Section (b) permits the payment of compensation by a seller to his broker or agent for services actually rendered in his behalf: Likewise by a buyer to his broker or agent for services in connection with the purchase of goods actually rendered in his behalf; but it prohibits the direct or indirect payment of brokerage except for such services rendered. It prohibits its allowance by the buyer direct to the seller, or by the seller direct to the buyer; and it prohibits its payment by either to an agent or intermediary acting in fact for or in behalf, or subject to the direct or indirect control, of the other.

V. SERVICE ALLOWANCES

Still another favored medium for the granting of oppressive discriminations is found in the practice of large buyer customers to demand, and of their sellers to grant, special allowances in purported payment of advertising and other sales-promotional services, which the customer agrees to render with reference to the seller's products, or sometimes with reference to his business generally. Such an allowance becomes unjust when the service is not rendered as agreed and paid for, or when, if rendered, the payment is grossly in excess of its value, or when in any case the customer is deriving from it equal benefit to his own business and is thus enabled to shift to his vendor substantial portions of his own advertising cost, while his smaller competitor, unable to command such allowances, cannot do so.

Sections (c) and (d) of the bill address this evil by prohibiting the granting of such allowances, either in the form of services or facilities themselves furnished by the seller to the buyer, or in the form of payment for such services or facilities when undertaken by the buyer, except when accorded or made available to all competing customers on proportionally equal terms.

The phrase "proportionally equal terms" is designed to prevent the limitation of such allowances to single customers on the ground that they alone can furnish the services or facilities or other consideration in the quantities specified. Where a competitor can furnish them in less quantity, but of the same relative value, he seems entitled, and this clause is designed to accord him, the right to a similar allowance commensurate with those facilities. To illustrate: Where, as was revealed in the hearings earlier referred to in this report, a manufacturer grants to a particular chain distributor an advertising allowance of a stated amount per month per store in which the former's goods are sold, a competing customer with a smaller number of stores, but equally able to furnish the same service per store, and under conditions of the same value to the seller, would be entitled to a similar allowance on that basis.

It should be noted, however, that there is nothing in this section or elsewhere in the bill to limit or restrict the widespread custom of manufacturers and others selling sources of supply to engage and pay for exhibit space at trade association exhibitions, or for advertising space in trade-association publications, nor to limit the freedom of newspaper or periodical advertising generally, so long as not employed in ways calculated to defeat the purposes of this bill.

VI. PROCEDURE

Section (e) down to the proviso merely lays down directions with reference to procedure including a statement with respect to burden of proof.

MEETING COMPETITION

This proviso represents a contraction of an exemption now contained in section 2 of the Clayton Act which permits discriminations without limit where made in good faith to meet competition. It should be noted that while the seller is permitted to meet local competition, it does not permit him to cut local prices until his competitor has first offered lower prices, and then he can go no further than to meet those prices. If he goes further, he must do so likewise with all his other customers, or make himself liable to all of the penalties of the act, including treble damages. In other words, the proviso permits the seller to meet the price actually previously offered by a local competitor. It permits him to go no further.

VII. COOPERATIVES

Section (f) affirms the right of cooperatives to distribute their net earnings resulting from their trading operations among their members on a patronage basis in proportion to their purchases or sales from, to, or through such cooperative association. While the bill contains elsewhere no provision either express or implied to the contrary, this section is added as a precautionary reservation in a spirit of encouragement to the cooperative movement.

CONCLUSION

In conclusion, your committee wishes to correct some important misapprehensions, and even misrepresentations, that have been broadly urged with regard to the probable effect of this bill. There is nothing in it to penalize, shackle, or discourage efficiency, or to reward inefficiency. There is nothing in it to fix prices, or enable the fixation of prices; nor to limit the freedom of price movements in response to changing market conditions.

Any physical economies that are to be found in mass buying and distribution, whether by corporate chain, voluntary chain, mail-order house, department store, or by the cooperative grouping of producers, wholesalers, retailers, or distributors—and whether those economies are from more orderly processes of manufacture, or from the elimination of unnecessary salesmen, unnecessary travel expense, unnecessary warehousing, unnecessary truck or other forms of delivery, or other such causes—none of them are in the remotest degree disturbed by this bill. Nor does it in any way infringe the seller's freedom to give a part or all of the benefit of the saving so effected to others with whom he deals, whether in higher prices paid to the producer from whom he buys his raw materials, or in higher wages to those who labor in production or handling of his goods, or in lower prices to the customer, including the ultimate consumer who buys them.

It is not believed that the restoration of equality of opportunity in business will increase prices to consumers. Unfair trade practices and monopolistic methods which in the end destroy competition, restrain trade, and create monopoly have never in all history resulted in benefit to the public interest. On the contrary, for the most part, they have been symbolic of lower wages, longer hours, lower prices paid producers, coercion of independent manufacturers, domination of that field of industry, and in the end high prices to consumers and large profits to the owners.

It is the design and intent of this bill to strengthen existing antitrust laws, prevent unfair-price discriminations, and preserve competition in interstate commerce. It is believed to be in the interest of producer, consumer and distributor. No business institution need have any fear of this legislation if it will conduct its business honestly and without the use of unfair trade practices, and unjust price discriminations.

In compliance with clause 2a of rule XIII there is printed below, first a comparison of the bill as introduced with existing law, and second a comparison of the committee amendment with existing law. Present law is in roman, matter proposed to be omitted in black brackets, and new matter in italics.

H. R. 8442 AS ORIGINALLY INTRODUCED

SEC. 2. (a) That it shall be unlawful for any person engaged in commerce, in the course of such commerce, either directly or indirectly, to discriminate in price *or terms of sale* between different purchasers of commodities [which] *of like grade and quality, where either or any of the purchases involved in such discrimination are in commerce, and where such* commodities are sold for use, consumption, or resale within the United States or any Territory thereof or the District of Columbia or any insular possession or other place under the jurisdiction of the United States: [where the effect of such discrimination may be to substantially lessen competition or tend to create a monopoly in any line of commerce;] *Provided,* That nothing herein contained shall prevent [discrimination] *differentials* in [price] *prices as* between purchasers [of commodities on account of differences in the grade, quality, or quantity of the commodity sold, or] *depending solely upon whether they purchase for resale to wholesalers, to retailers, or to consumers, or for use in further manufacture; nor differentials* [that makes] *which make* only due allowance for differences in the cost of [selling or transportation, or discrimination in price in the same or different communities made in good faith to meet competition] *manufacture, sale, or delivery resulting from the differing methods or quantities in which such commodities are to such purchasers sold or delivered: And provided further,* That nothing herein contained shall prevent persons engaged in selling goods, wares, or merchandise in commerce from selecting their own customers in bona fide transactions and not in restraint of trade.

(b) *That it shall be unlawful for any person engaged in commerce, in the course of such commerce, to pay or grant, or to receive or accept, anything of value as a commission, brokerage, or other compensation to an agent, representative, or other intermediary in connection with the sale or purchase of goods, wares, or merchandise, where such intermediary is acting therein for or in behalf or is subject to the direct or indirect control, of any party to such purchase and sale transaction other than the person by whom such compensation is so granted or paid.*

(c) *That it shall be unlawful for any person engaged in commerce to pay or contract for the payment of anything of value to or for the benefit of a customer of such person in the course of such commerce as compensation or in consideration for any services or facilities furnished by or through such customer in connection with the processing, handling, sale, or offering for sale of any products or commodities manufactured, sold, or offered for sale by such person, unless—*

(1) *such payment or consideration is offered on proportionally equal terms to all other customers competing in the distribution of such products or commodities; or unless*

(2) *the business, identity, or interests of such customers are in no way publicly associated, by name, reference, allusion, proximity, or otherwise, with or in the furnishing of such services or facilities, and the consideration paid therefor does not exceed the fair value of such services or facilities in the localities where furnished.*

(d) *For purposes of suit under section 4 of this Act, the measure of damage from any violation of this section shall, in the absence of proof of greater damage, be presumed to be the unit amount of the prohibited discrimination, payment, or grant concerned, multiplied by—*

(1) *the volume of business involved in such violation in case the plaintiff shall be in competition with the grantor therein in the distribution of the products or commodities concerned; and*

(2) *the volume of plaintiff's business in the respective products and commodities, and for the period of time concerned in such violation, in case the plaintiff shall be in competition with the grantee therein, or, in cases under paragraph (b) of this section, in competition with the intermediary or with the person for or under whose control such intermediary shall act therein.*

Committee Amendment to H. R. 8442

Sec. 2. (a) That it shall be unlawful for any person engaged in commerce, in the course of such commerce, either directly or indirectly, to discriminate in price between different purchasers of commodities [which] *of like grade and quality, where either or any of the purchases involved in such discrimination are in commerce, where such* commodities are sold for use, consumption, or resale within the United States or any Territory thereof, or the District of Columbia or any insular possession or other place under the jurisdiction of the United States, *and* where the effect of such discrimination may be [to] substantially *to* lessen competition or tend to create a monopoly in any line of commerce, [: *Provided,* That nothing herein contained shall prevent discrimination in price between purchasers of commodities on account of differences in the grade, quality, or quantity of the commodity sold, or that makes only due allowance for differences in the cost of selling or transportation, or discrimination in price in the same or different communities made in good faith to meet competition: *And provided further,*] *or to injure, destroy, or prevent competition with any person who either grants or receives the benefit of such discrimination, or with customers of either of them; and that it shall also be unlawful for any person, whether in commerce or not, either directly or indirectly, to discriminate in price between different purchasers of commodities of like grade and quality where in any section or community and in any line of commerce such discrimination may substantially lessen competition in commerce among either sellers or buyers or their competitors or may restrain trade or tend to create a monopoly in commerce or any line thereof; all subject to the following provisions:*

(1) *That nothing herein contained shall prevent or require differentials as between purchasers depending solely upon whether they purchase for resale to wholesalers, to retailers, or to consumers, or for use in further manufacture; for the purpose of such classification of customers as wholesalers or jobbers, or retailers, the character of the selling of the purchaser and not the buying shall determine the classification, and any purchaser who, directly or indirectly, through a subsidiary or affiliated concern or broker, does both a wholesale and retail business shall, irrespective of quantity purchased, be classified (1) as a wholesaler on*

purchases for sale to retail dealers only, not owned or controlled, directly or indirectly, by the purchaser; and (2) as a retailer on purchases for sale to consumers.

(2) That nothing herein contained shall prevent or require differentials which make only due allowance for differences in the cost of manufacture, sale, or delivery resulting from the differing methods or quantities in which such commodities are to such purchasers sold or delivered: Provided, however, That the Federal Trade Commission, after due investigation and hearing to all interested parties, following insofar as applicable the procedure and subject to the recourse of the courts, provided in section 11 of this Act, may issue an order fixing and establishing quantity limits and revising the same as it finds necessary, as to particular commodities or classes of commodities, and the foregoing shall then not be construed to permit differentials based on differences in quantities greater than those so fixed and established.

(3) That nothing herein contained shall prevent price changes from time to time where in response to changing conditions affecting the market for or the marketability of the goods concerned, such as but not limited to actual or imminent deterioration of perishable goods, obsolescence of seasonal goods, distress sales under court process, or sales in good faith in discontinuance of business in the goods concerned.

(4) That nothing herein contained shall prevent persons engaged in selling goods, wares, or merchandise in commerce from selecting their own customers in bona-fide transactions and not in restraint of trade.

(5) That the word "price," as used in this section 2, shall be construed to mean the amount received by the vendor after deducting actual freight or cost of other transportation, if any, allowed or defrayed by the vendor.

(b) That it shall be unlawful for any person engaged in commerce, in the course of such commerce, to pay or grant, or to receive or accept, anything of value as a commission, brokerage, or other compensation, or any allowance or discount in lieu thereof, except for services rendered in connection with the sale or purchase of goods, wares, or merchandise, either to the other party to such transaction or to an agent, representative, or other intermediary therein where such intermediary is acting in fact for or in behalf, or is subject to the direct or indirect control, of any party to such transaction other than the person by whom such compensation is so granted or paid.

(c) That it shall be unlawful for any person to discriminate in favor of one purchaser against another purchaser or purchasers of a commodity bought for resale, with or without processing, by contracting to furnish or furnishing, or by contributing to the furnishing of, any services or facilities connected with the processing, handling, sale, or offering for sale of such commodity so purchased upon terms not accorded to all purchasers on proportionally equal terms.

(d) That it shall be unlawful for any person engaged in commerce to pay or contract for the payment of anything of value to or for the benefit of a customer of such person in the course of such commerce as compensation or in consideration for any services facilities furnished by or through such customer in connection with the processing, handling, sale, or offering for sale any products or commodities manufactured, sold, or offered for sale by such person, unless such payment or consideration is available on proportionally equal terms to all other customers competing in the distribution of such products or commodities.

(e) Upon proof being made, at any hearing on a complaint under this section, that there has been discrimination in price, the burden of rebutting the prima-facie case thus made by showing justification shall be upon the person charged with a violation of this section, and unless justification shall be affirmatively shown, the Commission is authorized to issue an order terminating the discrimination: Provided, however, That nothing herein contained shall prevent a seller rebutting the prima-facie case thus made by showing that his lower price to any purchaser or purchasers was made in good faith to meet an equally low price of a competitor.

(f) Nothing in this section shall prevent a cooperative association from returning to its members, or a cooperative wholesale association from returning to its constituent retailer members, the whole or any part of the net earnings resulting from its trading operations, in proportion to their purchases or sales from, to, or through such association.

CONFEREES' COMMITTEE—SENATE AND HOUSE

SENATE

74TH CONGRESS—2ND SESSION. DOCUMENT NO. 267

PROHIBITION OF PRICE DISCRIMINATION

Mr. VAN NUYS, from the committee of conference, submitted the following

CONFERENCE REPORT ON THE BILL (H. R. 8442) TO AMEND SECTION 2 OF THE ACT ENTITLED "AN ACT TO SUPPLEMENT EXISTING LAWS AGAINST UNLAWFUL RESTRAINTS AND MONOPOLIES, AND FOR OTHER PURPOSES," APPROVED OCTOBER 15, 1914, AS AMENDED (U. S. C., TITLE 15, SEC. 13), AND FOR OTHER PURPOSES

JUNE 6, 1936.—Ordered to lie on the table and to be printed

The committee of conference on the disagreeing votes of the two Houses on the amendment of the Senate to the bill (H. R. 8442) to amend section 2 of the act entitled "An act to supplement existing laws against unlawful restraints and monopolies, and for other purposes," approved October 15, 1914, as amended (U. S. C., title 15, sec. 13), and for other purposes, having met, after full and free conference, have agreed to recommend and do recommend to their respective Houses as follows:

That the House recede from its disagreement to the amendment of the Senate and agree to the same with an amendment as follows:

In lieu of the matter proposed to be inserted by the Senate amendment insert the following:

That section 2 of the Act entitled "An Act to supplement existing laws against unlawful restraints and monopolies, and for other purposes," approved October 15, 1914, as amended (U. S. C., title 15, sec. 13), is amended to read as follows:

"SEC. 2. (a) That it shall be unlawful for any person engaged in commerce, in the course of such commerce, either directly or indirectly, to discriminate in price between different purchasers of commodities of like grade and quality, where either or any of the purchases involved in such discrimination are in commerce, where such commodities are sold for use, consumption, or resale within the United States or any

Territory thereof or the District of Columbia or any insular possession or other place under the jurisdiction of the United States, and where the effect of such discrimination may be substantially to lessen competition or tend to create a monopoly in any line of commerce, or to injure, destroy, or prevent competition with any person who either grants or knowingly receives the benefit of such discrimination, or with customers of either of them: Provided, That nothing herein contained shall prevent differentials which make only due allowance for differences in the cost of manufacture, sale, or delivery resulting from the differing methods or quantities in which such commodities are to such purchasers sold or delivered: Provided, however, That the Federal Trade Commission may, after due investigation and hearing to all interested parties, fix and establish quantity limits, and revise the same as it finds necessary, as to particular commodities or classes of commodities, where it finds that available purchasers in greater quantities are so few as to render differentials on account thereof unjustly discriminatory or promotive of monopoly in any line of commerce; and the foregoing shall then not be construed to permit differentials based on differences in quantities greater than those so fixed and established: And provided further, That nothing herein contained shall prevent persons engaged in selling goods, wares, or merchandise in commerce from selecting their own customers in bona fide transactions and not in restraint of trade: And provided further, That nothing herein contained shall prevent price changes from time to time where in response to changing conditions affecting the market for or the marketability of the goods concerned, such as but not limited to actual or imminent deterioration of perishable goods, obsolescence of seasonal goods, distress sales under court process, or sales in good faith in discontinuance of business in the goods concerned.

"(b) Upon proof being made, at any hearing on a complaint under this section, that there has been discrimination in price or services or facilities furnished, the burden of rebutting the prima-facie case thus made by showing justification shall be upon the person charged with a violation of this section, and unless justification shall be affirmatively shown, the Commission is authorized to issue an order terminating the discrimination. Provided, however, That nothing herein contained shall prevent a seller rebutting the prima-facie case thus made by showing that his lower price or the furnishing of services or facilities to any purchaser or purchasers was made in good faith to meet an equally low price of a competitor, or the services or facilities furnished by a competitor.

"(c) That it shall be unlawful for any person engaged in commerce, in the course of such commerce, to pay or grant, or to receive or accept, anything of value as a commission, brokerage, or other compensation, or any allowance or discount in lieu thereof, except for services rendered in connection with the sale or purchase of goods, wares, or merchandise, either to the other party to such transaction or to an agent, representative, or other intermediary therein where such intermediary is acting in fact for or in behalf, or is subject to the direct or indirect control, of any party to such transaction other than the person by whom such compensation is so granted or paid.

"(d) That it shall be unlawful for any person engaged in commerce to pay or contract for the payment of anything of value to or for the benefit of a customer of such person in the course of such commerce as compensation or in consideration for any services or facilities furnished by or through such customer in connection with the processing, handling, sale, or offering for sale of any products or commodities manufactured, sold, or offered for sale by such person, unless such payment or consideration is available on proportionally equal terms to all other customers competing in the distribution of such products or commodities.

"(e) That it shall be unlawful for any person to discriminate in favor of one purchaser against another purchaser or purchasers of a commodity bought for resale,

with or without processing, by contracting to furnish or furnishing, or by contributing to the furnishing of, any services or facilities connected with the processing, handling, sale, or offering for sale of such commodity so purchased upon terms not accorded to all purchasers on proportionally equal terms.

"*(f) That it shall be unlawful for any person engaged in commerce, in the course of such commerce, knowingly to induce or receive a discrimination in price which is prohibited by this section.*"

SEC. 2. *That nothing herein contained shall affect rights of action arising, or litigation pending, or orders of the Federal Trade Commission issued and in effect or pending on review, based on section 2 of said Act of October 15, 1914, prior to the effective date of this amendatory Act: Provided, That where, prior to the effective date of this amendatory Act, the Federal Trade Commission has issued an order requiring any person to cease and desist from a violation of section 2 of said Act of October 15, 1914, and such order is pending on review or is in effect, either as issued or as affirmed or modified by a court of competent jurisdiction, and the Commission shall have reason to believe that such person has committed, used or carried on, since the effective date of this amendatory Act, or is committing, using or carrying on, any act, practice or method in violation of any of the provisions of said section 2 as amended by this Act, it may reopen such original proceeding and may issue and serve upon such person its complaint, supplementary to the original complaint, stating its charges in that respect. Thereupon the same proceedings shall be had upon such supplementary complaint as provided in section 11 of said Act of October 15, 1914. If upon such hearing the Commission shall be of the opinion that any act, practice, or method charged in said supplementary complaint has been committed, used, or carried on since the effective date of this amendatory Act, or is being committed, used or carried on, in violation of said section 2 as amended by this Act, it shall make a report in writing in which it shall state its findings as to the facts and shall issue and serve upon such person its order modifying or amending its original order to include any additional violations of law so found. Thereafter the provisions of section 11 of said Act of October 15, 1914, as to review and enforcement of orders of the Commission shall in all things apply to such modified or amended order. If upon review as provided in said section 11 the court shall set aside such modified or amended order, the original order shall not be affected thereby, but it shall be and remain in force and effect as fully and to the same extent as if such supplementary proceedings had not been taken.*

SEC. 3. *It shall be unlawful for any person engaged in commerce, in the course of such commerce, to be a party to, or assist in, any transaction of sale, or contract to sell, which discriminates to his knowledge against competitors of the purchaser, in that, any discount, rebate, allowance, or advertising service charge is granted to the purchaser over and above any discount, rebate, allowance, or advertising service charge available at the time of such transaction to said competitors in respect of a sale of goods of like grade, quality, and quantity; to sell, or contract to sell, goods in any part of the United States at prices lower than those exacted by said person elsewhere in the United States for the purpose of destroying competition, or eliminating a competitor in such part of the United States; or, to sell, or contract to sell, goods at unreasonably low prices for the purpose of destroying competition or eliminating a competitor.*

Any person violating any of the provisions of this section shall, upon conviction thereof, be fined not more than $5,000 or imprisoned not more than one year, or both.

SEC. 4. *Nothing in this act shall prevent a cooperative association from returning to its members, producers, or consumers the whole, or any part of, the net earnings or surplus resulting from its trading operations, in proportion to their purchases or sales from, to, or through the association.*

And the Senate agree to the same.

FREDERICK VAN NUYS,
GEO. McGILL,
WM. E. BORAH,
WARREN R. AUSTIN,
Managers on the part of the Senate.

HUBERT UTTERBACK,
JNO. E. MILLER,
CHARLES F. McLAUGHLIN,
U. S. GUYER,
JOHN M. ROBSION,
Managers on the part of the House.

HOUSE OF REPRESENTATIVES

74TH CONGRESS—2ND SESSION. REPORT No. 2951

PRICE DISCRIMINATION

JUNE 8, 1936.—Ordered to be printed

Mr. UTTERBACK, from the committee of conference, submitted the following

CONFERENCE REPORT

[To accompany H. R. 8442]

The committee of conference on the disagreeing votes of the two Houses on the amendment of the Senate to the bill (H. R. 8442) to amend section 2 of the act entitled "An act to supplement existing laws against unlawful restraints and monopolies, and for other purposes," approved October 15, 1914, as amended (U. S. C., title 15, sec. 13), and for other purposes, having met, after full and free conference, have agreed to recommend and do recommend to their respective House as follows:

That the House recede from its disagreement to the amendment of the Senate and agree to the same with an amendment as follows:

In lieu of the matter proposed to be inserted by the Senate amendment insert the following:

That section 2 of the Act entitled "An Act to supplement existing laws against unlawful restraints and monopolies, and for other purposes," approved October 15, 1914, as amended (U. S. C., title 15, sec. 13), is amended to read as follows:

"SEC. 2. (a) That it shall be unlawful for any person engaged in commerce, in the course of such commerce, either directly or indirectly, to discriminate in price between different purchasers of commodities of like grade and quality, where either or any of the purchases involved in such discrimination are in commerce, where such commodities are sold for use, consumption, or resale within the United States or any Territory thereof or the District of Columbia or any insular possession or other place under the jurisdiction of the United States, and where the effect of such discrimination may be substantially to lessen competition or tend to create a monopoly in any line of commerce, or to injure, destroy, or prevent competition with any person who either grants or knowingly receives the benefit of such discrimination, or with customers of either of them: Provided, That nothing herein contained shall prevent differentials which make only due allowance for differences in the cost of manufacture, sale, or delivery resulting from the differing methods or quantities in which such commodities are to such purchasers sold or delivered: Provided, however, That the Federal Trade Commission may, after due investigation and hearing to all interested parties, fix and establish quantity limits, and revise the same as it finds necessary, as to particular

313

commodities or classes of commodities, where it finds that available purchasers in greater quantities are so few as to render differentials on account thereof unjustly discriminatory or promotive of monopoly in any line of commerce; and the foregoing shall then not be construed to permit differentials based on differences in quantities greater than those so fixed and established: And provided further, That nothing herein contained shall prevent persons engaged in selling goods, wares, or merchandise in commerce from selecting their own customers in bona fide transactions and not in restraint of trade: And provided further, That nothing herein contained shall prevent price changes from time to time where in response to changing conditions affecting the market for or the marketability of the goods concerned, such as but not limited to actual or imminent deterioration of perishable goods, obsolescence of seasonal goods, distress sales under court process, or sales in good faith in discontinuance of business in the goods concerned.

"(b) Upon proof being made, at any hearing on a complaint under this section, that there has been discrimination in price or services or facilities furnished, the burden of rebutting the prima-facie case thus made by showing justification shall be upon the person charged with a violation of this section, and unless justification shall be affirmatively shown, the Commission is authorized to issue an order terminating the discrimination: Provided, however, That nothing herein contained shall prevent a seller rebutting the prima-facie case thus made by showing that his lower price or the furnishing of services or facilities to any purchaser or purchasers was made in good faith to meet an equally low price of a competitor, or the services or facilities furnished by a competitor.

"(c) That it shall be unlawful for any person engaged in commerce, in the course of such commerce, to pay or grant, or to receive or accept, anything of value as a commission, brokerage, or other compensation, or any allowance or discount in lieu thereof, except for services rendered in connection with the sale or purchase of goods, wares, or merchandise, either to the other party to such transaction or to an agent, representative, or other intermediary therein where such intermediary is acting in fact for or in behalf, or is subject to the direct or indirect control, of any party to such transaction other than the person by whom such compensation is so granted or paid.

"(d) That it shall be unlawful for any person engaged in commerce to pay or contract for the payment of anything of value to or for the benefit of a customer of such person in the course of such commerce as compensation or in consideration for any services or facilities furnished by or through such customer in connection with the processing, handling, sale, or offering for sale of any products or commodities manufactured, sold, or offered for sale by such person, unless such payment or consideration is available on proportionally equal terms to all other customers competing in the distribution of such products or commodities.

"(e) That it shall be unlawful for any person to discriminate in favor of one purchaser against another purchaser or purchasers of a commodity bought for resale, with or without processing, by contracting to furnish or furnishing, or by contributing to the furnishing of, any services or facilities connected with the processing, handling, sale, or offering for sale of such commodity so purchased upon terms not accorded to all purchasers on proportionally equal terms.

"(f) That it shall be unlawful for any person engaged in commerce, in the course of such commerce, knowingly to induce or receive a discrimination in price which is prohibited by this section."

SEC. 2. *That nothing herein contained shall affect rights of action arising, or litigation pending, or orders of the Federal Trade Commission issued and in effect or pending on review, based on section 2 of said Act of October 15, 1914, prior to the effective date of this amendatory Act: Provided, That where, prior to the effective date of this amendatory Act, the Federal Trade Commission has issued an order requiring any person to cease and desist from a violation of section 2 of said Act of October 15, 1914, and such order is pending on review or is in effect, either as issued or as affirmed or modified by a court of competent jurisdiction, and the Commission shall have reason to believe that such person has committed, used or carried on, since the effective date of this amendatory Act, or is committing, using or carrying on, any act, practice or method in violation of any of the provisions of said section 2 as amended by this Act, it may reopen such original proceeding and may issue and serve upon such person its complaint, supplementary to the original complaint, stating its charges in that respect. Thereupon the same proceedings shall be had upon such supplementary complaint as provided in section 11 of said Act of October 15, 1914. If upon such hearing the Commission shall be of the opinion that any act, practice, or method charged in said supplementary complaint has been committed, used, or carried on since the effective date of this amendatory Act, or is being committed, used or carried on, in violation of said section 2 as amended by this Act, it shall make a report in writing in which it shall state its findings as to the facts and shall issue and serve upon such person its order modifying or amending its original order to include any additional violations of law so found. Thereafter the provisions of section 11 of said Act of October 15, 1914, as to review and enforcement of orders of the Commission shall in all things apply to such modified or amended order. If upon review as provided in said section 11 the court shall set aside such modified or amended order, the original order shall not be affected thereby, but it shall be and remain in force and effect as fully and to the same extent as if such supplementary proceedings had not been taken.*

Sec. 3. *It shall be unlawful for any person engaged in commerce, in the course of such commerce, to be a party to, or assist in, any transaction of sale, or contract to sell, which discriminates to his knowledge against competitors of the purchaser, in that, any discount, rebate, allowance, or advertising service charge is granted to the purchaser over and above any discount, rebate, allowance, or advertising service charge available at the time of such transaction to said competitors in respect of a sale of goods of like grade, quality, and quantity; to sell, or contract to sell, goods in any part of the United States at prices lower than those exacted by said person elsewhere in the United States for the purpose of destroying competition, or eliminating a competitor in such part of the United States; or, to sell, or contract to sell, goods at unreasonably low prices for the purpose of destroying competition or eliminating a competitor.*

Any person violating any of the provisions of this section shall, upon conviction thereof, be fined not more than $5,000 or imprisoned not more than one year, or both.

Sec. 4. *Nothing in this act shall prevent a cooperative association from returning to its members, producers, or consumers the whole, or any part of, the net earnings or surplus resulting from its trading operations, in proportion to their purchases or sales from, to, or through the association.*

And the Senate agree to the same.

Hubert Utterback,
Jno. E. Miller,
Charles F. McLaughlin,
U. S. Guyer,
John M. Robsion,
Managers on the part of the House.

Frederick Van Nuys,
Geo. McGill,
Wm. E. Borah,
Warren R. Austin,
Managers on the part of the Senate.

STATEMENT OF THE MANAGERS ON THE PART OF THE HOUSE

The managers on the part of the House at the conference on the disagreeing votes of the two Houses on the bill (H. R. 8442) to amend section 2 of the act entitled "An act to supplement existing laws against unlawful restraints and monopolies, and for other purposes," approved October 15, 1914, as amended (U. S. C., title 15, sec. 13), and for other purposes, submit the following statement in explanation of the effect of the action agreed upon by the conferees and recommended in the accompanying conference report:

The Senate amendment struck out all of the House bill after the enacting clause, and substituted for the matter struck out the provisions of the Senate bill. The House disagreed to the Senate amendment. The House conferees recommend that the House recede from its disagreement to the Senate amendment and agree to the same with an amendment which inserts in lieu of the matter proposed to be inserted, by the Senate, a substitute which has been agreed upon by the conferees.

The differences between the House bill, the Senate amendment, and the substitute agreed upon by the conferees are noted in the following discussion, except for clerical amendments and incidental changes made necessary to harmonize various provisions affected by the agreement reached.

SECTION 1

The first section both of the House bill and the Senate amendment amend section 2 of the Clayton Act, and divide said section 2 into a number of subsections. The subsections hereinafter mentioned, therefore, refer to the subsections into which it is proposed to divide section 2 of the Clayton Act.

SUBSECTION (A)

The Senate amendment made it unlawful to discriminate between purchasers "in price or terms of sale." The House bill did not contain the words "or terms of sale." The Senate receded, and the words "or terms of sale" were stricken. The managers were of the opinion that the bill should be inapplicable to terms of sale except as they amount in effect to indirect discriminations in price within the meaning of the remainder of subsection (a).

The Senate amendment made the law applicable only to commodities "manufactured or produced and sold for use, consumption, or resale." The House bill did not contain the words "manufactured or produced and." The Senate receded, and the words quoted are omitted. This leaves the clause the same as in present section 2 of the Clayton Act.

The word "knowingly" appears in the Senate amendment immediately before the words "receives the benefit of such discrimination." The House conferees accepted this amendment. Its purpose is to exempt from the meaning of the surrounding clause those who incidentally receive discriminatory prices in the routine course of business without special solicitation, negotiation, or other arrangement for them on the part of the buyer or seller, and who are therefore not justly chargeable with knowledge that they are receiving the benefit of such discrimination.

The following provision in the House bill was not contained in the Senate amendment:

and it shall also be unlawful for any person, whether in commerce or not, either directly or indirectly, to discriminate in price between different purchasers of commodities of like grade and quality where in any section or community and in any line of commerce such discrimination may substantially lessen competition in commerce among either sellers or buyers or their competitors or may restrain trade or tend to create a monopoly in commerce or any line thereof;

This was omitted, as the preceding language already covers all discriminations, both interstate and intrastate, that lie within the limits of Federal authority.

The next difference between the House bill and the Senate amendment consisted of the addition of a proviso in the Senate amendment under which commodities which "are sold for use in further manufacture and in the production of a new product to be sold to the public," were exempted from the provisions of the act. The Senate receded, and the proviso was stricken from the bill.

The Senate amendment also contained a provision for classification of buyers, on which they receded.

A minor change is the elimination as unnecessary of the words "or require" in the House bill after the word "prevent" in the sentence reading:

That nothing herein contained shall prevent differentials which make only due allowance for differences in the cost of manufacture, sale, or delivery resulting from the differing methods or quantities in which such commodities are to such purchasers sold or delivered.

In the sentence quoted in the foregoing paragraph the words "other than brokerage," which appeared in the Senate amendment immediately after the word "cost," are eliminated, for the reason that the matter of brokerage is dealt with in a subsequent subsection of the bill.

A clause dealing with market changes was contained in the Senate amendment, reading as follows:

nor differentials which are based exclusively upon recognized changes in the market price of the product or products sold:

This was also omitted, as its subject matter is fully covered in the last proviso of subsection (a) in the conference text.

Both the House bill and the Senate amendment contained a provision permitting the Federal Trade Commission, after investigation and hearing, to fix and establish quantity limits, above which differentials based on differences in quantities are not permitted. The Senate provision contained a rule for the Commission's guidance as follows:

where it finds that available purchasers in greater quantities are so few as to render differentials on account thereof unjustly discriminatory or promotive of monopoly in any line of commerce;

The House accepted the Senate provision as preferable.

The Senate bill contained a further proviso—

That nothing herein contained shall prevent discrimination in price in the same or different communities made in good faith to meet competition.

This language is found in existing law, and in the opinion of the conferees is one of the obstacles to enforcement of the present Clayton Act. The Senate receded, and the language is stricken. A provision relating to the question of meeting competition, intended to operate only as a rule of evidence in a proceeding before the Federal Trade Commission, is included in subsection (b) in the conference text as follows:

Provided, however, That nothing herein contained shall prevent a seller rebutting the prima-facie case thus made by showing that his lower price or the furnishing of services or facilities to any purchaser or purchasers was made in good faith to meet an equally low price of a competitor, or the services or facilities furnished by a competitor.

SUBSECTION (B)

Subsection (b) of the Senate amendment, relating to certain questions of procedure before the Federal Trade Commission, was identical with subsection (e) of the

House bill. In the conference report the subsection keeps the designation as subsection (b) which it had in the Senate amendment.

SUBSECTION (C)

Subsection (c) deals with brokerage. It is the same as subsection (b) in the House bill, which in turn is the same as subsection (c) in the Senate amendment, except that the words "except for services rendered," as contained in the House bill, do not appear in the Senate amendment. In the conference report these words are retained, so that, with adjacent language, it reads:

* * * any allowance or discount in lieu thereof, except for services rendered in connection with the sale or purchase of goods, wares or merchandise, * * *

With the words of the House bill thus retained, this subsection permits the payment of compensation by a seller to his broker or agent for services actually rendered in his behalf; likewise by a buyer to his broker or agent for services in connection with the purchase of goods actually rendered in his behalf; but it prohibits the direct or indirect payment of brokerage except for such services rendered. It prohibits its allowance by the buyer direct to the seller, or by the seller direct to the buyer; and it prohibits its payment by either to an agent or intermediary acting in fact for or in behalf, or subject to the direct or indirect control, of the other.

SUBSECTIONS (D) AND (E)

The House bill dealt in two subsections with both of the major types of abuses in furnishing and paying for advertising, services, and facilities.

Subsection (d) of the House bill prohibited payments by the seller to the buyer for such services or facilities when undertaken by the buyer unless available to all buyers on proportionally equal terms. This becomes subsection (d) in the conference text.

Subsection (c) of the House bill prohibited the furnishing of any services or facilities by a seller to a buyer upon terms not accorded to all buyers on proportionally equal terms. This becomes subsection (e) of the conference text.

Subsection (e) of the Senate bill set up a new measure of damages for violations of the law, whereas the House bill left the damages to be determined in accordance with the provisions of the existing Clayton Act. The Senate receded.

SUBSECTION (F)

Subsection (f) makes it unlawful for any person engaged in commerce knowingly to induce or receive a discrimination in price which is prohibited by this section. This subsection was not contained in the House bill, but is the same as subsection (f) in the Senate amendment, except that the words "or terms of sale" are eliminated to harmonize with subsection (a).

The Senate amendment contained a subsection (g) which in effect exempted from the operation of the Act sales or purchases of "crude mineral products or metals in the form in which they are loaded for shipment." The Senate receded, and this subsection was omitted.

SECTION 2

The provisions of section 2 of the House bill were agreed to without amendment by the Senate. Relating only to pending rights of action and proceedings, and being therefore temporary in purpose, it appears in the conference report as section 2 of the bill itself, rather than as part of the amendment to section 2 of the Clayton Act which is provided for in section 1 to the present bill.

SECTION 3

Subsection (h) of the Senate amendment, which was not contained in the House bill, was accepted by the House conferees, and, except for the paragraph relating to cooperatives, separately treated in section 4 below, appears in the conference report as section 3 of the bill itself. It contains the operative and penal provisions of what was originally the Borah–Van Nuys bill (S. 4171). While they overlap in some respects, they are in no way inconsistent with the provisions of the Clayton Act amendment provided for in section 1. Section 3 authorizes nothing which that amendment prohibits, and takes nothing from it. On the contrary, where only civil remedies and liabilities attach to violations of the amendment provided in section 1, section 3 sets up special prohibitions as to the particular offenses therein described and attaches to them also the criminal penalties therein provided.

Section 3 also makes it possible for the person subjected to a discrimination prohibited therein to cause the offender to be prosecuted in the Federal court of the district in which such violation is committed.

SECTION 4

Section 4 provides:

Nothing in this act shall prevent a cooperative association from returning to its members, producers, or consumers, the whole or any part of the net earnings or surplus resulting from its trading operations, in proportion to their purchase or sales from, to, or through the association.

Substantially this same provision is found in the House bill as subsection (g), and in the Senate amendment as a part of subsection (h). However, the words "or a cooperative wholesale association from returning to its constituent retail members," which appeared following the word "consumers" in the Senate amendment, have been eliminated. As so modified, this section serves to safeguard producer and consumer cooperatives against any charge of violation of the act based on their distribution of earnings or surplus among their members on a patronage basis. While the bill contains elsewhere no provisions, express or implied, to the contrary, this section is included as a precautionary reservation to protect and encourage the cooperative movement. Whether functioning as buyers or sellers, cooperatives also share under the bill the guaranties of equal treatment and equal opportunity which it seeks to accord to trade and commerce generally.

HUBERT UTTERBACK,
JOHN E. MILLER,
CHARLES F. McLAUGHLIN,
U. S. GUYER,
JOHN M. ROBSION,
Managers on the part of the House.

CONGRESSIONAL RECORD

Important and pertinent arguments, statements, and clarifying explanations of the Robinson-Patman Act culled from the Congressional Record, Volumes 79 and 80, during the Act's legislative history and debates, 1935–1936.

Reference pages in Congressional Record, Volume 80, regarding progress of the Robinson-Patman Act, S. 3154 in the Senate. (Introduced in the Senate, June 26, 1935 (Vol. 79, page 10129), and referred to Senate Committee on the Judiciary.)

Page		Date
1333	Reported with amendment (S. Rept. 1502)	Feb. 3, 1936
1458	Debated and passed over	Feb. 4, 1936
2430	Passed over	Feb. 20, 1936
3112	Debated	Mar. 3, 1936
3446	Debated	Mar. 9, 1936
4393	Passed over	Mar. 26, 1936
6275	Debated	Apr. 28, 1936
6279–88	Debated	Apr. 28, 1933
6327	Debated	Apr. 29, 1936
6346	Debated	Apr. 29, 1936
6425–36	Debated, amended and passed in Senate	Apr. 30, 1936
8418	Ordered to be printed	June 1, 1936

Reference pages in Congressional Record, Volume 80, regarding progress of the Robinson-Patman Act, H. R. 8442 in the House. (Introduced in the House, June 11, 1935 (Vol. 79, page 9081), and referred to House Committee on the Judiciary.)

Page		Date
3446	Remarks	Mar. 9, 1936
4685	Reported with amendment (H. Rept. 2287) . . .	Mar. 31, 1936
5184	Leave to file minority views	Apr. 8, 1936
7759	Remarks	May 21, 1936
8102–11	Made special order (H. Res. 523)	May 27, 1936
8111–40	Debated	May 27, 1936
8223	Debated	May 28, 1936
8242	Amended and passed House title amended . . .	May 28, 1936
8285	In Senate and ordered to lie on table	May 29, 1936
8403	Debated	May 30, 1936
8418	Passed Senate	June 1, 1936
8419	Senate insists on its amendment and asks conference .	June 1, 1936
8419 and		
8617	Ordered printed with the amendments of the Senate numbered and conferees appointed	June 1, 1936
8617	House disagrees to Senate amendments and agrees to conference	June 1, 1936
9413	Conference Report submitted in House (H. Rept. 2951) .	June 15, 1936
9413 and		
9422	Agreed to	June 15, 1936
9902	Conference report submitted in the Senate (S. Doc. 267) .	June 18, 1936
9902 and		
9904	Agreed to	June 18, 1936
10030 and		
10056	Examined and signed	June 19, 1936
10279	Presented to the President	June 19, 1936
10700	Approved (Public No. 692) (June 19, 1936) . . .	June 20, 1936

CONGRESSIONAL RECORD

RESOLUTION TO INVESTIGATE BIG-SCALE BUYING PRACTICES

(Vol. 79, page 8646, June 4, 1935)

House Resolution 239

Resolved, That House Resolution 203 (74th Cong., 1st sess.) is amended as follows: On page 5, line 10, before the semicolon, insert a comma and the following: "and to investigate the trade practices of individuals, partnerships, and corporations engaged in big-scale buying and selling of articles at wholesale or retail, and their associations."

THE INVESTIGATING COMMITTEE

(Page 8992)

Mr. PATMAN. Mr. Chairman, 2 or 3 weeks ago a special committee was appointed by the Speaker of the House. I was appointed chairman after the gentleman from Missouri [Mr. COCHRAN] resigned, being unable to serve on account of illness. On the committee are the gentleman from New York, Mr. SOL BLOOM; the gentleman from Illinois, Mr. LUCAS; the gentleman from California, Mr. DOCKWEILER; the gentleman from New Jersey, Mr. McLEAN; the gentleman from New York, Mr. COLE; and the gentleman from Wisconsin, Mr. BOILEAU.

PURPOSE OF THE COMMITTEE

(Page 8996)

Mr. SUMNERS of Texas. Is it proposed that this committee shall investigate in an effort to discover how these chain organizations are able to establish themselves to the elimination of independent stores—to find out, for instance, whether they get their strength from mass purchases, or how they are able to do it as an economic question?

Mr. PATMAN. We are going into that now, and I think we know pretty well how they do it. We expect to propose some legislation that will stop it.

DEBATE IN THE SENATE

PRICE DISCRIMINATION

Mr. LOGAN. Mr. President, sometime during the last session Senate bill 3154, known as the price-discrimination bill, was introduced by the Senator from Arkansas [Mr. ROBINSON]. In fact, it is a proposed amendment to the Clayton antitrust law.

Mr. President, in the consideration of any measure it is first necessary to understand the purposes sought to be accomplished. This can be done only through an analysis of the provisions of the bill and its relationship to other laws in existence. S. 3154 is a proposed amendment to an existing law known as the Clayton amendment to the Sherman Antitrust Act. I have given the proposed legislation the most careful study and analysis of which I am capable. I believe that the bill as proposed will serve a very useful purpose, and that it can do no harm to any legitimate business.

AMENDS CLAYTON ACT

(Page 3113)

The section of the Clayton Act which it is proposed to amend is section 2, which became a law October 15, 1914. Much of the criticism directed at the bill under consideration by those opposing it has been aimed at provisions of that law, apparently thinking that it was new matter. That section of the Clayton Act was intended to prevent discrimination in price between purchasers, and it is proper to set out the provisions of that section and then to show in what respect the bill under consideration modifies or adds to it. The language of that section is as follows:

It shall be unlawful for any person engaged in commerce, in the course of such commerce, either directly or indirectly to discriminate in price between different purchasers of commodities, which commodities are sold for use, consumption, or resale within the United States or any territory thereof or the District of Columbia or any insular possession or other place under the jurisdiction of the United States, where the effect of such discrimination may be to substantially lessen competition or tend to create a monopoly in any line of commerce: *Provided,* That nothing herein contained shall prevent discrimination in price between purchasers of commodities on account of differences in the grade, quality, or quantity of the commodity sold, or that makes only due allowance for difference in the cost of selling or transportation, or discrimination in price in the same or different communities made in good faith to meet competition: *And provided further,* That nothing herein contained shall prevent persons engaged in selling goods, wares, or merchandise in commerce from selecting their own customers in bona fide transactions and not in restraint of trade.

The Clayton Act prohibits discrimination in price, so the first change proposed by the bill is to add after "price" the words "or terms of sale." The next change in the text of the Clayton Act is to add after "commodities" the words "of like grade and quality, where either or any of the purchases involved in such discrimination are in commerce." The word "which" following commodities in the original act is changed to "where." The word "and" is inserted in the bill after "United States" to improve the language, and the word "to" before "substantially" is placed after it for the same reason. There is a clause added before the proviso immediately following the word "commerce" as follows: "or to injure, destroy, or prevent competition with any person who either grants or receives the benefit of such discrimination, or with customers of either of them." In the proviso the word "discrimination" in the original act is changed to "differentials" in the bill, and the word "price" is changed to "prices" and "as" is inserted before the word "between."

After "purchasers" are inserted the words:

Depending solely upon whether they purchase for resale to wholesalers, to retailers, or to consumers, or for use in further manufacture, nor differentials which make only due allowance for differences in the cost other than brokerage, of manufacture, sale, or delivery resulting from the differing methods or quantities in which such commodities are to such purchasers sold or delivered.

This language is substituted for the following language in the original act:

Of commodities on account of differences in the grade, quality, or quantity of the commodities sold, or that makes only due allowance for difference in the cost of selling or transportation, or discrimination in price in the same or different communities made in good faith to meet competition.

Then follows the second proviso conferring power upon the Federal Trade Commission, after due investigation and hearing all interested parties, to fix and establish quantity limits and revise the same as it finds necessary as to particular commodities, or classes of commodities, where it finds that available purchasers in greater quantities are so few as to render differentials on account thereof unjustly discriminatory or promotive of monopoly in any line of commerce.

The third proviso is identical with the proviso in the Clayton Act.

WEAKNESS OF THE CLAYTON ACT

As pointed out in the report of the Judiciary Committee, the weakness of section 2 of the Clayton Act is in that it places no limit upon differentials permissible on account of differences in quantity and in that it permits discriminations to meet competition and thereby tends to substitute the remedy of retaliation for that of law which results in destructive consequences to the main purposes of the bill.

To allow one seller to make prices below the actual cost of the article and thus drive others engaged in the same line of business into bankruptcy, or other disaster, is one of the worst practices found in trade today. The more powerful has a great advantage in being able to cut prices and thereby destroy competition in a particular locality and then recoup the loss by raising prices in another locality.

The bill would close many dangerous loopholes that were found in the Clayton Act, but would leave the fields of competition free and open to the most efficient and, in fact, would protect them the more securely against the aggressions of those having larger purchasing power. The language, "where either or any of the purchasers involved in such discrimination are in commerce," which is added by the bill to the provisions in the original section, is necessary in that it will extend the provisions of the law to discriminations between interstate and intrastate customers, as well as between those purely interstate.

Discriminations not in accord with sound economy generally involve an element of loss, either of the necessary minimum of profits or perhaps of the actual cost, and this loss of profits must be recouped from the business of customers which do not receive the benefits of such discriminations. If granted by a seller to his customers in other States and denied customers within the State, they involve the use of that particular interstate commerce to the burden and injury of the customers of the State not receiving the benefits of such discriminations. The converse is true. If the discriminations are granted to the customers in a particular State and denied to those outside of that State, that also casts a burden upon interstate commerce without the particular State.

Another important amendment in the body of the original section is to prevent a discrimination where its effect may be substantially to lessen competition, or tend to create a monopoly in any line of commerce, or to injure, destroy, or prevent competition with any person who either grants or receives the benefit of such discrimination, or with the customers of either of them.

This provision broadens a similar clause found in section 2 of the Clayton Act. The provision in the original section is too restrictive, in requiring a showing of general injury to competitive conditions in the line of commerce concerned, when the more important concern is in injury to the competitor who has suffered by the discrimination.

The Clayton Act permits the differentials contained in the bill now before us, but it places no limit on quantity differentials of any kind nor upon any differentials that do not affect general competition. Additional restrictions are imposed by the provisions of the bill. Thus a separate clause safeguarding differentials between different classes of purchasers is necessary.

New Bill Permits Price Differentials Limited to Differences in Cost

Differentials which accord equal treatment of all within the particular class do not bring about the competitive evils which the bill before us is intended to remedy. Differentials cannot be suppressed, as that would create an unwarranted interference with existing trade habits. The bill, therefore, contains the clause that differentials are not prohibited which make only due allowance for differences in the cost, other than brokerage, of manufacture, sale, or delivery resulting from the differing methods or quantities in which such commodities are sold or delivered to purchasers.

Brokerage

The words "other than brokerage" were inserted to harmonize this provision with subsection (b), considered below, which deals directly with the question of brokerage. This proviso leaves trade and industry free from any restriction or impediment to the adoption and use of more economic processes and to the translation of appropriate shares of any saving so effected from the source to the mouth of the stream of distribution for the benefit of the original producer and the ultimate consumer; and it also limits strictly the use of quantity price differences to that particular sphere, since beyond that sphere they may be so used as to become weapons of competitive oppression.

Does Not Require Differentials
(Page 3114)

The bill does not compel the granting of discriminations or differentials of any sort. It leaves those who wish to do so entirely free to sell to all at the same price, regardless of differences in cost, or to grant any differentials not in excess of such differences. It does not require the differential to be the equivalent of the difference in cost. It only requires that it shall not exceed the difference in cost.

The cost of manufacture, sale, or delivery resulting from the differing methods or quantities in which such commodities are sold or delivered defines the cost which may be considered in support of price differentials, and they are confined to those marginal differences provable as between the particular consumers concerned in the discrimination. It is intended, among other things, to preclude the granting of a discrimination to a particular customer equal to the whole saving in cost resulting to the seller's entire volume of business as augmented by that customer's patronage, and also to preclude differentials based on allocated or imputed differences in cost as distinguished from actual differences.

TEST OF PERMISSIBLE DIFFERENTIALS

As stated in the report, this provision is designed to leave the test of a permissible differential upon the following basis: If the more-favored customer were sold in the same quantities and by the same methods of sale and delivery as the customer not so favored, how much more per unit would it actually cost the seller to make such sale and delivery, his other business remaining the same? No particular customer should be permitted distinctively to claim the benefit nor required distinctively to bear the burden of the immediate use or nonuse of facilities which the seller must maintain for his business generally.

FEDERAL TRADE COMMISSION'S POWER TO SET QUANTITY LIMITS

The provision conferring power upon the Federal Trade Commission to make investigations is designed to enable the determination, when necessary, of quantity limits as to various commodities, beyond which quantity price differentials shall not be permitted, although supported by differences in cost. It is based upon the principle that where even an admitted economy is of a character that is possible only to a very few units of large size in a particular trade or industry, it may become in their hands meat upon which monopoly feeds, and that in forbidding its use and forgoing its benefits the public is but paying a willing price for its freedom from monopoly control. It is the same limitation that has been applied for half a century in the field of transportation, in refusing to extend rate differentials beyond the carlot quantity.

BROKERAGE

Now, turning to the provisions of the bill that seek more definitely to accomplish the purpose intended, I desire to refer to subparagraph (b) relating to rebates, or payments as a commission, brokerage, or other compensation, or any allowance in lieu thereof, in connection with the sale or purchase of goods, wares, or merchandise, either to the party to such transaction, or to an agent, representative, or other intermediary therein, where such intermediary is acting in behalf, or is subject to the direct or indirect control, of any party to such transaction other than the person by whom such compensation is paid.

The Clayton Act was intended to prevent discrimination in prices where such discrimination tended to create a monopoly. This bill forbids the payment or allowance of brokerage either to the other principal party, or to an intermediary acting in fact for or under the control of the other principal party to the purchase and sale transaction.

This is one of the most prevalent schemes to evade the provisions of the law. Some large buyers demand the allowance of brokerage direct to them on the purchases which they make, or the payment of such brokerage to some intermediary of such a buyer who is an employee, agent, or corporate subsidiary for the buyer which has been set up in the guise of a broker, and through which they require that sales to them must be made.

The legitimate broker has an important place in trade, and it is not intended to interfere at all with his legitimate business. Where he is employed by the buyer in the buyer in the field to find a source of supply, or by the seller to find a market, he is discharging a sound and reasonable function, and is entitled to appropriate compensation by the one he serves. It is an entirely different thing, however, to allow payment or allowance under the guise of brokerage where no such service is rendered, and where the supposed broker is only a dummy pointed out by the buyer to the seller, rather than one who brings the buyer to the seller. This scheme corrupts a legitimate function to the purposes of competitive discrimination. The relationship existing between a broker and his client is fiduciary. To allow a broker to collect from a client for services rendered to the adverse party is a violation of that relationship. Such rebates, fostered by schemes under the guise of brokerage, for the sole purpose of bringing about unfair discriminations, should not be allowed, and are prohibited by this bill.

ADVERTISING AND SERVICE ALLOWANCES

Another practice has grown up, used extensively for the purpose of evading the law, which may be termed advertising or service allowances. It is used for the purpose of granting unfair discriminations. It is the practice of some large buyers to demand such allowances, and the seller, whether willingly or otherwise, must grant them. The ostensible purpose of such allowances is for the payment of advertising and other sales promotional services which the buyer agrees to render in connection with the sale of the products of the seller, or perhaps with reference to his business generally.

If such allowance should be used for the purposes stated, it may be that it would be unobjectionable; but it is exceedingly unjust when the service is not rendered, although paid for, or, if in fact rendered, where the payment is grossly in excess of the value, or where the purchaser is deriving from such allowances equal benefits with the seller. These benefits often flow to his own business in other lines, as well as benefits to the particular line purchased from the one who made the allowance. In that way the purchaser is able to shift to the seller a large part of his own advertising cost, while the small competitor who cannot secure such allowances finds that his business has been severely damaged.

Subsection (c) is intended to prohibit the granting of such allowances unless made available to all other customers of the seller concerned on proportionately equal terms, or unless, in the rendition of the services, the purchaser's own business is not benefited other than to the extent of the particular goods purchased from the one making such allowances.

BUYER AND SELLER GUILTY?

Mr. GEORGE. Does the bill impose upon the taker of any rebate or any concession the same penalty that it imposes upon the giver?

Mr. LOGAN. The bill does not impose any penalty upon the giver, and it imposes no penalty upon the receiver. The buyer is the one who receives the benefits. No penalty is imposed other than in another provision which I shall reach later, under which the one who is damaged by the unlawful discrimination may go into court and file a suit to recover from the one who caused him the damage and get judgment for his loss, and the standard is set up in the bill.

Mr. GEORGE. Certain things are prohibited to the seller, and the same prohibitions extend to the acceptor?

Mr. LOGAN.   No; the prohibitions, of course, would apply to the seller under the general terms of the law, but the seller is not the one who is guilty of these practices; it is the buyer. The seller suffers at the hands of the buyer. The buyer has great purchasing power, and he forces the seller to make rebates and allowances under one device or another.

One of the favorite methods is what is known as the brokerage scheme. If some buyer goes to a seller desiring to buy a large quantity of goods, he may say to him, "You must sell through this broker over here," who is an employee of the buyer; "and you must pay him brokerage," which the seller does, to his loss. The supposed broker turns the brokerage over to the buyer, and in that way it amounts to a rebate on the price of the goods which were purchased, and, of course, it enhances the profits of the buyer.

Mr. GEORGE.   What I wanted to get perfectly clear, if I could, was whether the same prohibitions relate to both the giver and the taker of a rebate in any form.

Mr. LOGAN.   The prohibition is against its being done at all, and, of course, it would apply to the giver as well as to the taker, although there is no criminal penalty provided.

Mr. GEORGE.   No penalty is imposed?

Mr. LOGAN.   No penalty is provided in the bill, although there is a right to institute a suit for damages.

Mr. GEORGE.   And that right runs to whom?

Mr. LOGAN.   That right runs to the person who has been injured.

For instance, if I may illustrate to the Senator, let us assume there is a merchant who buys goods and who gets an illegal rebate in some form or other so his goods do not cost him as much as they would another customer buying from the same seller. The second merchant gets no rebate, so his business is damaged, because his competitor can sell his goods at a lower price than that for which he can sell them, without a loss. He may institute suit for actual damages against the one who has caused the damage, whether it be the seller or the buyer.

Mr. GEORGE.   Are the damages liquidated in the bill?

Mr. LOGAN.   Two standards are set up. One of them amounts to a liquidated damage, because if one customer bought goods and was entitled to a discount because another customer from the same seller had received a discount, the first would be entitled to recover whatever he was entitled to as a discount which had been denied him. The effect of that would be liquidated damages. There is another standard set up, which I will discuss when I reach the particular section.

Mr. GEORGE.   I had the impression that the bill did impose penalties on the giver of a rebate, and I wanted to know whether it imposed like prohibitions, or penalties, or whatever the bill provides, on the taker.

Mr. LOGAN.   The bill prohibits the act, and that prohibition would extend alike to all who are affected by it.

Mr. GEORGE.   Both to the giver and to the taker, of course?

Mr. LOGAN.   Yes; that is true.

NEWSPAPER ADVERTISING SPACE

(Page 3115)

Mr. GORE.   I should like to ask the Senator from Kentucky what application the provision now under discussion would have to newspapers which merely act as advertising mediums or agencies. Would it prevent a differential charge on their part respecting advertisers, based on or measured by the amount of advertising carried?

Mr. LOGAN.   No. The only thing the bill attempts to do regarding advertising is to provide that the allowance made for advertising purposes shall be used for the benefit of the seller, and for the benefit of the buyer no further than he is benefited by advertising the particular line of goods. The evil sought to be remedied is that these large advertising allowances are forced. If one is buying shoes and gets a large allowance, he does not only advertise his shoes but he advertises his other business with the money received advertising the shoes.

Mr. GORE.   It amounts to a bonus or subsidy?

Mr. LOGAN.   That is correct. The bill provides that as long as one uses the advertising allowance for the purposes intended, and it is not unreasonable, and is not such as to bring about an unfair discrimination among customers, it is not prohibited.

Mr. GORE.   Then, if a newspaper charged $10 an inch for 10 inches, it would not be required to charge $10 an inch for 100 inches?

Mr. LOGAN.   No; the bill does not require anything of that kind.

SENATE JUDICIARY COMMITTEE REPORT UNANIMOUS

Mr. WALSH.   I should also like to inquire whether the report of the Judiciary Committee to the Senate was unanimous.

Mr. LOGAN.   The report of the Committee on the Judiciary was unanimous, but there were one or two Senators who voted to report the bill who said they reserved the right, which a Senator always has, to look into it, or change their minds upon further investigation. There were 13 members of the Committee on the Judiciary present when the bill was discussed, and a yea-and-nay vote was requested. The yeas and nays were taken, and 13 voted affirmatively to report the bill favorably.

TO STRENGTHEN THE CLAYTON ACT

Mr. GORE.   I desire to ask the Senator whether the general purpose and object of the pending bill are to strengthen the provisions of section 2 of the Clayton Act, and to stop the loopholes and correct the abuses which time and experience have developed and disclosed in that legislation?

Mr. LOGAN.   I say to the Senator that the bill has no other purpose, and at the risk of perhaps repeating later what I am saying now, the bill has three things in view, all aimed at strengthening the Clayton Act.

Mr. GORE.   I was a member of the Committee on Interstate Commerce which prepared the Clayton Act, and was very much interested in section 2, and the abuses which it sought to correct.

Mr. LOGAN.   Let me tell what happened. The section of the act to which the Senator has referred was evaded by able lawyers representing those who controlled large purchasing power. One of the first schemes was to set up what they called a brokerage system, and compel a seller to use the services of a broker, who may have been an employee, who at least was under the control of the buyer, or it may have been some subsidiary corporation of the buyer.

One large chain received last year $6,000,000 or $8,000,000 in brokerage fees. The bill attempts to prohibit that scheme. That is one of the most important things it seeks to do. It does not interfere with legitimate brokerage, but it makes it an unfair discrimination to grant such a brokerage in the nature of a rebate to one and not grant it to another.

The next thing the bill undertakes to do is to prevent the evasion of the Clayton Act through service allowances, the point I was just discussing a moment ago when I was interrupted.

One concern which has been brought to my attention sells yeast—I believe in the form of the familiar little yeast cakes—and a buyer is forcing—I say "forcing" because I do not think the manufacturer would do it voluntarily—the payment of

$12,000 a month under the cloak of advertising. I could name hundreds of such instances developed by the Federal Trade Commission in its investigation and also by the House committee, but I will proceed for the moment and finish what I was saying about advertising.

PRICE FIXING?

(Page 3116)

Mr. GORE.   This bill does not authorize or contemplate price fixing?

Mr. LOGAN.   Not at all.

Mr. GORE.   And it does permit discriminations founded on actual difference in quantity sales?

Mr. LOGAN.   That is true. Another thing the bill does is to place a limitation on discounts based upon the difference in quantity purchases. That was one of the defects in the Clayton Act, and I think I will discuss that a little later.

Getting back to the advertising feature, it is the purpose of the bill to rid such practices of their discriminatory character.

PROPORTIONALLY EQUAL TERMS

Mr. COSTIGAN.   Before the able Senator from Kentucky leaves this part of his discussion may I recall a phrase of his that is also used in subdivision (1) of subsection (c) of section 2, on page 7 of the bill. There the bill offers relief from certain unlawful acts designated in the bill provided the person extends or offers to all other customers competing in the distribution of such products proportionally equal terms.

May I ask whether the expression "proportionally equal terms" has been judicially interpreted, and if not, what construction is placed upon it by the Senator from Kentucky?

Mr. LOGAN.   I do not think it has been judicially construed. But if the seller grants an advertising allowance to one customer there is no reason why he should not grant, under identical circumstances, the same allowance to another customer.

I continue further on the question of advertising. I have said it is the purpose of the bill to rid such practices of their discriminatory character and to leave open a legitimate field for the use of customer services by mere employees or agents in local advertising in lieu of salaried representatives sent from without or other local personnel not known by the seller. Limited advertising appropriations used for a legitimate purpose, and in a legitimate way, are not prohibited, but the purpose is to prevent service allowances when the use of them results in unfair discrimination. All buyers should be allowed proportionately the same service allowances as there is no other way to avoid the use of such allowances to bring about discrimination.

RECOVERABLE DAMAGES

Subsection (d) states a presumptive rule for the measurement of damages in private suits for violation of the law. It affords a simple remedy to the one who has been damaged by unfair discriminations in price.

I might say that this is a part of the bill as originally introduced by the Senator from Arkansas. Later an amendment was added to this provision. The practices against which the provisions of the bill are directed not only injure the public, but private parties will likewise be injured. For that reason one who has been damaged by reason of the violation of this law is allowed to recover such damages as may be proven in the courts. This is not unusual in antitrust legislation. The main purpose of the bill is the prevention of unjust discrimination, and it is in harmony with the provisions of the bill to allow those who have been directly damaged by a violation of the law to recover the amount of the damage from the one who caused it. This provision, perhaps, will go far toward preventing violations of the bill when enacted.

Mr. GORE.   That is practically the only penalty, is it not?

Mr. LOGAN.   There is no penalty. It simply provides that damages such as are probable in court shall be recoverable.

APPLIES TO ANY PERSON ENGAGED IN COMMERCE

Many have complained because the provisions of the bill apply to "any person engaged in commerce." Some of the special newspaper writers have called particular attention to what is termed a most drastic provision because it applies to any person engaged in commerce. The original Clayton Act contains that exact language, and it is carried into the bill under consideration. The language of the Clayton Act was used because it has been construed by the courts.

Yet there has been a terrific protest against using the phrase "any person engaged in commerce." Evidently for 22 years astute businessmen did not find out that we had such a law on the statute books.

SPECIAL DISCOUNTS AND ALLOWANCES TO BIG-SCALE BUYERS

(Page 3117)

The Federal Trade Commission, on page 36 of its report, in speaking of special discounts and allowances, made this statement:

The lower selling prices of chains as compared with independent distributors are largely possible because of the lower buying prices enjoyed by the chains as compared with the independent wholesaler, cooperative chain, or the independent retail buyer in those cases where the retailers buy directly from the manufacturer. In these lower buying prices special discounts and allowances play an important part.

In the first place, the Commission's figures indicate that more manufacturers make allowances to chains than to wholesalers. Secondly, although the number of wholesale-customer accounts involved in the Commission's study of discounts and allowances was far greater than the number of chain accounts, the proportion of chain accounts carrying allowances was far greater than the proportion of wholesale accounts.

Third, in all three of these lines of business, the percentage rates of allowances were very much higher on sales to chains than on those to wholesalers, whether the base to which the allowances were applied was the total sales of all manufacturers reporting, or only the sales of the manufacturers making allowances. In 1930, for example, the rate of special allowances on total sales of all reporting manufacturers to tobacco chains was 3.57 percent, as compared with 0.71 percent to wholesalers.

The discounts allowed to a chain store were five times the amount allowed to wholesalers in the tobacco trade.

In the grocery trade it was 2.02 percent per chain as compared with 0.91 percent for wholesalers—

Two and one-half times the discount allowed in the grocery trade—and in drugs, 5.10 percent compared with 1.11.

Five times as great discount on the same quality of goods, sold under the same circumstances and under the same conditions in every way. Here is a group of purchasers, because they have a tremendous purchasing power, getting five times as much allowance as the others who are entitled to exactly the same treatment.

Finally, the total amounts—

I am still continuing reading from the Federal Trade Commission:

Finally, the total amounts of the allowances made by all the manufacturers to chains greatly exceeded the amounts given to wholesalers. The interest of this last statement lies in the fact that the proportion of the total allowances paid to the chains was much higher, and that paid to the wholesalers was much lower, relatively, than the total quantities bought by each of these types of distributors, respectively.

It does not require the vision of a seer to look into the future far enough to understand that if the tendencies referred to are continued for a few years, there will be a complete monopoly of many of the necessities of life. When that time comes the consumer will be at the mercy of such monopoly, and the sensible thing to do is to prevent the coming of that day by attacking the problem in time. The result of such practices is easily discernible. Not only will the consumer eventually suffer but these large units controlling purchasing power may be entirely destroyed through unwise legislation, or through their taking advantage of conditions which have been created by their own unwise acts. They should be left free in the management of their affiairs, but one of the chief aims of government is to protect the people against aggressions that naturally follow the creation of a monopoly.

The bill does not interfere in any way with legitimate competition. It recognizes that those controlling large aggregations of capital may secure a legitimate advantage by reason of great purchasing power, but this advantage should be restrained by the adoption of sound economic rules, which will not allow the practice of using large purchasing power to destroy those with lesser purchasing power, thereby destroying competition and when, by such practices, competition has been destroyed, then monopoly must result.

Mr. GORE.   The pending bill permits differentials based on actual and bona-fide difference in quantity sales?

Mr. LOGAN.   Yes, sir.

Mr. GORE.   But it provides that the differential can be regulated and fixed so as not to be used to accomplish the evils described by the Senator?

Mr. LOGAN.   The Senator has made a correct statement.

Mr. Teegarden Explains Provisions of the Bill
(Page 3118)

On page 206 of the hearing held before the Committee on the Judiciary, House of Representatives, in July 1935, I find a statement in the testimony of Mr. H. B. Teegarden, counsel for the United States Wholesale Grocers' Association, which calls attention very forcibly to some of the provisions of the bill which those who oppose it seem to misunderstand. He there said:

After the various objections that have been raised against this bill by those who are opposed to it, I feel decidedly that the burden upon me just now is, perhaps, to tell you more of what the bill does not do than what it does do. The bill has been very badly misunderstood, whether intentionally or innocently, I am not to say.

But I want to point out categorically first what the bill does not do. The bill does not penalize efficiency. It has nothing whatever to do with any internal organization or conduct of chain stores or any other kind of merchants. It has nothing whatever to do with the selection of one kind of merchandising as against another, as being the more or less economical of the two.

Mr. Logan, Mr. Wood, Mr. Adams, all referred to the bill as penalizing or shackling efficiency. There is not a single economy or saving that the wit of man could devise in the process of distribution that could not, under the provisions of this bill, be translated along the chain of distribution to the ultimate consumer. It has nothing to do with that whatever.

The bill does not compel the observance of any differential between various classes of buyers; that is, between the wholesalers, retailers, manufacturers, and so on. It does not compel the granting of any quantity discounts. It does not prevent the granting of all quantity discounts.

I want to call the attention of the committee to a very remarkable piece of juggling that has been done in the reading of this bill by those who are opposed to it, as they have presented it to the committee. If the committee has the bill before them, if they will turn to the second page, line 12, after the general prohibition of discriminations: *"Provided,* That nothing herein contained shall prevent differentials."

Those are the words. And then it states two categories of things that shall not be prevented. First, differentials between wholesalers, retailers, and manufacturers; second, differentials on the basis of some cost saving or differences between the parties to the discrimination.

Now, here is what they do. Those same two words apply to both. They not only read the bill wrong but they do not read it the same way twice. They first say that these words "shall prevent" read "shall compel" differentials as between wholesalers, retailers, and manufacturers.

Mr. Teegarden states but the simple truth touching the provisions of the bill, and, while I do not have the honor of knowing the ability of Mr. Teegarden as a lawyer, I must confess he states with great clarity what the bill does not provide.

Further on, on page 207, he continues:

Instead of reading it "that nothing herein contained shall prevent differentials in prices," they say "this shall prevent differentials on account of differences in cost," and they say, therefore, that this bill does not permit quantity differentials based on cost differences and it penalizes efficiency.

Mr. Teegarden then continues his testimony:

The bill does not, therefore, prohibit any kind of quantity discounts or differentials justified by differences in cost or savings in cost in the chain of distribution of food or merchandise or goods or wares of any kind. The bill does not compel or restrict any form of distribution or merchandising, one as against another.

The bill has nothing to do with the fixation of prices. It says nothing whatever as to the prices to be maintained or the price relationship to be maintained or the trading relationship to be maintained as between the seller and another.

It governs only the relationship to be maintained by a seller between his various customers. It requires him to treat them on an equal basis, subject only to those differentials which are justified by differences in cost involved in the differing methods or quantities in which the goods are sold or delivered.

CONSTITUTIONALITY

Some suggestions have been offered to the effect that the bill is unconstitutional. I have given consideration to that question, and I have reached the conclusion that under the many decisions of the Supreme Court passing upon similar questions the bill is clearly within the power of Congress. If there should be an effort on the part of some Senator to prove by decisions of the Supreme Court that the bill is not constitutional, I shall be very glad to meet the argument, but until that time I shall withhold any comments on the constitutionality of the proposed bill.

STRENGTHEN CLAYTON ACT
(Page 3119)

Mr. GORE.   The pending bill is based to some extent on section 2 of the Clayton Act and is related to methods of procedure and administration?

Mr. LOGAN.   The Senator is correct. The purpose of the bill is to stop up loopholes found in section 2 of the Clayton Act. Section 2 of the Clayton Act has been abated. There was a provision in it, as Senators will remember, allowing the granting of price differentials to meet competition in a particular community. That was perhaps unwise, although at the time of the passage of the Clayton Act it was well designed to remedy the evils then in existence. However, since then time has proved that there are ways to evade the Clayton Act, and therefore it is necessary to strengthen its provisions; and the bill seeks to do nothing else.

Mr. GORE.   The principle underlying section 2 of the Clayton Act and section 2 itself have run the gauntlet of the courts and have been sustained by them.

Mr. LOGAN.   That is correct.

DEBATE IN THE HOUSE OF REPRESENTATIVES

HOUSE STEERING COMMITTEE ORGANIZED FOR BILL

(*Vol. 80, page 5714, April 20, 1936*)

Mr. MARTIN of Colorado.   Mr. Speaker, this morning about 80 Members met in the caucus room of the old House Office Building and organized a steering committee to facilitate the passage of the Robinson-Patman equal business opportunity bill (H. R. 8442), better known as the chain-store bill. Subcommittees were appointed and a brief statement formulated with reference to the provisions of the bill.

At this meeting Mr. PATMAN, of Texas, was elected chairman, and Mr. MARTIN of Colorado secretary.

Upon motion of Mr. DIES, of Texas, the chairman was authorized to appoint such committees as deemed necessary in order to expedite the consideration and passage of this legislation.

The following steering committee, which will be added to later, has already been appointed: Andresen, Minnesota; Utterback, Iowa; Cox, Georgia; Johnson, West Virginia; Ryan, Minnesota; Zimmerman, Missouri; Cannon, Missouri; Calwell, Florida; Ekwall, Oregon; Massingale, Oklahoma; Johnson, Oklahoma; Nichols, Oklahoma; Gassaway, Oklahoma; Mott, Oregon; Gray, Indiana; Jencke, Indiana; Lesinski, Michigan; Pittinger, Minnesota; Gilchrist, Iowa; Ford, California; Ayers, Montana; Sanders, Texas; Boileau, Wisconsin; Schulte, Indiana; Carlson, Kansas; White, Idaho; Luckey, Nebraska; Gillette, Iowa; Schneider, Wisconsin; Ramsay, West Virginia; Patterson, Kansas; Dies, Texas; Lambertson, Kansas; Gehrmann, Wisconsin; Maas, Minnesota; Hildebrandt, South Dakota; Rogers, Oklahoma; Martin, Colorado; Costello, California; Sabath, Illinois; McClellan, Arkansas; Keller, Illinois; Lundeen, Minnesota; Lemke, South Dakota; Starnes, Alabama; Peterson, Florida; Cannon, Wisconsin; Lamneck, Ohio; Christianson, Minnesota; Beiter, New York; Pierce, Oregon; Engel, Michigan; Thomason, Texas; Guyer, Kansas; Buckler, Minnesota; Lee, Oklahoma; Boehne, Indiana; Smith, Washington; Hook, Michigan; Cross, Texas; Mead, New York; Larrabee, Indiana; Turner, Virginia; Barry, New York; McFarlane, Texas; Stefan, Nebraska; Blanton, Texas; Weaver, North Carolina; Smith, Virginia; Haynes, Pennsylvania; Murdock, Utah; Greever, Wyoming; Scott, California; Knutson, Minnesota; Cochran, Missouri; Fiesinger, Ohio; Binderup, Nebraska; Randolph, West Virginia; Cravens, Arkansas; Robison, Kentucky; O'Leary, New York; Biermann, Iowa.

The following special committees have been appointed by the chairman in accordance with authority given him by the action of the above meeting:

EXECUTIVE COMMITTEE

Dies, Texas, chairman; Utterback, Iowa, vice chairman; Cox, Georgia; Sabath, Illinois; Cannon, Missouri; Schulte, Indiana; Nichols. Oklahoma; Martin, Colorado; Ekwall, Oregon; Boileau, Wisconsin, and Ramsay, West Virginia.

(Each member of this committee is vice chairman of the steering committee.)

PARLIAMENTARY COMMITTEE

(This committee is also charged with the duty of making an effort to secure a rule at an early date for consideration of the bill.)

Cannon, Missouri, chairman; Nichols, Oklahoma, vice chairman, and Mott, Oregon.

COMMITTEE TO COORDINATE ACTIVITIES WITH ADMINISTRATION AND SENATE LEADERS

Patman, Texas, chairman; Johnson, Oklahoma, vice-chairman; Dies, Texas; Martin, Colorado; Schulte, Indiana, and Cannon, Missouri.

INFORMATION COMMITTEE

(The purpose of this committee is to assemble and furnish information to both Members of Congress and interested parties upon request.)

Nichols, Oklahoma, chairman; Martin, Colorado, vice chairman; Maas, Minnesota; Sanders, Texas, and Quinn, Pennsylvania.

Representative Patman Explains the Bill
(Page 5715)

Mr. PATMAN, co-author of the bill, stated that this bill, as reported by the committee, is a result of months of hearings; hundreds of pages of testimony were taken and are now in printed form and available through the Judiciary Committee of the House; that witnesses were heard on both sides of the question and every question that can possibly arise was carefully considered; that the interest of the consumers was given first consideration; that the bill represents the combined thought and judgment of the best-informed people in America on this subject, including representatives of the trade, consumers, corporate chains, department stores, and trade organizations—including druggists, grocers, hardware, and dry goods, both retail and wholesale; that it also includes the mature judgment based upon years of experience of representatives from governmental departments that have for many years dealt directly with the questions involved, including the Federal Trade Commission and Anti-Trust Division of the Department of Justice.

AT LEAST 100 CO-AUTHORS OF BILL IN HOUSE

Mr. PATMAN further stated that as co-author he held the same position with reference to the bill as all other members of the steering committee and other parties who have contributed toward the perfection of the measure; that at least a hundred Members of the House are entitled to the same credit for this measure and have made the equal contributions toward its perfection as himself; that the bill is not a partisan measure but is nonpartisan; and our objectives should be the early passage of the bill in order to protect the consumers against monopoly and the independent merchants against extinction.

THANKS TO JUDICIARY COMMITTEE OF HOUSE

Mr. PATMAN further expressed appreciation especially to Congressmen UTTERBACK, RAMSAY, and SUMNERS of Texas, and all other friends on the Judiciary Committee of the House for the very effective work after weeks and months of extended and patient hearings on the proposed legislation.

DEBATE IN THE SENATE CONTINUED

SENATOR ROBINSON EXPLAINS THE BILL

(Page 6277, April 28)

Mr. ROBINSON. It has been said that there is a large number of measures dealing with this subject pending before the two Houses. There are several bills in the House, and I think there are more than two bills in the Senate, and each one of those measures reflects difference of opinion as to some details; but the purpose of this proposed legislation runs through all the bills, and that is to correct the defects in the Clayton Antitrust Act which undertook to prevent by law unfair price discriminations which gave to those who had the power to do so the opportunity to destroy their competitors and to gain a monopoly of the business in which they were interested, to the detriment of both dealers and consumers. Those who are sincerely interested in that purpose may stand on a common ground.

They may differ respecting some details, but if they are earnestly desiring to prevent the building up of monopolies in this country in the trade of the country they may adjust their differences and reach a fair conclusion.

During the course of this debate it will be shown that certain business organizations have been able to buy enormous quantities of articles going into commerce from large producers at prices from 25 to 50 per cent less than the sales agents of the seller are able to secure. That means that under the guise of brokerages that were never earned, brokerages charged for services that were never performed, gigantic organizations have driven into ruin and bankruptcy hundreds of small competitors. By reason of the unfair practices implied by the sellers granting a large brokerage fee where no brokerage service was earned large organizations have been able to sell at prices so low that the independent dealer could not continue in business.

All I ask is that this bill be taken up; that the Senate give it fair consideration and send it to the other House, which, as suggested by the Senator from Kentucky and, I think, by the Senator from Idaho, is likely to substitute its bill by striking out all after the enacting clause of the Senate bill and adopting as a single amendment the House proposal. That will throw the whole subject matter into conference and give the conferees the opportunity of reconciling the differences between the two measures. With that in view, I see no objection to incorporating as an amendment the provisions of the Borah–Van Nuys bill, so that if the conferees finally prefer the plan of that bill to either the House bill or the Senate bill—speaking now of the original measures—they will have the opportunity of doing so.

SENATOR LOGAN EXPLAINS THE BILL

(Page 6281)

Mr. LOGAN. I will tell the Senate as best I can what is in the bill. I have no desire but to give correct information, and if I am mistaken about any provision of the bill I shall be deeply grateful to any Senator who will find out the mistake I make.

It was in 1914 that the Congress enacted what has since been known as the Clayton Antitrust Act, or the Clayton amendment. The purpose of that act was to prevent unfair price discrimination. The purpose of the act was to prevent a seller disposing of his goods to one purchaser at one price and to another purchaser, under the same conditions and circumstances, at another price. The Clayton Act was to prevent discriminations in the prices of goods sold to customers.

Let me digress long enough to say that the bill now under consideration has nothing to do with competition between or among sellers. If one concern desires to sell to its customers at one price, and another concern handling the same line of commodities desires to sell to its customers at another price, there is not a thing in the Robinson bill that would interfere with that. The bill relates to the sale of goods by a seller to his own customers, and the Clayton Act originally related to that particular situation. The Clayton Act, however, contained a provision that there might be a discrimination in price based upon cost of manufacture, cost of transportation, and quantity sold. That sounded very well.

"Price Discrimination 'to Meet Competition'" Fatal to the Clayton Act

Then there was another provision in the Clayton Act which was fatal, namely, that price discrimination might be made in order to meet competition. That is where the chief defect in the Clayton Act is to be found. For instance, a seller has a customer, we will say, in Louisville, Ky., and he has a customer in Detroit, Mich. They are both in the same class or group of purchasers. Cost of transportation, cost of manufacture, and the quantity involved are all the same. The Clayton Act allows the seller to sell to the concern in Louisville at a less price than that at which he sells to the concern in Detroit, provided the seller's competitor in the same line is selling to customers in Louisville at a price making it necessary for the seller to cut prices in Louisville, while it is not necessary to cut prices in Detroit. The old Clayton Act, however, prohibited discrimination in prices except when based upon cost of production, cost of transportation, and quantity. Let us bear that in mind and see what change it is proposed to make by the provisions of the Robinson bill.

It was found by experience that those who were able to employ good lawyers could evade the provisions of the Clayton Act and could bring about unfair price discrimination, and that was done in several ways. The Robinson bill, which we are now considering, deals only with three of those methods of evading the Clayton Act, because there are other methods and ways of evading the Clayton Act which perhaps cannot be reached by Congress. We can reach only those things that relate to interstate commerce or have a direct bearing upon interstate commerce. The practice of using loss leaders, for instance, by a store in Kentucky or by a store in Arizona, could not perhaps be reached by an act of Congress.

The Clayton Act prohibited price discrimination. Let me say for purposes of brevity that under its provisions, where the purchasers were in the same group purchasing the same quantity, conditions all being the same, the seller could make no discrimination. He was, however, allowed to make discrimination based on cost, including overhead, distribution, transportation, and all that.

Discrimination might be made, but one might go no further than was justified by the cost and quantities sold.

How did some of them find ways to evade that provision? I say, "some of them." I do not refer to chain stores. The bill under consideration has been designated an anti-chain-store bill. It is nothing of the kind. It treats everyone alike. All who sell and all who buy from the same seller alike are placed in the same class. Therefore, it is of the utmost importance that the provisions of the bill be entirely fair, that the provisions of the bill do no harm to any group, sellers or buyers. The only thing the bill seeks to do is to make them be fair with each other. I may say to those listening to me that I realize that we may never be able to put into effect here on earth the Golden Rule as announced by the Christ. We may never be able to make men live according to the Golden Rule, but I believe no one should be blamed or condemned for trying to bring about the desired condition.

BROKERAGE

I now speak of the matter of brokerage. Let me say in the beginning that the bill does not affect legitimate brokerage either directly or indirectly. Where the broker renders service to the buyer or to the seller the bill does not prohibit the payment of brokerage. It is not aimed at the legitimate practice of brokerage, because brokerage is necessary. The broker has a field all his own and he should not be interfered with. In order to evade the provisions of the Clayton Act, however, it was found that while direct price discrimination could not be indulged in, the buyer, if he were sufficiently powerful, could designate someone and say, "That is my broker." Perhaps it was a clerk in his office. Perhaps it was a manager of a store. Perhaps it was a subsidiary corporation organized for the purpose. However, the buyer would say to the seller, "You must sell through that man, and you must pay him a certain percentage or amount of brokerage"; and when the so-called broker or dummy broker received what was paid him, he turned it over to the buyer, and in that way a price discrimination was brought about.

I undertake to say in this august body that there is not a Member of the Senate, there is not a Member of the House, who will not at once condemn a practice of that kind, which provides secret rebates under the guise of brokerage. A very important case was heard by the Federal Trade Commission recently, wherein the rebate, the brokerage, or whatever one may wish to call it, amounted almost to 40 percent, and one concern had been enabled to purchase automobile tires at an average of 40 percent less than independents could purchase tires throughout the country. What was the result of that practice? The independent dealers in the small towns and in some of the larger towns could not meet such competition as that; their businesses were destroyed; and there are wrecks of such businesses all over the country, growing out of that particular practice.

Do not tell me that any manufacturer willingly and gladly gives such tremendous sums to the purchaser. He is coerced into it by the fact that the purchasing power has become so great that the seller is afraid to antagonize it. He must yield to any demand that may be made by the great purchaser, and, if he does so, the purchaser gets an advantage so to build up his business and carry it on that monopoly must eventually result.

The first thing which the Robinson bill does—and it represents about one-third of the bill—is to provide that no buyer shall engage in this trick brokerage practice whereby a rebate may be made by the seller. Under the provisions of the bill no payment may be made to a man acting as a broker unless he actually is a broker. Is there anyone in the whole country, from one end of the Nation to the other, who will not heartily approve of the provisions of the bill aimed at fraudulent practices like that which tend toward the destruction of the small man and also tend toward the destruction of the seller himself in many instances? Should not such practices be prevented if we can prevent them? That is the first thing in the bill.

SERVICE ALLOWANCES TO THE PURCHASER

(Page 6282)

What else is there in the bill? One practice which has been indulged in to evade the provisions of the Clayton Act is for the seller to make certain service allowances to the purchaser. They may be called advertising allowances. When the purchaser had great purchasing power he could demand that great concessions be made to him; but here was the Clayton Act, which said, "You cannot make discriminations in prices." So there was devised a second scheme under which the seller said, "We will make you an advertising allowance or a service allowance which will bring about a discrimination in prices." That practice has been indulged in to such an enormous extent that I should hesitate to give Senators the facts, even if I had them available this afternoon, which I do not.

Advertising Allowances

The Robinson bill does not say that an allowance may not be made for advertising services. Legitimate allowances for advertising and matters of that nature may be made; but allowances must not be made for the purpose of giving the purchaser an opportunity to buy goods at a less price than others similarly situated may buy them. It is provided in the Robinson bill that money allowed for advertising purposes must be used to advertise the goods of the seller and not the purchaser's goods, except those which he secured from the seller. How does it work? What has been the result?

One man, who has a good business, demands a large advertising allowance. He does not use it to advertise the goods of the seller; he does not use it to service the seller's products; but he uses it to advertise his business in all lines—in the newspapers, by handbills, and by personal solicitation. One man gets that advantage while another man does not get it. Thus the one who gets that advantage shifts the advertising of his own business over to the seller, while the other man cannot do so; and consequently it amounts to a discrimination in price. The Robinson bill—that is Senate bill 3154— which the Senate now has under consideration, provides that the allowance for services or for advertising must be used for that purpose legitimately and cannot be used as an instrument of price discrimination.

I believe I may safely say that there is no businessman, there is no legislator in the Congress, there is no one who has ever given thought to the matter at all who will not heartily agree that fraudulent advertising allowances made for the purpose of bringing about price discrimination should be prohibited. That is the second thing the Robinson bill does. I am merely telling the Senator what the bill proposes to do. If Senators disagree with me let them read the bill. It is short; it can be read in 10 minutes. Do not listen to the voice of those who are opposed to such legislation; do not listen to the arguments of expert lawyers and skilled research workers who attempt to deceive you; read the bill and exercise your own judgment.

Quantity Discounts

Now, I have pointed out two things. There is another that may bring about some confusion, although it ought not to do so. There is nothing in the bill to prevent quantity discounts. They are allowed; they have to be allowed; they cannot be prohibited. It is well recognized that if one merchant buys a hundred thousand pairs of shoes he should receive a more generous discount than the merchant who only buys a thousand pairs. I mean by that that the discrimination or differential or price must be based upon the cost of handling the transaction, the cost of distribution, the cost of manufacture, the cost of overhead, the cost of transportation, and, yes, even the cost of brokerage. All those things may be taken into consideration, and in the quantity discount necessarily a man who buys a large quantity would get a larger discount. Nobody proposes to interfere with that; nobody objects to it; it is one of the laws of business; that must be so. But there may come such a condition after a while that that purchaser becomes so enormously large, his purchasing power is so tremendous, the quantity he buys may become so very great that the discount which he receives will enable him to drive all others out of business.

That ought not to be allowed; that brings monopoly; for if a man has such purchasing power than he can purchase $10,000,000 worth of goods or a hundred million dollars' worth of goods, he can force his own terms on the manufacturer and the seller and can crush out of existence all the independents, all the smaller organizations; yes, and all the big organizations.

FTC May Fix Quantity Limits

So under the Robinson bill there may be quantity discounts, just as under the Clayton Act; but the Robinson bill goes further and provides that in cases where there are so few purchasers of large quantities that one of them or a few of them may completely dominate and control the entire industry, then the Federal Trade Commission shall have the power to make an investigation and fix quantity limits as affecting prices.

Let me say to the Senate that there have been suggestions all over the country that this is a price-fixing bill. It has no relationship in the world to price fixing, and there is no man who can read and who can understand the simplest language who can reach the conclusion that the Robinson bill tends in any way to bring about price fixing. It does not do that.

There is one other feature of the bill, and just one other—and I think it is absolutely right—and that has to do with the measure of damage.

Mr. MURPHY. In the matter of discounts, to which the Senator has referred, in the case of the purchaser of a smaller quantity of shoes as related to the purchaser of a larger quantity of shoes, am I to understand from the Senator that the larger purchaser could have a discount of 5 percent on his purchase of shoes and the smaller purchaser have a discount of 2 percent?

Mr. LOGAN. My judgment is, I may say to the Senator from Iowa, that it will work out in that way. I do not say that that is right, but I do not know whether it can be prohibited, though the discount cannot be a greater percentage than the difference in the cost. If one merchant buys a thousand pairs of shoes and another merchant buys a hundred thousand pairs, the cost of manufacturing them would be the same; the cost of overhead might be the same; but the cost of transportation, of storage, of bookkeeping, and other items of that kind would be no greater, perhaps, on a hundred thousand pairs of shoes than on a thousand, and so there would, I think, legitimately be a distinction, and the larger purchaser would be entitled to receive a greater discount. For that reason—and I thank the Senator for mentioning that point —it is necessary to say that at some point the Federal Trade Commission shall step in and say, "You cannot go any further with those quantity discounts; you can make the discount, if you want to, but treat all alike, and when you get to a certain point you cannot go on and make a difference even based upon the cost." That is the Robinson bill.

Mr. BARKLEY. Let us take in any city or town two merchants; one of them is a small merchant with a little store, and he sells a certain brand of shoes, or clothing, or hats, or underwear, or whatever it is. By reason of the small purchases he makes— although he may make them frequently, and they might, over a long period, amount to as much in the aggregate as the purchases made less frequently but in larger quantities by his competitor in the same community—the small merchant, because of the size of his business as compared to that of the larger merchant, pays a larger unit price for the article which is sold by both of them. Of course, I can understand that if neither of them can undersell the other, and they both have to sell articles at the same price, the public is not injured, because they pay the same whichever store they go to; but what will be the effect on the small merchant? In view of the fact that he has to pay for what he buys a larger unit price than is paid by his larger competitor, who is able to obtain the goods at a smaller unit price because he can buy more at one time, how will that operate as between the two merchants in the way of competition?

Mr. LOGAN. I will say very frankly to my colleague that there is no way by legislation to afford protection to the less fortunate or less efficient merchant under a condition such as that.

We may go as far as we can to protect him, but if there be one merchant who is efficient, who saves by discounting his bills, and desires to use that saving by passing it on to the public, the man who cannot secure such advantages is apt to go under sooner or later, and we cannot help him by law.

This bill attempts to bring about fair treatment among those who are in the same condition. We cannot prevent efficiency; we cannot stop progress. Those who are efficient, those who are good businessmen, those who are skillful in their business are not restrained in any way. That is true even of the large seller and of the manufacturer. Everything that he can save through his efficiency he can use in making discounts to those to whom he sells under the provisions of this bill, and when he does that he will get an advantage over those who cannot manufacture so cheaply as he does. However, that is an advantage which is natural and to which he is entitled, and we cannot take it away from him by law.

Mr. BARKLEY. If any merchant in a city or elsewhere, who is able by reason of quantity purchases to get a lower unit price for what he buys, desires to pass that advantage on to the public by a reduction in the price which he charges the public, will he be prevented from doing so by anything contained in this bill?

Mr. LOGAN. Oh, no; not at all. It does not interfere with anything of that kind.

There are only three or four points in the Robinson bill. First, it prevents fraudulent discrimination. Second, it prohibits advertising that brings about discrimination in prices. Third, it attempts to regulate or fix limits on which quantity discounts may be made, so one may go to a certain point, but cannot go any further.

Mr. MURPHY. Reverting again to the question of quantity discounts, let us assume that a chain store buys 100,000 cases of a breakfast food and the unit cost of each package of that breakfast food after discount to the chain stores is 6 cents. Let us assume that a retail merchant doing his own buying has a unit cost of 8 cents per package. A chain store would be able in competing with the independent merchant and having a unit cost of only 6 cents per package to offer the package at a lower price to the trade than would the independent merchant. The bill is so drawn that quantity discounts could be taken advantage of, provided the seller and purchaser did not exceed the limitation as to discounts fixed by the Federal Trade Commission. Is not that true?

Mr. LOGAN. That is correct. The Senator has pointed out very carefully one of the important purposes of the bill.

Numerous Bills Introduced to Strike at the Same General Evils

(Page 6284)

Mr. HATCH. Is it not true, as the Senator has just pointed out about the different groups, that the various bills he has mentioned are all designed to, and do, strike at the same general evil?

Mr. LOGAN. Absolutely.

Perishable Goods

Mr. SCHWELLENBACH. I should like to say to the Senator, that the only objections I have recognized as having any merit came from those who are engaged in the production or distribution of perishable commodities. Because of the language of the first sentence of section 2 (a) of the amendment, there is fear upon the part of those who produce or sell perishable commodities that they will be left in this position:

A man is running a produce store. He goes along until 4 o'clock in the afternoon. He has sold to his customers at a certain price. He realizes that he has to dispose of all the perishables that afternoon, so he reduces his price; and it is feared that that will be forbidden by the bill.

I believe, from carefully reading the bill, that there is no legitimate basis for that fear. I have proposed an amendment, which I understand the Senator is perfectly willing to accept, taking care of recognized changes in market prices; but in view of the fact that the bill, if passed, must be administered, and there will be an interpretation by those who administer it, and possibly a judicial interpretation, I think we should have a legislative record by the Senator from Kentucky on that precise point. I shall appreciate it, therefore, if he will discuss that phase of the matter.

Mr. LOGAN.   I do not think there is anything in the Robinson bill which would prevent a man selling perishable goods at different prices on the same day as a result of different conditions arising, and I think the bill allows that; but let me say to the Senator from Washington that where there is doubt about a matter of that kind, and it can be clarified by a little simple language, the time and place to do it is before we get through with the matter. Therefore I shall gladly accept the Senator's suggested amendment, because it cannot do any harm.

Mr. SCHWELLENBACH.   Mr. President, the Senator feels that with that amendment there can be no question about that particular phase of the matter?

Mr. LOGAN.   Not a bit; and, in my judgment, there is no question about it without the amendment.

Mr. BARKLEY.   I was wondering whether the sales of perishable goods where the question of time is involved are not largely retail sales, anyway, and not by persons engaged in interstate commerce.

Mr. LOGAN.   That is largely true; but there are some sales of which it is not true. We ship strawberries from Bowling Green to Philadelphia, Boston and Washington, and that would be interstate commerce.

If a man receives a carload of strawberries from Kentucky and cannot sell all of them on one day, so he sells part of the crates on the first day, and the next day he sells some more of them, I think that transaction might come under the provisions of the bill; but I know it will be protected when the Senator from Washington [Mr. SCHWELLENBACH] presents his amendment.

Let me say another thing that seems to be important.

It has been suggested that the farm cooperatives, which are selling milk and things of that kind, made some complaint. They were afraid of something or other, and there was some suggested amendment in their behalf that I looked at. I do not know who prepared it or where it came from, but I do believe that insofar as possible this cooperative business should be encouraged. Mention was made a while ago of the quantity limits. If merchants are allowed to organize or other businessmen are allowed to organize or farmers are allowed to organize and then purchase through their combined purchasing power, and they are allowed quantity discounts, it will be a great benefit to them.

SENATOR LOGAN DISCUSSES POSSIBLE CHANGES IN ORIGINAL BILL

(Page 6285)

In the second section of the committee amendment there is a provision that in making discriminations or differentials, or whatever we may choose to call them, all costs other than brokerage shall be allowed; and it has been said that the words "other than brokerage" in that section ought to go out.

I have thought a good deal about that suggestion. I think perhaps legitimate brokerage ought to be allowed as a part of the costs; and I think when the bill was drafted—

I did not write the bill—perhaps in the amendment which was inserted by the Judiciary Committee of the Senate we had in mind dummy brokerage, sham brokerage. It may be that something should be done about that. I call it to the attention of the Senate, so that some of the other Senators may consider it.

On the question of advertising allowances, it has been said to me that the bill compels the making of proportionately the same allowance to all persons for advertising and that that will not work. Perhaps that is true in some instances. For instance, it has been said that you have a customer in one town down in Kentucky and there is a good newspaper there. He is a live merchant and you wish to have your goods advertised. You are introducing your goods and you make him a certain allowance, knowing that he will expend the money well, and for the purposes for which it may be expended under the provisions of the bill. Right next to him in another town you have a customer who has no newspaper facilities. He is not a very good merchant and if you allow him the same amount of service allowance for advertising purposes it will be wasted. I can see that side of the matter. It may be that something can be done about that.

Then there is another provision to which objections have been made, and that is that in the consideration of the costs which are to be used as the basis of price differentials which are allowed by the bill, the bill provides that there shall not be taken into consideration the part of a factory or business which is not used by the particular buyer, and that the allowance must be confined to the costs that can be charged up against a particular transaction. That has been suggested.

For instance, it has been said that here is a man who comes to a manufacturer and wishes to purchase a certain specific article of goods; it may be that it is a plow point, or a coulter, or something of like nature; and he says, "Here is what I want. I have my pattern all ready. I have my design; I have everything ready; and I am willing to buy and pay cash."

Those who are against the bill say the manufacturer has his designs prepared, his molds prepared, a lot of things ready, and this man, because he does not use the service, ought not to have charged up to him something which he does not use.

PENALTIES

(*Page 2686*)

Mr. O'MAHONEY. I observe that no special penalty is provided, and apparently the sanctions for the bill are to be found only in the provisions of the Sherman Act and of the Clayton Act. Am I correct in that?

Mr. LOGAN. No penalty is provided, but let me say to the Senator that there is provision for securing judgment against one who violates the provisions of the law and damages another's business. It is the thought of those who are interested in the bill that that would be a much more effective method of enforcing the provisions of the bill than a simple penalty.

If the Senator is engaged in business, let me say, and he is buying goods, and across the street is another merchant in the same business buying the same type of goods, and the Senator finds out after a while that the sellers have been allowing certain discriminations in prices to his opponents he is allowed under the bill to go into court and bring a suit and have the matter determined in a perfectly legal way as to how much he has been damaged.

Mr. O'MAHONEY. I was going to call the attention of the Senator to the fact that section 15 of title 15, United States Code, is the section which provides that—

Any person who shall be injured in his business or property by reason of anything forbidden in the antitrust laws may sue therefor in any district court of the United States in the district in which the defendant resides or is found or has an agent * * * and shall recover threefold the damages by him sustained * * *.

Would that provision apply under the pending bill?

Mr. LOGAN.   I think the Senator is right about that, I am frank to say.

WIDESPREAD DEMAND FOR THIS LEGISLATION
(Page 6287)

Mr. LOGAN.   Let me say in conclusion, Mr. President, that the interest in this proposed legislation is very widespread. I do not expect to place in the RECORD a large number of telegrams which come to my office every day. The Federal Trade Commission, however, this morning transmitted to the Senate Committee on the Judiciary photostatic copies of many telegrams which have been received by the President of the United States and transmitted to the Commission. At this time I shall not put them in the RECORD, but I will say that most of the States of the Union are represented in those telegrams.

I am anxious that the purposes sought to be accomplished by the bill shall be carried out, which are that false brokerage as a means of price discrimination must be ended, that fraudulent advertising allowances as a means of price discrimination must be ended, that quantity discounts must be regulated so that the concern of tremendous purchasing power may not drive out of business everyone in the same line as himself simply because his purchasing power is so great that others cannot compete.

WAS THE CLAYTON ACT EFFECTIVE?
(Page 6332, April 29)

Mr. ROBINSON.   That provision, of course, is retained in the section; and the substantial difference is with respect to the limitation that is sought to be imposed on quantity discriminations. Does the Senator think the Clayton Act has been effective for the accomplishment of the purposes for which it was written?

Mr. AUSTIN.   Mr. President, I must say that, as administered, I do not think it has been; but I think it could have been. Ever since the Van Camp decision I have believed that both the buyer and the seller are affected by that act.

The excuse for not administering it more effectively theretofore was that it was claimed that it did not affect the buyer as well as the seller; but in the Van Camp case, decided in 1929, the Court put an interpretation on the act which, I believe, would have enabled the Federal Trade Commission to put it into effect with the saving clauses in it.

Mr. ROBINSON.   If I understand the reply of the Senator to my former question, it is that the present law is adequate, but that it has not been properly administered. The Senator takes the position that there is really no necessity for further legislation. Is that correct?

Mr. AUSTIN.   Mr. President, if it were left to me to decide, I should certainly take the position that it is much better for the welfare of the country, for the welfare of all persons concerned in trade and commerce, to add nothing more to the law than is found in the Clayton Act and section 5 of the Federal Trade Commission Act. I think section 2 of the Clayton Act, section 5 of the Federal Trade Commission Act, and the Sherman antitrust law are wholly adequate to take care of unfair discrimination.

SELLING BELOW COST TO MEET COMPETITION

Mr. LOGAN.   Does the Senator believe that, in order to meet competition in good faith, the manufacturer or the seller should be permitted to sell his product below cost?

Mr. AUSTIN. I should say yes, under certain circumstances. From my personal observation, as well as from much evidence that came before the committee, there are occasions in trade when, if one were not permitted to sell below cost, he would have on his hands a great quantity of sirup, for example, which would perish, or a great quantity of fruit, or other perishable products, foodstuffs of all kinds.

Mr. LOGAN. Mr. President, I do not think any legislation would interfere with such a condition as that. What I ask is, in order to meet competition, should the seller be allowed to sell below cost?

Mr. AUSTIN. Mr. President, I did not apprehend the point in the question when I answered. That is a very difficult question of ethics, as well as of law. If the competition in business on one side is unfair and is not restrained by any governmental agency, I should like to ask this question in answer to the other: How can a man whose business life depends upon meeting that sort of competition do otherwise than sell below cost?

Mr. LOGAN. If he does it in order to meet legitimate competition, of course, he cannot continue very long, and he not only pulls his own temple down, but he pulls down the temple of all others. In a given community there may be a small dealer, perhaps, who is doing business in the community, and there may be a more powerful concern there, one which sells its products all over the country, and, realizing that the small fellow in the community is going to get some business, the larger concern deliberately goes out to meet competition, and sells goods in the community below cost, repeating what was done in the old days in the sale of petroleum. Should that be allowed? I mean, should any man be allowed to sell his product below cost for the purpose of meeting competition; that is, perhaps, to drive his competitor from the field?

Mr. AUSTIN. Mr. President, that is prohibited by law.

Mr. LOGAN. Not by the Clayton Act.

Mr. AUSTIN. It is prohibited by the Clayton Act. I trust the Senate will excuse me for differing.

Mr. LOGAN. In the Clayton Act, as I read it, it is provided that nothing in the act shall prevent one from selling below the standard fixed there in order to meet competition in good faith, which would allow one to sell for whatever he thought proper.

Mr. AUSTIN. Oh, yes, Mr. President, but that is the difference between the question asked and the law. "In good faith to meet competition" is something different from underselling one's opponent to drive him out of business. That is the point that is prohibited by the law. The Clayton Act was designed to prevent such unfair competition as that. The moment the competition enters the field of driving any one out of business, eliminating competition, or unreasonably reducing competition, a transgression of the law occurs which can be stopped by a cease and desist order, under the act.

Mr. LOGAN. The vice of the Clayton Act is that after making that provision it immediately exempts from the provisions of the law those who sell in a community in order to meet competition in good faith; and that is where the trouble is. There could always be competition in good faith, and then a seller could sell to the people in a community at prices lower than those at which he sells to people in some other community. In fact, such sellers can drive a competitor out of business in one community by lowering prices, and then increasing the prices of the products elsewhere in order to make up the loss. I do not think that ought to be allowed, although I realize the Senator is entitled to his own opinion.

Mr. AUSTIN. Answering on the assumption in the question, of a purpose to drive the other fellow out, I would agree with the learned Senator from Kentucky, with whom I find myself in agreement so often. I would not approve of that, and that is not my purpose in what I have to say here.

When I say that I think the Clayton Act is adequate to meet a condition of which the Senator speaks, it is because the Clayton Act in the prohibitory clause provides as follows:

It shall be unlawful for any person engaged in commerce * * * either directly or indirectly to discriminate in price between different purchasers of commodities * * * where the effect of such discrimination may be to substantially lessen competition.

Mr. LOGAN.   There is a proviso there, however, that if it is necessary in order to meet competition, they may do so.

Mr. AUSTIN.   Oh, yes; it takes care of the intent in good faith.

Mr. VANDENBERG.   Am I to gather from the colloquy between the Senator from Vermont and the Senator from Kentucky that the Robinson bill prohibits the sale of a commodity at any time below its cost of production?

Mr. AUSTIN.   I am impressed by the testimony with the idea that the bill was so interpreted.

Mr. VANDENBERG.   May I ask the Senator from Kentucky if that is the fact?

Mr. LOGAN.   No, Mr. President; that is not true. There is nothing in the Robinson bill which prohibits the sale of any commodity at any price at which a seller desires to dispose of it; but there is a provision against his selling, for example, to the Senator from Michigan at one price and to the Senator from Vermont at another price under the same conditions and the quality of the goods being the same. However, so far as the Robinson bill is concerned, the seller may sell at any price he desires. The purpose of the bill is to compel the treatment of all customers exactly alike when the same situation applies to all of them.

Mr. VANDENBERG.   Would that apply equally to a customer in the United States and a customer out of the United States?

Mr. LOGAN.   I do not think it applies to a customer out of the United States.

Mr. VANDENBERG.   The Senator does not think the provision he is talking about would prevent sales of surplus products abroad at lower prices?

Mr. LOGAN.   I do not. As I recall, the provisions of the bill are confined specifically to the United States and possessions of the United States.

BORAH–VAN NUYS BILL INTRODUCED AS A FURTHER AMENDMENT TO THE ROBINSON-PATMAN BILL
(Page 6346)

Mr. BORAH.   Mr. President, I desire to call the attention of the Senate to the matter now pending before the Senate. I direct attention to Senate bill 4171, which will be offered as an amendment to the bill now before the Senate. It will be offered either by the Senator from Indiana [Mr. VAN NUYS] or myself at the appropriate time.

Section 2 of the proposed amendment reads as follows:

SEC. 2. It shall be unlawful for any person engaged in commerce, in the course of such commerce, to be a party to, or assist in, any transaction of sale, or contract to sell, which discriminates to his knowledge against competitors of the purchaser, in that, any discount, rebate, allowance, or advertising service charge is granted to the purchaser over and above any discount, rebate, allowance, or advertising service charge available at the time of such transaction to said competitors in respect of a sale of goods of like grade, quality, and quantity; to sell, or contract to sell, goods in any part of the United States at prices lower than those exacted by said person elsewhere in the United States for the purpose of destroying competition, or eliminating a competitor in such part of the United States; or, to sell, or contract to sell, goods at unreasonably low prices for the purpose of destroying competition or eliminating a competitor.

Nothing in this section shall prevent a cooperative association from returning to producers or consumers, or a cooperative wholesale association from returning to its constituent retail members, the whole, or any part of, the net surplus resulting from its trading operations in proportion to purchasers from, or sales to, the association.

Then violations of the terms of the proposed amendment are made punishable by fine of not more than $5,000 or imprisonment for not more than 1 year or both.

Mr. President, the amendment is designed to cover certain specific matters which we think ought to be inhibited as a matter of law, certain things which we think ought to be prohibited without the intervention of the discretionary power of the Federal Trade Commission or other bureau. The matters which we propose to prohibit that of allowing discount or rebate or allowance for advertising service charge to one purchaser without making it available to each and every other purchaser. That, it seems to me, should be prohibited as a matter of law, and that there need not be any discretion laid anywhere with reference to the execution of that kind of law. That is the distinction really between the bill which is now pending and the proposed amendment.

It is not our purpose to embarrass or impede the action upon the main measure, but we shall ask that it be adopted as an amendment, believing that the two propositions can be reconciled when the bill goes to conference, and that we can save the principle of both.

Mr. President, I do not think the principle of this amendment is in conflict with the principle of the main bill. It does contain, however, specific provisions of law violation of which would constitute an offense; and the person violating them may be taken into court instead of being taken before the Federal Trade Commission.

Mr. President, I am not offering the amendment with the view that it would be accepted in lieu of the Robinson bill; but I should like, so far as it is possible, to have incorporated into law a positive prohibition covering certain of these practices, such as making allowances, and so forth. I should like to have that prohibition positive. I should like to have it so worded that if the prohibition is violated the person violating it may be taken into court. If a small merchant is compelled to come here from Omaha, or some other point in the Middle West, or any far distant point, and make his showing before the Federal Trade Commission, and get his relief, that in itself is a very burdensome requirement.

Mr. LOGAN.   I agree with the Senator; but under the Robinson bill the merchant may bring suit in the courts to recover damages. However, the only question that arises in my mind just now is as to how the Senator's amendment should be included in the Robinson bill.

Mr. BORAH.   I will offer it as a new section.

Mr. LOGAN.   That would be satisfactory to me, I am quite sure.

Mr. KING.   Does the Senator perceive any incongruity between the bill which he has offered—and I refer particularly to the penal provision—and the so-called Robinson bill, where the remedy is by suit for damages, based upon whatever damages may be sustained by reason of so-called discrimination?

Mr. BORAH.   My view is that there are certain practices so obviously improper and unjust that they ought to be prohibited by specific provision of law, and that indulging in them ought to constitute a crime. There are things like the granting of quantity discounts which are difficult to cover by a specific provision of law and make the violation punishable, but when we come to the special discount allowance, or rebate allowance, or service-charge allowance, or advertising allowance, to one party and the refusal of it to another, that is a fraudulent transaction.

Mr. KING.   It seems to me that the Clayton Act, particularly section 2, and the Sherman antitrust law, pretty effectively deals with the evils of which the Senator complains and which this proposed bill seeks to prevent.

Mr. BORAH.   In a sense, that is correct, but when the businessman knows positively that if he does a thing he will be subject to criminal prosecution, that is a great deterrent. And it is not a thing about which he might be honestly misled. If he makes these allowances to one and refuses them to another, if he makes rebates to one and refuses them to another, it is a matter wholly within his knowledge, and done after full consideration and full knowledge of what he is doing.

Mr. LOGAN. Mr. President, may I interrupt the Senator to ask whether it is unusual to provide, for violation of a statute, a criminal prosecution and also a right to sue for damages? The two are not inconsistent.

Mr. BORAH. No; we have such a provision in the Sherman antitrust law.

PRICE CHANGES TO MEET CHANGING MARKET CONDITIONS
(Page 6426, April 30)

THE LEGISLATIVE CLERK. On page 6 of the committee amendment, line 14, after the word "trade," it is proposed to insert a colon and the following:

And provided further, That nothing herein contained shall prevent price changes from time to time where in response to changing conditions affecting the market for or the marketability of the goods concerned, such as but not limited to actual or imminent deterioration of perishable goods, obsolescence of seasonal goods, distress sales under court process, or sales in good faith in discontinuance of business in the goods concerned.

Mr. AUSTIN. Mr. President, the purpose of my amendment is very simple. It is to take care of recognized changes in market conditions, as well as to take care of seasonal and perishable goods.

Mr. ROBINSON. Mr. President, this is a general amendment and, I think, a very valuable one. It does make provision in general language for a number of conditions which might arise, and to meet which amendments excepting certain commodities from the provisions of the bill have been proposed. I prefer this general language, and I am sure the Senator from Kentucky [Mr. LOGAN], who is familiar with the subject, also does.

I have no objection to the amendment.

Mr. LOGAN. I think the amendment offered by the Senator from Vermont is in proper form and will be helpful to the bill.

FURTHER DEBATE ON PRICE CHANGES IN GOOD FAITH TO MEET COMPETITION

The PRESIDING OFFICER. The Senator from Oregon offers an amendment to the amendment of the committee, which the clerk will state.

The CHIEF CLERK. In the amendment of the committee at the end of section 2 (a) it is proposed to strike out the period, insert a colon, and add the following proviso:

And provided further, That nothing herein contained shall prevent discrimination in price in the same or different communities made in good faith to meet competition.

Mr. McNARY. Mr. President, it is very obvious and readily observed that this is a restoration of the language of the Clayton Act so far as it is possible to make it applicable in the matter of competition in a given line. The Senator from Arkansas suggested that it might be included in the phraseology of the amendment offered by the Senator from Vermont [Mr. AUSTIN], but, in my opinion, the amendment of the Senator from Vermont does not include the proposal I have just submitted and which has been read by the clerk.

The Senator from Kentucky [Mr. LOGAN] this morning thought the same idea was carried in the so-called Borah–Van Nuys amendment. Of course, if that is the situation, I do not desire to press the amendment; I am willing to trust the judgment of the Senator who has the bill in charge and, if that is his view, there are either of two courses he could take. One would be to accept the amendment or state specifically that, in his best judgment, it is already a part of the amendment that has been incorporated in the pending bill.

Mr. ROBINSON.   I cannot say that I think the amendment which the Senator from Oregon has proposed is identical in effect with the amendment of the Senator from Vermont which the Senate has just agreed to; but I do say that I think the purpose which the Senator has in mind is accomplished by the amendment that has been agreed to.

I myself would not be able to accept at this juncture language that is so general as that contained in the pending amendment proposed by the Senator from Oregon. I should prefer that the Senator withhold the amendment until opportunity can first be afforded for its further consideration, if the Senator has no objection to that course.

The PRESIDING OFFICER.   The Senator from Oregon temporarily withdraws his amendment.

Mr. ROBINSON.   Mr. President, I feel it due to repeat what I thought I said a while ago, that I do not wish to imply by any statement I have made that I find myself in a position to agree to the amendment. I should like an opportunity of making a further study of it.

Mr. McNARY.   Nothing that I have said would indicate that the Senator from Arkansas had accepted the amendment. I understood the Senator simply wanted a little additional time to consider the amendment before determining what course he would pursue in compliance with the request. I have temporarily withdrawn the amendment.

MAKING THE BUYER LIABLE UNDER CERTAIN CONDITIONS
(Page 6428)

Mr. COPELAND.   Mr. President, I move to insert at the bottom of page 8, the amendment which I send to the desk.

(e) That it shall be unlawful for any person engaged in commerce, in the course of such commerce, knowingly to induce or receive a discrimination in price or terms of sale, which is prohibited by this section.

Mr. ROBINSON.   This amendment makes the person who knowingly receives an unfair, discriminatory price also liable; and I think it is sound in principle.

PERMITTING A VIOLATOR "REBUTTING A PRIMA FACIE CASE BY OFFERING EVIDENCE OF GOOD FAITH TO MEET COMPETITION"
(Page 6435)

Mr. MOORE.   Mr. President, I offer the amendment, which the clerk has at his desk, and which I ask to have read.

(e) Upon proof being made, at any hearing on a complaint under this section, that there has been discrimination in price, or services or facilities furnished, the burden of rebutting the prima facie case thus made by showing justification shall be upon the person charged with a violation of this section, and unless justification shall be affirmatively shown, the Commission is authorized to issue an order terminating the discrimination: *Provided, however,* That nothing herein contained shall prevent a seller rebutting the prima facie case thus made by showing that his lower price or the furnishing of services or facilities to any purchaser or purchasers was made in good faith to meet an equally low price of a competitor, or the services or facilities furnished by a competitor.

Mr. MOORE.   Mr. President, all over the United States there has been great difficulty about the prices of milk. In New Jersey that was true. The producers of milk in New Jersey were starving. At the time I had the honor of being Governor of New Jersey we had a milk-control board. Prices were made that would permit these men just to live. The difference between poverty and prosperity was just 1 cent.

We have built up this system in New Jersey, New York, in Pennsylvania, and possibly in other States of the Union. The milk producers in New Jersey feel that unless this amendment is adopted all of their work for all these years will mean nothing; that they will go back again to where they were. The amendment merely provides that if they charge more to one person than to another, or are accused of discrimination, they shall have a right to prove justification. I think the amendment goes just a little farther than the Borah–Van Nuys amendment or the amendment of the Senator from Oregon [Mr. McNary].

Mr. ROBINSON.   Mr. President, the amendment of the Senator from New Jersey appears to be consistent with the McNary amendment and other amendments which have heretofore been agreed to. There is one feature of the amendment about which I am in doubt; and little opportunity is afforded to study the proposition, as I have not seen the amendment before it was brought forward here. I see no objection to its incorporation in the bill, so that the conferees may consider it.

DEBATE IN THE HOUSE OF REPRESENTATIVES CONTINUED

UNANIMITY OF AGREEMENT THAT IT IS IMPORTANT PROPOSED LEGISLATION
(*Page 8109, May 27*)

Mr. SUMNERS of Texas.   Mr. Speaker, whatever may be the attitude of Members of Congress with regard to this proposed legislation, there must be unanimity of agreement that it is important proposed legislation.

I do not believe that any student of economics in this country can be unconcerned as to what is happening. At one extreme we find ourselves drifting toward an economic feudalism and on the other extreme drifting toward an attitude of dependence upon the Government or somebody else. These two tendencies together are identical, in my judgment, with certain things that happened long ago when the world came to live under a feudalism.

This bill proposes, and its purpose is definite, to try to give to the little man in business and industries a better opportunity to survive than he now has. No student of our system of government can fail to recognize that we have a definite choice. We cannot preserve a democracy in government unless we preserve a democracy in opportunity.

Mr. Speaker, the proposed legislation, in my humble opinion, is in the interest of private property. In days gone by private property was secure behind the line of defense held by smaller men in business and industry. Whenever there was a red agitation, these little fellows gathered about them their schoolmates, their friends, and their kin folk established and held the line of defense. Behind that line private investments were safe. But under this drift the number of those defenders of private property is continuing to be reduced, and these aggregations are getting bigger and bigger, and are attracting more and more attention. If this thing continues, I venture my life on the prophecy the time is not far distant when some men, some opportunists, will take advantage of the psychology of the situation and led by a spirit of revolution will take over these big industries and aggregations of capital. If they have not the money to pay for them, they will use the printing press. Is it possible these great captains of business do not appreciate this peril or will ignore it?

There is not anything in human economy that makes men more dependable than responsibility. Perhaps that statement is not quite right. There is not anything that makes people dependable like responsibility or so willing to fight for a thing as having an ownership interest associated with responsibility. Human beings do not fight for a boarding house as they fight for their firesides. Somehow, some way, in America we have to begin to build from these two extremes toward the middle, and we have not a split second to spare. We have been going along here dreaming that conditions which obtain in other sections of the world and in other ages of the world have by some mysterious sort of process been excluded from us. That is a foolish dream. It may prove to be a fatal dream.

There is much to indicate that the generation in which we live must grapple with the same major problems which have challenged the genius of those who lived in the other great crises of the world and which wrecked nations and civilizations in days gone by. There has not been an age in all the history of time as stupendous as this. There has not been a time that challenged men to be statesmen more than this age challenges us. It is not to protect an individual, it is not to give the little fellow more money, it is not to take something from somebody else, but it is to build strong again the foundation of our Government and our civilization. That is the job presently before us. You cannot have it with a few great economic overlords to whom everybody else owes economic allegiance. They are not reading the signs of the times, they are not looking beyond their noses. If they will but read the history of the past, if they will only study the signs of the present, those people who are not blinded by greed and lust for power would come in here and assist us.

Mr. FITZPATRICK. Apropos of the gentleman's statement a moment ago, is there anything in the pending act that would compel a merchant or manufacturer to sell to the little man if the manufacturer or merchant did not want to do so?

Mr. SUMNERS of Texas.   No; but let me tell you right now that if ever those people in this country defy public opinion and deny to the little man a chance to buy they will be committing economic suicide and the gentleman better tell them so. [Applause.] The American people are not going to stand for a few lords of industry destroying this country. [Applause.] I am not an enemy of these people; I am trying to be their friend. They are not more happy. They are not more secure. They are building for themselves an aggregate of opposition from which they will not escape. If they will not allow the existence of the small businessman, their only possible defenders, they, and they alone, will then be the authors of their own destruction.

Mr. GREENWOOD.   Mr. Speaker, I agree with the previous speaker that there is no room in this country for commercial feudalism because we live in a country of democracy, which some have called rugged individualism, where we believe in fair play for all groups and classes that are engaged in the same kind of endeavor.

Along this line, I recall a professor who was beloved very much, just before I left school, gave this instruction to his class:

You may forget some of the general maxims of the law which I have taught you, but I want you to remember at all times that the supreme function of the law is to protect the weak and to restrain the strong.

This is the purpose of this bill. I trust the rule will be adopted and this bill enacted into law by the Congress.

The Clayton Act undertook to regulate monopoly and prevent unfair trade practices. There has grown up in the more than 20 years since it was enacted certain concentrations of wealth that are not satisfied with the economic power they have of concentrated credit and management. They desire the advantages of being able to buy at a lower figure than other competitive classes that are entitled to the same treatment, and there have grown up certain practices which this bill proposes to remedy. It is contended that because of quantity purchases they should have great discounts. This bill does not undertake to destroy that right, but it does say that another class or group that buys the same amount in quantity shall have the same privilege of purchase. If a bunch of farm cooperatives organized into an association buys as much in quantity as a chain store, they should have the same privileges of a quantity discount, and this bill undertakes to classify and treat them in the same way.

There are certain schemes that have been carried on of allowing fictitious brokerage fees. Some firm that buys in large quantities goes to a manufacturer and says he would like to buy at a fixed price. The manufacturer says, "I cannot sell you at that price, because this is my price," and he says, "I know, but I am giving you my exclusive business and it can be arranged by some agent of mine coming to you and by your paying him a brokerage fee."

This is a false and fictitious fee, and in order to end such trade practices this bill undertakes to eliminate fictitious brokerage fees.

The same is true with reference to service allowances and advertising fees used as a subterfuge to give an unjust discount to someone who uses coercion and says to the manufacturer, "We are buying altogether from you and taking a large portion of your output and therefore you must give us this advantage through this subterfuge."

This bill undertakes to correct this situation. We must have trade practices of fair competition.

Farm cooperatives will not be injured by this bill. If farm cooperatives that are associated together can buy the same quantity from a manufacturer, they will receive the same treatment as a chain-store or mail-order houses or any other centralization of economic power.

Labor is never injured by fair-trade practices. Labor will take care of itself if these fair-trade practices are enacted into law.

BURDEN OF PROOF PLACED ON ACCUSED

(Page 8110)

Mr. GREENWOOD.   This bill provides that a prima-facie case shall be made out against a manufacturer or wholesaler and after a prima-facie case is made out the burden shifts to the other party, which is offset by proper proof. This is the proper procedure for this kind of case. This is not a criminal case, this is a case between two classes of businessmen and when they have satisfied the rule as to burden of proof, then the wholesaler or the one against whom the complaint is made shall come in and rebut that prima-facie case by introducing his evidence. This is the way it should be handled and in a judicial way it is all in the hands of the Federal Trade Commission.

LEGISLATIVE HISTORY AND PURPOSE

(Page 8111)

Mr. PATMAN.   Mr. Chairman, those of us who are interested in this legislation appreciate the fact that the Speaker of the House, the majority leader, and the Rules Committee and the Judiciary Committee have cooperated with us in our desire to get this legislation properly considered.

The bill was introduced almost a year ago. The Judiciary Committee held hearings lasting over several months. The questions involved were discussed by those against as well as those in favor, and the committee hearings are available, printed in two volumes, to every Member of the House. Every person who desired to be heard in behalf of the legislation or against it was heard by the Judiciary Committee.

NOT PRICE FIXING

This bill is opposed to price fixing. It is an anti-price-fixing bill. The only time I have ever said that manufacturers would give the same price to retailers is in the case where the independent is in a position to purchase the same quantity as the corporate chains. We are making no effort in this bill to fix the price.

NOT CLASS LEGISLATION

It is not a bill that discriminates against any class or group. It is not a bill that will shelter the independent merchants of this country or reward the inefficient retail merchant, but it is a bill to give equal rights, equal privileges, and equal benefits to all alike who are in the same position, purchase the same quantities under the same circumstances. I venture to say that not one member of this Congress will get on this floor and say that he is opposed to the main purposes of this bill.

PURPOSES OF BILL

What are the objectives of this bill? Mr. Chairman, there has grown up in this country a policy in business that a few rich, powerful organizations by reason of their size and their ability to coerce and intimidate manufacturers have forced those manufacturers to give them their goods at a lower price than they give to the independent merchants under the same and similar circumstance and for the same quantities of goods. Is that right or wrong? It is wrong. We are attempting to stop it, recognizing the right of the manufacturer to have a different price for a different quantity where there is a difference in the cost of manufacture. There is nothing in this bill to prohibit it but the bill expressly provides that the manufacturer may have a difference in price where there is a difference in cost of manufacture. There is only one exception to that, which I shall discuss after I have finished discussing the other purposes of the bill, and that is advertising allowances.

One great concern in America last year compelled manufacturers to pay it $8,000,000 in pseudo-advertising allowances and pseudo-brokerage charges. That amount of benefits the independent merchants of the country were not entitled to receive from the same manufacturers, purchasing the same quantity under the same conditions. You are in favor of giving the citizens the same right as the corporations in this country, and that is all that we are asking in this bill.

Mr. COX.   In effect that practically forces the independent buyer to provide the fund that goes by way of rebate and advertising to the big buyer, giving him an advantage.

Mr. PATMAN.   That is right, giving him an advantage in that way.

DUMMY BROKERAGE

There is a merchant in Virginia representing potato growers. He sells thousands of cars of potatoes a year, and our investigation has disclosed that he had a secret contract with a large mass corporate chain buyer by which he obligated himself to sell every car of those potatoes of those farmers to this large buyer. At what price? Oh, at the market price. That sounds good, but fortunately for the large mass buyer, he was big enough to make the market price. They do make the market in those localities. This man representing the farmers sold those potatoes to that mass buyer, fixing the price himself, and what did he get out of it? He got a secret rebate of $2.50 to $5 on every car that the farmers knew nothing about, and the trade was, "If I don't deliver you every car, for every car that I do not deliver you I will be penalized $5." That is the kind of dummy brokerage arrangement we are trying to prohibit in this bill.

QUANTITY PURCHASES

Next is quantity purchases. This bill expressly provides that there shall be price differentials, but against discrimination; a different price for a different quantity, if there is a difference in cost of manufacture. But there is one exception to that. That exception you will approve, I believe, if you understand it as those of us who have been sponsoring this bill understand it.

RAILROAD REBATES

Fifty years ago there was a clamor in this country for legislation to prohibit rebates and discrimination in freight rates, to prevent favoritism in freight rates. The people of this country demanded that the Congress pass a law that would stop such discriminatory practices. The Congress met. The argument then was made on the floor of this House that will today be made against this bill. This argument was made:

Oh, if you do that, these big fellows will not get these cheap freight rates, and that will cause prices to go up, and the consumer will pay the bill. It will raise prices hundreds of millions of dollars a year.

They made those same arguments against that law that they are making against this bill today. But the people were aroused. They were against this cheating and chiseling for the purpose of helping a few large buyers, through discriminatory freight rates, create a monopoly. So Congress passed that law creating the Interstate Commerce Commission. The Interstate Commerce Commission said:

Hereafter we are going to fix the carload as the quantity limit, and whoever causes one carload to be transported will pay the same price per car for transportation as one who causes 100,000 carloads to be transported.

The large shippers came in. They said:

If we have a train load shipped from Chicago to New York in one direct run, it will only cost about 50 percent per car for transportation that it would cost if you shipped in and out in single cars from Chicago to New York.

They were right about it. The Interstate Commerce Commission did not take issue with them, because they knew it was the truth; but the Interstate Commerce Commission said:

Yes; but if you permit that you will create a worse condition in this country. We have to look into the future. If we permit that, a few large shippers will get all the special prices and the large dealers will destroy the small dealers and we will have a monopoly in this country, and we are not going to permit it. So we are going to stay by that one-carload-quantity limit.

The Supreme Court of the United States, in the case of *I. C. C.* v. *B. & O.* (145 U. S. 263), although not passing on the question directly, expressed itself in favor of what I am saying today. This is what they said:

If, for example, a railway makes to the public generally a certain rate of freight and to a particular individual residing in the same town a reduced rate for the same class of goods, this may operate as an undue preference, since it enables the favored party to sell his goods at a lower price than his competitors, and may even enable him to obtain a complete monopoly of that business. Even if the same reduced rates be allowed to everyone doing the same amount of business, such discrimination may, if carried too far, operate unjustly upon the smaller dealers engaged in the same business, and enable the larger ones to drive them out of the market.

That is what the Supreme Court of the United States said. I will read what the Commission said in another case, the *Anaconda Copper* case (19 I. C. C. 592):

Whatever difference there may be in cost to the carrier between traffic in trainloads and traffic in carloads, it appears to the Commission that to give greater consideration to trainload traffic than to carload traffic would create preferences in favor of large shippers, and be to the prejudice of the small shippers and the public.

Those are two expressions, one from the highest court of this land and the other of the Interstate Commerce Commission, saying that you must not give special rates to trainloads, admitting there is a difference in cost per car, because if you do it, it will create a monopoly in this country and the large dealers will be enabled to crush and destroy the business of the small dealers, and that is against the public and against the consumers.

That is exactly the point involved in this bill. We permit differences in price for different quantities, based upon cost up to one point. What is that point? To the point where a few large buyers can buy at such a low price that they can create a monopoly, just like they had a chance to create through railroad freight rates. We placed a provision in this bill which provides that when that stage is reached the Federal Trade Commission may fix a quantity limit on that particular commodity. The Federal Trade Commission will have nothing to do under this provision unless there is danger of monopoly. I am sure you are in favor of curbing and stopping monopolies. If the Commission believes there is danger of monopoly, then the Commission can fix a quantity limit on that particular commodity, just as they did on freight rates, whether it be 1 carload or 10 carloads, or a few pounds or a thousand pounds, depending on the commodity. It makes no difference. They will be permitted to fix quantity limits above which anyone purchasing that particular quantity receives the same price under the same conditions.

That has already been approved by the Supreme Court of this country and by the Interstate Commerce Commission. It is absolutely fair. Who is there on this floor who will say we should not stop a monopoly, and if it is necessary to do it, that we should fail to give the Federal Trade Commission this power which would permit them to curb a monopoly in the same way that the Interstate Commerce Commission was given the power to curb that monopoly?

A SUMMARY OF THE MAIN PROVISIONS

In this bill, Mr. Chairman, we are asking for those main points, to eliminate these pseudo advertising allowances, given only for the purpose of favoring the large corporate chains. We are asking that the dummy brokerage be eliminated to the extent that it cannot be used as a bribe to make one person go back upon the person who employed him and betray him. That is, if you are against deceit and trickery and treachery, you certainly ought to be against this dummy brokerage.

We are providing further that quantity purchases shall be permitted up to the limit where a monopoly will possibly be caused; and then the Federal Trade Commission may, not shall, may adopt rules and regulations that will prohibit that monopoly from being created. These are the main points in the bill.

PERISHABLES

(Page 8114)

Mr. ROBERTSON.   Subsection 3 of section 2 allows price differentials on perishables that are deteriorating.

Mr. PATMAN.   Yes. This does not prohibit price changes. You may change your price every minute of the day so long as you are not using it to discriminate in favor of one customer as against another one. [Applause.]

Mr. ROBERTSON.   Suppose one merchant would buy one barrel of apples and you would sell it to him at $3 a barrel. Suppose a chain store would say, "We will take the 10,000 barrels that you have for sale."

Mr. PATMAN.   There is a difference in the cost of distribution, and you would have a right to permit a differential in price where there is a difference in manufacturing and distribution cost. There would be a difference in the cost of distribution in the case to which the gentleman refers, and they would have the right to make that change in price, but if the same amount was sold to a competitor they would have to give him the same price. If the sales are made in different markets there cannot be a discrimination. Prices can be changed any time so long as it is not done for the purpose of discriminating.

It [the bill] simply enforces common honesty in business. It prohibits things that every man should be prohibited from doing.

Mr. PALMISANO.   I am in sympathy with the object of the bill, but I would like to know if the gentleman from Texas can explain what effect this bill would have on dealings within the limits of a particular State.

Mr. PATMAN.   Of course, it will not apply to intrastate commerce. There is only one exception where it could apply, and that is where the transactions within a State would affect the price of the commodity that was sold interstate, on the same theory as railroad freight rates. This is the only way it could apply to intrastate transactions.

WHO ARE IN COMPETITION?

(Page 8123)

Mr. BOILEAU.   I am referring to subsection (d), on page 9. At the end of the paragraph it says:

Unless such payment or consideration is available on proportionally equal terms to all other customers competing in the distribution of such products or commodities.

Customers competing in the distribution of such products or commodities.

That means the same city or community, with competitors in the same town. But it does not mean that an advertising allowance to a customer on a corner in New York must be made to one in my home town in Wisconsin. They do not compete.

ADVERTISING ALLOWANCES

Mr. BLOOM.   I am simply looking for information. Will the gentleman tell me in what part of the bill it says anything about advertising at all? Where is the word "advertising" used?

Mr. BOILEAU.   We can talk about advertising allowances without using the word "advertising." If you want to find it read section (d) with that thought in mind, and you will find that it fully covers advertising allowances.

Mr. BLOOM.   And yet you can find no place in the bill where it uses the term "advertising."

Mr. BOILEAU.   No; but the Judiciary Committee discussed the bill and the provisions in paragraph (d) with relation to advertising allowances, and any member of that committee will tell you that that section refers to advertising allowances.

Mr. CRAWFORD.   Even if the Judiciary Committee claimed that these provisions on pages 8 and 9 did not import advertising allowances the fact remains that it does embrace it?

Mr. BOILEAU.   There is no question about that.

Mr. CRAWFORD. The gentleman made the statement that this advertising allowance would have to be granted to each dealer in a town.

Mr. BOILEAU.   I say "competing."

Mr. CRAWFORD.   The gentleman means that each customer?

Mr. BOILEAU.   Each customer.

Mr. CRAWFORD.   In other words, I do not have to allow it to people who are not my customers?

Mr. BOILEAU.   No.

Mr. CRAWFORD.   I could select a single customer in a single town and grant it to him?

Mr. BOILEAU.   The advertising allowance?

Mr. CRAWFORD.   Yes.

Mr. BOILEAU.   No; you could not. If you grant an advertising allowance to one customer in that community who is competing, you must grant it to all his competitors.

Mr. CRAWFORD.   Then why the language on line 5:

To all other customers competing.

Mr. BOILEAU.   All other customers competing in the distribution of such commodities.

Mr. CRAWFORD.   But he must be my customer?

Mr. BOILEAU.   All persons with whom you deal, and if you offer such an advertising allowance, it is my opinion that you must offer it to all customers of yours in that community.

Mr. CRAWFORD.   I can select one customer?

Mr. BOILEAU.   If you are only selling to one customer.

Mr. CRAWFORD.   In a given town?

Mr. BOILEAU.   I believe you could do that; yes.

Mr. BLOOM.   You only think he can do it?

Mr. BOILEAU.   No; I am stating that if you have only one customer in a community, that is the only person to whom you have to offer it.

Mr. BLOOM.   You will have to give it proportionately to all other persons in that town.

Mr. BOILEAU.   All other customers with whom you deal.

Mr. MILLER.   Yes; his customer.

Mr. BOILEAU.   That is all.

HOUSE STEERING COMMITTEE OFFERS AMENDMENTS ON THE FLOOR

(Page 8139)

Mr. MILLER.   Mr. Speaker, the amendments to the committee amendment, which will be offered by the Committee on the Judiciary, are as follows:

On page 6 of the committee amendment strike out all of lines 4 to 17, both inclusive, which is designated as subsection (1) of section 2 of the committee amendment.

This is the so-called classification subsection and the Committee on the Judiciary on May 21, 1936, decided to offer an amendment to strike the same from the bill as reported.

The second amendment which the Committee on the Judiciary will offer is to lines 20 and 23 on page 7 of the committee amendment to the bill, and the amendment will be a motion to strike said lines 20 to 23, both inclusive, therefrom.

This particular section which the committee will seek to strike out is designated as subsection (5) on page 7, and is what is commonly called the basing-point provision.

The third amendment which the Committee on the Judiciary will offer is to subsection (2) of the committee amendment on page 9, and is as follows:

After the word "price," in line 9, page 9, insert the words "or services or facilities furnished." In line 16, page 9, after the word "price," insert the words "or the furnishing of services or facilities." Immediately following the word "competitor," in line 18, page 9, add a comma and the following: "or the services or facilities furnished by a competitor."

This would make subsection (E) of the committee amendment to the bill, on page 9, read as follows:

(E) Upon proof being made, at any hearing on a complaint under this section, that there has been discrimination in price or services or facilities furnished, the burden of rebutting the prima-facie case thus made by showing justification shall be upon the person charged with a violation of this section, and unless justification shall be affirmatively shown, the Commission is authorized to issue an order terminating the discrimination: *Provided, however,* That nothing herein contained shall prevent a seller rebutting the prima-facie case thus made by showing that his lower price or the furnishing of services or facilities to any purchaser or purchasers was made in good faith to meet an equally low price of a competitor or the services or facilities furnished by a competitor.

FTC SPONSORS AMENDMENT
(*Page 8140*)

At the request of the Federal Trade Commission I propose to offer an amendment which will add two new sections to the committee amendment. These have not been presented to the Committee on the Judiciary because I have not had an opportunity to do so, and they will not be offered as amendments bearing the approval of the Committee on the Judiciary, but will be offered by me upon my own responsibility. However, I may add that I do not think the Committee on the Judiciary would have any objection to the amendment. The proposals which I expect to offer, adding sections (2) and (3) to the committee amendment, are as follows:

SEC. 2. That nothing herein contained shall affect rights of action arising, or litigation pending, or orders of the Federal Trade Commission issued and in effect or pending on review, based on section 2 of said act of October 15, 1914, prior to the effective date of this amendatory act: *Provided,* That where, prior to the effective date of this amendatory act the Federal Trade Commission has issued an order requiring any person to cease and desist from a violation of section 2 of said act of October 15, 1914, and such order is pending on review or is in effect either as issued or as affirmed or modified by a court of competent jurisdiction, and the Commission shall have reason to believe that such person has committed, used, or carried on, since the effective date of this amendatory act, or is committing, using, or carrying on, any act, practice, or method in violation of any of the provisions of said section 2 as amended by this act, it may reopen such original proceeding and may issue and serve upon such person its complaint, supplementary to the original complaint, stating its charges in that respect. Thereupon the same proceedings shall be had upon such supplementary complaint as provided in section 11 of said act of October 15, 1914. If upon such hearing the Commission shall be of the opinion that any act, practice, or method charged in said supplementary complaint has been committed, used, or carried on since the effective date of this amendatory act, or is being committed, used, or carried on, in violation of said section 2 as amended by this act, it shall make a report in writing in which it shall state its findings as to the facts and shall issue and serve upon such person its order modifying or amending its original order to include any additional violations of law so found. Thereafter the provisions of section 11 of said act of October 15, 1914, as to review and enforcement of orders of the Commission shall in all things apply to such modified or amended order. If upon review as provided in said section 11 the court shall set aside such modified or amended order, the original order shall not be affected thereby, but it shall be and remain in force and effect as fully and to the same extent as if such supplementary proceedings had not been taken.

SEC. 3. If any part, clause, sentence, or paragraph of this act shall, for any reason, be adjudged by any court of competent jurisdiction to be invalid, such judgment shall not affect, impair, or invalidate the remainder thereof, but shall be confined in its operation to the part, clause, sentence, or paragraph thereof directly involved in the controversy or proceeding in which such judgment shall have been rendered.

The above proposals are self-explanatory, but I may add that section 2 will be offered to protect the proceedings that have already been had in the Goodyear Tire & Rubber Co. case, and section 3 is merely the separability amendment.

BASING-POINT PROVISION STRICKEN OUT
(Page 8223, May 28)

Mr. CITRON.   Mr. Chairman, if this provision remains in the bill, it would result in forcing f. o. b. prices on manufacturers; but with this provision eliminated they will not be forced to charge f. o. b. prices. Otherwise, many would not be able to compete with foreign manufacturers, for instance, from Canada, who would not be subject to this provision if it remained in the bill.

The paragraph in this bill that we are eliminating is as follows:

(5) That the word "price" as used in section 2 shall be construed to mean the amount received by the vendor after deducting freight or other transportation, if any, allowed or defrayed by the vendor.

I believe that there are very important reasons why this paragraph should be eliminated entirely, not only for the reason that there is already under consideration a bill which has separately and wholly to do with the basing-point price method, and on which committee hearings have been held, but also for the reason that the basing-point price method has some economically sound merits, and to prohibit the legitimate carrying on of this pricing system by industries will have serious consequences in many industries doing business within the confines of the United States. There is still a further most important reason why this particular definition of price should be eliminated from the instant bill, which is that it would compel all manufacturers and wholesalers under the jurisdiction of the United States Government to ship all their merchandise on an f. o. b. point of origin basis and the consequences of such a statute would be to place many of our manufacturers and wholesalers at a serious disadvantage when competing with foreign manufacturers and exporters who do business in the United States.

But this paragraph involves more than the so-called basing-point system. All this system does is to equalize the freight which the customers of a given manufacturer or wholesaler pay, thereby giving an opportunity to all customers to operate on the same equal basis. There is an economic justification of this system, because it provides an open and aboveboard method for manufacturers and wholesalers to meet competition outside of their own local freight area. Second, whatever the cost of equalizing freight may be, it is more than offset by the economies of volume production and volume distribution which the greater trading area provides. In other words, the volume production thus obtained lowers the manufacturers' and wholesalers' per-unit cost and enables them to make lower prices to their customers in their own local trading areas.

But a more serious consequence of the inclusion of this definition of price, as previously stated, would be to compel all manufacturers to ship f. o. b. shipping point, and therefore compel the very definite localization of operations of all manufacturers and wholesalers, which would have the immediate effect of increasing costs as the result of seriously limited volume production.

Volume production is the very lifeblood of many types of industries. If the products they manufacture cannot be made in large volume, upon which the low cost is dependent, the cost of the finished product would be so high that it would seriously curtail, if not entirely prohibit, their consumption.

This paragraph would seriously affect the publishers of national magazines, because it may mean that the national publishers cannot sell their magazines not only for the reason that the freight charges on the magazines to distant points will be so great as to prohibit the sale of the magazines at those points, but also for the reason that the magazines are dependent upon advertising revenues derived from national distributors whose operations will be seriously curtailed by this definition of price.

If this paragraph remains in this bill, it will mean the increased centralization of manufacturing in the more thickly populated industrial centers.

Some people say these consequences can easily be offset by manufacturers and wholesalers establishing wholesale-distributing points all over the United States. However, this would mean increasing the number of operations and the amount of handling, all of which entails increased cost which the consumer must pay, and only the larger manufacturers in the country could finance the cost, and it would mean the further submergence of the small industry and the small businessman, which would actually tend to enhance monopoly in all branches of industry.

Another very serious objection to this paragraph is that in many instances our manufacturers and wholesalers would be placed at a serious disadvantage in meeting competition of manufacturers in other countries. Take an instance from my own State—the Scoville Manufacturing Co., a large and old established concern which manufactures thousands of different kinds of metal products, from articles for personal use—such as buttons—to parts to be used in the manufacture of other merchandise. Under the terms of this definition of price in the instant bill, they would be compelled to charge freight from Connecticut to New York City, to Baltimore, to New Orleans, to San Francisco, to Detroit, or to Chicago, just to mention a few major manufacturing centers. A manufacturer in the same kind of business, located in Canada or in Europe, or any other industrial country, and who is not subject to the jurisdiction of our Federal statutes, would be able to deliver his products f. o. b. to every one of these industrial cities which I have mentioned for the reason that they are all direct ports of entry into the United States. By the wording of this definition of price in this paragraph, the Scoville Manufacturing Co. could not meet the foreign competition, nor could any other manufacturer in the United States, under like conditions, meet that competition. The only way open to them would be to set up manufacturing branches in Canada, which would have the effect of further increasing unemployment in the United States.

Because of the reasons that I have given, I also favor the exclusion of this paragraph.

Mr. MILLER.   I think the amendment ought to be adopted. I doubt whether that provision ought ever to be in this kind of bill anyway.

The CHAIRMAN.   I would like to submit as part of my remarks the letter of the Acting Chairman of the Federal Trade Commission.

FTC CHAIRMAN'S LETTER PROPOSES AMENDMENT
(*Page 8125*)

FEDERAL TRADE COMMISSION,
Washington, May 1, 1936.

HON. HATTON W. SUMNERS,
    Chairman of the Judiciary Committee,
        House of Representatives, Washington, D. C.

MY DEAR CHAIRMAN: I am handing you herewith suggested amendments to H. R. 8442, but which the Commission deems important amendments to whatever bill passes amending section 2 of the Clayton Act.

The principal suggested amendment is to make sure that any amendment of section 2 will not impair orders heretofore issued by the Commission under that section, notable among which is the recent order against the Goodyear Tire & Rubber Co. We deem it important not only that these existent orders be not affected by amendments to section 2, but also that provision be made whereby full competitive conditions may be restored or brought about by virtue of the amendments to section 2 by reopening the old case and thus avoid re-proof of facts that may be common to both the original and supplementary proceedings. Hence the proviso.

The other amendment is the usual provision covering possible partial invalidity of the provisions of the bill.

Sincerely yours,

W. A. AYRES, *Acting Chairman.*

Price Discrimination Clarified
(Page 8229)

Mr. BOILEAU. Mr. Chairman, for the purpose of clarifying the congressional intent, I have taken this time to get the opinion of the distinguished gentleman from Arkansas as to his understanding of the meaning of the language at the beginning of section 2 (a), page 5, of the bill. The section starts out as follows:

Sec. 2. (a) That it shall be unlawful for any person engaged in commerce, in the course of such commerce, either directly or indirectly, to discriminate in price between different purchasers of commodities of like grade and quality—

And so forth. My understanding of that language is that the sellers may not discriminate, but they may, nevertheless, charge different prices in different communities to persons who are not competitors. In other words, as I understand it—and I ask the gentleman whether or not this is his opinion— a seller may sell a commodity in one community at one price and sell it in another community at a different price, because those two purchasers, even though they are purchasers for resale, are not competitors, and therefore there is no discrimination in price. Is that the understanding of the distinguished gentleman from Arkansas [Mr. MILLER]?

Mr. MILLER. They are operating in different markets. I do not think there is any doubt about the language.

Mr. BOILEAU. I am asking these questions at the request of certain farm organizations, and I want to show the congressional intent.

Mr. MILLER. As indicated by the gentleman from Nebraska [Mr. McLAUGHLIN], the gentleman from Iowa [Mr. UTTERBACK], the gentleman from Nebraska [Mr. McLAUGHLIN], the gentleman from Michigan [Mr. MICHENER], and some others were appointed as a special subcommittee to work on this bill. That was our understanding. We undertook to draft a bill that would deal with the three principal things with which we are all familiar. It was not our intention to injure the organizations about which the gentleman is speaking. The gentleman has the right interpretation of the bill.

Mr. BOILEAU. In this particular letter, which refers to this particular section, I quote as follows:

We are fearful that this section, viewed in the light of the committee report, might be construed to mean that different prices could not be charged by the same seller in different markets.

Is it the gentleman's opinion that their fears in this respect are without foundation?

Mr. MILLER. They are entirely unfounded.

Advertising Allowances
(Page 8230)

Mr. BOILEAU. Mr. Chairman, the farm organizations have one further objection that needs clarification along the same line, and that is with reference to advertising allowances. They refer to sections 5 (c) and (d) insofar as these particular paragraphs affect advertising allowances.

In their communication they state as follows:

We are unwilling to have our operations put in a strait jacket under legislation which might require that if an advertising campaign is put on in Washington, D. C., a similar program must be followed in each market in the United States in which our cooperatives operate.

In other words, it is my understanding that under the language of the bill having to do with advertising allowances, paragraphs 5 (c) and (d), particularly (d), a manufacturer or other seller may give advertising allowances to stimulate trade in one community, but because he gives such advertising allowances in one community he is not required to give an identical, a similar, or a proportional advertising allowance to a customer in another community who is not in competition with the persons in the community in which the advertising allowances are granted.

Mr. MILLER.   The gentleman is correct, and I call attention to the specific provision of the act, which appears in lines 3 to 6, inclusive, page 9, reading as follows:

(d) By such person, unless such payment or consideration is available on proportionally equal terms to all other customers competing in the distribution of such products or commodities.

Competing in the distribution on that market, in that community, and in that place.

Do Not Weaken Robinson-Patman Act by Restoration of "Meet Competition" Clause Which Destroyed Effectiveness of Clayton Act
(Page 8231)

Mr. PATMAN.   Mr. Chairman, I rise in opposition to the amendment.

Mr. Chairman, it was just such amendments as this that led to the entire destruction of the Clayton Act in 1914. They commenced to put this plausible amendment in and that plausible amendment in, and by the time the Clayton Act was passed all the teeth were taken out and it was not enforceable.

We are trying to make the act enforceable. This sounds like a plausible amendment, but do you think the farmers are going to discriminate against anybody? Do you think there is a farmer in this country who is big enough so that he is going to take advantage of somebody through advertising allowances and dummy brokerages and quantity discounts? There is not one in this Nation who is large enough for that, and although there are some large and important livestock producers in the gentleman's district, there is not one so large that he can take advantage of Swift and Armour and the big packers in the markets of Kansas City.

The argument of the gentleman from Texas sounds plausible, but this bill is not to affect cases like that. It only applies to discriminations. It is enforcing honesty, and honesty should apply to the farmers and stock raisers, I will say to my dear friend from Texas, just the same as it applies to the businessman. I am not willing to exempt the farmers from a provision requiring common honesty, and that is all we are doing here, and if they are violating the rule of common honesty, they should suffer the penalty just the same as anyone else.

Now, with regard to the matter of burden of proof, that is an argument that sounds very plausible. Just such arguments as that have destroyed every antitrust law that has ever been presented to the American Congress.

Let me analyze that for you. What does that mean? It means exactly the rule of law today. It is a restatement of existing law. So far as I am concerned you can strike it out. It makes no difference. It is the law of this land exactly as it is written there. If the gentleman were to have a farmer or a livestock grower so large that he would discriminate, become dishonest, treat his customers unfairly, and there should be a charge or complaint filed against him before the Federal Trade Commission, what would he have to do? They would write him a letter and send him a copy of the charges, and under this bill he would rebut that by a statement of the actual facts, and that is all there is to it. If he is not dishonest, if he has not treated his customers unfairly, there will be nothing else in the world to it.

I hope you will not start amending this bill. The Judiciary Committee has worked on the bill for months and months. The subcommittee spent nights and days and Sundays and all the time in the world that a committee could give to legislation the committee gave to this bill. Now, if you start here with amendments that are hastily drawn and quickly considered, you are just as likely to have a law that will not be worth the paper it is written on like the present Clayton Act. Therefore I plead with you not to amend this bill; leave it like it is. It is a good bill.

We have considered what the gentleman from Texas has said. The committee has considered that matter. We are just as much interested in the welfare of the farmer and the stock grower and the others involved as is the gentleman. We yield to no man on questions of that kind and I hope the gentleman will withdraw the amendment. I think the gentleman should withdraw it in order that not one stone may be thrown in the way of passing this legislation that is very much needed, and needed now. For what? To save the business of the independent merchants of this country who are rapidly becoming victims no. 1, and to save the wage earners who will be forced to pauper wages if something is not done.

The farmers are forced to sell at a price that causes them to do without the comforts and necessities of life. The farmers and the wage earners are victim no. 2. Whenever a monopoly is created there will be another victim, and that will be the consumer. He will be victim no. 3. He will be a victim because the monopoly will pay the producer whatever they want to pay and they will charge the consumer the price they want to charge in order to make up the high bonuses they pay their officers. So I ask you to defeat this amendment.

Mr. MILLER. I do not think there is any reason for the amendment proposed by the gentleman from Texas [Mr. JONES]. I want to call your attention to the theory of this bill. What are we trying to do in this bill? I call your attention to the first section on page 5. I want to say further to you that the farmer selling livestock, or corn, or cotton, or anything else cannot possibly come under this act unless he is creating a monopoly, and if he is creating a monopoly, a monopoly created by a farmer is just as bad as a monopoly created by a manufacturer.

Let me call your attention to this language:

It shall be unlawful for any person engaged in commerce, in the course of such commerce, either directly or indirectly, to discriminate in price between purchasers of commodities of like grade and quality, where either or any of the purchasers involved in such discrimination are in commerce, where such commodities are sold for use—

Under certain conditions—

and where the effect of such discrimination may be substantially to lessen competition or tend to create a monopoly in any line of commerce, or to injure, destroy, or prevent competition with any person who either grants or receives the benefit of such discrimination.

Then I call your attention to something else. This bill does this, and this only: It prevents unfair quantity discounts, it prevents pseudo advertising allowances, it does away with fraudulent brokerage allowances, and that is all it does do. That is the theory of this bill. Of course, you can go out and dig up all kinds of scarecrows. You can set up all kinds of straw men and knock them down if you want to. You can bring in the farmer, you can bring in every class, but, after all, the question is this, whether or not we are going to let the monopolistic tendencies of the last 20 years continue.

I have no pride of authorship in this bill, although we worked very hard on it. They talk about apples and perishable goods. Let me call your attention to page 7, paragraph 3. It says:

That nothing herein contained shall prevent price changes from time to time where in response to changing conditions affecting the market for or the marketability of the goods concerned—

That takes care of the livestock people. It takes care of the things that the gentleman from Texas [Mr. JONES] is attempting to cure.

Then it says further:

such as but not limited to actual or imminent deterioration of perishable goods, obsolescence of seasonal goods, distress sales under court process.

Now, that is the situation that is confronting us here. I come from a rural district. If I ever return to the House it will be by the votes of the farmers. The largest town in my district is 6,000. Farmers are opposed to monopolies, and you cannot prevent monopolies if you pass an act like the old Clayton Act and shoot it full of provisos and amendments and loopholes.

DO NOT WEAKEN ROBINSON-PATMAN ACT BY INSERTING "PURCHASED UNDER LIKE CONDITIONS"
(Page 8235)

Mr. CELLER. Mr. Chairman, I offer an amendment.
The Clerk read as follows:

Amendment offered by Mr. CELLER: Page 5, line 8, after the word "quality," insert "purchased under like conditions"; also on page 5, line 22, after the word "quality," insert "purchased under like conditions."

Mr. CELLER. I maintain, and will maintain to the end of the discussion of this bill, that from what we have heard there is no question but that there can be no right to anyone selling goods to make any different prices to different customers where the goods are of like grade and quality and quantity, the gentleman from Texas notwithstanding.

The distinguished gentleman from Texas [Mr. PATMAN] put in the RECORD yesterday the following language:

Now, with regard to the statement made by the distinguished gentleman from New York [Mr. CELLER], here is what I said. I said that manufacturers would have to treat their customers alike and give them the same price, and I still say that. For what? For the same quantity under the same conditions. This is the part that the gentleman did not bring out. He simply failed to tell it all.

Now, I simply put his exact language in this amendment, and I say that where the goods are purchased thus under like conditions there can be no discrimination. When they are purchased under unlike conditions, the inference is there can be discrimination and change in price. That is logical and reasonable.

Now, if what the gentleman said this afternoon is so, he should not object to the amendment, as I have put his exact language in my amendment.

We know that goods may be of the same quantity, of the same quality, but may be purchased under unlike conditions. There may be different items of credit. One man may be entitled to a 60-day dating, while another man may be entitled only to cash on delivery. There may be questions of delivery datings. One man may want his deliveries within 10 days; another may want his deliveries in 60 days or 6 months or may want them daily. Certainly, where there are these different conditions, there ought to be the right given to effect a different price. He may want his goods with samples or he may want them without samples. There may be accorded the right to furnish demonstrators for toilet articles or similar goods or there may be no demonstrators. A man may have a strike on his hands or there may be a lock-out, or there may be no labor difficulties.

Certainly, if there are like conditions, there should be no discrimination, but if there are unlike conditions, which is the inference of my amendment, a man should have the right to contract under our Constitution as he sees fit and allow for these different conditions by a difference in price.

The bill, as now drafted, will not allow these differences and I urge upon you sincerely that you allow such differences, because of differing or unlike conditions. Put in the words to which the gentleman from Texas always adverts, namely "like conditions." He reiterates, "Under the same or like conditions." Put them in now. He questioned me yesterday and took me to task because I did not include these words. I include them now in the amendment and I offer them for your judicial and earnest consideration.

Mr. PATMAN.   Mr. Chairman, I rise in opposition to the amendment.

Mr. Chairman, the gentleman from New York is conscientiously opposed to this bill, and, naturally, he is going to do what he can to weaken it. If you were to adopt this amendment he would not vote for the bill. Therefore, he is trying to perfect it for us. So if it is already satisfactory to those of us who have been working on it in the committee and with the other sponsors of the legislation, why should he not let us have the bill we want.

If you put these words in the place where he proposes to insert them, without a sufficient explanation, you will just confuse the bill. You will have confusing language by placing them where he has proposed to put them.

What are the conditions? Delivery by truck, delivery over the railroad, delivery on a barge, delivery at a certain point that is a few miles removed from the other competitor. Any condition like this would remove the case from a question of discrimination if you were to adopt the gentleman's amendment.

The committee worked on this bill for months and a subcommittee worked on it for months. It is true they agreed to some amendments, but they have got a bill they think is all right, and I hope you do not amend it by putting in the weasel phrases and these statements that sound all right, but upon second thought or upon reflection or upon analysis, you find some of them are destructive of the purposes of the bill.

The CHAIRMAN.   The question is on the amendment offered by the gentleman from New York [Mr. CELLER].

The amendment was rejected.

ADVERTISING ALLOWANCES
(Page 8236)

Mr. BLOOM.   Mr. Chairman, I would like to call the attention of Members to paragraph (d). At no place in the bill is the word "advertising" used. It might refer to advertising, but it does not specifically say so. Now, clause (d) reads, as follows:

(d) That it shall be unlawful for any person engaged in commerce to pay or contract for the payment of anything of value to or for the benefit of a customer of such person in the course of such commerce as compensation or in consideration for any services or facilities furnished by or through such customer in connection with the processing, handling, sale, or offering for sale of any products or commodities manufactured, sold, or offered for sale by such person, unless such payment or consideration is available on proportionally equal terms to all other customers competing in the distribution of such products or commodities.

"Proportionally," it says. In other words, if the Coca Cola Co. should make a contract with a store, whether a drug store or grocery store or whatever it may be, and should say, if you buy $100 worth of goods we will give you a sign, then the fellow in the next street, or on the next corner, if he purchased only $50 worth of goods, according to this proposed bill, could have only half a sign. That is what it says. You cannot get away from the fact that this is not workable.

Mr. RAMSPECK.   Is there anything to keep the Coca Cola Co., or any other company, from going to drug stores and saying they want a certain amount of space?

Mr. BLOOM.   No; you cannot do that under this section. You prevent it from being done.

Mr. MICHENER.   The gentleman says that it cannot be done. The Coca Cola Co. under this bill could give anybody all the space they saw fit, but they could not give a discount or a lower price to someone for space which is not used.

Mr. BLOOM.   That has nothing to do with this section. This is for services or facilities furnished. It has nothing to do with price.

Mr. MICHENER.   But that is where these phony discriminations come in. They claim they render a service which they do not render.

To finish this up, that is one of the troubles and discriminations here—that one of these manufacturers will sell to one store, say, a million units, provided they do so much advertising, and then, in turn, will exchange checks and pay the purchaser for doing the advertising, and the advertising consists in hanging up a 2 by 4 sign.

ADVERTISING ALLOWANCES
(*Page 8237, May 28*)

Mr. RAMSPECK.   I do not read anything in this bill which would prevent the Coca Cola Co., for instance, from going to a druggist and making an agreement with him to put a sign across the top of his window. They can either pay him for it or they could do it for nothing. Am I correct?

Mr. McLAUGHLIN.   That is correct. But there must be no discrimination. He has to do it under such terms and conditions that there is no discrimination between competitors.

Mr. RAMSPECK.   The gentleman does not understand my question. I say if he goes there, not in connection with the sale of Coca Cola, but goes to the merchant and says, "I want to put a Coca-Cola sign across the top of your window," but it has no connection with a sale, there is nothing to prevent that, is there?

Mr. McLAUGHLIN.   They would no doubt take into consideration whether or not that was a subterfuge in a sale or an independent transaction.

CONSTITUTIONALITY
(*Page 8240*)

Mr. GILCHRIST.   Mr. Chairman, I want to call attention to the Sugar Institute case relied upon by the distinguished attorney from New York [Mr. CELLER], who stated, on page 8342 of the RECORD, that any lawyer worth his salt would have to say that this bill is unconstitutional. He gave us an excerpt from that case which in itself, if properly applied, shows the contrary and that this bill is really constitutional.

But I want to call attention to another thing that the Supreme Court said in that case:

The restrictions imposed by the Sherman Act are not mechanical or artificial. We have repeatedly said that they set up the essential standard of reasonableness. (*Standard Oil Co.* v. *United States,* 221 U. S. 1; *United States* v. *American Tobacco Co.,* 221 U. S. 106.) They are aimed at contracts and combinations which "by reason of intent or the inherent nature of the contemplated acts, prejudice the public interests by unduly restraining competition or unduly obstructing the course of trade" (*Nash* v. *United States,* 229 U. S. 373, 376; *United States* v. *American Linseed Oil Co.,* 262 U. S. 371, 388, 389). Designed to frustrate unreasonable restraints, they do not prevent the adoption of reasonable means to protect interstate commerce from destructive or injurious practices and to promote competition upon a sound basis.

This bill is exactly in line with that decision. It is an attempt to adopt reasonable means to protect interstate commerce from destructive and injurious practices and to promote competition on a sound basis. It is designed to do away with fraudulent practices and secret rebates. It prevents unfair and destructive discriminations which work against the small country storekeeper and in favor of the big and powerful merchant. It prevents unfair discriminations only. It allows and upholds fair and open practices. For example, it allows proper and reasonable discounts and allowances for quantity purchasing. But such discounts and allowances must not be tricky and fraudulent ones. They must not be allowances which are discriminatory. The jobber, under the bill, will have a perfect right to give discounts resulting from quantity purchases provided that these discounts have a reasonable relation to the transaction itself and are based on the difference in the cost of manufacture or of sale or of delivery. What else ought they to be based upon? The manufacturer can give a discount to quantity purchasers if it is based upon a difference in the cost of manufacturing a large quantity instead of the small amount; or if it is based upon the difference in selling a large quantity instead of a small amount; or if it is based upon the difference in cost of delivering a quantity instead of a small amount. The bill has been misrepresented in this respect. And these are the very kind or character of things that were upheld in the Sugar Institute case. In that case the lower court enjoined the sugar-refining companies from engaging in some 45 activities. About 2 months ago the Supreme Court of the United States passed upon it and upheld about 42 or 43 of these injunctions, and thereby appellants were prevented from doing many things that were in restraint of interstate and foreign commerce in violation of the Sherman Antitrust Act. Instead of being an authority against the legality of the present proposal, the Sugar Institute case undoubtedly warrants us in saying that the present bill is constitutional. Just why the distinguished jurist and gentleman from New York [Mr. CELLER] cited it and quoted from it is very strange. And when he said in his speech that any lawyer worth his salt would have to agree that the present bill is unconstitutional, he was undoubtedly indulging in hyperbole, which in rhetoric is defined to be a figure of speech in which the expression is exaggerated fancifully through excitement or for effect.

Along the same line, something has been said in argument about the burden of proof, and it has been asserted that the bill is not constitutional because those who have specific and certain knowledge of their own good faith are permitted to prove it. We should distinguish between the duty of going forward with the evidence and the burden of proof. It is often wise to place the burden of producing evidence on the party best able to sustain it. It is very often held that where the party who does not have the original burden of proof, but who does possess positive and complete knowledge concerning the existence of facts which his opponent is called upon to negative; or, where, for any reason, the evidence to prove a fact is chiefly, if not entirely, within the control of the party who does not have the general or original burden of proof, then the burden of going forward with and producing this evidence rests upon him who does have the facts primarily and chiefly within his possession.

Paragraph (e) of section 2 of the bill does not provide that the burden of proof shall shift at any stage of the proceedings. On the other hand, it provides that, after it has been shown that a discrimination in price has really occurred, then the duty of going forward with the evidence to show justification and good faith rests upon the party who has almost exclusive possession of such evidence of good faith, and who has easy means of proving it. We should pass the bill and send it to conference.

BILL PASSES 290 TO 16
(Page 8242)

The SPEAKER. The question is on the passage of the bill.

The question was taken; and on a division (demanded by Mr. DIES) there were ayes 290 and noes 16.

So the bill was passed.

FURTHER EXPLANATION OF THE BILL
(Page 9415, June 15)

Mr. UTTERBACK. Mr. Speaker, I want to state for the convenience of the Members and, so far as I can, in terms that can be understood and applied by the man in the street some of the outstanding features of the practical operation of the bill. In so doing I want to address myself first to the three principal objections which opponents have urged against the bill. I refer to the claims, first, that it will injure the cooperative movement; second, that it will raise prices to consumers; and, third, that it will ruin small manufacturers.

BENEFIT TO COOPERATIVES

I need not pause to describe the cooperative movement. You are all familiar with it, whether it be a cooperative of farmers to buy what they need or to sell what they produce; a cooperative of consumers to purchase the necessities of life; or a cooperative of independent merchants to buy what they propose to sell across the counter to their consumer customers. I need only remind you that in its essential character the cooperative movement is a device whereby individual smaller units in production, distribution, or consumption associate themselves together in a collective activity for the purpose of achieving the economies and price advantages of larger scale operations. This bill reserves those advantages and expressly authorizes their translation into differences in price wherever those differences represent real economies.

This bill will afford positive protection to cooperatives in two ways: First, it will reduce the menace of oppressive discrimination in favor of larger corporate competitors against which cooperative activity is now defensively necessary; second, it will insure to cooperatives enterprise the fuller fruits of its activity. It will guarantee to it the achievement of the full economies and price advantages to which the size and scale of its operations actually entitle it as compared with its larger corporate competitors.

So far as concerns freedom to organize cooperative enterprises, freedom of those enterprises to deal with others, either in the purchase of needs for their members, or in the sale of their members' products; and so far as concerns full freedom to distribute among their members any earnings or surplus resulting from their trading operations, there is nothing whatever in the bill to impede or limit those activities. There is, on the contrary, an express reservation, denying any intent or effect to limit cooperatives in the distribution of their earnings or surplus to their members on a patronage basis.

It is evident, upon a full examination of the bill, that not only is there nothing in it to hurt cooperatives, but that there is much in it to protect and assist them.

BENEFIT TO THE CONSUMER

Equally unfounded is their claim that the bill will increase consumer price levels. Upon what do consumer prices depend? Fundamentally upon the physical economies and efficiencies of production and distribution. There is nothing in this bill to affect them. Its opponents insist that it shackles efficiency. On the contrary, it expressly reserves the rewards of efficiency and economy, whether in manufacture, sale, or distribution, and authorizes their transmission into price differences in favor of the buyer whose methods or quantities make them possible. But they say it will compel the chain to pay more for its goods and they will therefore have to charge more to their customers. It will compel them to pay more only where they are now getting lower prices at the expense of their competitors only where through those lower prices they are now not paying their proper share of the seller's burden of cost, which he must therefore recover in higher prices from his other buyers, to wit: the competitors of the chains. If the bill will compel the chains to pay more for their goods, it will enable their competitors to buy for less and therefore to sell to their consumer customers for less. Remember, that not all chains receive these forbidden allowances. It is only the largest who do so. Out of the several hundreds of corporate chains in the food field, probably not more than 25 receive allowances and discriminations of the kind this bill would forbid; and out of those the larger receive them disproportionately to the smaller. If this bill will raise prices to the consumer who purchases from the few big chains, it will lower prices to the consumers who purchase from all other merchants.

But in any case this claim assumes that the discriminations in price granted to large mass buyers are actually passed on in lower prices to the consumer. There is no evidence that this is true. There is, on the contrary, evidence that it is not true. In the first place, it is still an open question whether the consumer prices offered by large chains and mass distributors are on an average lower than those of their efficient independent competitors, or whether they are due to the elimination of services such as delivery and credit, which throw a corresponding burden upon the consumer, and to unfair merchandising such as the skillful use of the loss-leader, a bargain held out as bait to lure the customer into the store where she buys before she leaves a variety of other and higher-priced articles upon which the real profit is made. But assuming for the moment that big chain prices are lower on the whole than independent competitor prices, and assuming what they also claim, namely that chain methods of distribution are more efficient and economical than those of their independent competitors, then those lower prices may well be accounted for on the basis of that very efficiency; and that efficiency this bill does not in the least disturb.

But there is nothing to indicate that the discriminations and allowances, such as this bill will forbid, ever find their way to any great extent into price reductions to the consumer. There is, on the other hand, a great deal to indicate that those discriminations and allowances go instead to make up the excessive salaries paid to mass buyer executives, and the excessive profits paid to their owners. Hearings before the House Judiciary Committee and the Patman Special Investigating Committee showed that one large chain received in one year discriminations and allowances aggregating over $8,000,000. Where did it go? Evidently $2,000,000 of it went to pay a list of its chain executives, each of whom received more than $100,000 a year. The other $6,000,000 went to inflate its net profits to a total of $16,000,000 on that year's operations, and of that $16,000,000, 90 to 95 percent evidently went into the pockets of two men, who are its principal stockholders. The remainder went to a few of its employees who share the remainder of its technical ownership.

BENEFIT TO THE SMALL MANUFACTURER

Now as to the small manufacturer. Discriminatory prices and allowances are a millstone around the neck of the manufacturer, large or small; because in granting favors to a selected few of their customers, they give those few a competitive advantage over the rest, and enable them gradually to drive the rest out of business and thereby to destroy them as customers. In granting such discriminations the manufacturer is therefore committing a form of slow suicide, and many a manufacturer has discovered that to his sorrow after it is too late. But so far as they constitute a weapon of competition, they are by nature most effective in the hands of the larger manufacturer against his smaller competitor. Discriminations of the kind forbidden by this bill involve a loss to the seller of his necessary profit and cost on the favored customer's business; and that loss the seller is compelled to make up in higher prices to his other customers, or his business will land in the red. The more far-flung his operations, the larger his business, and the greater his list of customers, the more reserve has he at his disposal on which to absorb those losses, and the deeper the price cut he can afford rather than lose a large customer's business to a competitor. Likewise the deeper the price cut he can afford to offer the larger customers of his various competitors, to induce them to switch their business to him.

Scan the list of manufacturers who were revealed in the hearings of the Patman committee as granting these excessive allowances, and you will note that they are in nearly every case the leading and largest manufacturers in their respective commodity fields. Where smaller ones also give these allowances, they are compelled to do so in self-defense. But it is frequently physically impossible for them to do so.

But it is further claimed that the provisions of the bill with regard to advertising allowances work a hardship on the small manufacturer, in that they require such allowances to be granted to all competing customers on proportionally equal terms. But proportional to what? Proportional naturally to those customers' purchases and to their ability and equipment to render or furnish the services or facilities to be paid for. But the small manufacturer is small either because he has fewer customers or because their purchases are small, and in either case his responsibilities under this bill are correspondingly small. Here again the freedom to favor large customers with discriminatory advertising allowances is a peculiar advantage to the large manufacturer, just as it is to the large customer; for whatever he sacrifices of necessary cost or profit in granting such an allowance, he can the more easily make up in the profits from his other business—on the business of smaller customers to whom such allowances are denied.

Thus, the menaces to the cooperative, to the farmer, the consumer, and the small manufacturer, which some claim to see in this bill, lose their substance and turn out to be advantages instead. It is, indeed, not without significance to those who have followed the hearings on this subject before the committees of this House, and listen to its debate upon this floor, that fears of its injury to the farmers came not from the farmers themselves or from their representatives in Congress, but from the metropolitan centers; that fears of injuries to cooperatives came not from the rank and file of cooperatives themselves, but from corporate interests who buy and sell in competition with cooperatives; and that fears of its injury to the consumer came not from the consumer as such, but from a few who pocket millions in salaries and profits reaped from selling to the consumer his necessities of life.

But the real value of this bill is not to be measured in dollars and cents, nor determined by the price levels offered by particular manufacturers or merchants. Seventy-five millions of our people live in urban and rural communities under 25,000 population. These communities depend primarily upon local enterprise for the support of their social, educational, and spiritual institutions, their schools, their churches, their hospitals, their civic enterprises of all kinds. The backbone of that local enterprise is the local independent businessman, whether manufacturer, merchant, or producer of raw materials. It is a mistake to assume that he is less efficient just because he is small. For that very reason, on the contrary, he is often the more efficient. He has less overhead, less of a top-heavy, unwieldy organization, less of his activities devoted to the crushing of competition rather than to services really productive. Yet his nonresident competitor, armed with the privilege of price discriminations and allowances now permitted by law, with the financial resources furnished by metropolitan banks, and with the ability to absorb losses with excessive profits in noncompetitive territory, is able to come into that local community, plant a competing enterprise next door to the local manufacturer or merchant, cut prices below cost, and crush his superior efficiency with no other weapons than those of greater size and the power of outside resources. In the assurance of equal opportunity and fair play which this bill gives to local independent business, it guarantees the integrity and wholesomeness of local community life against corruption and impoverishment by these sinister influences.

OPERATION OF PARTICULAR PROVISIONS

Let us turn now to the bill itself and examine the operation of its particular provisions.

DISCRIMINATION

In its meaning as simple English a discrimination is more than a mere difference. Underlying the meaning of the word is the idea that some relationship exists between the parties to the discrimination which entitles them to equal treatment, whereby the difference granted to one casts some burden of disadvantage upon the other. If the two are competing in the resale of the goods concerned, that relationship exists. Where, also, the price to one is so low as to involve a sacrifice of some part of the seller's necessary costs and profit as applied to that business, it leaves that deficit inevitably to be made up in higher prices to his other customers; and there, too, a relationship may exist upon which to base the charge of discrimination. But where no such relationship exists, where the goods are sold in different markets and the conditions affecting those markets set different price levels for them, the sale to different customers at those different prices would not constitute a discrimination within the meaning of this bill.

BETWEEN PURCHASERS

The bill prohibits such discriminations where either or any of the purchasers involved in such discrimination are in interstate commerce. Where a manufacturer sells only to customers within the State, his business is beyond the reach of Federal authority and is not included within the provisions of this bill. This exemption, however, is not important for practical purposes. He may not sell to a mass buyer at discriminatory prices for delivery within the State and shipment then to other States, since such sales are, by long-settled law, interstate commerce. Moreover, the important discriminations here forbidden are of a kind that can only be granted to some at the expense of the rest. The small manufacturer, operating purely within the State, ordinarily lacks the diversified list of customers which he must have in order to absorb from them his losses in price cuts to a favored few. Since his smaller customers can always go to the interstate seller, even within the same State, and demand the same prices granted to his larger interstate buyers, the small intrastate seller is precluded from raising his prices to his smaller customers sufficiently to absorb such losses.

Where, however, a manufacturer sells to customers both within the State and beyond the State, he may not favor either to the disadvantage of the other; he may not use the privilege of interstate commerce to the injury of his local trade, nor may he favor his local trade to the injury of his interstate trade. The Federal power to regulate interstate commerce is the power both to limit its employment to the injury of business within the State, and to protect interstate commerce itself from injury by influences within the State.

I shall deal later with the question of discrimination to meet competition.

EFFECT ON COMPETITION

The discriminations prohibited by this bill are those whose effect may be:

1. Substantially to lessen competition in any line of commerce; or,
2. To tend to create a monopoly in any line of commerce; or,
3. To injure, destroy, or prevent competition:

   (a) With any person who either grants or knowingly receives the benefit of such discrimination; or,

   (b) With customers of either of them (i. e., the grantor or grantee).

Effects nos. 1 and 2 above correspond to those required to be shown under the old section 2 of the Clayton Act. Generally speaking, they require a showing of effect upon competitive conditions generally in the line of commerce and market territory concerned, as distinguished from the effect of the discrimination upon immediate competition with the grantor or grantee. The difference may be illustrated where a nonresident concern opens a new branch beside a local concern, and with the use of discriminatory prices destroys and replaces the local concern as the competitor in the local field. Competition in the local field generally has not been lessened, since one competitor has been replaced by another; but competition with the grantor of the discrimination has been destroyed. The present bill is, therefore, less rigorous in its provisions as to the effect required to be shown in order to bring a given discrimination within its prohibitions.

DIFFERENCES IN COST

The bill expressly exempts from its prohibitions, however, price differentials.

Which make only due allowance for differences in the cost of manufacture, sale, or delivery resulting from the differing methods or quantities in which such commodities are to such purchasers sold or delivered. (That is, in which the commodities concerned are sold or delivered to the purchasers between whom the price differential is made.)

It is through this clause that the bill assures to the mass distributor, as to everyone else, full protection in the use and rewards of efficient methods in production and distribution in return for depriving him of the right to crush his efficient smaller competitors with the power and resources of mere size. There is no limit to the phases of production, sale, and distribution in which such improvements may be devised and the economies of superior efficiency achieved, nor from which those economies, when demonstrated, may be expressed in price differentials in favor of the particular customers whose distinctive methods of purchase and delivery make them possible. They apply as between purchasers of materials for use in manufacture, as well as between those who purchase purely as retail or wholesale distributors. As between purchasers in equal quantities, for example, where one takes multiple store-door delivery, and the other single warehouse delivery, with consequent savings in trucking or other delivery costs to the seller, that saving may be expressed in a price differential. Or where one places a single order calling for periodic deliveries over an extended period of time, whereas the other places smaller successive orders requiring more frequent and therefore more costly salesman solicitation, such a difference in cost may be expressed in a price differential. Or where one customer, devoid of storage facilities, requires spot deliveries during the rush of the season, for which the manufacturer must produce in advance and store himself in order to make the fullest utilization of his plant capacity; while another customer orders for delivery in off seasons, handling the storage himself and saving the manufacturer that cost, such a saving may be expressed in a price differential.

Or where one customer orders from hand to mouth during the rush of the season, compelling the employment of more expensive overtime labor in order to fill his orders; while another orders far in advance, permitting the manufacturer to use cheaper off-season labor, with the elimination of overtime, or perhaps to buy his raw materials at cheaper off-season prices, such savings as between the two customers may likewise be expressed in price differentials. So also where a manufacturer or merchant sells to some customer through traveling-salesman solicitation, to others across the counter, and to others by mail order from catalog, price differentials may be made to reflect the differing costs of such varying methods of sale. These examples are illustrative of the way in which the bill permits the translation of differences in cost into price differentials as between the customers concerned, no matter where those differences arise.

But the bill does not permit price differentials merely because the quantities purchased are different, or merely because the methods of selling or delivery are different, or merely because the seasons of the year in which they enable production are different. There must be a difference in cost shown as between the customers involved in the discrimination, and that difference must be one "resulting from the differing methods or quantities in which such commodities are to such purchasers sold or delivered." A customer granted the benefit of a discrimination may receive it only on the basis of the difference between his methods or quantities of purchase and delivery and those of other customers not receiving the differential.

Such a difference cannot be claimed on the basis of a difference in cost in the seller's entire business with and without the purchases of the customer in question. If his purchases so increase the seller's volume as to make possible a reduction in unit cost upon his entire business, other customers are entitled to share also in the benefit of that reduction. The differential granted a particular customer must be traceable to some difference between him and other particular customers, either in the quantities purchased by them or in the methods by which they are purchased or their delivery taken.

Where the methods of delivery are the same, but the distance is different, price differences in such cases may of course be made to reflect those differences. In such case the price is really paid both for the commodity itself and for its delivery, and the differing freight rates or commercial trucking rates applicable to the different delivery distances involved, are of course differences in cost which may be reflected in differences in such delivered prices.

QUANTITY LIMITS

One proviso of the act authorizes the Federal Trade Commission to fix quantity limits as to various commodities, and when so fixed further price differentials are not permitted on account of quantities purchased in excess of those limits. The rule laid down for the Commission's guidance in this respect is that it find—

That available purchasers in greater quantities are so few as to render differentials on account thereof unjustly discriminatory or promotive of monopoly in any line of commerce.

This limitation, however, does not become effective as to any commodity until the Federal Trade Commission has acted under this authority with respect to the commodity in question. Until then the granting of price differentials between purchasers of such commodities remains subject only to the other limitations under the bill, the chief of which is the requirement that they be supported by a showing of differences in cost as between the methods of sale or delivery or the quantities purchased by the buyers concerned.

SELECTION OF CUSTOMERS

The bill contains the proviso already contained in the present Clayton Act permitting sellers to select their own customers in bona-fide transactions and not in restraint of trade. This permits, however, the selection of customers and not the selection of what shall be sold to them. It is intended to protect the buyer against customers who are troublesome in their methods or insecure in their credit. It does not permit the buyer, once he has accepted a customer, to refuse discriminatorily to sell to him particular distinctions of quality, grade, or brand which the seller has set aside for exclusive sale at more favorable prices to selected customers in evasion of the purposes of this bill. Nor does it permit absolute refusal to sell to particular customers, where the facts are such as to show that it is done for the purpose of injuring or destroying them and that the elimination of their competition effects a restraint of trade.

MARKET CHANGES, PERISHABLES, ETC.

Although the present Clayton Act has never been differently construed, Congress has in the fullness of caution inserted in the present bill a proviso exempting from its prohibitions—

Price changes from time to time where in response to changing conditions affecting the market for or the marketability of the goods concerned, such as but not limited to actual or imminent deterioration of perishable goods, obsolescence of seasonal goods, distress sales under court process, or sales in good faith in discontinuance of business in the goods concerned.

This, however, is intended for protection of purely legitimate trade movements. The merchant or manufacturer who resorts to it as a cloak for price discriminations contrary to the spirit and purpose of this bill is likely to pay dearly for the lessons of experience. Wherever there are suspicious circumstances to indicate that such was the intent, the burden of proof, as in the case of other provisos granting exemptions from the bill, is upon the seller or other offender claiming the benefit of the proviso. The liberty of "price changes from time to time," as herein conferred, may not be held to extend, for example, to a price drop placed in effect one-half hour before the expected arrival of a large buyer representative whom it is desired to favor, with its restoration upward a half hour after his departure. Whether price changes are of a character justified by the causes here described is a question of fact, and where that question comes to issue, the burden of proof is upon the offending party claiming its protection.

BURDEN OF PROOF

Owing to a body of court decisions to the effect that the legal rules of evidence do not in certain respects apply to hearings before administrative commissions, and to the uncertainty thus suggested, the bill contains a subsection stating the rule as to burden of proof, substantially as suggested above, as applicable to hearings before the Federal Trade Commission.

MEETING COMPETITION

In connection with the above rule as to burden of proof, it is also provided that a seller may show that his lower price was made in good faith to meet an equally low price of a competitor, or that his furnishing of services or facilities was made in good faith to meet those furnished by a competitor. It is to be noted, however, that this does not set up the meeting of competition as an absolute bar to a charge of discrimination under the bill. It merely permits it to be shown in evidence. This provision is entirely procedural. It does not determine substantive rights, liabilities and duties. They are fixed in the other provisions of the bill. It leaves it a question of fact to be determined in each case, whether the competition to be met was such as to justify the discrimination given, as one lying within the limitations laid down by the bill, and whether the way in which the competition was met lies within the latitude allowed by those limitations.

This procedural provision cannot be construed as a carte blanche exemption to violate the bill so long as a competitor can be shown to have violated it first, nor so long as that competition cannot be met without the use of oppressive discriminations in violation of the obvious intent of the bill.

To illustrate: The House committee hearings showed a discrimination of 15 cents a box granted by Colgate-Palmolive-Peet Co. on sales of soap to the A. & P. chain. Upon a complaint and hearing before the Federal Trade Commission, this proviso would permit the Colgate Co. to show in rebuttal evidence, if such were the fact, an equally low price made by a local soap manufacturer in Des Moines, Iowa, to A. & P.'s retail outlets in that city; but this would not exonerate it from a discrimination granted to A. & P. everywhere, if otherwise in violation of the bill.

But the committee hearings show a similar discount of 15 cents a case granted by Procter & Gamble to the same chain. If this proviso were construed to permit the showing of a competing offer as an absolute bar to liability for discrimination, then it would nullify the act entirely at the very inception of its enforcement; for in nearly every case mass buyers receive similar discriminations from competing sellers of the same product. One violation of law cannot be permitted to justify another. As in any case of self-defense, while the attack against which the defense is claimed may be shown in evidence, its competency as a bar depends also upon whether it was a legal or illegal attack. A discrimination in violation of this bill is in practical effect a commercial bribe to lure the business of the favored customer away from the competitor, and if one bribe were permitted to justify another, the bill would be futile to achieve its plainly intended purposes.

BROKERAGE

The bill prohibits payment or allowance of brokerage or commission except for services rendered. As explained more fully in the report of the House Committee on the Judiciary, this refers to true brokerage services rendered in fact for the party who pays for them, whether he be an agent employed and paid by the seller to find market outlets or one employed and paid by the buyer to find sources of supply. As the bill further enumerates, it prohibits the payment or allowance of commissions or brokerage on the purchase or sale of goods either to the other party to the transaction or to an intermediary who is acting in fact for or under the control of the other party to the transaction; that is, the party other than the one who pays the commission or brokerage in question. There is nothing in the bill that requires the employment of a broker; there is nothing to prevent sales direct from seller to buyer. But if an intermediary is employed, and is in fact acting for or under the control of the buyer, then the seller cannot pay him. Or if he is acting for or under the control of the seller, then the buyer cannot pay him. And where sales are made from buyer to seller, in the nature of the case no brokerage services are rendered by either, and no payment or allowance on account thereof can be made by either party to the other.

SERVICES OR FACILITIES PAID FOR

The bill prohibits the seller from paying the customer for services or facilities furnished by the latter in connection with the seller's goods, unless such payment is available on proportionally equal terms to all other competing customers. The existing evil at which this part of the bill is aimed is, of course, the grant of discriminations under the guise of payments for advertising and promotional services which, whether or not the services are actually rendered as agreed, results in an advantage to the customer so favored as compared with others who have to bear the cost of such services themselves. The prohibitions of the bill, however, are made intentionally broader than this one sphere, in order to prevent evasion in resort to others by which the same purpose might be accomplished, and it prohibits payment for such services or facilities whether furnished "in connection with the processing, handling sale, or offering for sale" of the products concerned.

SERVICES AND FACILITIES FURNISHED

The bill also prohibits the seller from furnishing services or facilities to the purchaser in connection with the processing, handling, or sale of the commodities concerned unless they are accorded to all purchasers on proportionally equal terms. Again the last phrase has reference to the several purchasers' equipment and ability to satisfy the terms upon which the offer is made, or the services, or facilities furnished to any other purchaser.

There are many ways in which advertising, sales, and other services and facilities may be either furnished or paid for by the seller upon terms that will at once satisfy the requirements of the bill concerning equitable treatment of all customers, and at the same time satisfy the legitimate business needs of both the seller and the purchaser.

THE BUYER'S LIABILITY

The closing paragraph of the Clayton Act amendment, for which section 1 of this bill provides, makes equally liable the person who knowingly induces or receives a discrimination in price prohibited by the amendment. This affords a valuable support to the manufacturer in his efforts to abide by the intent and purpose of the bill. It makes it easier for him to resist the demand for sacrificial price cuts coming from mass buyer customers, since it enables him to charge them with knowledge of the illegality of the discount, and equal liability for it, by informing them that it is in excess of any differential which his difference in cost would justify as compared with his other customers.

This paragraph makes the buyer liable for knowingly inducing or receiving any discrimination in price which is unlawful under the first paragraph of the amendment. That applies both to direct and indirect discrimination; and where, for example, there is discriminaton in terms of sale, or in allowances connected or related to the contract of sale, of such a character as to constitute or effect an indirect discrimination in price, the liability for knowingly inducing or receiving such discriminaton or allowance is clearly provided for under the later paragraph above referred to.

SECTION 2. PENDING CASES

Section 2 of the bill—not section 2 of the Clayton Act, which section 1 of this bill proposes to amend—imposes temporary procedural requirements applicable to pending rights of action, complaints, or litigation, and is designed to enable the revision of existing or future orders of the Federal Trade Commission arising out of such claims harmoniously with the provisions of this amendment without the necessity of instituting a new proceeding.

SECTION 3. PENAL PROVISIONS

Section 3 of the bill sets aside certain practices therein described and attaches to their commission the criminal penalties of fine and imprisonment therein provided. It does not affect the scope or operation of the prohibitions or limitations laid down by the Clayton Act amendment provided for in section 1. It authorizes nothing therein prohibited. It detracts nothing from them. Most of the acts which it does prohibit lie also within the prohibitions of that amendment. In that sphere this section merely attaches to them its criminal penalties in addition to the civil liabilities and remedies already provided by the Clayton Act.

SECTION 4. COOPERATIVES

Section 4 represents another provision added to the bill in the fulness of caution to protect the distribution of cooperative earnings or surplus among their members on a patronage basis. In the dealings of cooperatives with others they share, of course, the protections and guaranties of the bill as to equal treatment and equal opportunity which it extends to producers, manufacturers, and merchants in trade and commerce generally. It leaves the members of cooperatives free to seek through cooperative endeavor the economies and savings of mass operations and assures to them, as compared with their larger corporate competitors, any real economies and savings to which those mass operations entitle them, and which they often now do not receive. There is nothing in the last section of the bill that distinguishes cooperatives, either favorably or unfavorably, from other agencies in the streams of production and trade, so far as concerns their dealings with others.

HOUSE ACCEPTS CONFEREES' REPORT

Borah–Van Nuys Amendment

(Page 9421)

Mr. MILLER. Section 3 is the Borah–Van Nuys amendment. We accepted that amendment for this reason and this reason only. The first section of the bill as reported back here amends section 2 of the Clayton Act. That is the House bill substantially, and when I say to you it is substantially the House bill, every amendment that was offered in the Senate to the Patman bill was receded from by the Senate.

Triple Damages

Mr. MASSINGALE. Does the bill as agreed to by the conferees carry the penalty of triple damages and also a penalty under the criminal law?

Mr. MILLER. The penalty of triple damages is the old law. In other words, we made no change in that particular provision of the Clayton Act. Section 3, which the gentleman from New York talks about, is the Borah–Van Nuys amendment, and that is the criminal section of this bill. The first part of the bill has nothing to do with criminal offenses. It deals primarily, in my opinion, with the authority of the Federal Trade Commission to regulate and enforce the provisions of section 2 of the Clayton Act, as amended. Section 3 in the bill is placed in an effort to make the criminal offense apply only to that particular section, and I believe that is a reasonable construction, if you will look at the bill.

Criminal Offense

Mr. MASSINGALE. There is no criminal offense involved for anything outside of what is contained in that section?

Mr. MILLER. In section 3.

Mr. HANCOCK of New York. Is it not perfectly clear that any vendor who discriminates in price between purchasers is guilty of a crime and is also subject to triple damages to anyone who claims to be aggrieved?

Mr. MILLER. That is true, but the criminal part is included in section 3 and section 3 only.

Mr. HANCOCK of New York. But it is a part of the same act?

Mr. MILLER. Of course it is, but it is not a part of the Clayton Act as amended by section 2. It ought to be, as far as that is concerned, if a seller willfully discriminates.

Mr. MILLER. Mr. Speaker, I want to say if the Congress really wants a bill amending the Clayton Act, and desires to retain the three objectives of the House bill, the conferees on the part of the House, excluding myself, did a good job and brought back to the House a bill which thoroughly represents, in their opinion, and in my opinion, the expressed will of the House as indicated by the passage of the Patman bill. [Applause.]

FINALE
(Page 9422)

Mr. PATMAN.   Mr. Speaker, a million and a half independent retail dealers in this country are interested in this bill, including druggists, grocers, and others. They are not asking for special privileges, special rights, or special benefits. They are just asking for a fair, square deal. That is all they are asking for and that is all this bill will give them. It will not deprive any person of any privilege or benefit that he is now receiving and which he is as a matter of right entitled to receive. It will help farmers, wage earners, and the consumers generally.

This bill grants each and every one the opportunity to do an honest, legitimate business, and protects him from cheaters and racketeers. It is not going to hurt any manufacturer or producer who is doing an honest business and treating all of his customers in the same fair, square way that he should treat all of them.

This is a good bill. I commend the House conferees, Congressmen UTTERBACK, MILLER, McLAUGHLIN, SUMNERS, GUYER, and ROBSION, for the good agreement they reached with the Senate conferees. It is a better bill than it was when it passed the House. The Borah–Van Nuys provision is separate and distinct. It is section 3 of this bill. It does not in the way it is inserted hurt the bill or injure it in any way, but strengthens the bill. I am pleased that the provision is in there in the way the conferees have put it in.

This bill passed the House by the enormous majority of 290 for, to only 16 against, and I hope this conference report will be accepted by this House by an even greater majority. This bill has heretofore been fully discussed and I hope this report is adopted without further delay.

Mr. UTTERBACK.   Mr. Speaker, I move the previous question on the adoption of the conference report.

The previous question was ordered.

The conference report was agreed to.

A motion to reconsider was laid on the table.

TABLE OF CASES CITED

MISCELLANEOUS CITATIONS

CONGRESSIONAL HEARINGS

CONGRESSIONAL REPORTS

CONGRESSIONAL RECORD

BOOKS

ARTICLES

INDEX

391